Children's Eyewitness Memory

KF
9672
C47
1987

Children's Eyewitness Memory

Edited by
Stephen J. Ceci, Michael P. Toglia,
and David F. Ross

6/9/88 mw

CALIFORNIA SCHOOL OF PROFESSIONAL PSYCHOLOGY LOS ANGELES

Springer-Verlag
New York Berlin Heidelberg
London Paris Tokyo

Stephen J. Ceci
Department of Human Development
  and Family Study
Cornell University
Ithaca, New York 14853 USA

Michael P. Toglia
Department of Psychology
State University of New York
  at Cortland
Cortland, New York 13045 USA

David F. Ross
Department of Human Development
  and Family Study
Cornell University
Ithaca, New York 14853 USA

Library of Congress Cataloging in Publication Data.
Children's eyewitness memory.
  Bibliography: p.
  Includes index.
  1. Children as witnesses—United States.
2. Memory in children—United States. I. Ceci,
Stephen J. II. Toglia, Michael P. III. Ross,
David F., 1959–
KF9672.C47   1987   345.73'066'088054   86-24852
                        347.30566088054

© 1987 by Springer-Verlag New York Inc.
All rights reserved. This work may not be translated or copied in whole or in part without the written permission of the publisher (Springer-Verlag, 175 Fifth Avenue, New York, New York 10010, USA), except for brief excerpts in connection with reviews or scholarly analysis. Use in connection with any form of information storage and retrieval, electronic adaptation, computer software, or by similar or dissimilar methodology now known or hereafter developed is forbidden.

The use of general descriptive names, trade names, trademarks, etc. in this publication, even if the former are not especially identified, is not to be taken as a sign that such names, as understood by the Trade Marks and Merchandise Marks Act, may accordingly be used freely by anyone.

Typeset by Publishers Service, Bozeman, Montana.
Printed and bound by R.R. Donnelley & Sons, Harrisonburg, Virginia.
Printed in the United States of America.

9 8 7 6 5 4 3 2 1

ISBN 0-387-96429-0 Springer-Verlag New York Berlin Heidelberg
ISBN 3-540-96429-0 Springer-Verlag Berlin Heidelberg New York

Preface

This volume grew out of a 1985 American Psychological Association symposium that was devoted to the issue of children's eyewitness testimony. The symposium itself was organized in response to a growing concern among professionals over the limited state of knowledge about the reliability and validity of children's eyewitness and earwitness memory and jurors' implicit beliefs about this. Increasingly, the courts are calling upon young children to provide testimony in an ever-widening range of cases, including capital offenses. As state after state abandons its rules requiring children's testimony to be corroborated by a third party, the need to learn more about factors that might influence the accuracy of children's recollections becomes increasingly acute.

This volume comprises a collection of chapters that lie at the crossroads of psychology and criminal justice. All of the chapters deal with children's recollections, at least in some fashion. Some authors have described research involving children's recollections under emotionally neutral circumstances (e.g., Ceci, Ross, and Toglia; King and Yuille; Zaragoza); others have made the most of naturally occurring stressful situations, such as trips to the dentist's office or to the hospital to have blood work done (Peters; Goodman, Aman, and Hirschman). Some of the chapters, we believe, have provided fresh insights into adults' intuitions regarding the reliability of children's recollections and the extent to which a child-witness' recollections are instrumental in juror determinations of guilt or innocence (Leippe and Romanczyk; Ross, Miller, and Moran). Finally, several chapters focus on casting children's recollections into a broader theoretical framework: the ability to distinguish fact from fantasy, or to monitor external and internal states (Lindsay and Johnson). We believe this volume constitutes some of the best and most interesting research to date on these issues.

One feature of this volume deserves comment. It is the inclusion of three commentaries by well-known psycholegal researchers—Chapters 10, 11, and 12. From the moment we decided to edit this volume, we were committed to assembling the best work available. We attempted to accomplish this in two ways. First, each of us critiqued every chapter. Second, we invited critical commentaries on the chapters from three independent, and highly respected researchers. This form of peer commentary has the advantage of encouraging authors to prepare their submissions with maximum care and attention to theory in order to avoid being chastized in print by one of the commentators. We think that the plan was successful. Every one of the chapters in this volume is *very* strong.

The commentaries themselves are treasure troves of insight. Cole and Loftus, Melton and Thompson, and Turtle and Wells have done an outstanding job digesting and synthesizing the various issues raised in the chapters. Moreover, they have sought, with some success, to embed these findings into larger, more integrative, theoretical frameworks. Our anticipation is that comments made by the discussants will resurface in countless articles and doctoral dissertations. Although we have made our feelings clear about the quality of these chapters and commentaries, it remains for the reader to decide whether we are correct or merely suffering from the sort of euphoria that accompanies the completion of a 15-month endeavor.

The reader might ask what role such a volume has today. Is it intended as a compendium of empirical observations that will be used to guide the criminal justice system, or is it primarily an incremental growth in our understanding of children's memory abilities? Clearly, it is the latter, but to what extent can these chapters be viewed as foundations for amending legal procedures or guiding jurors' beliefs? It has become a standard rallying cry of those who work in this area to caution readers against an uncritical acceptance of research findings. After all, there are many important differences between children's recollections as part of their actual testimony and the type of recollections observed in experimentally contrived testing situations. For instance, in cases of child sexual abuse, the modal case involves a child who was molested by a well-known relative, repeatedly, and over a long period of time. The events were often highly charged with emotion. In such instances there is little doubt about a child's ability to identify the perpetrator. In many experimentally contrived situations, however, children's identification of fleeting, emotionally neutral, and frequently unimportant details is assessed. Numerous other "mismatches" between actual testimony and experimental paradigms can be described, but the point is simply that if one's goal is to generalize from experimental findings to the actual courtroom performance of children, then careful consideration of the ecological validity of those findings is not only warranted but necessary.

The other side of this argument is equally worth bearing in mind. Although experimental studies often involve the observation of children in strange places by strange persons for brief periods of time, this is not unlike some of the circumstances surrounding actual cases. It is easy to forget that determinations of guilt or innocence often hinge on a child's recollection of a detail that, at the time of its occurrence, was unimportant and fleeting. A good example of this is the recent case of the alleged practice of witchcraft by parents in Bakersfield, California. During pretrial hearings involving child-witnesses to acts of parental sexual abuse, animal sacrifice, and torture, much was made of the children's accuracy in recalling fairly unimportant details, such as articles of clothing worn by the defendants. (This is not unlike many of the experimental studies of memory for central and incidental details.) Similarly, individuals have been asked to recollect events that occurred under emotionally neutral circumstances, such as whether the defendant was wearing swimming trunks that contained a pocket (see Ross et al., Chapter 8). So, the absence of high degrees of stress, the use of incidental details, and so on, may be relevant for some types of testimony even if they are not for other types. The job of those involved in child-witness research is to decide when a set of findings is appropriate for generalization and when it is not.

While we are on this topic of relevance, another point bears mentioning. In our efforts to mold our experimental paradigms to "the real world," we may be missing opportunities to alter existing legal practices in ways that would be beneficial. For example, if researchers exclusively concentrated on "what is," as opposed to "what might be," then the potential for research to inform legal practice may be lost. A case can be made that researchers should not worry whether their practices conform to current legal procedures because their findings may suggest that the best course of action is to change those procedures. (Admittedly, this optimism for the potential of research is dissipated by the recent Supreme Court ruling concerning "death qualified juries," in which solid experimental and correlational research findings were apparently ignored in the Court's decision.) But researchers should not be mesmerized by what has been the reluctance of judges and policy makers to implement research findings. We are still at an early stage in the research enterprise, and the future holds promise for a greater reliance on experimental findings.

January 1987

Stephen J. Ceci
Michael P. Toglia
David F. Ross

Contents

Contributors

Christine Aman
Department of Psychology
University of Denver
Denver, CO 80208 USA

Stephen J. Ceci
Department of Human Development
  and Family Study
Cornell University
Ithaca, NY 14853 USA

Carol B. Cole
Department of Psychology
University of Washington
Seattle, WA 98195 USA

Gail S. Goodman
Department of Psychology
University of Denver
Denver, CO 80208 USA

Jodi Hirschman
Department of Psychology
University of Denver
Denver, CO 80208 USA

Marcia K. Johnson
Department of Psychology
Princeton University
Princeton, NJ 08540 USA

Mary Ann King
Department of Psychology
University of British Columbia
Vancouver, British Columbia
V6T 1W5 Canada

Michael R. Leippe
Department of Psychology
Adelphi University
Garden City, NY 11530 USA

D. Stephen Lindsay
Department of Psychology
Princeton University
Princeton, NJ 08540 USA

Elizabeth F. Loftus
Department of Psychology
University of Washington
Seattle, WA 98195 USA

Gary B. Melton
Department of Psychology
University of Nebraska
Lincoln, NE 68588 USA

Beth S. Miller
Department of Human Development
  and Family Study
Cornell University
Ithaca, NY 14853 USA

Patricia B. Moran
Department of Human Development
   and Family Study
Cornell University
Ithaca, NY 14853 USA

Douglas P. Peters
Department of Psychology
University of North Dakota
Grand Forks, ND 58262 USA

Ann Romanczyk
Department of Psychology
Adelphi University
Garden City, NY 11530 USA

David F. Ross
Department of Human Development
   and Family Study
Cornell University
Ithaca, NY 14853 USA

Karen J. Saywitz
UCLA School of Medicine
Division of Child and Adolescent
   Psychiatry
Harbor, UCLA Medical Center
Los Angeles, CA 90049 USA

Ross A. Thompson
Department of Psychology
University of Nebraska
Lincoln, NE 68588 USA

Michael P. Toglia
Department of Psychology
State University of New York
   at Cortland
Cortland, NY 13045 USA

John W. Turtle
Department of Psychology
University of Alberta
Edmonton, Alberta
Canada T6G 2E9

Gary L. Wells
Department of Psychology
University of Alberta
Edmonton, Alberta
Canada T6G 2E9

John C. Yuille
Department of Psychology
University of British Columbia
Vancouver, British Columbia
Canada V6T 1W5

Maria S. Zaragoza
Department of Psychology
Kent State University
Kent, OH 44240 USA

1
Child Sexual and Physical Abuse: Children's Testimony

GAIL S. GOODMAN, CHRISTINE AMAN, and JODI HIRSCHMAN

In Miami, Florida last year a highly sensational case of child sexual abuse captured public attention. The case, known locally as the Country Walk case, involved a young woman, Ileana, and her husband, Frank, who ran a babysitting service in their home. The case was first brought to the attention of authorities when parents became suspicious that something strange was happening at the babysitters'. The parents noticed that their children acted oddly and sometimes had a rash or even a fever upon returning home. The parents began to talk among themselves and to question the children. None of the children said anything unusual was going on.

Finally, one parent became so concerned that she called the authorities, and an investigation began. The children, who ranged in age from about 2 to 5 years, were brought to two developmental psychologists who interviewed them repeatedly, recording each interview on videotape. Some of their questioning was quite leading, although most was not. At first, the children maintained that nothing had occurred. Gradually, however, they began to recount acts of sexual abuse. With the aid of anatomically correct dolls, the children demonstrated how they had been assaulted by Ileana and Frank. They described "pee pee" and "caca" games; they described acts of oral sex and digital penetration; they described nudity and being filmed. Sometimes the children said outrageous, fanciful things—that, after the assaults, Frank and Ileana ate the children for dinner, for example.

As the trial approached, Frank and Ileana's attorneys prepared their defense. Experts were called in who, according to their depositions, planned to say that the children's statements were unreliable, that the children had never spontaneously claimed sexual abuse but did so only when pressured through suggestive questioning, and that anatomically correct dolls might have elicited false accounts of sexual abuse from the children. The experts' statements were based in part on research concerning children's eyewitness testimony.

The particular case described above would indeed lead many experts to question the children's word. But, shortly before the trial was to commence, Ileana confessed, corroborating the children's testimony. She explained that the children— including Frank's 6-year-old son from a former marriage, who was found to have gonorrhea of the throat—had been threatened into silence. At the trial, Ileana, only 17 years of age herself, testified against Frank, describing how she had been beaten into submission to perform the sexual acts. Frank had a previous history of violence against adults and children. He was found guilty and received what amounted to several consecutive life sentences (Hollingsworth, 1986).

In what way does the research literature on children's eyewitness testimony lead many to doubt children's statements about sexual and physical abuse, such as in the Country Walk case? Such doubts are not new, of course. There has been a history in the field of psychology of not believing children. Children have been viewed as being highly suggestible (Berenda, 1950; Binet, 1900; Small, 1896; Stern, 1910; Varendonck, 1911), unable to differentiate fantasy from reality (Piaget, 1932; Werner, 1948), and prone to fantasize sexual events (Freud, 1905). In this chapter we will examine research relevant to these claims. We will also evaluate some important ways in which current research differs from actual incidents and investigations of child sexual and physical abuse. Finally, we will discuss several new studies, conducted in our laboratory, that examine the testimony of child "victims" under more ecologically valid conditions than heretofore established.

We concentrate on children's testimony in cases of child abuse because children appear to be most likely to testify as witnesses at trials connected with this kind of crime (Whitcomb, Shapiro, & Stellwagen, 1985). Their greater likelihood of testifying in such cases derives from the fact that the child is often not only the victim but also the only eyewitness; these cases therefore revolve largely around the child's statements. Even if corroborating physical evidence is available—and often it is not (Whitcomb et al., 1985)—it typically must be tied to the defendant through the child's testimony.

Child Sexual and Physical Abuse

In order to examine how research on children's testimony relates to actual cases of child abuse, it is necessary to know something about this set of crimes. Child abuse is commonly divided into two broad catgories: physical abuse and sexual abuse. (We do not explicitly deal with neglect cases in this chapter.) The child abuse literature is vast and growing (e.g., Bulkley, 1985; Finkelhor, 1984; Gerbner, Ross, & Zigler, 1980; Helfer & Kempe, 1976; Kempe & Kempe, 1984; Mrazek & Kempe, 1981), so only a summary can be provided here.

Recent research indicates that the prevalence of child abuse is alarmingly high. If abuse is more common than previously recognized, perhaps we should pay greater heed to children's reports than we have in the past. While precise prevalence rates are extremely difficult to obtain, relevant information is available. For child sexual abuse, Russell's (1983) study is considered to be the most technically sound. She interviewed 930 randomly selected adult women about their sexual experiences as children. Extrafamilial child sexual abuse was defined as unwanted sexual experiences with persons unrelated to the respondent, ranging from petting to rape, before the age of 14 years, and completed or attempted forcible rape from the ages of 14 to 17 years. Intrafamilial child sexual abuse was defined more broadly as any kind of exploitive sexual contact between the respondent and a relative before the respondent turned 18 years of age. Russell found that "38% of the women reported at least one experience of intrafamilial and/or extrafamilial sexual abuse before the age of 18 years, and 28% reported at least one such experience before 14 years of age" (p. 137). Other research lends support to these shockingly high figures (Finkelhor, 1979).

For child physical abuse, a survey study by Straus, Gelles, and Steinmetz (1980) provides prevalence estimates. A nationally representative sample of 1,143 homes with children between the ages of 3 and 17 years was selected, and parents were interviewed about their means of discipline. Abusive violence was defined as acts having a high probability of injuring the child, such as kicking, biting, trying to hit or hitting the child with an object, beating up the child, and threatening to use or using a gun or knife. Straus et al. found that 3.8% of the parents engaged in at least one act of abusive violence in the year prior to the study. When abuse occurred, it was often repeated: The median number of violent acts in abusive homes was 4.5 times per year. When this rate was projected to all children between the ages of 3 and 17 years, in American homes, it was estimated that 1.4 million children experience physical abuse each year.

This estimate, while disturbing, is probably low. As Gelles and Cornell (1985) point out, the survey omitted measurement of violence against children below the age of 3 years, who are often considered to be at high risk for abuse. The survey included only intact families. Several forms of violence, such as burning, were not investigated. Furthermore, and most important, since the study involved self-report of violence, one might expect that the true incidence was higher than indicated.

Given that child abuse does occur, and at distressingly high rates, what are its typical characteristics? Research on sexual abuse indicates that (a) perpetrators are most likely to be people who are familiar to the child—not strangers (DeFrancis, 1969; Finkelhor, 1979); (b) the majority of abused children do not spontaneously tell their parents about the abuse (Finkelhor, 1984); (c) the abuse is often repeated—it is seldom a one-time event (Herman, 1981); (d) lower socioeconomic families are overrepresented in cases of reported abuse (Finkelhor, 1979); (e) child sexual abuse can occur at virtually any age, from infancy to adolescence (DeJong, Hervada, & Emmett, 1983); (f) children are most likely to report that the abuse was unpleasant and that they were frightened (Browne & Finkelhor, 1986; Herman, 1981); and (g) the abuse itself typically consists of fondling rather than rape (Finkelhor, 1979, 1984).

Child physical abuse presents a similar pattern (see Gelles & Cornell, 1985, and Kempe & Helfer, 1974, for reviews). One difference between the two forms of abuse is that women are slightly more likely than men to physically abuse children—a finding probably reflecting women's greater contact with children—whereas men are overwhelmingly more likely than women to sexually abuse children (Finkelhor, 1984; Straus et al., 1980).

Do the events studied in psychological research on children's testimony simulate acts of abuse? Are the subject samples tested representative of children reported to be abuse victims? Are the memory tests given and the type of questions asked similar to those that children would experience in police or social service investigations? To the extent that the accuracy of children's testimony varies as a function of these factors, psychological research may over- or underestimate children's abilities as witnesses. In the following sections we examine many of the studies to date with these questions in mind.

Children's Eyewitness Testimony

Most published studies of eyewitness testimony, whether they concern children's or adults' performance, use slides, films, or stories as stimuli (e.g., Buckhout, Alper, Chern, Silverberg, & Slomovits, 1974; Cohen & Harnick, 1980; List, 1986; Loftus, Miller, & Burns, 1978; Loftus & Palmer, 1974; McCloskey & Zaragoza, 1985). Moreover, the witness is not actively involved in the event but is merely a neutral bystander. Take, for example, a study by Cohen and Harnick (1980). Children, aged 9 and 12 years, and adults were asked to view a 12-minute black-and-white film of petty crimes, specifically, shoplifting and failure to return a purse. The participants then completed a multiple-choice test that included 11 nonsuggestive and 11 suggestive questions. One week later, the participants' memory was examined in a series of four-alternative, multiple-choice questions to determine if the misleading information influenced their responses. It was found that the younger children's memory was worse than that of the older age groups and that the younger children were more suggestible. Are there important factors related to abuse, not included in studies such as this, that might have profound effects on children's memory, conformity, and suggestibility? In addressing this question, we consider three broad types of factors—demographic, degree of involvement, and task factors.

Demographic Factors

AGE

In most studies of age differences in eyewitness testimony and suggestibility, a relatively restricted age range is tested. We know little about very young children's or adolescents' abilities to provide eyewitness reports. For example, only a few studies have included children as young as 3 years of age (Ceci, Ross, & Toglia, Chapter 5, this volume; Goodman & Reed, 1986; Peters, Chapter 7, this volume; Zaragoza, Chapter 4, this volume). Yet in many cases of abuse—such as purported sexual assault at preschools and day-care centers—very young children are involved. Fortunately, the number of studies in which very young children are included is growing. Adolescents remain under-studied.

SOCIOECONOMIC STATUS (SES)

While child abuse occurs at all SES levels, low-income families are over-represented in *reported* cases of abuse (Steinmetz, 1971; Straus et al., 1980). Researchers who investigate children's eyewitness reports rarely state the SES level of the participants in their studies. It is possible that a relationship exists between SES and memory performance or between SES and suggestibility. For example, to the extent that, on average, children from low-SES families possess poorer intellectual skills as assessed on standardized intelligence tests, they might not perform as well as children from higher-SES families. Alternatively, disadvantaged children might be more attuned to real-life events than to school tasks and thus perform well in eyewitness testimony situations.

RACE/ETHNIC GROUP

Child abuse occurs across a wide range of racial and ethnic groups (e.g., see Straus et al., 1980). Most studies of children's testimony do not indicate the racial and ethnic background of the individuals tested. Not only does this limit the representativeness of the samples tested, but it does not permit one to examine certain interesting effects, such as cross-racial identification. While a few developmental studies of cross-racial identification exist (see Chance & Goldstein, 1984, for a review), they have typically involved the presentation of briefly exposed pictures rather than actual people.

A meager literature exists on the relationship between race and conformity, and these few studies have relied on fairly artificial tasks. For example, Iscoe, Williams, and Harvey (1964), in contrasting black children's and white children's conformity, found that young black females were the least conforming when tested in an Asch-like experiment.

In sum, the samples tested in most experiments are probably not representative of children who typically become involved in police or social service investigations or who testify in courts of law. Because so few relevant studies have been done, it is impossible to tell at the moment how important or unimportant these demographic factors may be. The few studies in which very young children have been tested suggest, however, that age is an important factor.

Degree of Involvement

PERSONAL SIGNIFICANCE

The events viewed in most studies of children's or adults' testimony are unlikely to have personal significance to the individuals tested. In addition, the witnesses often know that they are involved in an experiment and that their responses will have little actual or potential impact on their lives. For example, they know that the characters in the stories, slides, or movies will not hurt them. They do not directly interact with the people they will later have to identify. The theme of the events may not be remarkable, as when a child is read a story (Ceci et al., Chapter 5, this volume), watches a person enter a room and water a plant (King, 1984), or views cartoons (Dale, Loftus, & Rathbun, 1978; Duncan, Whitney, & Kunen, 1982). While it is possible to learn something interesting about memory from these studies, the findings may underestimate children's ability to provide accurate testimony for personally significant events.

Several studies suggest that the personal significance of an event does indeed influence memory (e.g., Keenan & Baillet, 1980; Linton, 1982). For example, Linton (1982) reports that the following kinds of events produce memories that will endure: events that lead to strong emotion and are salient at the time they occur, events that influence one's subsequent life course, and events that are relatively unique and remain so. Many acts of abuse meet one or more of these criteria. For example, sexual assault and physical abuse are likely to raise strong emotion in the child and to be salient at the time they occur. These events may influence a child's subsequent life course, in that they may serve as the turning point when a criminal investigation begins or the child is taken away from home. Especially if the abuse occurs only once, the events will be unique.

Unfortunately, only a few studies have examined the effects of personal significance on memory, and several studies that have attempted to examine it are flawed. For example, Brown and Kulik (1977) claim that events of high personal signifiance may create "flashbulb" memories, that is, memories that stay vivid over time. They use as an example people's memory for where they were and what they were doing at the time of President Kennedy's death. Since an objective record of people's whereabouts and actions at the time of the assassination is unavailable, the reality of flashbulb memories is difficult to evaluate.

Another suggestion that personally significant events are remembered well, even by children, is offered by Wallerstein (1985). In a 10-year follow-up of children's reactions to divorce, she states that "Perhaps the most striking [finding] was the accessibility of memory, especially memories of the separation, which for 40% of these young people had remained surprisingly fresh as if, in fact, the incidents had occurred very recently. It may well be, in fact, that we have altogether overestimated the effect of time in muting experiences and painful feelings and that memories or perhaps some memories do not fade" (p. 549). Unfortunately, Wallerstein's comments were not supported with data.

One index of personal significance might be the interest value of an event. A recent study by Renninger and Wozniak (1985) indicates that children's attention and memory is affected by their interest in the materials presented. Renninger and Wozniak determined which toys children were most interested in from the toys available at their preschool. These toys were then used in a series of experiments that assessed the children's attention, recognition memory, and free recall. It was found that children paid greater attention to the high-interest toys and were more likely to recognize and recall them correctly, in contrast to toys of lower interest value. In the typical study of children's testimony, no attempt is made to determine whether the stimuli are of equal, or any, interest to the children and adults, or if the children and adults are paying equal attention to the stimulus materials.

Two other factors related to the personal significance of an event concern the event's meaningfulness to the child and the child's degree of active involvement. Istomina (1975) combined these two factors in a study of children's memory. Children in her study fell into two groups. Like the children in so many laboratory experiments, half were simply asked to remember a list of words. The list consisted of grocery items. The children in the second group were read the same list of words but, in addition, were required to obtain the items from a play store. The children in the latter group displayed greater use of mnemonic strategies (e.g., rehearsal) and better memory (but see Weissberg & Paris 1986).

TRAUMA

Also related to personal significance is the degree of trauma associated with an event. Crimes against children are often traumatic. Until recently (Goodman, Hepps, & Reed, 1986; Peters, Chapter 7, this volume), there have been no scientific studies of children's memory for traumatic events. Instead we have had to rely on clinical reports. Perhaps the most famous of these are Terr's (1979, 1983) studies of the children of Chowchilla. These children were victims of a school bus kidnapping. Terrorized by their abductors, who were armed with rifles, the children and their school bus driver were buried alive in an enclosed truck. Fortunately, the children and driver escaped. Terr interviewed the children approximately 6 to 13 months after the ordeal. She reports that some distortions occurred in their memory, but the children were largely correct in their statements. Of course, by the time Terr arrived in Chowchilla, the children had had a chance to talk among themselves and see local news stories about the kidnapping. Thus, their memories may have been enhanced or contaminated by other sources.

The paucity of controlled, laboratory research on trauma and memory results from obvious ethical considerations. Researchers cannot, and presumably would not want to, bring children into their laboratories and terrorize them so that the children's memory could be tested. Although we believe there are ways to overcome these problems in studying human memory (see below), the field has generally relied on studies with animals that (according to current ethical guidelines) can be traumatized.

The Yerkes-Dodson law, for example, was first developed in connection with research involving mice (Yerkes & Dodson, 1908), but it has been used to predict the relation between trauma and memory in people. This law predicts that performance on a complex task will increase at optimal levels of stress but decrease as stress becomes high. Easterbrook (1959) interpreted the Yerkes-Dodson law in terms of changes in attentional focus, claiming that attention to relevant cues increases at optimal levels of stress, but then decreases as stress becomes high. A review of the testimony literature, however, provides only inconsistent support for the Yerkes-Dodson law (Deffenbacher, 1983), and, to our knowledge, the law has not been tested on children.

The effects of stress on suggestibility are largely unknown. The only study we have found on this topic was conducted before current ethical standards were established. Estabrooks (1929) subjected boys (mean age approximately 13 years) to four tasks designed to tap suggestibility. One of the tasks involved electric shock; the other tasks were less aversive. In the electricity task, the child put his fingers across two "handles" and was given a shock, which, "while not severe, was strong enough to make him withdraw his fingers" (p. 122). Unbeknown to the child, the electricity was then turned off. Next, the child put his hand back on the handles and was told that, across trials, the experimenter would turn on the electricity, but in graduated strength. On each trial, Estabrooks measured whether the child removed his hand. The scores on the electricity task formed a "U-shaped" curve, indicating an "all-or-none" response pattern. The curves for the other tasks tended to become normal as emotion declined. In addition, when the children's scores on the electricity task were correlated with their scores on the other tasks, the correlations were nonsignificant. Estabrooks stated that "Emotion plays a big role in suggestion" (p. 120) and that "the type of curve obtained when the suggestion is backed by a strong emotion is totally different from that in which the suggestion has no such feeling-tone involved" (p. 135). Unfortunately, the task used in this study is quite different from the ones child witnesses face in investigations or in courts of law.

In sum, there is very little scientific work on the effects of trauma on children's memory or suggestibility.

PARTICIPATION

Research on children's testimony has almost invariably investigated bystander witnesses. Yet, abuse against children involves direct interaction of the child with a perpetrator. We know of only one study that has explicitly examined the role of participation in a real-life event, and this study was conducted by MacWhinney, Keenan, and Reinke (1982) with adult subjects. MacWhinney et al. found that participants' memories were stronger than those of bystanders. We suspect that the same findings would hold for children.

As can be seen from this brief review, the degree of a child's involvement in an event—whether the event is personally significant, interesting, meaningful, traumatic, or it directly involves the child—is likely to be related to the strength of a child's memory. But much more research along these lines is needed.

Task Factors

TYPE OF STIMULUS MATERIALS AND TYPE OF TEST

As mentioned earlier, most studies of children's testimony and suggestibility have used stories, slides, or films as stimuli rather than real-life events. The majority of studies on children's conformity have used even more artificial stimuli: for example, lines (Berenda, 1950), lights (Hamm & Hoving, 1969), and metronome clicks (Iscoe et al., 1964). In the eyewitness testimony literature, however, there are a growing number of exceptions (e.g., Dent, 1977; Goodman & Reed, 1986; King, 1984; Marin, Holmes, Guth, & Kovac, 1979). In any case, memory may be stronger for real-life events than for stories, slides, or movies.

Baggett (1979) has shown that surface information in visually presented materials (films) has a slower decay function than does surface information in equivalent verbal stories (see also Bates, Masling, & Kintsch, 1978). In Baggett's study, there was evidence of visual surface memory as long as six weeks after presentation. There is also evidence that memory for the surface form of sentences in real-life events lasts longer than would be predicted by studies of prose memory (Keenan, MacWhinney, & Mayhew, 1977). As suggestibility may be exacerbated when memory is poor (Loftus, 1975), suggestibility may be reduced for a real-life event as opposed to a story or even a film.

The type of test used may also influence memory. In some laboratory studies, these tests are not the same as those typically used by police or in courts of law. In these real-life legal settings, free recall and objective and suggestive questioning are most likely to be employed. In many studies, multiple-choice or pictorial recognition tests are used instead (e.g., Cohen & Harnick, 1980; Duncan et al., 1982). The type of test can have important effects on memory performance (Goodman, 1980; Price & Goodman, 1985; Tulving, 1983). For example, memories that might otherwise be lost can become accessible under the right testing conditions (e.g., McCloskey & Zaragoza, 1985).

TYPE OF INFORMATION TESTED

There may be important differences between children's and adults' ability to answer questions about various kinds of information. Marquis, Marshall, and Oskamp (1972) found that adults were more accurate and resistant to suggestion when questions concerned central as opposed to peripheral information. It is possible that, in studies showing deficits in children's memory, the deficits largely concern peripheral information and that children are closer to adults in their ability to remember central information.

Moreover, the questions asked should ideally be similar to those asked in actual investigations. In abuse cases, an investigator would want to know if the child had been hit, kissed, or touched, for example. In many studies of children's testimony, the questions asked of the witnesses are not reported, making it difficult to know what kind of information was asked about.

TEMPORAL FACTORS

In studies of children's eyewitness testimony, researchers often expose children to brief events. In a study by Marin et al. (1979), for instance, children witnessed a 15-second argument between two adults. The Cohen and Harnick (1980) study cited earlier used one of the longest exposure durations, 12 minutes. In real-life cases of abuse, the events will involve more than a few seconds and are more likely to last minutes or hours.

Moreover, the abuse is often repeated. Studies of children's eyewitness testimony have not investigated repeated events, but studies of children's "scripts" have done so (see Nelson & Gruendal, 1981, and Nelson, Fivush, Hudson, & Lucarello, 1983, for reviews). Children, especially young ones, provide only skeletal reports of repeated events, and there is some evidence that they can report what generally happens in scripted events better than they can report specific episodes (Fivush, 1984). Children show many of the same confusions that adults show when recalling repeated events. For example, in some studies children and adults hear stories describing familiar acts, but the acts are presented out of their typical order (e.g., a story about eating at a restaurant in which the bill is paid before the customers are served their meal). The children and adults both tend to recall the acts in their canonical order (Hudson & Nelson, 1983; Mandler, 1984).

Another important temporal factor is the delay interval between experiencing an event and having one's memory tested. The delay intervals used in studies of children's testimony are relatively limited. In some studies, the children were tested immediately (Cohen & Harnick, 1980; Dale et al., 1978; Duncan et al., 1982). In others, a delay of a few days or weeks was imposed (Dent & Stephenson, 1979; Goodman & Reed, 1986). Although, in actual cases, children may be interviewed the day of the abuse or within a few days or weeks, it is not uncommon for many weeks, months, or years to elapse between the event and the child's initial report or courtroom testimony (Herman, 1981; Whitcomb et al., 1985). Moreover, interviews are often repeated over a period of months or years (Whitcomb et al., 1985). Because research on children's memory and suggestibility has generally not investigated performance after long delays (but see Myles-Worsley,

TABLE 1.1. Mean performance of 3- and 6-year-olds and adults on the memory tests.

Test	3 years	6 years	Adults
Objective questions: number of correct answers (out of 17)	10.00_a	11.75_b	12.63_b
Suggestive questions: number of correct answers (out of 4)	1.35_a	2.21_b	3.06_c
Free recall: amount of information correctly recalled	0.83_a	5.50_b	17.68_c
Free recall: number of intrusion errors	0.61_a	0.91_a	2.25_b
Photo identification: proportion of correct identifications	0.38_a	0.93_b	0.75_b
Photo identification: number of false identifications	5.00_d	1.00_d	3.00_d

Note: Within each row, condition means with the same subscript did not differ significantly, $p = .05$ or less. Subscripts "a" through "c" indicate planned comparisons. Subscript "d" indicates a chi square test.

Note: From "Age Differences in Eyewitness Testimony" by G. S. Goodman and R. S. Reed, 1986, *Law and Human Behavior, 10*, 317–332. Reprinted by permission.

Cromer, & Dodd, 1986), we do not know whether loss of memory continues indefinitely or levels out. Bahrick (1984) reports that adults' memory for academically learned material shows a decline over the first 5 or 6 years, but that the forgetting curve then levels off, with nothing more forgotten for 25 years. We do not know if the same function would be found for children or, regardless of age, for different types of information. Moreover, studies have not investigated whether young children's forgetting occurs at a faster rate than that of older children or adults.

In summary, a variety of task factors reduce the ecological validity of studies of children's testimony. It is thus unclear whether findings from current studies accurately reflect children's abilities. While the studies we have reviewed above may provide valuable information for theory building, the generalization of the findings to real-life cases of abuse must be made with caution.

Research on Child Victims' Testimony

In our laboratory, several studies concerning the testimony of child "victims" and participants have been conducted. Three will be briefly described here. All examine the testimony of children who were actively involved in an event and who interacted with an unfamiliar confederate. While the studies do not remedy all of the existing research gaps, we have attempted to make gains in ecological validity while maintaining scientific rigor.

The first study was conducted by Goodman and Reed (1986). The goal of the study was to examine age differences in testimony for a relatively neutral experience but one in which the participants were more than mere bystanders. In addition, we wanted to compare young children's performance to that of adults. In the study, children, 3 and 6 years of age, and adults interacted with an unfamiliar adult male for 5 minutes. The interaction consisted of a brief conversation followed by a game similar to Simon Says. After a delay of 4 or 5 days, the participants were questioned about the event. Objective and suggestive questions were asked, free recall elicited, and a five-person photo-identification task administered. Free recall followed, rather than preceded, questioning to determine if suggested information would appear in the witnesses' reports.

The findings of the study are presented in Table 1.1. Adults and 6-year-olds performed equivalently in answering objective questions and in identifying the confederate in the lineup. The 6-year-olds were significantly more suggestible than the adults, but the absolute difference in their performance was small. Sharp differences between these two groups appeared in the amount of information recalled, with the adults recalling more correct *and* more incorrect information than 6-year-olds.

The 3-year-olds performed poorly compared to the other two groups on virtually every measure. They answered the fewest objective and suggestive questions correctly, recalled little, recognized the confederate relatively poorly, and made the most false identifications. The only way in which they surpassed adults was that, in free recall, they did not produce as many errors. Although the 3-year-olds answered fewer objective questions correctly than did the older age groups, the absolute differences in performance were not large. Even the 3-year-olds offered information that might have been useful in a real criminal case.

Although the children, especially the 3-year-olds, were more suggestible than adults (as measured by their ability to resist false information offered in our suggestive questions), the suggested information was quite unlikely to appear in their own free reports. This finding is of considerable interest because it is often feared that once information is suggested to and accepted by children, they will later report it as true. Moreover, when the children conformed to the suggestive questions, it was typically with a hesitant "yes" or "no," without further incorrect elaboration. The children were more likely to elaborate on their correct responses.

The results of this study corroborate other findings (Marin et al., 1979) that children say less than adults in free recall but that what they say is largely correct. Because children say little, an interviewer's natural tendency is to question them more rigorously. As long as the questions are not too suggestive, even 3-year-olds can produce many reliable answers. The 3-year-olds' photo identifications were not very reliable, however. Only a third of these young children made an accurate identification. It should be noted, however, that many of the 3-year-olds were quite shy and so had spent less time looking at the confederate than the older subjects did. This more limited exposure to the confederate may have influenced the 3-year-olds' performance.

While the Goodman and Reed study provides information on children's testimony when witnesses interact with an unfamiliar man, the research was still somewhat artificial. Unlike a victimization situation, the man did not touch the participants and no one was hurt. In our most recent research, we have examined children's memory for events that resemble in many ways an attack on a child. Specifically, we have investigated children's memory for receiving either "venipuncture" (blood drawing) at a hospital ambulatory clinic or an inoculation at an immunization clinic. The children were all prescheduled for the medical procedures; we did not impose them. By taking advantage of these situations, however, we were able to study children's testimony for stressful events.

Children are often quite frightened of receiving venipuncture or inoculations, as were many of the children in our study. Many of them cried and a number had to be held down, sometimes by two people in addition to the laboratory technician or nurse who administered the medical procedure. Especially when receiving inoculations, some of the children became nearly hysterical. There was considerable variance in the reactions, however; some children were quite stoical, did not cry, and said "it didn't hurt."

In the venipuncture study (Goodman et al., 1986; Hepps, 1985), two groups of children were tested—an experimental group and a control group. Most of the children were white and from middle- to upper-middle-class families. The experimental-group children, who ranged in age from 3 to 7 years, were the only ones to experience venipuncture. The control children were matched with the experimental children in age, sex, race, time in the venipuncture room, and laboratory technician seen, but merely had a washable design, similar in appearance to a tattoo, gently rubbed onto their arm. The control group was included so that we could examine the effects of stress on memory. Specifically, we were interested in testing the predictions of the Yerkes-Dodson law and Easterbrook's explanation of it. Based on Easterbrook's theorizing, we predicted that because the experimental-group children would be under greater stress, their attention would become narrowly focused on the main event and they would remember it well but to the exclusion of peripheral information. The control-group children were expected to maintain a broader attentional focus and thus be able to remember central and peripheral information more equally.

The nine experimental-group children were solicited from among those who came to the clinic for medical reasons. None were seriously ill or running a fever. Rather, we selected children who were having their blood tested for such reasons as exposure to hepatitis or because they were candidates for growth hormone treatment. When the child entered the venipuncture room, he or she was typically seated on a parent's lap with the laboratory technician facing the child. Virtually all the children were noticeably nervous. In an attempt to relax the child, the technician engaged him or her in a brief conversation, explained what was going to be done, and then asked or, with the help of the child's parent and/or another technician, forced the child to extend his or her arm. A rubber tourniquet was wrapped around the child's arm before the needle was inserted. The length of time blood was taken varied, depending on the amount needed. Sometimes several attempts to find the child's vein had to be made. The child was then permitted to leave. The entire event lasted 4 minutes on average.

Parents provided ratings of their children's stress on a 6-point scale, with 1 indicating that the child was "extremely happy or relaxed" and 6 indicating that the child was "extremely frightened or upset." The average rating for the experimenal children was 3.7; the ratings ranged from 2 to 6.

The control group was treated similarly except that design placement substituted for venipuncture. The children had been told ahead of time that they would not have their blood tested or receive a shot. The parents of the nine control-group children also rated their children's stress. The average rating was 2.9; the ratings ranged from 1 to 4.

For both groups, families were initially told that the study concerned children's reactions to medical procedures. It was not until Session 2—held 3 or 4 days later—that the parent and child learned that the study actually concerned memory. At that time, the children were brought to a university laboratory for memory testing. They were first given a digit span test to determine if there were reliable differences between the groups on an independent test of memory. (There were not.) The children were then asked to recall what happened, to answer objective questions (e.g., "Was your mom or dad in the room with you?") and suggestive questions (e.g., "The person didn't touch you, did she?"), and to identify the technician from a photo lineup.

TABLE 1.2. Mean performance for the experimental and control groups in the venipuncture study.

Test	Experimental	Control
Digit span	8.29	8.00
Free recall: amount of information correctly recalled	4.33	3.89
Objective questions: proportion of correct answers		
Person	0.55	0.55
Room	0.67	0.65
Actions	0.91	0.83
Central information	0.81	0.76
Peripheral information	0.49	0.56
Suggestive questions: proportion of correct answers	0.60	0.71
Photo identification: proportion of correct identifications	0.53	0.67
Photo identification: proportion of false identifications	0.00	0.11

Note: There were no significant differences between the groups.

The main results of the study are presented in Table 1.2. As can be seen, there were no significant differences between the groups. The predicted interaction of group membership and type of information (central vs. peripheral) failed to emerge, although the means were in the expected direction. That is, in answering the objective questions, the experimenal group remembered more central information than the control group, and the control group remembered more peripheral information than the experimental group, but the differences were not significant. Instead, both groups remembered significantly more central than peripheral information. (The result did not change when we divided the groups into "stressed" and "nonstressed" groups based on the parents' stress ratings.)

Central and peripheral information was determined by having an independent group of adults rate the questions as to the type of information queried. Actions tended to be rated as central and aspects of the room as peripheral, whereas questions about the technician were split between the two categories. Memory for actions was significantly better than memory for the room or the technician. Of particular interest were two questions about the technician's actions that might be asked in actual cases of child physical and sexual abuse: "Did the person hit you?" and "Did the person put anything in your mouth?" One hundred percent of the children answered these questions correctly.

The two groups did not differ significantly in suggestibility. Unfortunately, so few children qualified for the study (e.g., did not have a serious illness), that we could not include age as a factor in our main analyses. We did, however, calculate correlations between age and resistance to suggestion and between age and correct answers to objective questions. Both were significant, $r = .59, p < .05$, and $r = .54, p < .05$. Age did not correlate with correct or incorrect free recall, nor with the ability to make a correct or false photo identification. Only one false identification was made.

The results of this study do not support the notion that stress interferes with a victim's memory (e.g., Deffenbacher, 1980). At least within the levels of stress experienced by the children in our study, the two groups were equivalent in their performance. It is possible, of course, that more extreme levels of stress in the experimental group and larger differences in stress between the two groups would have produced differences. Moreover, because of the relatively small number of children tested, we had limited statistical power to uncover differences that may well exist.

In any case, the results again point to the conclusion that when young children (e.g., 3-year-olds) are compared to older children, significant age differences in the ability to provide correct answers to objective and suggestive questions emerge.

Because so few children qualified for the venipuncture study, we moved the project to an immunization clinic. We have so far tested 48 children, all in the experimental group, in this new "inoculation study." The children who participated were prescheduled for the inoculation either as part of their normal medical care or as a requirement to attend public school. Like the children most subject to abuse (at least as indexed by reports to authorities; see Gelles & Cornell, 1985), the children in our study were mainly from low-SES families. A variety of racial and ethnic groups were represented in the sample. The children ranged in age from 3 to 6 years.

At the clinic, each child was escorted into the inoculation room by his or her parent. When receiving their shot, the children were typically either restrained on their parent's lap or held down on a medical examination table. The inoculations were given in the child's arm or thigh. Sometimes two shots were endured. Most of the children also received an oral polio vaccine. The event lasted about 3 or 4 minutes, on average. As in the venipuncture study, the families did not initially know the true purpose of the study.

The parents and experimenters rated the children's stress on the same scale as used in the venipuncture study. The average stress rating made by the parents was 3.7; the average rating made by the experimenters was 4.0. The ratings ranged from 2 to 6.

Because we anticipated being able to test a much larger sample of children at the immunization clinic than at the hospital, we decided to include a delay factor in the study. Some researchers claim that memory for arousal-producing events increases over time (e.g., Kleinsmith & Kaplan, 1963). To examine this possibility, the children were brought to the University for questioning after a 3- to 4- or 7- to 9-day delay. The children were asked to recall the event, answer objective and suggestive questions, and identify the nurse from a six-person photo lineup. The questions were basically the same as asked in the venipuncture study, although a few were changed to fit the new situation and a few were added to increase the similarlity of the questions to those asked in child sexual abuse cases. For example, the children were now asked if the nurse kissed them.

The children were also asked a set of legal questions. These mimicked some of the questions typically asked of children during "competence examinations" in court. Before children can testify in court, they are usually interviewed to determine if they are competent witnesses. The examination, conducted by the judge and/or attorneys, serves in place of an oath but is also used as a means to predict the accuracy of the child's testimony. If the judge decides that the child is incompetent as a witness, the child will not be permitted to testify. The legal questions we asked were: "Do you know the difference between the truth and a lie?"; "If you said the nurse kissed you, would that be the truth or a lie?"; "What happens if you tell a lie?"; and, "Is everything you said today the truth?" The purpose of including these questions was to determine if they predicted the accuracy of the children's testimony.

A summary of the results of this study appears in Table 1.3. To analyze the data, the 3- and 4-year-olds were grouped together, as were the 5- and 6-year-olds. When the children were grouped in this way (and when they were treated as four separate groups as well), there were no significant age differences in the children's ability to recall the event, and their recall did not deteriorate over time. Moreover, the children's reports were quite accurate.

Significant age differences did appear in the ability to answer objective and suggestive questions, however. The older children answered more objective ques-

TABLE 1.3. Mean performance for the 3- to 4-year-olds and the 5- to 6-year-olds on the memory tests as a function of delay in the inoculation study.

Test	Delay 1		Delay 2	
	3.4 years	5.6 years	3.4 years	5.6 years
Free recall				
Number correct	3.13_a	3.38_a	3.75_a	3.60_a
Number incorrect	0.00_a	0.00_a	0.08_a	0.13_a
Objective questions (proportion correct)				
Person	0.47_a	0.65_b	0.48_a	0.64_b
Room	0.69_a	0.78_a	0.67_a	0.77_a
Actions	0.85_a	0.79_{ab}	0.68_b	0.79_{ab}
Central information	0.77_{ab}	0.84_b	0.66_a	0.83_b
Peripheral information	0.56_a	0.57_a	0.48_a	0.53_a
Suggestive questions (proportion correct)				
Person	0.50_a	0.90_b	0.50_a	0.62_a
Room	0.50_a	0.54_a	0.47_a	0.60_a
Actions	0.56_a	0.69_{ab}	0.54_a	0.80_b
Photo identification				
Correct identification	0.50_a	0.54_a	0.17_{ad}	0.53_a
False identification	0.50_a	0.31_a	0.67_a	0.33_a

Note: Within each row, condition means with the same subscript ("a" through "c") did not differ significantly, $p = .05$ or less, planned comparisons. Subscript "d" indicates difference from chance was nonsignificant.

tions correctly, and the younger children showed a decline over the delay in their ability to answer questions about the actions involved. Regardless of age, objective questions about central information were answered more accurately than were such questions about peripheral information.

Four objective questions were included that would be of particular interest in investigations of child sexual and physical abuse: "Did the person kiss you?"; "Did the person hit you?"; "Did the person put anything in your mouth?"; and "Did the person touch you anywhere other than your arm/thigh?" The children were quite accurate in their responses to most of these questions, scoring 96%, 100%, 81%, and 50% correct, respectively. When a mistake was made, it tended to be an error of omission as, for example, when a child who had been given an oral polio vaccine later claimed that the nurse had not put anything in the child's mouth or when a child who had been touched by the nurse on the leg claimed to having been touched only on the arm. In total, only 2% of the mistakes made in response to these questions—all made by 3- and 4-year-olds—were errors of commission. Of course, in the legal system, errors of commission are considered to be more grievous than errors of omission.

In response to the suggestive questions, the older children showed greater resistance to the misleading information than did the younger children. Interestingly, suggestibility also varied with the type of information queried. Resistance to suggestion was significantly greater for the actions involved and for the nurse's physical appearance than for characteristics of the room. Averaging across the two delay conditions, the 5- and 6-year-olds, for example, were resistant to 75% and 76% of the leading questions concerning the actions and the nurse's appearance, respectively, but to only 57% of the leading questions concerning the room. These findings are notable because in most investigations, the actions that took place and the description of the culprit are of particular importance.

On the photo-identification task, the children performed above chance except for the 3- and 4-year-olds at the longer delay. In contrast to the 5- and 6-year-olds' performance, which remained at a constant level across the delay, the 3- and 4-year-olds' performance dropped markedly. The 3- and 4-year-olds also made more false identifications than the older children, although not significantly so.

Correlational analyses were conducted to examine the effects of stress on memory. The correlations concerning the children's rated stress during the inoculations and their accuracy of recall, ability to answer objective and suggestive questions, and photo-identification accuracy were all nonsignificant.

The legal questions proved to be poor predictors of children's performance, as can be seen in Table 1.4. Note that Question 4 was scored in two ways. The preferred answer in a court of law—the one that would presumably contribute to a judge deeming a child competent—would be "yes." On the other hand, one could consider Question 4 to be a metamemory question. Can the children accurately reflect on their performance to know whether everything they said on our memory tests was correct or not? Since we could evaluate the accuracy of the children's testimony, we also coded their answers to Question 4 in terms of their

TABLE 1.4. Correlations between responses to the legal questions and performance on memory tests in the inoculation study.

Question	Correct recall	Correct answers to objective questions	Correct answers to suggestive questions	Identification	
				Correct	False
1. "Do you know the difference between the truth and a lie?"	.10	.04	−.07	.10	.06
2. "If you said the nurse kissed you, would that be the truth or a lie?"	.10	−.02	−.02	.06	−.10
3. "What happens if you tell a lie?"	.19	.37*	.22	.16	−.16
4a. "Is everything you told me today the truth?" (scored "yes" vs. "no")	.26	.01	−.15	−.19	.12
4b. "Is everything you told me today the truth?" (scored for accuracy of child's response)	.00	.22	.34*	.13	.03

*$p < .05$, two-tailed test.

metamemory. In any case, only two correlations out of the 25 were significant. These findings lend support to the recent trend toward dropping the requirement of a competence examination for children.

The results of the inoculation study are in strong agreement with those of the other studies we have described in this chapter. When children as young as 3 years of age are included, significant age differences emerge in the ability to answer objective and suggestive questions accurately. The inoculation study also indicates that some of these age differences are exaggerated over time, so that, for example, the younger children are more likely to lose the ability to correctly identify the "culprit." Interestingly, the inoculation study further demonstrates that children are not equally suggestible about all types of information. Their suggestibility is greater for characteristics of the room in which an event occurred than for the actions that took place or the physical characteristics of the "culprit." Interestingly, across the studies, children never made up false stories of abuse even when asked questions that might foster such reports.

One consistent difference between the studies concerned age differences in free recall. In neither of the studies that examined stress were there age differences, while there was such a difference in the study that examined a more neutral event, even when the 3- and 6-year-olds were compared. The reason for this disparity is unclear. One possibility is that the stressful as opposed to the neutral events examined in our studies were more familiar to the children and this familiarity eliminated age differences in free recall.

Our studies have the advantage of examining children's testimony in situations that, in a number of ways, mimic victimization. In terms of demographic factors, we have studied a wide age range (3 years to adulthood) and have included children who varied in race, ethnicity, and SES. The degree of involvement of the children was high in all three studies. Particularly in the venipuncture and inoculation studies, many of the children in the experimental groups were stressed. As far as task factors are concerned, the children did not know that their memory would be tested, and the questioning paralleled that used by police. The temporal factors—duration of the event and recall delay—were more realistic than in many studies. The event lasted more than a few seconds, and the delay intervals that elapsed before testing were consistent with delays that can occur in actual criminal investigations.

Conclusions

We believe that researchers interested in children's testimony must squarely face the issue of ecological validity if their studies are to be applied to actual cases. Not only is this scientifically sensible, it is forced on us by the kinds of questions addressed to expert witnesses by rival attorneys in the courtroom. The studies described in this chapter attempt to bring the field closer to that goal. Because children who testify in court will often be victims of criminal acts, research like that described here is needed, which focuses on the child victim's testimony for personally significant events. To the extent that children's testimony still falls short of adults', techniques need to be developed to bolster the accuracy and completeness of children's statements and identifications.

In our studies we have been able to simulate only a few of the characteristics of child abuse and of investigations of alleged abuse. Our studies did not examine children's testimony for repeated events or for acts carried out by familiar people in familiar settings. In future studies we hope to extend the duration of the incidents and the delays before testing. Although the events themselves were often stressful, we did not attempt to investigate the effects of several kinds of stress that children may experience as part of police or social service investigations. One form of stress concerns the experience of being repeatedly interviewed by a variety of strange adults (e.g., police officers, detectives, social service workers, and attorneys). Stress may also arise when acts of abuse cause embarrassment to the children or involve threats, as in the Country Walk case described at the beginning of this chapter. In these situations, children may be quite hesitant to talk about what happened and may only gradually come to tell their "secrets." In laboratory experiments, the children and adults have nothing to hide and thus, from the start, are likely to tell the experimenter all they remember. But this may not be characteristic of child abuse victims. For example, one child in the Country Walk case claimed over many interviews that *he* had not been molested but had only watched as the others played the games. It was only after multiple interviews and multiple tests of his parents' reactions that he finally admitted that the acts of abuse had been perpetrated against him, too. During the disclosure, he described a game Frank played with the children called "Who's going to lose their head?" In the game, Frank wielded a knife. After describing the game, the boy made a comment that probably explained his former silence: "I don't want to die. I'm only five years old . . ."

Acknowledgments. We are grateful to many people for their assistance with the research projects described in this chapter. For studies 1 and 2, Division Chief Donald Mulnix of the Investigative Unit of the Denver Police Department provided stimulus materials. For study 2, the following individuals—all from Children's Hospital in Denver, Colorado—graciously gave their time and support: Dr. Steven Poole, Director of the Ambulatory Clinic; Dr. Ed Orsini, Pathologist; Bette Jamieson, Hematology Supervisor; and laboratory technicians Vern Ashbaugh, Glenda Cattarello, Venita Jensen, and Gerri Simpson. Jim Vissar, former Investigator for the Denver District Attorney's Office, reviewed our questions for their legal relevance. For study 3, members of the staff of the Colorado State Department of Health and Hospitals' Immunization Clinic provided invaluable assistance: Dr. Franklin Judson, Director Disease Control Center; Marilyn Shahan, Head Nurse; and Fran Moore, Annette Rossi, Ann Schempf, Mayme Tagawa, and Sherry Wiggins, the nurses at the clinic who, along with Marilyn Shahan, served as our confederates. Debra Hepps, Rebecca S. Reed, Annette Rice, and Christine Wilson provided valuable assistance. This research was supported in part by a grant to Gail S. Goodman from the Developmental Psychobiology Research Group of the University of Colorado Health Sciences Center, Department of Psychiatry, and the Academic Research Center of the University of Denver.

References

Baggett, P. (1979). Structurally equivalent stories in movie and text and the effect of the medium on recall. *Journal of Verbal Learning and Verbal Behavior, 18*, 333–356.

Bahrick, H. P. (1984). Semantic memory content in permastore: Fifty years of memory for Spanish learned in school. *Journal of Experimental Psychology: General, 113*, 1–29.

Bates, E., Masling, M., & Kintsch, W. (1978). Recognition memory for aspects of dialogue. *Journal of Experimental Psychology: Human Learning and Memory, 4*, 187–197.

Berenda, R. W. (1950). *The influence of the group on the judgments of children*. New York: King's Crown Press.

Binet, A. (1900). *La suggestibilité*. Paris: Schleicher-Frères.

Brown, R., & Kulik, J. (1977). Flashbulb memories. *Cognition*, *5*, 73–99.

Browne, A., & Finkelhor, D. (1986). The impact of child sexual abuse: A review of the research. *Psychological Bulletin*, *99*, 66–77.

Buckhout, R., Alper, A., Chern, S., Silverberg, G., & Slomovits, M. (1974). Determinants of eyewitness performance on a lineup. *Bulletin of the Psychonomic Society*, *4*, 191–192.

Bulkley, J. (1985). Evidentiary and procedural trends in state legislation and other emerging legal issues in child sexual abuse cases. In J. Bulkley (Ed.), *Papers from a national policy conference on legal reforms in child sexual abuse cases* (pp. 153–165). Washington, DC: American Bar Association.

Chance, J. E., & Goldstein, A. G. (1984). Face-recognition memory: Implications for children's eyewitness testimony. *Journal of Social Issues*, *40*, 69–85.

Cohen, R. L., & Harnick, M. A. (1980). The susceptibiity of child witnesses to suggestion. *Law and Human Behavior*, *4*, 201–210.

Dale, P. S., Loftus, E. F., & Rathbun, L. (1978). The influence of the form of the question on the eyewitness testimony of preschool children. *Journal of Psycholinguistic Research*, *7*, 269–277.

Deffenbacher, K. (1980). Eyewitness accuracy and confidence: Can we infer anything about their relationship? *Law and Human Behavior*, *4*, 243–260.

Deffenbacher, K. (1983). The influence of arousal on reliability of testimony. In B. R. Clifford & S. Lloyd-Bostock (Eds.), *Evaluating eyewitness evidence* (pp. 235–251). Chichester, England: Wiley.

DeFrancis, V. (1969). *Protecting the child victim of sex crimes committed by adults*. Denver: American Humane Association.

DeJong, A., Hervada, A., & Emmett, G. (1983). Epidemiological variations in childhood sexual abuse. *Child Abuse and Neglect*, *7*, 155–162.

Dent, H. R. (1977). Stress as a factor influencing person recognition in identification parades. *Bulletin of the British Psychological Society*, *30*, 339–340.

Dent, H. R., & Stephenson, G. M. (1979). An experimental study of the effectiveness of different techniques of questioning child witnesses. *British Journal of Social and Clinical Psychology*, *18*, 41–51.

Duncan, E. M., Whitney, P., & Kunen, S. (1982). Integration of visual and verbal information in children's memory. *Child Development*, *53*, 1215–1223.

Easterbrook, J. A. (1959). The effects of emotion on the utilization and organization of behavior. *Psychological Review*, *66*, 183–201.

Estabrooks, G. H. (1929). Experimental studies in suggestion. *Journal of Genetic Psychology*, *36*, 120–139.

Finkelhor, D. (1979). *Sexually victimized children*. New York: Free Press.

Finkelhor, D. (1984). *Child sexual abuse: New theory and research*. New York: Free Press.

Fivush, R. (1984). Learning about school: The development of kindergartners' school scripts. *Child Development*, *55*, 1697–1709.

Freud, S. (1905). Three essays on the theory of sexuality. In J. Strachey (Ed.), *The standard edition of the complete psychological works of Sigmund Freud* (Vol. 7, pp. 125–245). London: Hogarth Press.

Gelles, R. J., & Cornell, C. P. (1985). *Intimate violence in families*. Beverly Hills: Sage Publications.

Gerbner, G., Ross, C. J., & Zigler, E. (1980). *Child abuse: An agenda for action*. Oxford: Oxford University Press.

Goodman, G. S. (1980). Picture memory: How the action schema affects retention. *Cognitive Psychology*, *12*, 473–495.

Goodman, G. S., Hepps, D., & Reed, R. S. (1986). The child victim's testimony. In A. Haralambie (Ed.), *New issues for child advocates* (pp. 167–177). Phoenix, AZ: Arizona Association of Council for Children.

Goodman, G. S., & Reed, R. S. (1986). Age differences in eyewitness testimony. *Law and Human Behavior,10*, 317–332.

Hamm, N. H., & Hoving, K. L. (1969). Conformity of children in an ambiguous perceptual situation. *Child Development, 40*, 773–784.

Helfer, R. E., & Kempe, C. H. (1976). *Child abuse and neglect: The family and the community.* Cambridge, MA: Ballinger.

Hepps, D. L. (1985). *Children's eyewitness testimony: Effects of trauma on children's memory.* Unpublished manuscript, University of Denver, Colorado.

Herman, J. L. (1981). *Father-daughter incest.* Cambridge, MA: Harvard University Press.

Hollingsworth, J. (1986). *Unspeakable acts.* New York: Contemporary Books.

Hudson, J., & Nelson, K. (1983). Effects of script structure on children's story recall. *Developmental Psychology, 19*, 625–635.

Iscoe, I., Williams, M., & Harvey, J. (1964). Age, intelligence, and sex as variables in the conformity behavior of negro and white children. *Child Development, 35*, 451–460.

Istomina, Z. M. (1975). The development of voluntary memory in children of preschool age. *Soviet Psychology, 13*, 5–64.

Keenan, J. M., & Baillet, S. D. (1980). Memory for personally and socially significant events. In R. S. Nickerson (Ed.), *Attention and performance* (Vol. 8, pp. 651–669). Hillsdale, NJ: Erlbaum.

Keenan, J. M., MacWhinney, B., & Mayhew, D. (1977). Pragmatics in memory: A study of natural conversation. *Journal of Verbal Learning and Verbal Behavior, 16*, 549–560.

Kempe, C. H., & Helfer, R. E. (Eds.). (1968/1974). *The battered child.* Chicago: University of Chicago Press.

Kempe, R. S., & Kempe, C. H. (1984). *The common secret: Sexual abuse of children and adolescents.* New York: W. H. Freeman.

King, M. A. (1984). *An investigation of the eyewitness abilities of children.* Unpublished doctoral dissertation, University of British Columbia, Vancouver, Canada.

Kleinsmith, L. J., & Kaplan, S. (1963). Paired associated learning as a function of arousal and interpolated interval. *Journal of Experimental Psychology, 65*, 190–193.

Linton, M. (1982). Transformations of memory in everyday life. In U. Neisser (Ed.), *Memory observed: Remembering in natural contexts* (pp. 77–91). New York: W. H. Freeman.

List, J. A. (1986). Age and schematic differences in the reliability of eyewitness testimony. *Developmental Psychology, 22*, 50–57.

Loftus, E. F. (1975). Leading questions and the eyewitness report. *Cognitive Psychology, 7*, 560–572.

Loftus, E. F., Miller, D. G., & Burns, H. J. (1978). Semantic integration of verbal information into a visual memory. *Journal of Experimental Psychology: Human Learning and Memory, 4*, 19–31.

Loftus, E. F., & Palmer, J. C. (1974). Reconstruction of automobile destruction: An example of the interaction between language and memory. *Journal of Verbal Learning and Verbal Behavior, 13*, 585–589.

MacWhinney, B., Keenan, J. M., & Reinke, P. (1982). The role of arousal in memory for conversation. *Memory and Cognition, 10*, 308–317.

Mandler, J. (1984). *Stories, scripts and schemes.* Hillsdale, NJ: Erlbaum.

Marin, B. V., Holmes, D. L., Guth, M., & Kovac, P. (1979). The potential of children as eyewitnesses. *Law and Human Behavior, 4*, 295–305.

Marquis, K. H., Marshall, J., & Oskamp, S. (1972). Testimony validity as a function of question form, atmosphere, and item difficulty. *Journal of Applied Social Psychology*, *2*, 167–186.

McCloskey, M., & Zaragoza, M. (1985). Misleading postevent information and memory for events: Arguments and evidence against memory impairment hypotheses. *Journal of Experimental Psychology: General*, *114*, 1–16.

Mrazek, P. B., & Kempe, C. H. (Eds.). (1981). *Sexually abused children and their families*. New York: Pergamon Press.

Myles-Worsley, M., Cromer, C. C., & Dodd, D. H. (1986). Children's preschool script reconstruction: Reliance on general knowledge as memory fades. *Developmental Psychology*, *22*, 22–30.

Nelson, K., & Gruendel, J. (1981). Generalized event representations: Basic building blocks of cognitive development. In A. Brown & M. Lamb (Eds.), *Advances in developmental psychology* (Vol. 2, pp. 131–158). Hillsdale, NJ: Erlbaum.

Nelson, K., Fivush, R., Hudson, J., & Lucarello, J. (1983). Scripts and the development of memory. In M. Chi (Ed.), *Trends in memory development research* (pp. 52–70). Basel: Karger.

Piaget, J. (1932). *The moral judgment of the child*. New York: Harcourt Brace Jovanovich.

Price, D. W. W., & Goodman, G. S. (1985, April). *Children's event representations for recurring episodes*. Paper presented at the Society for Research in Child Development, Toronto, Canada.

Renninger, K. A., & Wozniak, R. H. (1985). Effect of interest on attentional shift, recognition, and recall in young children. *Developmental Psychology*, *21*, 624–632.

Russell, D. E. H. (1983). The incidence and prevalence of intrafamilial and extrafamilial sexual abuse of female children. *Child Abuse and Neglect*, *7*, 133–146.

Small, M. (1896). The suggestibility of children. *Pedagogical Seminary*, *4*, 176–220.

Steinmetz, S. K. (1971). Occupation and physical punishment: A response to Straus. *Journal of Marriage and the Family*, *33*, 664–666.

Stern, W. (1910). Abstracts of lectures on the psychology of testimony and on the study of individuality. *American Journal of Psychology*, *21*, 273–282.

Straus, M., Gelles, R., & Steinmetz, S. K. (1980). *Behind closed doors: Violence in the American family*. Garden City, NY: Anchor Press.

Terr, L. (1979). Children of Chowchilla: A study of psychic trauma. *The Psychoanalytic Study of the Child*, *34*, 547–623.

Terr, L. (1983). Life attitudes, dreams, and psychic trauma in a group of "normal" children. *Journal of the American Academy of Child Psychiatry*, *22*, 221–230.

Tulving, E. (1983). *Elements of episodic memory*. New York: Oxford University Press.

Varendonck, J. (1911). Les témoignages d'enfants dans un procès retentissant. *Archives de Psychologie*, *11*, 129–171.

Wallerstein, J. S. (1985). Children of divorce: Preliminary report of a ten-year follow-up of older children and adolescents. *Journal of the American Academy of Child Psychiatry*, *24*, 545–553.

Weissberg, J. A., & Paris, S. G. (1986). Young children's remembering in different contexts: A reinterpretation of Isotomina's study. *Child Development*, *57*, 1123–1129.

Werner, H. (1948). *Comparative psychology of mental development*. New York: International Universities Press.

Whitcomb, D., Shapiro, E. P., & Stellwagen, C. D. (1985). *When the victim is a child: Issues for judges and prosecutors*. Washington, DC: National Institute of Justice.

Yerkes, R. M., & Dodson, J. D. (1908). The relation of strength of stimulus to rapidity of habit-formation. *Journal of Comparative Neurological Psychology*, *18*, 459–482.

2
Suggestibility and the Child Witness

MARY ANN KING and JOHN C. YUILLE

Until recently, children were generally viewed as unable to supply trustworthy testimony. Legal authors dating back to the Middle Ages have voiced concerns about children's abilities as witnesses, citing their proneness to invention, their inability to distinguish fact from fantasy, and their incompetence for accurately recalling events uncontaminated by suggestion (Goodman, 1984). Legal rulings on the admissibility of children's testimony reflect these long-standing assumptions about children. In Canada, for instance, the law states clearly that the testimony obtained from "witnesses of tender years" is subject to special conditions and particular scrutiny (Canada Evidence Act, R.S.C. 1970, c E-10, S.16).

Although legal experts still can be found to support this pessimistic assessment of the abilities of child witnesses, the pendulum of opinion has recently swung to giving credence to the evidence of children. The impetus for this change is multifaceted. Mounting demands for prosecution of child sexual and physical abuse offenses has increased the courtroom appearances of children and has precipitated a debate about the credibility of the child witness. Archival studies like the recent work of Jones (1985) are challenging ingrained assumptions, such as the view that children frequently fabricate allegations of abuse. In a preliminary analysis of 576 sexual abuse cases, Jones found only 7.81% of the cases were proven to be fictitious. Of these, 6.25% were allegations made by an adult, and only 1.56% were fictions generated by children.

Social workers and psychologists working with actual child witnesses have commended the quality of children's testimony, arguing "that children, even very young ones, can give valuable testimony if they are properly prepared and interviewed" (Berliner & Barbieri, 1984, p. 129). Until recently little research evidence existed to support such claims. Over the last decade, however, researchers have begun to isolate those special instances in which children have problems as witnesses from the many situations in which their performance equals adults. In this chapter we present the findings from two separate investigations of the eyewitness abilities of children. What emerges from this work is a composite picture of children's strengths and weaknesses. Our results and our understanding of the findings of other investigators have convinced us that increased sensitivity to the cognitive and situational factors that influence children may ameliorate the problems related to their testimony. In this chapter we outline what we consider the most important of these factors, while emphasizing the necessity of integrating our knowledge of cognitive and social considerations in our interviews of children.

Suggestibility: The Core Issue

In the two studies we have conducted (King & Yuille, 1986; Yuille, Cutshall, & King, 1986) we presented a simulated event (described below) to children of varying ages, and then assessed children's ability to describe the event and to describe and identify an actor from the event. In both cases the children were interviewed individually, following standard police procedures. Each child gave a free account of the event, and this was followed by a series of direct questions about specific aspects of the event. Photospreads were included to examine the identification abilities of the children. Finally, both studies examined the suggestibility of children through the use of leading questions.

Suggestibility may be the most widely expressed concern regarding the child witness. Children, it is believed, are especially susceptible to confusions and distortions as a result of postevent influences and suggestions (see Ceci, Ross, & Toglia, Chapter 5, this volume). While there is some legal sensitivity to the problem of suggestibility in adults, as evidenced by the cautionary use of leading questions, suggestibility is believed to be a particularly serious and unavoidable feature of childhood (Bigelow, 1967).

We initially conceptualized suggestibility as a straightforward characteristic that could be measured through responses to leading questions. After analyzing our findings, however, we realized suggestibility is a recurring concern throughout all aspects of the eyewitness interview and hence an organizing motif for many of the research findings relating to child witnesses.

In our first study (King & Yuille, 1986) the investigation of suggestibility drew from the developmental literature on inference (e.g., Paris, 1978; Paris & Lindauer, 1977). The development of pragmatic inferences has been studied extensively in the context of memory for prose. In this research, children's memories for stories are examined through questions that tap their ability to infer various consequences, entailments, instruments, and so on implied by the explicit content of the narrative. The findings reveal a developmental increase in children's inferential constructions while reading prose. Thus, with increasing age, children become better at reading between the lines, supplying inferences derived from their knowledge of the world. Transposing this finding to the processing of real-world events raises the possibility that young children might be more "databound" than older people when perceiving an event. Children may be less capable of drawing inferences about the connections, motives, and causes for occurrences than older individuals who filter the world through a more elaborated knowledge base. Different inferential processes could affect both the memory of the event and the susceptibility of the child to suggestion. In fact, there could be situations where the adult, because of his or her inferences, might be more suggestible than the child. This would occur when a suggestion is consonant with the adult's inference.

To investigate the relation between inference and suggestibility, we included some questions in our study that suggested erroneous but plausible inferences about the witnessed event. The event was witnessed individually by children from four age groups (ages 6, 9, 11, and 16 to 17 years). Each child was seated alone in a room when a stranger entered with plant-care equipment and tended some plants. Before leaving, the stranger noted the time, indicated that it was late and he had to leave. During the subsequent interview the child was asked the following leading question: "On which arm did the man wear his watch?" He had not worn a watch. On the basis of the developmental literature concerning narrative inferences, we hypothesized that younger children might be more resistant to this leading question than older witnesses in the study because they would be less likely than older individuals to infer the existence of a watch from the stranger's remarks.

Two such leading questions were embedded in our postevent interview. The second question asked whether scissors had been used to remove a leaf. In fact, a leaf had been removed, but by hand, and the scissors, which were in clear view, were not used. Contrary to our expectations it was the younger children who were most affected by the leading questions. The 6-year-olds in the study were significantly more likely to agree with the misleading suggestions. The oldest age group of 16- and 17-year-olds, in contrast, typically answered these questions by saying that they had not noticed the particular detail. In this instance, at least, it appears that inference is not the basis of suggestibility.

For comparison purposes we included a condition that mirrored the paradigm developed by Loftus (1979) for measuring the influence of postevent suggestion upon adults' accounts of an event. In this condition, children saw a slide sequence (depicting a man bumping into a woman and in the resulting confusion stealing a wallet from her purse). Embedded in one of the questions from the subsequent interview was the suggestion that the woman in the slide sequence had been carrying a briefcase. (She had not been carrying one.) The children were later shown a series of slides of the woman including one distractor in which the woman was shown carrying a briefcase. Younger children were more likely than older children to select this incorrect slide as one they had seen in the original series. Thus, with both a live event and a slide event we found younger children more suggestible than older children (see also Cohen & Harnick, 1980; Dale, Loftus, & Rathbun, 1978).

The results of our suggestibility manipulations require further scrutiny in terms of the salience of the aspects of the events focused upon. It has been observed that the effect of leading questions depends upon the aspect of the event the question probes (e.g., Duncan, Whitney, & Kunen, 1982). Leading questions are less effective if they deal with central or salient aspects of the event (Dodd & Bradshaw, 1980; Yuille, 1980). We inadvertently provided evidence for this in our second study. In this instance (Yuille et al., 1986), we presented a staged bicycle theft to small groups of children in three age groups (8- and 9-year-olds, 11- and 12-year-olds, and 13- and 14-year-olds). A thief entered the room, used a pair of cutters to break a chain, and removed a bicycle from the room. The subsequent interview of each child included two misleading questions intended to investigate the effect of salience on suggestibility. One of the questions supplied misleading information about the thief's hat. (He had not been wearing one.) Given the usual strong attention to faces (Shepherd, Davies, & Ellis, 1981) it was assumed that the presence of a hat would be a salient characteristic and not readily susceptible to suggestion. The second question contained misleading information about the thief's boots. (He had worn running shoes.) We assumed that footwear was less salient than headwear. It was expected that the less salient misleading question would prove more effective in influencing the responses of the younger children.

It turns out that we had not effectively manipulated salience. Neither misleading question had an effect on the witnesses. As expected, we were unable to mislead the children about the thief's headwear. Unexpectedly, however, footwear turned out to be an important sartorial concern for these children. Many of them spontaneously reported during their free recall the color and style of the thief's running shoes, including the brand name. These results demonstrate that younger children are capable of resisting suggestions about matters that are salient and memorable (Johnson & Foley, 1984). The findings of the first study suggest that this resistance decreases for less salient aspects of the event.

The influence of salience implicates the role that memory plays in determining susceptibility to suggestion. Explanations for the suggestibility of children have pointed to the developmental trends in the initial perception and coding of the event (e.g., Cohen & Harnick, 1980), the rate of memory decay (e.g., Loftus & Davies, 1984), and the ability of the child to retrieve information from memory (e.g., Marin, Holmes, Guth, & Kovac, 1979). A deficiency in any one of these aspects of the coding and retrieval of an event will leave the child at a disadvantage when required to evaluate the veracity of a postevent suggestion. In short, according to these explanations the less a child remembers about the event the more he can be misled, and the younger the child the less he will remember.

Other findings from our two studies bear on this conclusion. The results of both studies confirm that witnesses at all ages provide more accurate information during their free report than in response to direct questions about particular aspects of the event. Dent and Stephenson (1979) have argued that this frequently reported decrement in accuracy (from free recall to direct questioning) is a demonstration of the implicit suggestiveness of all forms of direct questions, leading and nonleading, with younger children. Consider, for example, a witness who does not spontaneously volunteer any information about the hair color of a suspect in her free report and later is asked to indicate if she remembers seeing blond, brunette, or black hair. Indirectly, this witness is being told that hair color is important and something she should be able to provide. An adult may resist this implicit demand; a younger child may misinterpret the interviewer's intentions and end up providing what he or she feels is an appropriate answer.

The suggestive effect of direct questioning is clearly seen in the children's response to our photo-identification task. Our first study (King & Yuille, 1986) examined identification performance using an eight-item photo lineup, including a photograph of the stranger who had entered the room. The results showed that the 6-year-olds were significantly less likely to correctly identify the stranger than older individuals. This finding by itself could lead to an inappropriate conclusion if we had not included a blank lineup (see Wells & Lindsay, 1984) in the second study (Yuille et al., 1986). That is, half of the witnesses to the bicycle theft saw a lineup that did not include the thief. It is important to note that all the children were cautioned that the thief's picture might not be included and that a rejection of the photospread was a legitimate response. Averaged over the three age groups, the children correctly identified the thief 80% of the time from the stranger-present lineups. Only 10% of these witnesses made an incorrect choice from the photospread. However, only 40.5% of the children correctly rejected the photospread when it did not contain the thief's image. Further, the high rate of false identifications was age-related. Children between 8 and 11 years of age made a choice from the blank photospread on 74% of their opportunities. However, the oldest group (13- and 14-year-olds) made this error only 36% of the time.

It is our contention that the task demands of a photo-lineup presentation may be quite confusing to young children. Children may assume that an adult would not present such a task to them without the target being present among the options. Or they may interpret the task as requiring them to select an option that looks most like the person they viewed earlier. For whatever reason, the presentation of a photo lineup may be, in effect, like a leading question for younger children, one that will likely elicit a choice response. If the lineup is blank, of course, the choice will result in a mistaken identification.

The Dynamics of the Interview Situation

An appreciation of the potential suggestiveness of questioning and of identification tasks has convinced us that any memorial or cognitive deficits in children are amplified by the structural dynamics operating in the interview situation. This point was made evident to us when, on several occasions, we found children accepting misleading suggestions, despite evidence from their free-recall protocols, that they had recalled information that directly contradicted the suggestion (King & Yuille, 1986). Moreover, on several occasions we received unprompted admissions from children that they had "gone along" with a misleading suggestion. Thus, in answer to the question about the watch, although they had no recollection of seeing a watch, they provided an answer to the question. We have no information about how often such conscious acquiescence occurs. Clearly we need to determine the incidence of this phenomenon and explore the factors contributing to its occurrence.

Some direction in this inquiry can be gleaned from the developmental psychological literature. Developmental researchers are explicitly involved in the business of interviewing and eliciting information from children. What has emerged from this literature is an appreciation of the potential for a mismatch between the interviewer's or experimenter's goals and the child's own perception of what is being required of him or her. Variations in lineup array characteristics, the phrasing of questions, and the child's own assumptions about the purpose of the interview task can all influence the nature of the task the child receives and performs. That is, the child's interpretation of the language and intentions of an interviewer is powerfully affected by the interview context. This state of affairs has prompted McGarrigle, Grieve, and Hughes (1978) to make a distinction between received and intended tasks. The intended task is the task the adult wishes the child to complete, the received task is the task the child in fact completes. In the interview situation there are many aspects that can widen the gap between the received and the intended task.

Adults, according to Donaldson (1978), are generally unaware of the interpretive demands they place upon children. One reason for this "egocentricity" is our overestimation of the child's linguistic fluency. There is a considerable difference between the child as speaker and the child as listener. A child who speaks voluntarily is in control of the topic, the ideas, and the presentation. The child's performance in monologue can cause us to overestimate his or her linguistic competence. As a listener in a child-adult conversation the child is not in control and must use all the cues available, verbal and nonverbal, to aid in understanding the message. Children are enormously adept at drawing upon all available information in such situations, and the results are usually an intelligible interchange. At times, however, this contextual sensitivity can result in confusions and misinterpretations.

An excellent example of the subtle cues to which children are responsive is provided by the standard Piagetian conservation task (Piaget & Inhelder, 1974). This task involves presenting a child with two quantities (e.g., two balls of clay). The child is asked to judge the similarity of the two objects on some dimension (e.g., are they the same weight?). Following this judgment, a modification is made that changes the perceptual appearance of one object (e.g., to a sausage shape), and the child is again asked to make the comparative judgment. Younger children (e.g., 6-year-olds) will typically not display conservation, that is, they will appear to believe that the weight of an object changes when its appearance changes. Thus, they will answer the comparison question with a "yes" before the objects are changed, and a "no" when the shape of one of them is changed. However, Rose and Blank (1969) suspected that asking the same question both before and after the manipulation might suggest to children that they should change their answer. They conducted a study that included a single-question condition after the manipulation in the Piagetian task. The results bore out their suspicions as they found 6-year-olds were more likely to make a correct conservation response with the single-question version of the task. Donaldson (1978) has concluded that "the child is not concerned to weigh especially what the words of the question mean in isolation, . . . he is rather interpreting the whole situation: what the experimenter says, what he does, what he may be reasonably thought to intend" (p. 63).

It is possible to create an interview context that minimizes meaningful cues and children still appear to do their best to make sense of the situation. Hughes and Grieve (1980) interviewed 5- and 7-year-olds using nonsensical questions such as "Is mild bigger than water?" and "Is red heavier than yellow?". One might anticipate that children's responses to such queries would be an "I don't know" or puzzled silence. Instead, virtually all the children responded in a serious, reasoned manner, stating for example, "Milk is bigger because it has more color" or "Yellow is heavier because the red cushion is smaller than the yellow cushion there".

These responses, Hughes and Grieve argue, reflect what is likely a well practiced skill for children. Because of the developing state of their language abilities, children become quite proficient at using extra-linguistic cues, their knowledge about the world, and so on, in order to make sense of the comments, questions, and answers directed to them. Such findings underscore the need for viewing the child as an active interpreter of linguistic input rather than a passive recipient of interview questions.

This conclusion casts new light on Varendonck's (1911) classic studies of childhood suggestibility. In one, oft cited investigation, Varendonck asked school-age children for the color of a familiar teacher's beard. Despite the fact that the individual in question was clean shaven, the majority of children answered with a color choice.

Varendonck (1911) used findings such as these to support his claim that children's evidence is intrinsically unreliable. We are proposing alternatively that the term suggestibility can be considered a legal or forensic term for what developmentalists refer to as sensitivity to context. Further, we suggest that the effect of leading questions can be seen as one instance of context sensitivity. Context sensitivity is present throughout the life span. For adults it is particularly noticeable when we are dealing with unfamiliar situations, and we lack the skills to assimilate the unfamiliar. Relative to adults, children are more suggestible because they find themselves in more situations in which they are unfamiliar. As a consequence, children are likely to pay attention to anyone (especially an adult) who they believe knows how to behave in that situation. Thus, children will be more attuned to the social, linguistic, and pragmatic context because it is their means of learning about the world, anticipating appropriate responses, and making the unfamiliar familiar. Consequently, younger children can be expected to be particularly sensitive to contextual cues in a verbal situation where the child is supposed to listen and respond to questions and instructions from an interviewer. If children are interviewed concerning events they have understood, that is, an event they could assimilate to their level of social and cognitive competence, and if they are interviewed in a manner that is consistently meaningful and not contradicted by nonverbal cues, then they should be no more suggestible than adults.

In fact, when children's competence exceeds the adults' (e.g., about cartoons, or children's stories) they may even recall more about the event than adults (e.g., Lindberg, 1980). But if a child lacks competence concerning the event, and/or the interviewer is not adept at anticipating potential confusions, then problems will arise. Thus, the child will be susceptible to leading questions and may make an erroneous choice from a lineup, even if it is "blank," or he or she may invent answers to questions.

Three Methods for Improving Interviews

Our current research efforts are concentrating upon ways of eliciting information from children that are sensitive to the potential confusion and misdirection of the typical eyewitness interview. An additional consideration not alluded to as yet is the fact that the younger the child the less information is contained in their free reports (Brown, 1979; Chi, 1983; Todd & Perlmutter, 1980). In both of our studies the youngest groups provided less information. The younger children were just as accurate as the older witnesses—they simply said less in their free reports. The dilemma for the forensic investigator is that, because they provide fewer details, younger children are the witnesses most likely to require the use of specific questions and probes. Yet, as our previous discussion indicated these are the witnesses for whom such questioning should be avoided. With these two concerns—amount of recall and suggestibility—in mind there are three considerations guiding our research, and we offer these to others with similar interests.

First, insufficient attention has been given to innovative interview techniques that represent a compromise between free recall and more directed questioning. A prime example is the use of reconstruction techniques. The developmental literature demonstrates that reconstructive cues are useful memory aids for young children. Variations of these procedures have been used with children as young as 3 years of age in the investigation of cognitive maps (Goldbeck, 1983; Hazen, Lockman, & Pick, 1978; Rogoff & Waddell, 1982). In these studies, children are provided with small-scale models of people, furnishings, objects, and settings. Children use these props to reconstruct the event or situation of interest. A similar procedure could be developed to assist children in their recall of a personally witnessed event. The memory literature would lead one to expect a higher level of recall with such supportive techniques (Piaget & Inhelder, 1973). The largely nonverbal nature of such a task would make it an especially valuable means of minimizing confusion in communication. Still, the possible suggestiveness of these techniques will have to be assessed. For example, anatomically correct dolls have become popular as aids for younger children when describing sexual offenses. However, the dolls serve the function of a suggestive question with young children. The genitals and orifices of the dolls suggest a play pattern to children, and that play may be misinterpreted as evidence for abuse. Interviewers of younger children must be alert to this problem.

A second consideration for future research concerns the complexity of human memory. Psychologists (e.g., Tulving, 1983) have become aware of the multifaceted nature of human memory. Different aspects of memory appear at different points in development. Thus, what Tulving (1983) has called episodic memory (memory for specific episodes, involving one's own experience) does not appear until the third year. Generally, it is episodic memory that is of interest in eyewitness situations. But a still later-appearing aspect of memory is often involved when children have been sexually abused: script memory. The utility of this notion is suggested from work by Nelson and Gruendel (1981). These researchers have pioneered work on children's knowledge of the scripts for certain regularly occurring events in their lives. Their research has shown that children develop script knowledge of sequences such as birthday parties and restaurant meals from a very early age. Although naturalistic observations of children (Todd & Perlmutter, 1980) have shown that very young children are capable of recalling single-occurring events, what is provocative about the script research is that young children find it easier to describe a script for a familiar sequence than a memory for a specific instance of that script. In other words, young children can more easily provide the script for going to McDonald's than they can remember the specifics of their last meal there on Saturday. This finding has considerable significance for cases where very young children are queried about a crime to which they may have had repeated exposure, such as sexual abuse. A question for investigation is whether more information can be obtained from young children by using an interview that is directed at assessing the child's script knowledge of the events in question (e.g., What happens when Daddy puts you to bed?) rather than specific details (When did Daddy last do . . .?). This point has particular significance, as it is this latter type of question that is often asked of the child who makes an allegation of sexual abuse. Moreover, interviewers will often base their estimation of a child's credibility on his or her ability to supply detailed information about the alleged incidences. Interviewers may find that in the case of repeated abuse, assessing the script memory first may be beneficial. Details of specific episodes could be recalled by the child later, using the script as a guide.

Reconstruction techniques and the use of a script format during interviewing may prove useful as a less directive means of increasing the quantity of information obtained from children, so it is only realistic to expect that direct and specific questioning will be required. As we have already noted, however, inaccuracy and suggestiveness can result from this questioning. A third important area for investigation, therefore, is the development of effective means of communicating to children the intent and purpose of such interviewing, as well as dispelling any misinterpretations of the interviewer's intentions when certain questions are posed. Children need to understand that the interviewer is only interested in what the child remembers and that admissions of memory failure and memory gaps are expected.

Again the developmental literature may be a useful source of ideas for more effective techniques for reducing errors in children's testimony. A typical procedure when conducting a study with children is to provide some preliminary sample tasks to familiarize the child with the type of materials involved in the task and to ensure that the child understands what is expected of him or her. It may be possible to develop a similar sort of preliminary demonstration of modeling before an eyewitness interview with a child. Before a photo-identification task it may be possible to present two mock lineups to the child, one containing the target, perhaps the interviewer's face, and another blank lineup that does not contain the interviewer's face. Some discussion about these two types of lineups may help to communicate to children the actual purpose of the test and the existence of the two possibilities. Similar sorts of procedures could be developed and tested for their effect in minimizing confusion and possible suggestiveness with features of an eyewitness interview, such as direct questions.

Conclusion

The challenge for researchers and practitioners involved with child witnesses is the integration of the legal requirements of the judicial system with our knowledge of the developing memorial, linguistic, and intellectual capabilities of children. We see the use of prompts, script-oriented interviews, and practice tasks as having promise in helping younger children to optimize their response to an eyewitness interview, and in maximizing the value of their testimony.

Acknowledgments. The research reported in this chapter was supported by a grant to JCY from the National Sciences and Engineering Research Council of Canada. We would like to thank the Vancouver and Charlottetown School Boards for their cooperation, as well as the children, teachers, and principals of Spring Park Elementary, West Kent Elementary, and Colonel Grey High School (all of Charlottetown, Prince Edward Island) and False Creek Elementary, and Lord Tennyson Elementary (of Vancouver, British Columbia) for their participation in the research.

References

Berliner, L., & Barbieri, M. K. (1984). The testimony of the child victim of sexual assault. *Journal of Social Issues, 40(2)*, 125-137.

Bigelow, S. (1967). Witnesses of tender years. *Criminal Law Quarterly, 9*, 298-306.

Brown, A. L. (1979). Theories of memory and the problem of development: Activity, growth, and knowledge. In F. I. M. Craik & L. Cermak (Eds.), *Levels of processing.* Hillsdale, NJ: Erlbaum.

Canada Evidence Act, R.S.C., cE-10, S.16 (1970).

Ceci, S. J., Ross, D. F., & Toglia, M. P. (This volume). Age differences in suggestibility; Narrowing the uncertainties. In S. J. Ceci, M. P. Toglia, & D. F. Ross (Eds.), *Children's eyewitness memory.* New York: Springer-Verlag.

Chi, M. T. H. (Ed.). (1983). *Trends in memory development.* Basel: Karger.

Cohen, R. L., & Harnick, M. A. (1980). The susceptibility of child witnesses to suggestion. *Law and Human Behavior, 4(3)*, 201–210.

Dale, P. S., Loftus, E. F., & Rathbun, L. (1978). The influence of the form of the question on the eyewitness testimony of preschool children. *Journal of Psycholinguistic Research, 7*, 269–277.

Dent, H. R., & Stephenson, G. M. (1979). An experimental study of the effectiveness of different techniques of questioning child witnesses. *British Journal of Social and Clinical Psychology, 18*, 41–51.

Dodd, D. H., & Bradshaw, J. M. (1980). Leading questions and memory: Pragmatic constraints. *Journal of Verbal Learning and Verbal Behavior, 19*, 695–704.

Donaldson, M. (1978). *Children's minds*. London: Fontana.

Duncan, E. M., Whitney, P., & Kunen, S. (1982). Integration of visual and verbal information in children's memories. *Child Development, 53*, 1215–1223.

Goldbeck, S. L. (1983). Reconstructing a large-scale spatial arrangement: Effects of environment organization and operativity. *Developmental Psychology, 19(4)*, 644–653.

Goodman, G. (1984). Children's testimony in historical perspective. *Journal of Social Issues, 40(2)*, 9–32.

Hazen, N. L., Lockman, J. J., & Pick, Jr., H. L. (1978). The development of children's representations of large-scale environments. *Child Development, 49*, 623–636.

Hughes, M., & Grieve, R. (1980). On asking children bizarre questions. In M. Donaldson, R. Grieve, & C. Pratt (Eds.), *Early childhood development and education*. Oxford: Basil Blackwell.

Johnson, M. K., & Foley, M. A. (1984). Differentiating fact from fantasy: The reliability of children's memory. *Journal of Social Issues, 40(2)*, 33–50.

Jones, D. P. H. (1985, November). *Reliable and fictitious accounts of sexual abuse in children*. Paper presented at the Seventh National Conference on Child Abuse and Neglect, Chicago, IL.

King, M. A., & Yuille, J. C. (1986). *An investigation of children's eyewitness abilities*. Manuscript submitted for publication.

Lindberg, M. (1980). Is knowledge base development a necessary and sufficient condition for memory development? *Journal of Experimental Child Psychology, 30*, 401–410.

Loftus, E. F. (1979). *Eyewitness testimony*. Cambridge, MA: Harvard University Press.

Loftus, E. F., & Davies, G. M. (1984). Distortions in the memory of children. *Journal of Social Issues, 40(2)*, 51–67.

Marin, B. V., Holmes, D. L., Guth, M., & Kovac, P. (1979). The potential of children as eyewitnesses. *Law and Human Behavior, 3*, 295–305.

McGarrigle, J., Grieve, R., & Hughes, M. (1978). Interpreting inclusion: A contribution to the study of the child's cognitive and linguistic development. *Journal of Experimental Child Psychology, 26*, 528–550.

Nelson, K., & Gruendel, J. (1981). Generalized event representations: Basic building blocks of cognitive development. In A. Brown & M. Lamb (Eds.), *Advances in Developmental Psychology* (Vol. 1, pp. 131–158). Hillsdale, NJ: Erlbaum.

Paris, S. G. (1978). The development of interference and transformation as memory operations. In P. A. Ornstein (Ed.), *Memory development in children*. Hillsdale, NJ: Erlbaum.

Paris, S. G., & Lindauer, B. K. (1977). Constructive aspects of children's comprehension and memory. In R. V. Kail & J. W. Hagen (Eds.), *Perspectives on the development of memory and cognition*. Hillsdale, NJ: Erlbaum.

Piaget, J., & Inhelder, B. (1973). *Memory and intelligence*. New York: Basic Books.

Piaget, J., & Inhelder, B. (1974). *The child's construction of quantities: Conservation and atomism*. New York: Basic Books.

Rogoff, B., & Waddell, K. J. (1982). Memory for information organized in a scene by children from two cultures. *Child Development, 53*, 1224–1228.

Rose, S. A., & Blank, M. (1969). The potency of context in children's cognition: An illustration through conservation. *Child Development, 40*, 383–406.

Shepherd, J., Davies, G., & Ellis, H. (1981). Studies of cue saliency. In G. Davies, M. Ellis, & J. Shepherd (Eds.), *Perceiving and remembering faces*. London: Academic Press.

Todd, C. M., & Perlmutter, M. (1980). Reality recalled by preschool children. In M. Perlmutter (Ed.), *Children's memory: New directions in child development (No. X)*. San Francisco: Jossey-Bass.

Tulving, E. (1983). *Elements of episodic memory*. New York: Oxford University Press.

Varendonck, J. (1911). Les témoignages d'enfants dans un procès retentissant. *Archives de Psychologie, 11*, 129–171.

Wells, G. L., & Lindsay, R. C. L. (1984). On estimating the diagnosticity of eyewitness nonidentifications. *Psychological Bulletin, 88*, 776–784.

Yuille, J. C. (1980). A critical examination of the psychological and practical implications of eyewitness research. *Law and Human Behavior, 4(4)*, 335–345.

Yuille, J. C., Cutshall, J. L., & King, M. A. (1986). Age-related changes in eyewitness accounts and photo-identification. In press.

3
Children's Testimony: Age-Related Patterns of Memory Errors

KAREN J. SAYWITZ

Courtroom testimony by children has been the focus of long-standing controversy. In recent years, children have begun to testify in many cases where they are likely to be the only witness, as in cases of child abuse. Although cultural stereotypes lead us to be skeptical of trusting children's testimony, judges are called upon to determine how best to use children's testimony in court (Goodman, 1984; Goodman, Golding, & Haith, 1984). Employing their discretion on a case-by-case basis, judges must often predict which aspects of a child's testimony will be trustworthy and comparable to adult performance, as adult testimony, too, can be unreliable (Loftus, 1979).

Courts often presume that anyone over 14 years of age is competent to testify. For children under 14 years (and in some states under 10 years) of age, the judge determines whether the witness is competent to testify by interviewing the child. (In some states, the judge can listen to the child's entire testimony before making a determination of competency). These legal practitioners have little guidance in making decisions about the competence of a child as a witness. The findings of experimental studies, despite their limitations, may offer one source of assistance by describing some of the strengths and weaknesses that a child may bring to the task of testifying.

Empirical findings from the field of developmental psychology cannot offer sufficiently reliable and valid conclusions on which to base legal recommendations concerning age limits for competence. Researchers have not found a simple relation between age and eyewitness performance, but a growing body of literature in memory development suggests that the interaction between age and other factors (e.g., knowledge base, task demands, situational factors) is important for eyewitness memory. These findings may be used to begin to describe some of the relative strengths and weaknesses one can expect from child witnesses of various age groups.

In order to predict and evaluate the performance of a child witness, we need to operationalize the task of testifying and consider whether the capabilities of children at given developmental levels match task requirements. The type of memory often involved in testimony is currently characterized not as an instant replay of the event, but as a reconstruction (and at times construction) of the facts based on context cues, past experiences, inferences, and existing world knowledge (Chi, 1983; Loftus, 1979; Paris & Lindauer, 1977). Studies of children's memory for real-life events, televised action-adventures, and stories support this reconstructive view of memory, as well as the conceptual framework of schema theory that is widely utilized as an explanation for many aspects of memory for events (McCartney & Nelson, 1981; Nelson, 1978; Newcomb & Collins, 1979; Stein, 1978). Schema theory posits that schemata describe the way in which general knowledge is organized and how this organization influences subsequent processing of information. Nelson, Fivush, Hudson, & Lucariello (1983) describe schemata as

spatially-temporally organized sets of expectations about what things will look like or the order in which events will occur. These expectations are organized in terms of a series of variables or slots which can be instantiated with greater or lesser degrees of probability. (p. 53)

Within this framework, repeated experiences (e.g., routines) are organized into hypothetical cognitive structures, termed *scripts*, that are based on real-life experience (Shank & Abelson, 1977). This view is highly pertinent for eyewitness performance when one considers whether children have scripts for crimes, whether their scripts are similar to adults' scripts, and whether children have similar expectations about (slots for) weapons, victims, perpetrators, bystanders, and so forth. Preexisting scripts are proposed to influence both the selection of information to be remembered as well as the organization of recall.

Many studies have demonstrated the developmental invariance of underlying schemata that guide reconstruction for both children and adults. For example, Nelson and her colleagues conducted a series of studies on children's memory for personally meaningful routine events (e.g., eating lunch at McDonald's). Findings suggested that memories of very young children are not fragmented or jumbled, but are highly organized (Nelson, 1978, 1981; Nelson et al., 1983; Nelson & Gruendel, 1980). Children from 3 to 8 years of age showed the same basic structure of scripts as adults. Although the descriptions of 3- to 4-year-olds were shorter and skeletal, the basics of the script were evident. Older children, aged 5 to 8 years, gave longer, more detailed accounts and used more complex language than younger children.

In studies of story recall, similar results have been found. Children seem to utilize the same basic categories of organization as adults (Brown, Smiley, Day, Townsend, & Lawton, 1977; Mandler, 1978; Stein & Glenn, 1978). In these studies, stimuli are often constructed according to story grammars that are thought to characterize the major components of scripts for stories, according to rules and categories of information (e.g., beginning, reaction, attempt, outcome, and ending) (Mandler & Johnson, 1977). Although significant developmental differences exist in the amount of information recalled from simple stories, the pattern of recall for story-grammar categories is highly consistent across age from first grade to adulthood (Mandler & Johnson, 1977; Stein, 1978; Stein & Nezworski, 1978).

The present study employed a story-recall paradigm. Stimuli were constructed according to the rules of the Stein and Glenn (1978) story grammar. The use of schemata via story grammars as an algorithm provides a psychological rather than a linguistic basis for constructing prose stimuli. Comparability across studies is facilitated, providing a method of controlling what types of information are deleted and left to inference, and what types of information are made explicit in the stimuli. For example, Stein (1977) studied the differential effects of systematically deleting each category of information from a story. She reported age-related differences in recall, depending upon which category of information had been deleted.

Schema-driven processing of new information presents both advantages and disadvantages for accurate remembering. Memory is biased toward information consistent with existing schema knowledge, so that schema-consistent information is easier to recall accurately. However, the disadvantage of a schematic memory style is that the bias toward information predicted by and consistent with the schema may distort memory when, in reality, the data are inconsistent with schematic expectations. Thus, errors are created.

While the predominant memory error for both children and adults is one of omission, the addition of new information and the distortion of original material also occur in the memories of both children and adults (Stein & Nezworski, 1978). The tendency to make errors by modifying recall in this way, with information from general knowledge, is well documented for both children and adults. For example, Bartlett (1932) investigated the relation between adults' socio-historical knowledge base and recall for an American Indian legend. The non-Indian subjects tended to rearrange the story to fit their culturally logical and conventional style (i.e., schema), whereas the American Indians did not make such distortions. Stein (1977) reported that, when specific categories of information were deleted from a story, children, like adults, made inferences to fill in the missing information and transformed the original story ideas to make them conform to the new information. There is a need for studies that compare children and adults on the proportion of their reports that are distorted or embellished.

Given that children and adults both tend to modify memory with information from general knowledge, do children make such errors more frequently? Do children make qualitatively different types of errors than adults? Collins and his colleagues have carried out a program of research demonstrating age-related patterns of errors made by second- through ninth-graders recalling televised action-adventures (Collins, 1970; Collins & Wellman, 1982; Collins, Wellman, Keniston, & Westby, 1978). Older subjects' errors more often involved confusion about items unique to the program, whereas younger children's errors reflected what they expected to happen based on general knowledge. The researchers concluded that younger children tended to fill in gaps in comprehension with stereotyped information, failing to notice when the program actually departed from their scripted expectations.

Older children and adults may possess the ability to monitor their productions and screen out distortions and additions of inaccurate information by discriminating between actual input and their own elaborations (Flavell, 1981; Markman, 1981). In a study of second- through seventh-graders' memories for ambiguous passages, younger subjects had more difficulty than older subjects in distinguishing between their own embellishments and the actual story content (Brown et al., 1977). The ability to make such discriminations and to monitor output for potential errors may be a metamemory skill that develops gradually. Empirical research is needed to examine age-related differences in the ability to monitor productions for potential errors.

It is well documented that children spontaneously recall less information than adults in free recall. However, very young children are relatively proficient at recognition tasks, especially when stimuli are familiar and meaningful (Lindberg, 1980; Myers & Perlmutter, 1978; Perlmutter & Lange, 1978). This suggests that, when children are asked to "tell what happened" in an open-ended narrative form, the young child's account will not only be less complete than the adult's, but also a less complete rendition than they may be capable of providing. In order to uncover critical pieces of (potentially accessible) information, adults often ask children more specific (e.g., possibly leading) questions or give cues to stimulate and structure retrieval (e.g., recognition tasks, multiple choice questions). Thus, there is a great need for research concerning how to provide such cues in the least biasing fashion possible and a need to examine any errors these cues may generate.

For application to the legal setting, we need a greater understanding of the types of memory errors that are developmentally invariant (i.e., lack age differences in performance) and the types of errors that are age-related. It may be that certain more primitive errors decrease with age and that other more sophisticated error types increase with age. Still other types of errors may be found equally among the memories of both younger and older subjects. On the one hand, it could benefit legal practitioners who interact with child witnesses to be aware of possible age-related patterns in performance. On the other hand, these research paradigms may differ greatly from the task of testifying on important variables, reducing generalizability to the legal setting.

This chapter will present a study that employed a story-recall paradigm to investigate children's memory for a description of a crime. Few studies use crimes as stimuli because of the ethical concerns involved in exposing young children to models of criminal activity. However, the use of crimes as stimuli is important in generalizing to the legal setting because there is evidence to support the notion that children change their conceptions of events when damages or consequences are severe, as in crimes, in comparison to more innocuous situations. Piaget's (1932) early work on moral development, as well as numerous studies that replicated and extended his results, suggest that, when damages are high or outcomes are out of the ordinary (e.g., crimes), children change their explanations of causality, intent, motive, blame, and punishment (see Keasey, 1977, for a review).

In the present study, third-, sixth- and ninth-graders were compared on their memory for a description of a crime, in an effort to assess age-related patterns of memory errors that might have implications for the legal setting. These errors include patterns of recognizing information, omitting information, distorting original information, and adding novel information to recall. This study examined the quality of what was recalled, specifically (a) whether younger children distort more of what they freely recall than older subjects and (b) whether they fill in gaps in memory by adding more extraneous ("made-up") material to their accounts than older subjects. An exploratory aspect of the study investigated whether younger subjects are more susceptible than older subjects to intrusions of inaccurate information that has been embedded in questioning at a prior date.

Recall of a Crime Episode

Method

SUBJECTS

Seventy-two students in the average range of intelligence participated in the study: 24 subjects each in third, sixth, and ninth or tenth grade (mean chronological ages were 8.25, 11.5, and 15 years, respectively).[1] These three groups were chosen because the mean ages of children in these grades are just above and just below the common legal age limits for competency to testify, which are 10 and 14 years of age. In other words, in all states the ninth- and tenth-graders (14- to 16-year-olds) are treated as adult witnesses. Third-graders (8- to 9-year-olds), and in some jurisdictions sixth graders as well (11- to 12-year-olds), can only testify if the judge determines by interviewing them that they are competent.

MEASURES

The stimulus story describes two episodes (counterbalanced for presentation order) in which a character commits a theft. Pilot work indicated that the episodes were similar in level of interest and plausibility for both third-graders and college students when rated on a 5-point scale. The story contained 36 propositions and was constructed at the second-grade reading level. Episodes were controlled for story-grammar categories, word frequencies (using Thorndike and Lorge Junior Count norms for children) (Thorndike & Lorge, 1944), and repetition of propositions.

Of the original 36 propositions, 24 formed the true items in the recognition test. False items were generated, controlling for word frequency and category-instance typicality, according to the Battig and Montague (1969) category norms (e.g., T = "Bob ran out of the *bedroom*"; F = "Bob ran out of the *bathroom*"). The recognition test items were randomly ordered with half the subjects at each grade level receiving this order and half the reverse order. Subjects were

---

[1]The oldest age group included students from both ninth and tenth grades because the high school classrooms in which subjects were tested were a mixture of both grades.

also asked six direct questions about a specific character, three of which contained suggestive misleading information that did not appear in the original story (e.g., "What color was the *old* man's hair?" is a suggestive question because his age was not mentioned in the story). Five days later, they were asked to describe this character in detail. Responses were examined for intrusions of the suggested information.

PROCEDURE

Subjects were tested on two occasions. At the initial time of measurement, they listened to the story presented on audiotape and then received three written tasks that followed the presentation of the story: (a) a free-recall task, (b) a recognition test, and (c) six direct questions about a specific character.[2] Five days later, the free-recall and recognition tasks were readministered. Subjects were then asked to describe the character in as much detail as possible.

Subjects were first presented with a free-recall and then a recognition task on both times of measurement because it was felt that this paradigm more closely reflects the experience of the child witness. Often children are first asked by parents or police to tell what happened in an open-ended narrative. In an effort to elicit additional information, adults often ask specific questions that provide recognition cues. Later, children are again questioned in this same pattern by attorneys and judges at hearings and trials.

In coding the free-recall protocols, each of the 36 original stimulus propositions was coded into one of three categories: (a) Omitted from subject's memory, (b) Accurately recalled, or (c) recalled in Distorted form. A fourth general category of Additions was created to include all remaining propositions in recall that were not in the original story. Propositions were coded as accurately recalled if the same wording was used as in the original proposition or if there were minor syntactic changes that did not alter the semantic content of the proposition. Propositions were coded as distorted when the general idea of the original proposition was retained, but details were determined by coders to be slightly or grossly distorted. Distortions were further subdivided into nine types, based in part on the taxonomies developed by Brewer (1977) and Omanson, Warren, and Trabasso (1978). These were collapsed into two major types: (a) distortions due to inference (e.g., pragmatic or evaluative inferences) and (b) distortions due to modifier errors (e.g., the omission, replacement, or addition of prepositions, adjectives, or adverbs, individually or in phrases).

---

[2]Under incidental memory instructions subjects were asked to imagine that they were watching the story happen in their minds as they listened to the story on audiotape. This instruction was designed to aid in controlling for imaginability of stimuli across grade levels, as young children are often aided by imagery instructions and often do not spontaneously employ metamemory strategies to aid recall. See Pressley and Levin (1980) for a discussion of imagery prompts during encoding and retrieval. Subjects were also asked to count backward aloud from 20 to 1 after stimuli presentation, in an effort to reduce short-term memory and recency effects.

Results

Two raters (blind to the hypotheses of the study) coded the 24 free-recall protocols of 12 subjects (2 boys and 2 girls were randomly selected from each grade).
The free-recall scoring system was determined to be highly reliable, based on
Cohen's (1960) coefficients of interrater reliability ($M = .97$). There were no significant effects of presentation order on either the free-recall or recognition tests,
nor did the order of items on the recognition tests produce reliable effects. Free-
recall and recognition data showed no evidence of ceiling or floor effects. Subjects of all ages remembered more propositions on recognition tasks ($M =
70.5\%$, $SD = 8.3\%$) than on free-recall tasks ($M = 55\%$, $SD = 15\%$).

Unless otherwise stated, grade differences were analyzed in a repeated-
measures analysis of variance (ANOVA) with grade as the independent variable
(IQ was treated as a covariate when performance on memory tasks and IQ scores
were related).[3] Post hoc comparisons were made by using the Newman-Keuls test
($p = .05$).

A grade-related pattern of errors emerged on a number of tasks in which third-
graders differed significantly from sixth- and ninth-graders, while sixth- and
ninth-graders did not significantly differ from each other (see Table 3.1). First,
as expected, the free recall of third-graders was less complete (significantly more
omissions and fewer accurately recalled propositions).

A repeated-measures ANOVA was computed on the number of omissions, with
grade and the two times of testing as the independent variables. There was a significant effect of grade ($F = 3.34, p < .04$), but not time ($F < 1$), and no interaction between time and grade ($F < 1$). Because there was no effect of time and no
interaction, the sum of omissions from both times of measurement was treated as
the dependent variable in a one-way ANOVA. There was a significant effect of
grade ($F = 6.05, p < .004$), with third-graders omitting significantly more
propositions than the two older groups.

A repeated-measures ANOVA was computed for the number of propositions
accurately recalled, with grade as the independent variable. There was a marginally significant effect of grade ($F = 2.44, p < .08$), no effect of time ($F < 1$), and
no interaction between grade and time ($F = 1.42, p < .28$). Because there was
no effect of time and no interaction between grade and time, the sum of accurately
recalled propositions at immediate and delayed testing was treated as a dependent
variable in a one-way ANOVA, with grade as the independent variable. There was
a significant effect of grade ($F = 4.88, p < .01$), with third-graders recalling significantly fewer propositions accurately than the older children.

A repeated-measures ANOVA was computed on percent correct free recall.
Again, there was a significant effect of grade ($F = 3.45, p < .04$), but not of time
($F < 1$), and no interaction between grade and time ($F < 1$).

---

[3]For third- and sixth-graders, cognitive abilities were measured by standard age scores
($M = 100$, $SD = 16$) on the Cognitive Abilities Test, companion test to the Iowa Test of
Basic Skills. Cognitive abilities of ninth- and tenth-graders were measured by the SRA
Education Ability Series, companion test to the SRA Achievement Series.

TABLE 3.1. Significant grade-related patterns in means of recalled proposition types at each retention interval.

| | Grade[a] | | | | | |
| | Immediate memory test | | | Delayed memory test | | |
Proposition type	3	6	9	3	6	9
Omitted[b]						
M	19	[15]	[15]	19	[15]	[15]
SD	5	4	7	5	5	7
Accurately recalled[b]						
M	8	[11]	[11]	8	[11]	[12]
SD	5	4	7	5	5	7
Logs of added propositions[b]						
M	1.2	[.82]	[.75]	1.6	[1.1]	[.89]
SD	.6	.6	.6	1.0	.5	.6
Percent correctly recalled[bc]						
M	46	[59]	[57]	48	[58]	[59]
SD	14	12	19	13	15	19

Note: There were 36 propositions in the stimulus story. The means in brackets are not significantly different from each other at the $p < .05$ level of significance.

[a] $n = 24$ for each grade. [b] Adjusted for IQ. [c] Percent correctly recalled was computed by adding the propositions recalled in accurate and distorted form, dividing by 36, and then multiplying by 100.

The second finding of importance is that the third-graders tended to provide significantly more additional propositions in their recall than did the two older age groups. On the immediate free-recall test, the overall number of additions ranged from 0 to 10 ($M = 2.1$), and 5 days later they ranged from 0 to 50 ($M = 3.9$). In view of the highly skewed distribution, analyses of these data were computed following a log transformation of each subject's number of additional propositions. (An ANOVA for within-group variances that are not assumed to be equal was calculated.) There was a significant effect of grade ($F = 4.24, p < .01$) and time ($F = 7.56, p < .007$), and no interaction between time and grade ($F < 1$). In two one-way ANOVA's, grades differed significantly from each other at both immediate ($F = 4.21, p < .01$) and delayed ($F = 5.06, p < .009$) testings, with systematic decreases in the amount of additional propositions with age. The number of additions of extraneous information increased for all grades over the course of retention interval. There were 54% more additions after 5 days elapsed, while the amount of accurate information remained stable over time.

The third finding of consequence is that the third-graders were significantly more variable in the tendency to embellish recall, compared to the other grades. Many third-graders made no additions at all, but others added as many as 30 to 50 propositions. (Recall that there were 36 propositions in the original story.) Despite the reduction in variability that accompanied the log transformation, a test for equal variances was significant for the delayed test ($F = 4.14, p < .01$). It is possible that immediate-recall and recognition testing may have contaminated delayed performance, contributing to the significant number of additions in the delayed free-recall protocols. However, careful examination of the additions reveal that they did not resemble false recognition test items from the immediate recognition test.

In contrast to the aforementioned findings, there was a lack of significant grade-related differences in (a) percent correct recognition; (b) the ratio of distorted to accurate free recall (the ratio rather than the absolute number of distortions was used because of the expected lower recall of propositions by younger subjects—the ratio controls for the amount of accurate recall); (c) the various types of distortions made in free recall; and (d) intrusions of suggested misleading information. (See Table 3.2.)

A univariate ANOVA with repeated measures was computed on percent correct recognition. There was a significant effect of time ($F = 9.5, p < .003$), but not grade ($F = 1.29, p < .28$), and no interaction between grade and time ($F < 1$).

Although 8- to 9-year-olds provided fewer propositions in free recall, the proportion of distorted recall to accurate recall did not differ significantly from that of older subjects ($F < 1$). In fact, the types of distortions examined did not vary across grade levels ($F < 1$). Subjects of all ages made the same types of distortions.

TABLE 3.2. Means of variables showing no significant grade-related effects at each retention interval.

	Grade[a]					
	Immediate memory test			Delayed memory test		
Variable	3	6	9	3	6	9
Percent recalled in distorted form						
M	52	44	49	52	49	47
SD	12	11	17	10	14	11
No. of distortions						
M	11	14	13	12	15	14
SD	3	4	4	3	5	4
No. of inference errors						
M	3	4	4	3	4	4
SD	2	2	2	1	2	2
No. of modifier errors						
M	8	9	9	8	10	9
SD	2	3	3	3	4	3
Percent correctly recognized[b]						
M	72	70	73	67	69	72
SD	9	6	10	9	9	9
No. of intrusion errors[c]						
M				.04	.25	.33
SD				.21	.44	.56

Note: There were 36 propositions in the stimulus story.

[a]$n = 24$ for each grade. [b]Adjusted for IQ. [c]A total of three inaccurate propositions were suggested to the children in questions at the time of the immediate memory test. These propositions served as the stimuli for the intrusion error data collected during the delayed memory test.

For all grades, approximately 70% of the subjects' distortions were due to modifier errors (i.e., replacing, omitting, or adding adjectives, adverbs, adjectival or adverbial phrases—e.g., "he left" being recalled as "he left quickly" or "brown hair" being recalled as "blonde"). Approximately 25% of the distortions were due to either (a) pragmatic inferences (i.e., a plausible inference was drawn; however, coders determined that other inferences were equally plausible—e.g., the man in the store being referred to as the owner when his job title was not mentioned and one could easily have inferred that he was a salesman or manager) or (b) evaluative differences (e.g., the man being referred to, in recall, as "mean," and distorting "the man said" into "the man screamed").

Overall, subjects proved to be resistant to the suggested misleading information. At most, each subject could have made three such errors, resulting from the three inaccurate propositions embedded in prior questioning. The mean number of errors for each grade was less than 1 (see Table 3.2). Only 14 out of 72 subjects produced any of the suggested misleading propositions in their descriptions 5 days later.

The effect of grade on number of suggested misleading propositions was marginal, indicating a tendency in the direction of younger children being less susceptible ($F = 2.92, p < .07$). This trend was not an artifact of amount produced. (The mean number of words per description did not significantly differ across grades ($F < 1$), and there were no significant differences between the descriptions of the 14 subjects who made intrusions and the 58 subjects who were resistant to the suggested information.) However, the mean values were quite small.

As expected, percent correct recognition decreased significantly over time ($F = 9.5, p < .003$), with no significant effect of grade and no interaction between grade and time. However, the expected decrease in amount of free recall over the retention interval did not occur. Accurate recall did not decrease over the retention interval, and omissions did not increase over time. The effect of the 5-day delay may have been attenuated by the fact that subjects received the first recognition test before the second free-recall task. The immediate-recognition test is likely to have provided retrieval cues, which aided memory in the delayed free-recall task and may have interfered with any decrease over time in amount of free recall that otherwise might have taken place. It is also possible that the retention interval was not long enough for expected decreases in amount of free recall to emerge.

Discussion

Overall, the findings are consistent with past findings on story recall that have used innocuous situations rather than crimes as stimuli. Children under 10 years old provided less complete free recall, but were able to use recognition cues effectively to remember propositions not reported in free recall and also to retrieve as many propositions as the 11- to 16-year-olds. In this study, broad semantic category cues, based on the Battig and Montague (1969) category typicality norms, were the basis for successful elicitations of additional accurate propositions in the recognition task. This suggests that common semantic categories (e.g., weather, clothing) could be used in investigative interviewing as cues to direct the child's attention toward general area of content that they might not otherwise have realized were relevant to the crime (e.g., one might ask "is there anything about the weather that you think is important to tell?" rather than the more leading version "It was raining that night, wasn't it?"). Clearly, more research is needed to determine the amount of correct versus incorrect information specific category cues would generate, prior to implementing this suggestion.

Young children often demonstrate a discrepancy between underlying competence and performance (Flavell, 1970). Older children and adults seem to be able to rely on their own retrieval strategies to gain access to information available in memory to a greater degree than younger children. Studies of children's use of organizational strategies, with the aid of selective reminding paradigms, free versus constrained recall, and external cues, have demonstrated the extent to which young children can improve their recall of word lists and sentences, with category cues and props provided by adults (Corsale & Ornstein, 1980; Kobasigawa, 1974, 1977; Paris & Lindauer, 1976). There is a need for a similar line of investigation of memory for real-life events; Price (1984) describes one study of this type. Of course, it is necessary for further research to document the rate at which specific cues generate both accurate and inaccurate information before we can determine the usefulness of specific retrieval cues for the legal setting.

In this study, both additions and distortions are defined as memory errors. However, the data reveal clear differences in the developmental patterns of these two variables. Although 8- to 9-year-olds did not exhibit a greater proportion of distorted to accurate recall, they did add significantly more extraneous information to their recall than older subjects. These embellishments ranged from repetitious exaggerations to blatantly false contradictions (e.g., one child added that "the boy got on a bus" after he stole the item, when the story actually ends without commenting on what the boy did after the theft, and another subject added that "he ate dinner and went to bed," and still another added that "nobody saw him steal it").

McCartney and Nelson (1981) presented anecdotal reports of similar errors in which kindergartners and second-graders added information not in the stimulus story by continuing the story past its ending. For example, the story ended with bedtime, but in recall the subject included that the character got up the next morning and had breakfast. Following the recall task, children were asked what they would change about the story. For the most part, children added information that better matched their own bedtime routine, supporting the notion that children's errors reflect scripted expectations. These researchers did not find any age differences between kindergartners and second-graders in number or type of changes. The results of the present study suggest that age-related differences in this error type may not emerge until some time between the third and sixth grades.

We have been discussing the error type referred to in this study as additions. These seem to be less constrained by the actual stimuli and farther from the truth than those errors identified as distortions, which may be more subtle and difficult for judges and jurors to detect. It is beyond the scope of this chapter to assess which type of error is more likely to deter the course of justice when included in a witness's testimony. However, there may be ways to prepare children for testimony and to educate judges and jurors so that the memory errors that are more frequent in the reports of younger children will interfere less with the course of justice. For example, if third-graders add more extraneous information to their recall because they assume that "more" means "better," and try to please an adult by increasing the size of their production, then they could be cautioned against this tendency with prequestioning instructions. The child could be warned that the investigator does not want more information, but rather accurate information. It may be that, given such instructions, young children can reduce their additions, in contrast to children who did not receive these instructions.

There is some evidence to suggest that instructions prior to testifying may be useful in improving young children's performance. Research findings suggest that prior training, cues/prompts, and adult commentary at retrieval can improve young children's performance on laboratory tasks (Buss, Yussen, Mathews, Miller, & Rembold, 1983; Collins, Sobol, & Westby, 1981; Field & Anderson, 1985; Paris & Lindauer, 1977). Studies are needed that examine the feasibility of using similar techniques to improve memory for real-life situations. The results of studies that have trained children in referential communication and comprehension monitoring skills suggest that children can be trained to improve performance and maintain improvements over time within specific contexts (Asher & Wigfield, 1981; Harris, Kruithof, Terwogt, & Visser, 1981). Young children are limited in generalizing to new contexts. Training studies in these areas can serve as heuristic models for studying the kinds of instructions that children can be given to prepare them for court appearance. Even if children cannot generalize these skills outside the context of testimony, they may benefit during the course of testifying. However, for application to the legal setting, researchers will need to document that instructions and training do not also facilitate additional inaccurate information.

In this study, younger children were particularly likely, at both immediate and delayed testings, to produce recall errors by adding information not in the original stimuli. Over time, subjects of all ages demonstrated this phenomenon. These findings may be explained by the difficulty in distinguishing between what actually occurred and what might have occurred, based on one's expectations or schemata. When subjects are exposed to a stimulus, other related pieces of information resident in memory are activated as well. These are typically other aspects of the schema that have been frequently associated with the stimulus item in the person's past experience. Over time, the activated connections weaken, and the subject loses the ability to discriminate between the original stimulus and additional information that was activated at the time of encoding to provide the frame or context in which to make sense of the stimulus. Thus, over time, subjects' reconstructions rely more on general knowledge and less on uniquely experienced data. They begin to modify their reports over time with additional information (Myles-Worsley, Cromer, & Dodd, 1986).

From the outset, younger children may have a less well-developed ability to discriminate original material from additionally activated pieces of information that might have been part of the original material. Their schemata may be less enriched and less elaborate due in part to inexperience. In addition, younger children may not have been able to effectively monitor their output for the detection and inhibition of novel additions. This may be a metamemory skill that develops gradually. It is also possible that young children may try to compensate for their smaller output by increasing the size of their productions. The result may be embellished reports, similar to those produced by older subjects after memory begins to fade. Each of these hypotheses lacks empirical data to be tested adequately in the present study.

In our study, not only were third-graders more likely to embellish recall, but they were significantly more variable in their tendency to do so than the other two grades. High variability among younger children suggests the need for developing more sensitive screening techniques for judges to use in determining competency. If this higher variability among younger children can be related to systematic differences between children, then one could devise interview questions that judges could administer to witnesses under 10 years old to screen out the less able witnesses among this group. If children who tend to add extraneous material still are permitted to testify, it may be advisable to avoid the use of leading questions that are likely to produce distortions in witnesses of all ages. At the very least, the practice of asking the child "What else?" may only encourage some children to add extraneous, and in some instances contradictory, information to their accounts.

While the third-graders showed distinct differences from the older two grades, none of the post hoc comparisons between sixth- and ninth-graders reached significance. This was not because of a ceiling effect. On this task, 11- to 12-year-olds were as capable reporters as 14- to 16-year-olds. In many states, the legal system treats their testimony differently. This finding raises questions about this legal practice. Some of the skills utilized in testimony may not require the abstract reasoning skills that are thought to develop between 11 and 15 years of age. Instead, some aspects of testifying may involve a more concrete task on which children 11 to 12 years of age perform comparably to 14- to 16-year-olds. A careful task analysis of testifying would address this question.

In summary, the results of this study suggest relative weaknesses in the free-recall skills of 8- to 9-year-olds, who tended to remember less and embellish more. This may present unique problems for the court that are not found in the testimonies of adults. On the other hand, 8- to 9-year-olds did not distort more of what they recalled than older subjects, and they were able to utilize recognition cues to recognize as many propositions as 11- to 16-year-olds. There was a striking absence of strong developmental differences in the ratio of distorted to accurate recall, in the rate and type of distortions in recall, and in the susceptibility to suggested misleading information. These findings suggest several variables on which children under the common legal age limits for testimony (8- to 9-year-olds) perform comparably to subjects whose competence to testify is not questioned (14- to 16-year-olds). In addition, the results indicated few differences in the performance of 11- to 12-year-olds in comparison with the 15- to 16-year-olds. Yet, in many jurisdictions, only the latter group's testimony will be automatically considered competent in court.

Implications for Future Research

While the generalizability of these findings beyond the story-recall task remains unexplored, preliminary age-related trends emerging initially in laboratory studies, can serve as a springboard for more ecologically valid investigations of memory development that examine the underlying psychological processes of change and growth. In the effort to enhance the generalizability of normative developmental data for application to the legal system, researchers need to undertake a careful analysis of the task of testifying. This can be done through the study of courtroom transcripts of children being questioned on the stand. For example, studies are needed to compare the reliability of reports from subjects who receive questions modeled after direct versus cross-examination. Cross-examination is likely to be a more difficult task for young children, requiring more advanced metamemory skills. We need to identify what kinds of conceptual, memory, language, and social skills are commonly required of child witnesses and how well the capabilities of children at given developmental levels match what the task requires. Another rich source of data lies in interviews with child witnesses about their courtroom experiences and with legal practitioners who question children for investigative and legal purposes.

Current trends in memory development research are moving away from standard laboratory tasks with schoolchildren toward more naturalistic settings and with subjects who have actually witnessed traumatic events. However, before generalizing to the legal setting, a transitional phase of research is needed, using tasks in well-controlled paradigms that are designed to reflect more closely those with which the child witness is presented in testifying (e.g., experimental environments that model more closely the context of the courtroom at retrieval and the role of affect—fear, anxiety—in recall, studies of scripts for crimes, rather than innocuous situations; and memory for stressful real-life events).

The results of the present study suggest the need for additional data concerning (a) the nature of embellishments and the extent to which they are contradictions, exaggerations, and so on; (b) jurors' ability to sort through children's reports in order to evaluate, and perhaps discount, extraneous, contradictory embellishments; (c) children's ability to benefit from prequestioning cautions against embellishment; (d) techniques to identify children who are more prone to embellish recall; and (e) the rate at which specific retrieval cues generate accurate and inaccurate information.

The findings of the studies suggested above could then be applied in (a) constructing judicial criteria for determining competency; (b) developing techniques for questioning children that enhance accuracy and minimize distortion; and (c) developing instructions that prepare children for the courtroom experience in ways that reduce their stress and enhance the accuracy of their report. The data and ideas discussed in this chapter suggest several areas in which developmental psychology can contribute to the ability of the criminal justice system to better manage the special needs of the increasing number of cases in which young children are called to testify.

References

Asher, A., & Wigfield, A. (1981). Training referential communication skills. In W. P. Dickson (Ed.), *Children's oral communication skills* (pp. 105–126). New York: Academic Press.

Bartlett, F. C. (1932). *Remembering*. London: Cambridge University Press.

Battig, W., & Montague, W. (1969). Category norms for verbal items in 56 categories: A replication and extension of the Connecticut category norms. *Journal of Experimental Psychology, 80*(3, Pt. 2).

Brewer, W. (1977). Memory for the pragmatic implications of sentences. *Memory & Cognition, 5*(6), 673–678.

Brown, A., Smiley, S., Day, J., Townsend, M., & Lawton, S. (1977). Intrusion of thematic idea in children's comprehension and retention of stories. *Child Development, 48*, 1454–1466.

Buss, R., Yussen, S., Mathews, S., Miller, G., & Rembold, K. (1983). Development of children's use of a story schema to retrieve information. *Developmental Psychology, 19*(1), 22–28.

Chi, M. (Ed.). (1983). *Trends in memory development research*. Basel: Karger.

Cohen, J. (1960). A coefficient of agreement for nominal scales. *Educational and Psychology Measurement, 20*, 266–281.

Collins, A. W. (1970). Learning of media content: A developmental study. *Child Development, 41*, 1133–1142.

Collins, A. W., Sobol, B., & Westby, S. (1981). Effects of adult commentary on children's comprehension and inferences about a televised aggressive portrayal. *Child Development, 52*, 158–163.

Collins, A. W., & Wellman, H. (1982). Social scripts and developmental patterns in comprehension of televised narratives. *Communication Research, 9*(3), 380–398.

Collins, A. W., Wellman, H., Keniston, A., & Westby, S. (1978). Age-related aspects of comprehension and inference from a televised dramatic narrative. *Child Development, 49*, 389–399.

Corsale, K., & Ornstein, P. (1980). Developmental changes in children's use of semantic information in recall. *Journal of Experimental Child Psychology, 30*, 231–245.

Field, D., & Anderson, D. (1985). Instruction and modality effects on children's television attention and comprehension. *Journal of Educational Psychology, 77*, 91–100.

Flavell, J. (1970). Developmental studies of mediated memory. In H. Reese & L. Lipsitt (Eds.), *Advances in child development and behavior* (Vol. 5, pp. 182–211). New York: Academic Press.

Flavell, J. (1981). Cognitive monitoring. In W. P. Dickson (Ed.), *Children's oral communication skills* (pp. 35–60). New York: Academic Press.

Goodman, G. (1984). The child witness: Conclusions and future. *Journal of Social Issues*, *40*(2), 157–176.

Goodman, G., Golding, J., & Haith, M. (1984). Juror's reactions to child witnesses. *Journal of Social Issues*, *40*(2), 139–156.

Harris, P., Kruithof, A., Terwogt, M., & Visser, T. (1981). Children's detection and awareness of textual anomaly. *Journal of Experimental Child Psychology*, *31*, 212–230.

Keasey, C. (1977). Children's awareness and usage of intentionality and motive. In *The Report of Nebraska Symposium on Motivation* (pp. 220–259). Lincoln: University of Nebraska Press.

Kobasigawa, A. (1974). Utilization of retrieval cues by children in recall. *Child Development*, *45*, 127–134.

Kobasigawa, A. (1977). Retrieval strategies in the development of memory. In R. Kail & J. Hagen (Eds.), *Perspectives on the development of memory and cognition* (pp. 177–202). Hillsdale, NJ: Erlbaum.

Lindberg, M. (1980). Is knowledge-base development a necessary and sufficient condition for memory development? *Journal of Experimental Child Psychology*, *30*, 401–410.

Loftus, E. (1979). *Eyewitness testimony.* Cambridge, MA: Harvard University Press.

Mandler, J. (1978). A code in the node: The use of a story schema in retrieval. *Discourse Processes*, *1*, 14–35.

Mandler, J., & Johnson, N. (1977). Remembrance of things parsed: Story of structure and recall. *Cognitive Psychology*, *9*, 111–151.

Markman, E. (1981). Comprehension monitoring. In W. P. Dickson (Ed.), *Children's oral communication skills* (pp. 61–84). New York: Academic Press.

McCartney, K., & Nelson, K. (1981). Children's use of scripts in story recall. *Discourse Processes*, *4*, 59–70.

Myers, N., & Perlmutter, M. (1978). Memory in the years from two to five. In P. Ornstein (Ed.), *Memory development in children* (pp. 191–218). Hillsdale, NJ: Erlbaum.

Myles-Worsley, M., Cromer, C., & Dodd, D. (1986). Children's preschool script reconstruction: Reliance on general knowledge as memory fades. *Developmental Psychology*, *22*, 22–30.

Nelson, K. (1978). How children represent knowledge of their world in and out of language: A preliminary report. In R. Siegler (Ed.), *Children's thinking: What develops?* (pp. 255–348). Hillsdale, NJ: Erlbaum.

Nelson, K. (1981). Social cognition in a script framework. In L. Ross & J. Flavell (Eds.), *The development of social cognition in childhood*. New York: Cambridge University Press.

Nelson, K., Fivush, R., Hudson, J., & Lucariello, J. (1983). Scripts and the development of memory. In M. Chi (Ed.), *Trends in memory development research* (pp. 52–70). Basel: Karger.

Nelson, K., & Gruendel, J. (1980). At morning it's lunchtime: A scriptal view of children's dialogues. *Discourse Processes*, *2*, 73–94.

Newcomb, A., & Collins, A. W. (1979). Children's comprehension of family role portrayals in televised dramas: Effects of socioeconomic status, ethnicity and age. *Developmental Psychology*, *15*(4), 417–423.

Omanson, R., Warren, W., & Trabasso, T. (1978). Goals, inferential comprehension and recall of stories by children. *Discourse Processes, 1*, 337–354.

Paris, S., & Lindauer, B. (1976). The role of inference in children's comprehension and memory for sentences. *Cognitive Psychology, 8*, 217–227.

Paris, S., & Lindauer, B. (1977). Constructive aspects of children's comprehension and memory. In R. Kail & J. Hagen (Eds.), *Perspectives on the development of memory and cognition* (pp. 35–60). Hillsdale, NJ: Erlbaum.

Perlmutter, M., & Lange, G. (1978). A developmental analysis of recall-recognition distinctions. In P. Ornstein (Ed.), *Memory development in children* (pp. 243–258). New York: Wiley.

Piaget, J. (1932). *The moral judgment of the child.* New York: Harcourt Brace Jovanovich.

Pressley, M., & Levin, J. (1980). The development of mental imagery retrieval. *Child Development, 51*, 558–560.

Price, D. (1984). *The development of children's comprehension of recurring episodes.* Unpublished doctoral dissertation, University of Denver, Colorado.

Shank, R., & Abelson, R. (1977). *Scripts, plans, goals, and understanding.* Hillsdale, NJ: Erlbaum.

Stein, N. (1977, March). *The role of structural variation in children's recall of simple stories.* Paper presented at the meeting of the Society for Research on Child Development, New Orleans.

Stein, N. (1978). *How children understand stories: A developmental analysis.* (Tech. Rep. No. 69). Urbana: University of Illinois, Center for Study of Reading.

Stein, N., & Glenn, C. (1978). *The role of temporal organization in story comprehension* (Tech. Rep. No. 71). Urbana: University of Illinois, Center for Study of Reading.

Stein, N., & Nezworski, L. (1978). The effects of organization and instructional set on story memory. *Discourse Processes, 1*, 177–193.

Thorndike, E., & Lorge, I. (1944). *Teacher's work book of 30,000 words.* New York: Bureau of Publications.

4
Memory, Suggestibility, and Eyewitness Testimony in Children and Adults

Maria S. Zaragoza

Eyewitness's ability to accurately perceive, remember, and report witnessed events has received a great deal of attention from experimental psychologists over the last decade (Bekerian & Bowers, 1983; Christiaansen & Ochalek, 1983; Christiaansen, Sweeney, & Ochalek, 1983; Clifford & Hollin, 1981; Loftus 1975, 1977, 1978, 1979a, 1979b; Loftus, Miller, & Burns, 1978; Loftus & Zanni, 1975; McCloskey & Zaragoza, 1985; Weinberg, Wadsworth, & Baron, 1983; Yarmey, 1979). While we have learned much about eyewitness testimony in adults as a consequence, there has been relatively little parallel work on the reliability of eyewitness testimony in children. Nevertheless there is a critical need for up-to-date research on the reliability of children's testimony. Attempts to prosecute cases of physical or sexual abuse, in which the child involved may be the only witness, have brought to the fore issues pertaining to the accuracy and reliability of their testimony (Melton, 1981). Laws for dealing with child witnesses are currently in transition, and the courts are turning to social scientists for information and advice (see Goodman, 1984, for an extensive review of past and present laws concerning child witnesses).

In the past, much of the empirical work on adult eyewitness testimony has focused on the influence of misleading suggestions on testimony. The typical study presents misleading verbal information after a witnessed event through the use of leading questions or an erroneous summary, and then the person's report of the original event is tested. The results of these studies underscore the ease with which misleading suggestions can lead to inaccuracies in subsequent testimony. These studies of "misleading information effects" are purportedly a laboratory analog of changes in testimony that could theoretically be brought about in the court situation by, for example, questioning by the police, attorneys, or other people.

With children, the study of suggestibility becomes all the more critical. The belief that children are more suggestible than adults is pervasive, despite a serious lack of scientific evidence to support this notion. Recent studies, of which there are only a few, have failed to uncover any simple relationship between suggestibility and age. Nevertheless, the presumed suggestibility of children is one of the primary reasons children have historically been barred from testifying in court.

Understanding children's suggestibility is especially important in light of the fact that children are asked more leading questions in courts than adults (Thomas, 1956). Indeed, there are many jurisdictions where leading a child witness is permissible (Goodman, 1984). This practice stems from the fact that the child's spontaneous narrative report is limited and disorganized, and it is therefore often necessary to probe the child for more information to determine all he or she knows. Clearly, there is a critical need for up-to-date research concerning the suggestibility of young children. In particular, it is necessary to determine whether young children are more suggestible than adults and, if so, to determine the ways in which they are more suggestible. This research can provide information badly needed in our judicial system for gauging the reliability of children as eyewitnesses and for developing the most effective methods of dealing with child witnesses.

Although current research on children's suggestibility is scanty, there is a substantial literature concerning the effects of misleading suggestions on adult testimony. We have, as a consequence, made considerable progress in understanding the causes of misleading information effects in adults. This progress is due in part to the development of methodologies that have allowed us to examine separately some of the factors responsible for these effects. This chapter outlines our current understanding of misleading information phenomena in adults to show how the conceptual and methodological tools that have already been developed can profitably be applied to the study of suggestibility in children.

Misleading Postevent Suggestions and Testimony— Research With Adults

An eyewitness to a crime or traffic accident is often asked to recall the details of the witnessed event. Many times the witness will have been exposed to new information about the event (through questioning, conversations, or the media) before testimony. The results of numerous studies over the past decade have shown that witnesses will readily incorporate this new, often false, information into their eyewitness reports if the "postevent" information is presented by a credible source (Bekerian & Bowers, 1983; Bowers & Bekerian, 1984; Christiaansen & Ochalek, 1983; Loftus, 1977, 1978, 1979a, 1979b; Loftus & Loftus, 1980; Loftus et al., 1978; McCloskey & Zaragoza, 1985; Weinberg et al., 1983). This research has typically involved exposing subjects to a film or slide sequence depicting an event such as a traffic accident or a robbery. After witnessing the event, some subjects are exposed to false or *misleading* information that contradicts selected aspects of the original event. The misleading information is typically embedded in questions about the event or descriptions of the event. For example, in a well-known study by Loftus et al. (1978), subjects viewed a series of slides of a traffic accident in which a car failed to stop at a stop sign. Afterward some viewers were asked, "Did another car pass the red Datsun when it was stopped at the yield sign?," thus erroneously implying the presence of a yield sign. On a subsequent memory test, all viewers were asked whether they had seen a stop sign or a yield sign in the slides. Subjects exposed to misleading information were more likely than control subjects to erroneously identify the yield sign as having been in the slide sequence. These experiments, and others using variations of this procedure (e.g., Dodd & Bradshaw, 1980; Loftus & Palmer, 1974; Loftus, 1975), show that witnesses will readily pick up new information and incorporate it into their reports.

Factors Contributing to Misleading Information Effects

The finding that subjects who are exposed to misleading suggestions after viewing an event are likely to report this information on later tests of memory for the event is known as "the misleading information effect" (or "misinformation effect"). Much of the research on eyewitness testimony has been directed toward understanding the causes of this effect (e.g., Loftus et al., 1978; McCloskey & Zaragoza, 1985). Until recently, it was widely accepted that changes in testimony following misleading information come about because misleading information impairs the witness' ability to remember the original event. According to this memory impairment hypothesis, misled subjects report the misleading information more often than control subjects (who have not been misled) because exposure to misleading information impairs subjects' ability to remember what they originally saw. One version of the memory impairment hypothesis (Loftus, 1979a; Loftus & Loftus, 1980) assumes that misleading information alters the original information in memory so that the original information is lost from memory. According to this view, a subject who reports the misleading information "yield sign," instead of the original information "stop sign," does so because the yield sign has erased the stop sign information from memory. An alternative version of the memory impairment hypothesis (e.g., Bekerian & Bowers, 1983; Christiaansen & Ochalek, 1983) assumes that the misleading information renders the original information inaccessible, that is, difficult or impossible to retrieve. The inaccessibility view holds that the original information still resides in memory but can no longer be retrieved. Both versions of the memory impairment hypothesis do, however, share the basic assumption that misinformation effects reflect changes in the witness' ability to remember the original event that are caused by exposure to misleading information.

More recently, McCloskey and Zaragoza (1985) pointed out that memory impairment is only one of several potential causes of misinformation effects. In particular, they showed that misinformation effects can also be the result of at least two other factors. One possible cause of misinformation effects results from the fact that misleading suggestions may cause subjects who can remember what they saw to report, nevertheless, the misleading information. As an example, consider a witness who views a petty theft involving a maintenance man holding a hammer. The hammer in this case is the *critical item* on which subjects will later be tested. The witness is subsequently exposed to false information implying that the man was in fact holding a screwdriver. Finally, on a later test the subject is asked whether the man was holding a hammer or a screwdriver. In this situation, the subject who remembers both the original information "hammer" and the misleading information "screwdriver" may decide to select the misleading information "screwdriver" on the test. In particular, the subject is likely to think that the experimenter believes the critical item was a screwdriver, and the subject, wishing to be viewed favorably by the experimenter, may therefore agree with the experimenter's suggestion (cf. Weinberg et al., 1983). Alternatively, the subject may merely trust the information provided by the experimenter more than his or her own memory and therefore select the misleading alternative on the test. In sum, because there are a number of social pressures operative in this situation, misleading information may lead subjects who are able to remember correctly what they have seen to report instead the misleading information.

The second cause of misinformation effects results from the fact that under the conditions of the typical misleading information experiment, some subjects will remember the critical detail, and some subjects will not. This failure to remember some piece of information may result because the subject never encoded the information, or perhaps because the subject has forgotten the information in the period of time between the initial presentation and the test. The testimony of subjects who cannot remember the original detail is bound to be profoundly affected by exposure to misleading suggestions, thus leading to greater inaccuracies among misled subjects than the corresponding control subjects who cannot remember the original detail. To understand why misleading information may lead to poorer performance among subjects who do not remember the original information, consider first how control subjects who do not remember the original information (and have not been misled) can be expected to perform on this test. Control subjects who do not remember the information being queried will be forced to guess on the test. Subjects who guess can be expected to select the correct answer at a probability equal to chance. In contrast, the test performance of misled subjects who cannot remember the original information, but have been exposed to misleading information, is likely to be considerably less than chance. Some of these subjects, while unable to remember the original information, will nevertheless be able to remember the misleading information. These subjects who remember only the misleading information will systematically select the incorrect response on the test. For example, consider once again the situation where subjects witness the theft involving the maintenance man holding the hammer, and are subsequently exposed to misleading information concerning a screwdriver. At the time of test there are some subjects who no longer remember the original information "hammer," but do remember the misleading information "screwdriver." When asked whether the man was holding a hammer or a screwdriver, how will these subjects respond? Instead of guessing like the corresponding subjects who were not misled, these subjects will in all likelihood select the incorrect alternative "screwdriver." These subjects have no reason to mistrust the misleading information because they have no memory of the original information to contradict it. Because these subjects are responding on the basis of the misleading information alone, they will systematically select the incorrect alternative on the test. Hence misled subjects' accuracy as a group will be much lower than that of control subjects as a group because control subjects will select the incorrect alternative only by chance. Consequently, in all situations where some subjects do not remember the original information, one can expect to obtain poorer misled than control performance whenever the misleading information is presented by a credible source and is an alternative on the test.

Because misled subjects will perform more poorly than control subjects on this test whether or not their memory has been impaired, one is unable to determine to what extent, if at all, these decrements in performance are due to memory impairment. Nevertheless, a determination of whether or not memory is impaired by misleading information is critical to understanding the causes of these effects in the real world. In addition, determining the extent to which memory is impaired by misleading information is important for gauging the reliability of memory. Even though memory is only one of several factors that influence testimony, testimony can ultimately be only as reliable as the witness' memory. To the extent that a person's memory is impaired by misleading information, inaccuracies in testimony would be an inevitable consequence of misleading suggestions, and little could be done to prevent them. If, however, decrements in test performance following misinformation are due to changes in the subjects' responses as opposed to changes in the subjects' ability to remember, these inaccuracies could presumably be remedied by creating test situations that tap their ability to remember.

Because performance in the traditional test situation, like testimony in the real world, is influenced by a variety of factors other than the subjects' ability to remember what they saw, this procedure cannot be used to determine whether misleading information impairs memory. What is needed to evaluate the memory impairment hypothesis is a test that is sensitive only to memory impairment.

McCloskey and Zaragoza (1985) recently developed a test procedure—they call the *Modified Test* procedure—that can be used to determine the extent to which misinformation effects are caused by memory impairment alone. With the Modified Test the performance of misled and control subjects will differ only if the proportion of subjects who remember the original information in each group differs. The Modified Test procedure is identical to the test procedure traditionally used in misleading information experiments (which will be referred to here as the Original Test procedure), except that the misleading information (e.g., screwdriver) is not provided as an alternative on the test; test questions about the original detail provide subjects with a choice between the originally-seen item (e.g., hammer) and a new item (e.g., wrench). For misled subjects who remember both the original and misleading information, the Modified Test eliminates the social pressure to agree with the experimenter's suggestion, because the misleading information is not a choice on the test. Hence, on the Modified Test, misled subjects who remember the original information will, like the corresponding control subjects, indicate so on the test. Similarly, the Modified Test procedure ensures that misled subjects who do not remember the original information will indicate so by guessing as the corresponding subjects in the control group do. Because the misleading information is not an option on the test, all the misled subjects who do not remember the original information will guess on the test, whether or not they remember the misleading information.

The Modified Test procedure is thus ideally suited for determining whether exposure to misleading postevent information impairs people's ability to remember details from an originally-seen event. If misleading information does not impair subjects' ability to remember original events, the Modified Test ensures that misled and control performance will not differ. If, on the other hand, misleading information does cause memory impairment, misled subjects will perform more poorly than control subjects on the Modified Test. This is because misled subjects whose memory has been impaired will perform no better than chance on this test, whereas the control subjects whose ability to remember remains intact will select the correct answer on the test.

McCloskey and Zaragoza (1985) recently reported the results of six experiments employing the Modified Test procedure. The results of these experiments are presented in Table 4.1. With the Modified Test procedure McCloskey and Zaragoza (1985) found no evidence that memory impairment plays a role in misinformation effects. Misled and control performance never differed in any of the experiments or when the data were collapsed across experiments. However, as can also be seen in Table 4.1, they were nevertheless able to replicate the results of previous studies showing large misinformation effects when the Original Test procedure is used. Apparently, subjects who report the misleading information under the conditions of the Original Test procedure do so either because they do not remember the original item, or because they decide to go along with the experimenter's suggestion rather than their own memory.

More recently, Zaragoza, McCloskey, and Jamis (1987) reported several experiments in which they attempted to evaluate the memory impairment hypothesis in a recall situation. Zaragoza et al. (1987) reasoned that a recall test would be a more sensitive test of memory impairment because a recall test does not provide the potent retrieval cues present in a recognition test situation. Consequently, a recall test should be more likely to reveal potential retrieval difficulties that might be minimized under the conditions of a recognition test.

However with recall tests, like recognition, it is not a simple matter to determine whether memory is impaired by misleading suggestions. This is because most recall tests, like the Original Recognition Test, cannot ensure that differences in misled and control subjects' performance reflect differences in their ability to remember original details. In fact, whether or not memory is impaired by misleading information, misled subjects are likely to perform more poorly than control subjects on a recall test for the same reasons misled subjects are likely to perform more poorly than control subjects on the Original Recognition Test. This becomes apparent if we again consider the expected recall performance of misled

TABLE 4.1. Results obtained by McCloskey and Zaragoza (1985) in the Original Test and Modified Test conditions of Experiments 1–6.

Modified Test Condition

Item	Slides	Narrative	Test
Control	Hammer	_____	Hammer vs. wrench
Misled	Hammer	Screwdriver	Hammer vs. wrench
Experiment	Misled	Control	Difference
1	66	71	5
2	71	77	6
3	77	73	$\frac{2}{3}$4
4	74	81	7
5	70	68	$\frac{2}{3}$2
6	71	77	6
Mean	72	75	3

Original Test Condition

Item	Slides	Narrative	Test
Control	Hammer	_____	Hammer vs. screwdriver
Misled	Hammer	Screwdriver	Hammer vs. screwdriver
Experiment	Misled	Control	Difference
1	40	67	27
2	40	72	32
3	35	70	35
4	42	75	33
5	30	75	45
6	36	75	39
Mean	37	72	35

Note. Adapted from "Misleading Postevent Information and Memory for Events: Arguments and Evidence against Memory Impairment Hypotheses" by M. McCloskey and M. Zaragoza, 1985, *Journal of Experimental Psychology: General, 114*, p. 7. Copyright 1985 by the American Psychological Association. Adapted by permission.

and control subjects who do and do not remember the original information at the time of test.

On a recall test, misled subjects who remember the original information may nevertheless report the misleading information, for example, because of the demand pressures of the experimental situation. Thus misled subjects who remember the original information may perform more poorly than the corresponding subjects in the control group. Second, misleading information is likely to bias the responses of subjects who fail to remember the original information at the time of test. Whereas control subjects who have not been misled have some probability of guessing the correct answer by chance, subjects in the misled condition who do not remember the original information but do remember the misleading information will presumably report the misleading information on the test. These subjects, instead of having some chance of responding correctly by guessing, will be uniformly incorrect. Thus, as long as the probability of guessing correctly in a recall situation is greater than zero, performance for subjects who do not remember the original information will be worse in the misled condition than in the control condition. Consequently, even if an equal number of misled and control subjects can remember the original information, overall performance on the recall test will be lower in the misled condition.

To determine whether misleading information impairs memory in a recall situation, Zaragoza et al. (1987) devised a recall procedure that ensures that the performance of subjects in the misled and control condition will differ only if the proportion of subjects who remember the original information in each group differs. This was accomplished by constructing stimulus materials and test questions in such a way that the items used as misleading information were not appropriate responses to the critical test questions. As an illustration of the procedure used by Zaragoza et al. (1987), consider once again the situation involving the original information "hammer," and the test question, "Beneath what tool did the man hide the calculator?" However, assume now that the misleading postevent information is not "screwdriver," but rather, "sandwich."

With this procedure, misled subjects who remember the original information "hammer" will presumably report "hammer" on the test whether or not they also remember the misleading information "sandwich." Thus misled subjects who remember the original information should, like the corresponding control subjects, respond correctly on the test. Similarly, with this test procedure misled subjects who do not remember "hammer" should, like the corresponding subjects in the control group, guess on the test. Because the misleading information "sandwich" is not an appropriate response to the critical test question, misled subjects who do not remember the original information "hammer" must guess, whether or not they remember the misleading information. Thus, the recall procedure employed by Zaragoza et al. (1987) ensures that if misleading information impairs subjects' ability to remember original information, misled subjects will perform more poorly than controls. However, this recall procedure also ensures that if misleading information does not impair subjects' ability to recall the original event, misled and control performance will not differ.

Zaragoza et al. (1987) report that in two experiments employing this recall procedure performance in the misled condition was virtually identical to performance in the control condition. Mean percent correct was 33% for both misled and control items in Experiment 1, and 60% versus 58% for misled and control items, respectively, in Experiment 2. In both experiments they also obtained large misinformation effects when the Original Recognition Test procedures were used. The results of these recall experiments, in conjunction with the results obtained with the Modified Test for recognition (McCloskey & Zaragoza, 1985), strongly suggest that memory impairment does not play a role in misinformation effects in adults.

To summarize, research on the effects of misleading postevent information has shown that there are many circumstances under which misinformation will lead to inaccurate testimony. In particular, misinformation is likely to lead to inaccurate performance under any testing situation, be it recall or recognition, which allows the person to report the misleading information. These detrimental effects of misinformation on testimony are robust, highly reliable, and of widespread interest in their own right. Subsequent research has focused on determining why these effects occur. In particular, there has been considerable interest in understanding the role memory plays in the occurrence of these phenomena.

Three possible causes of misinformation effects have been identified. One possible cause is that misleading information impairs subjects' ability to remember originally-seen details. A second possible cause of misinformation effects is if demand or other sorts of social pressures lead some subjects who remember the original detail to nevertheless go along with the misleading information. A third source of misinformation effects results from the influence of misleading suggestions on the reports of subjects who cannot remember the original information. Subjects who do not remember the relevant detail are likely to accept new information from a credible source and report this information when subsequently tested on their memory for the event. Given these possibilities, misinformation effects could be the result of one, two, or all three factors, with each factor contributing to varying degrees. At this time there is considerable evidence to suggest that memory impairment is not one of the factors responsible for these effects. There is no evidence that in adults misleading information causes a memory impairment of any kind (McCloskey & Zaragoza, 1985; Zaragoza et al., 1987). It appears then that misinformation phenomena in adults are due entirely to the other two factors described above, namely, the social pressures to conform to misleading suggestions and the biasing of the responses of subjects who cannot remember the original detail.

Misleading Information and Children's Testimony

Of the recent studies which have attempted to investigate developmental trends in suggestibility, nearly all have utilized some variation of the Original Test procedure. Developmental differences are assessed by determining for different age groups the extent to which misleading information influences subsequent testimony. The measure of primary interest is the difference between misled and control performance at each age group. These studies are reviewed briefly below.

Subjects aged 5 to 22 years were included in a realistic study in which subjects witnessed a brief altercation between a confederate and one experimenter over the use of the testing room (Marin, Holmes, Guth, & Kovak, 1979). Each subject was asked to give a narrative account of the event and answer some questions. Two of the questions were given in either a leading or nonleading form; one implied the presence of a nonexistent object ("Was the package the man carried small?" versus "Did the man carry a package?"), and the other implied a nonexistent event ("Did the man slam the door as he closed it?" versus "Did the man close the door as he left?"). On a later test of memory for the original event, subjects of all ages who were exposed to misleading information performed worse than subjects who were not misled. The authors reported that for all age groups approximately half the subjects previously exposed to leading questions agreed with the erroneous information on the final test. They concluded, on this basis, that there were no developmental differences in suggestibility. However, because Marin et al. (1979) did not report control performance for the various age groups separately, one cannot determine whether differences between misled and control performance varied with age. Thus, although this study was able to demonstrate suggestibility effects across different age groups, several factors limit the extent of their conclusions. Particularly problematic is their use of only one misleading question per subject.

A study by Cohen and Harnick (1980) involved 9- and 12-year-old and college-age subjects who viewed a film of a petty crime and were later exposed to misleading questions. Developmental differences were assessed with the familiar method whereby subjects were exposed to either suggestive (i.e., misleading) or nonsuggestive (i.e., control) questions and subsequently were tested with a multiple-choice test that included the misleading information as an alternative. Their results showed that, although misled/control performance differences were larger for the 9-year-olds than for the older subjects, this developmental trend was not significant. Interpretation of this weak developmental trend is complicated by the fact that performance of the 9-year-old subjects on the nonsuggestive (control) questions was reliably worse than was that of the other two groups. Based on this result one would expect the 9-year-old subjects to more readily incorporate the misleading suggestions into their subsequent testimony because they are less likely to have a memory of the original event to contradict the misleading suggestion, but this was not the case. An additional interpretative difficulty noted by the authors is that the control performance of the two oldest age groups may have been at ceiling, thus minimizing misled/control performance differences that may have otherwise been observable. Obviously, Cohen and Harnick (1980) found no clear evidence of a developmental trend in the extent to which misleading information influences subjects' subsequent test performance.

In a study by Duncan, Whitney, & Kunen (1982) subjects aged 6, 8, and 10 years, & college-age were shown slide sequences of cartoons, were asked a series of questions, some of them leading, and were subsequently tested with verbal and visual recognition tests to determine the impact of the leading questions. When all of the data are considered, control performance improved with age but no developmental differences in the effect of postevent information were found. That is to say, misled/control performance differences were equivalent for the different age groups. However, in a second analysis that included only the subjects who had demonstrated good memory for the original event, the younger subjects were found to be less influenced by misleading suggestions.

Obviously, the developmental studies of suggestibility that have been done to date have failed to produce clear or consistent results. One might suppose that this inconsistency is due to procedural differences among the different experiments, for example, differences in the materials used, the age groups employed, test delay, or other factors. However, systematic attempts to compare the available studies on all these dimensions have failed to uncover any variable or combination of variables that can predict the occurrence or absence of developmental differences in suggestibility effects (Loftus & Davies, 1984).

The failure to find clear developmental trends across these experiments is probably due to some limitations inherent in the methodology. In particular, these interpretive difficulties are probably due to the fact that differences in the size of misinformation effects obtained for various age groups are not necessarily due to differences in suggestibility. The lack of a one-to-one relationship between the size of misinformation effects and degree of suggestibility stems from the fact that the magnitude of misinformation effects is to some extent dependent on the level of control performance; the lower control performance is, the larger the expected misled/control performance difference. To see why this is the case, consider a hypothetical situation involving a group of children and a group of adults, in which the children have poorer memory for the original event than the adults. Assume that 20% of the children can remember the original information but 40% of the adults can remember. Further assume that in both age groups all of the misled subjects who fail to remember the original information will accept the misleading information on a later test. Note that we are assuming that all subjects accept the misleading information for purposes of simplicity only—the same point can be made by assuming any probability of accepting the misleading information. The important point for our purposes is the assumption that the children and adults are equally suggestible.

Consider next the expected misled/control performance differences for the children versus the adults, when the final test is a two-alternative forced choice. For children in the control condition, performance will be 60% correct. This is because the 20% who remember the original detail will select the correct alternative, and the 80% who do not remember will guess on the test. Among the subjects who do not remember the original information, approximately half (or 40%) will select the correct alternative by chance on a two-alternative test. Thus overall control performance for the children will be 20% + 40%, or 60%. Performance for the corresponding children in the misled group will be 20% correct on the final test; the 20% who remember the original information will select the correct alternative, and the 80% who do not remember will select the misleading alternative. Hence the expected misled/control performance difference (or suggestibility effect) for the children will be 60% (control) − 20% (misled) or 40%.

By using the same logic we can estimate expected misled/control performance differences in the adult group. Because 40% of the adults remember the original information, performance for subjects in the control condition will be approximately 70% correct, and performance for subjects in the misled condition will be approximately 40% correct. The misled/control performance difference for the adults will thus be 70% − 40% or 30%, a much smaller misinformation effect than the 40% obtained for the children. In this example we have assumed that the children's ability to remember the original event was inferior to that of adults merely to illustrate that the size of misled/control performance differences will vary with differences in memory for the original event. In a situation where children's memory for the original information is superior to adults', they will appear less suggestible than adults. Thus given two groups that do not differ in suggestibility, but do differ in memory for the original detail, the size of the misinformation effect will be larger in the group with poorer memory for the detail. Because children differ from adults in what they select for attention and storage in memory, children and adults are likely to differ in their memory for original details. To the extent that they differ in this regard, the size of misinformation effects will vary even when there are no differences in suggestibility.

Given these interpretive difficulties, it is perhaps not at all surprising that studies which have attempted to assess developmental differences in suggestibility in this way have failed to obtain consistent results. But even in circumstances where children and adults are able to remember original details equally well it is difficult to assess developmental differences by comparing misinformation effects. This is because the influence of misleading suggestions on the performance of subjects who do not remember original details is only one of a variety of other cognitive and social factors that determine the occurrence and magnitude of these effects. Suggestibility is not constant for any age group, but will depend on the extent to which each of these factors comes into play in a particular situation. Determining whether there are developmental differences in suggestibility is a considerably complex problem because it is possible that children are more suggestible than adults in some ways but not in others. For example, it is possible, if not likely, that children may be more easily swayed by pressure to conform to misleading suggestions. Children, because of their dependent status, may be more easily intimidated or coerced into agreeing with information provided by an authority figure. It is possible, then, that children's testimony will be more suggestible than that of adults to the extent that overt social pressures are present. On the other hand, children may be less susceptible to other variables that influence suggestiblity in adults. Adults will readily include in their reports of a witnessed event new information about the event acquired from credible sources, especially when they have no memory of their own to contradict the new information. Children, on the other hand, may be less likely to integrate relevant information acquired from different sources (cf. Paris & Upton, 1976). Consequently, children may be less suggestible than adults in situations where the relevance of the new information to the original event is less obvious, for example, when exposure to new sources of information are spread out over time.

These examples of possible diffrerences in adults' and childrens' suggestibility illustrate the difficulty of determining whether children are more suggestible than adults by comparing absolute differences in suggestibility effects for different age groups. The suggestibility effects observed for the different age groups, even if equal in magnitude, may occur for entirely different reasons. Therefore, it is not possible to predict from such findings under what circumstances developmental differences in suggestibility will or will not be observed. To determine whether children will be more suggestible than adults requires an understanding of how children differ from adults with respect to each of the variables that contribute to suggestibility effects. Thus, an assessment of potential developmental differences in suggestibility would seem to require asking a number of more specific questions about developmental differences in the various factors that contribute to the size and nature of suggestibility effects.

In children, as in adults, one critically important determinant of subjects' testimony is their memory for the witnessed event. Although testimony is influenced by a variety of factors other than memory, the accuracy and completeness of a person's memory ultimately determines how accurate testimony can be under ideal circumstances. One of the important ways in which children may be more sugestible than adults is if exposure to misleading suggestions causes them to forget what they originally witnessed. As we have seen, although adults' testimony can be dramatically influenced by misleading suggestions, misleading information does not impair their ability to remember originally-witnessed details. Although laboratory experiments have amply demonstrated that children's testimony can, like that of adults, be dramatically influenced by misleading suggestions, it is not known whether these effects are due to memory impairment.

Children's Susceptibility to Memory Impairment

It is not clear from the literature on the development of memory whether young children's memories are more susceptible to forgetting caused by misleading information than adults. Generally speaking, forgetting does not occur more rapidly in young children over the short-term (Belmont & Butterfield, 1969) or over the long-term (Bach & Underwood, 1970; Fajnsztein-Pollack, 1973; Hasher & Thomas, 1973; Rogoff, Newcombe, & Kagan, 1974). Furthermore, it is well established that children as young as 4 or 5 years can, under some circumstances, perform as well as adults on recognition memory tasks (Brown, 1973; Brown & Campione, 1972; Brown & Scott, 1971; Corsini, Jacobus, & Leonard, 1969; Nelson, 1971; Perlmutter & Meyers, 1974, 1975, 1976), and that children's recall performance can be comparable to that of adults when they are given direct cues, such as specific direct questions, to stimulate recall (Emmerich & Ackermann, 1978; Kobasigawa, 1974; Perlmutter & Ricks, 1979; Ritter, Kaprove, Fitch, & Flavell, 1973). Nevertheless, young children generally do have greater difficulty than adults in retrieving information from long-term memory in free-recall situations (e.g., Brown, 1979; Chi, 1976; Goodman, 1980; Johnson & Foley, 1984). These retrieval difficulties stem from the fact that young children do not deal with memory tasks in a strategic fashion (i.e., they do not rehearse, generate images, spontaneously organize). A great deal of the development of the strategic skills necessary for recall occurs between the ages of 5 and 10 years (Brown, 1979).

It is possible that young children's relative lack of retrieval skills may make them more susceptible to forgetting caused by exposure to misleading suggestions. As Loftus and Davies (1984) suggest, it may be the case that misleading information, because it is more recent, would at the time of test be more accessible than the original information. Young children might therefore retrieve the misleading information instead of the original information. Thus exposure to misleading suggestions might interfere with the child's ability to retrieve originally-seen details, especially in tests of recall that have a large retrieval component. Clearly, determining whether children are more susceptible than adults to forgetting caused by misleading information is critically important to evaluating the reliability of children's testimony.

The Modified Test procedure offers several advantages over the Original Test procedure as a tool for asking more specific questions about potential development differences in the suggestibility of memory. The Modified Test allows us to determine whether exposure to misleading information causes children to forget what they saw because it allows us to assess forgetting independent of other factors that influence performance in these situations. In particular, because the Modified Test minimizes pressure to comply with the misleading suggestion, the effects of misleading suggestions on children's ability to remember what they saw can be separated from questions about the extent to which children's testimony can be swayed by pressure or intimidation.

If misleading information does impair children's performance on the Modified Test, this would imply that mere exposure to misleading suggestions causes children to forget what they saw, whether or not there are social pressures to conform to the misleading suggestions. Because it is well established that adults' memories are not impaired by misleading suggestions under the conditions of the Modified Test (cf. McCloskey & Zaragoza, 1985), the finding that children's memories are impaired under these conditions would provide strong evidence that children are more suggestible than adults.

We recently conducted two studies to determine whether young children are as resistant to forgetting caused by misleading information as adults are. To do so we tested preschool children between the ages of 3 and 6 years in experiments employing the Modified Test that were analogous to experiments previously conducted with adults. This age group was of particular interest because the testimonial accuracy of children this age is the most controversial. Furthermore, it seems reasonable to assume that if developmental differences in resistance to impairment do exist, they would be most readily observed among preschoolers.

The experiments employed the three-phase procedure traditionally used in misleading information studies with adults: all subjects (a) first viewed a slide sequence depicting an event, (b) were subsequently exposed to neutral or misleading information about selected aspects of the original event, and (c) were tested on their memory for the original event.

In an effort to make the original event appropriate for young children, the slide sequence that served as the original event was constructed from the pictures of a children's story book. The resulting slide sequence consisted of 29 black-and-white slides that depicted the story of a young girl who explores a city park while riding her toy giraffe. No words or sentences appeared on any of the slides. Four of the 29 slides were *critical slides* that subjects would later be tested on. For example, one of the critical slides was a picture of a boy playing in the park with a basketball. For each critical slide there were three different versions. The critical slides and the three versions of each were (a) an old man in the park holding either a cane, an umbrella, or a broom; (b) a construction man holding either a hammer, screwdriver, or a saw; (c) a boy playing with either a basketball, baseball, or a football; and (d) a toy airplane, boat, or train. The critical slides and the alternate versions of each can be seen in Figures 4.1a–d. All the subjects saw only

FIGURE 4.1a. The three versions of the "old man" slide employed as a critical item in Experiments 1 and 2. (Illustrations and adapted illustrations from pages 9, 16, 18, 26 from *The Girl on the Yellow Giraffe* by Ronald Himler. Copyright © 1976 by Ronald Himler. Reprinted by permission of Harper & Row, Publishers, Inc.)

FIGURE 4.1b. The three versions of the "tool" slide employed as a critical item in Experiments 1 and 2. (Illustrations and adapted illustrations from pages 9, 16, 18, 26 from *The Girl on the Yellow Giraffe* by Ronald Himler. Copyright © 1976 by Ronald Himler. Reprinted by permission of Harper & Row, Publishers, Inc.)

one of the versions of each critical item, and across the experiment an equal number of children saw each version of each critical item.

At the beginning of the experiment the children were instructed to pay close attention to the story and the pictures on the screen. The slides were then presented at a rate of 10 seconds per slide while the experimenter narrated the story. Following presentation of the slides and the story, the children were given a 10-minute filler task during which they colored in coloring books. Following the filler task, each child was tested individually. Two experimenters were employed so that both children could be tested simultaneously. During the test phase the children were told that they were going to be asked some questions about the

FIGURE 4.1c. The three versions of the "ball" slide employed as a critical item in Experiments 1 and 2. (Illustrations and adapted illustrations from pages 9, 16, 18, 26 from *The Girl on the Yellow Giraffe* by Ronald Himler. Copyright © 1976 by Ronald Himler. Reprinted by permission of Harper & Row, Publishers, Inc.)

story and the pictures they had seen earlier. They were further told that the experimenter would first briefly review what happened in the story to make sure they could remember the story. Care was taken to make the synopsis appropriate for children through the use of simple vocabulary and sentence structure. The synopsis of the story was identical for all subjects except for references to the critical items. The synopsis provided by the experimenter included false or *misleading* information about two of the critical items, and neutral information about the other two critical items. When subjects were misled about one of the original items, the alternate versions of the critical items were always used as misleading information. For example, for subjects who saw the boy playing with

FIGURE 4.1d. The three versions of the "toy" slide employed as a critical item in Experiments 1 and 2. (Illustrations and adapted illustrations from pages 9, 16, 18, 26 from *The Girl on the Yellow Giraffe* by Ronald Himler. Copyright © 1976 by Ronald Himler. Reprinted by permission of Harper & Row, Publishers, Inc.)

the basketball and were misled about this item, the experimenter may have referred to the "boy playing with the football" or the "boy playing with the baseball." For subjects who were not misled about the type of ball the boy was playing with, the experimenter merely referred to the "boy playing with a ball." Across subjects, each version of each critical item served equally often as the misleading information.

After subjects were given the synopsis of the story, they were told that they would see pairs of pictures and that they were to select the picture they saw in the original slide sequence. The test consisted of four pairs of 7 inch × 8 inch pictures reproduced from the story book. Each pair consisted of the version of the critical slide the child had seen in the original slide sequence and a nearly identical picture, which depicted an alternate version of the critical item. To ensure that the subjects detected the critical difference between the two pictures, the experimenter asked each subject to identify the difference. After pointing out the difference, the subject was asked to point to the picture he or she had seen in the original slide presentation. Across the experiment, each version of each critical item was used equally often as a test picture.

In the first experiment we tested two groups of subjects, with 24 subjects in each group. The two groups were treated identically except for the final recognition test. Subjects in the Original Test group were given the test traditionally used to assess the influence of misleading suggestions on testimony. At the time of test, subjects in the Original Test group were asked to choose between a picture of the critical item they saw originally and a picture of the critical item presented as misleading information for subjects in the misled condition. For example, for subjects in the Original Test condition who saw the boy playing with a basketball and were misled with "football," the choices on the test were a picture of the boy with a basketball (original item) and a picture of the boy with a football (misleading item). This group was included to ensure that misleading information would influence testimony under these circumstances. Subjects in the Modified Test condition received a test that did not include a picture of the misleading information. Subjects were instead given a choice between a picture of the critical item originally-seen and a picture of a new item. For example, for subjects in the Modified Test condition who originally saw the boy playing with the basketball and were misled with football, the choices on the test were a picture of the boy playing with a basketball (original item) and a picture of the boy playing with a baseball (new item).

The results for subjects in the Modified Test group indicated that the children's memory for the original event was not impaired by exposure to misleading information. These results parallel those obtained previously in similar experiments with adults. In the Modified Test condition subjects' performance on Misled items was as accurate as their performance on Control items; Misled performance was 69% correct and Control performance was 70% correct. The results also indicated that children's responses were influenced by exposure to misleading information when the misleading alternative was included as an option on the test. In the Original Test condition performance on Control items was 77% correct but performance on Misled items was only 54% correct. The latter finding confirms that the children did in fact attend to and encode the misleading information.

The results of the first study failed to provide any evidence that misleading information impairs children's ability to remember original information. However, because this experiment employed only a limited number of subjects, we conducted a second study to further test the hypothesis that misleading information causes memory impairment in young children. The second study was identical to the one described above except for one change designed to make the misleading information more interfering. Because retroactive interference increases with the number of presentations of the interfering material (cf. Crowder, 1976; Keppel, 1968), we exposed subjects to the misleading information twice by presenting the synopsis twice. The experimenter merely told the children that she wanted to go over the story "one more time" to make sure they remembered the story. The synopsis was sufficiently short that the children's interest and attention was maintained through the second presentation.

This replication served not only as a stronger test of the hypothesis that children's memories are impaired by misleading postevent information, but also provided another opportunity to compare children's memories with those of adults. McCloskey and Zaragoza (1985) found in several experiments that even after subjects read the postevent narrative twice, misleading information did not affect their ability to remember original information.

Forty-eight subjects between the ages of 3.5 and 6 years (mean age = 4.7 years) were tested in the Modified Test condition. The results of Experiments 1 and 2 are presented in Table 4.2. Experiment 2's results replicated those of the first experiment, by showing that children's ability to remember original details was not at all impaired by exposure to misleading information. Mean performance on Control items was 73% correct and mean performance on Misled items was 74% correct. Taken together, the results of both experiments support the idea that, at least in this situation, children's memories are just as resistant to forgetting as those of adults.

Clearly the present results cannot rule out the possibility that there are some situations in which children's memories might be more susceptible to forgetting caused by misleading information than adults' memories are. Indeed, Ceci, Ross, and Toglia (Chapter 5, this volume) report the results of two studies employing the Modified Test where young children's recognition performance was impaired by misleading suggestions. Furthermore, it is entirely possible that young children's memory would be impaired by misleading information in situations that require the children to recall the original information, even if they are asked specific direct questions that would provide cues to aid their recall. Recognition tests like those employed here, because they provide the original information at the time of test, also provide abundant retrieval cues that are not present in situations where subjects are required to retrieve information. Given that children generally have greater difficulty than adults in retrieving information from long-term memory (e.g., Brown, 1979; Chi, 1976; Goodman, 1980; Johnson & Foley, 1984) presentation of misleading information might impair children's ability to

TABLE 4.2. Misled and control recognition performance for preschool children in the Modified Test and Original Test conditions.

| Experiment | Modified Test condition | | | Original Test condition | | |
	Misled	Control	Difference	Misled	Control	Difference
1	69%	70%	1%	54%	77%	23%
2	74%	73%	−1%			

retrieve original information. Because several studies have already shown that adults' ability to recall original details is not impaired by exposure to misleading suggestions (Zaragoza et al., 1987) determining whether young children's ability to recall original information is impaired under similar circumstances could provide useful information about potential developmental differences in suggestibility. This possibility is currently being investigated in our laboratory.

More research is clearly needed to determine whether children are as resistant as adults to forgetting caused by misleading suggestions. Nevertheless, at this point it can be concluded with some confidence that young children are not more suggestible than adults in all circumstances.

An Approach to Assessing Suggestibility in Children

The legal system has long suspected that children's testimony is easily modified by misleading suggestions. Recent studies of misinformation effects obtained with the Original Test procedure (and variants of this procedure) have amply demonstrated that adult testimony is also dramatically influenced by misleading suggestions (Christiaansen et al., 1983; Loftus, 1975, 1977, 1978, 1979a, 1979b; Loftus et al., 1978; Loftus & Palmer, 1975; Loftus & Zanni, 1975; McCloskey & Zaragoza, 1985; Weinberg et al., 1983). These misinformation phenomena are robust and highly reliable; they have been shown to occur across a wide variety of stimulus events, different types of misleading information, and different methods for presenting the new information. These phenomena undoubtedly show that people have a strong tendency to incorporate different sources of information about an event in producing a response. To the extent that new information is inaccurate, people's testimony is bound to be inaccurate as well. Clearly, in many cases, misleading suggestions can seriously undermine the accuracy of adult testimony.

Studies employing the Original Test procedure in experiments with children have shown that their testimony can also be profoundly influenced by exposure to misleading suggestions. However, determining whether children are more heavily influenced by misleading suggestions than adults is difficult to determine by simply examining age differences in testimonial accuracy. To succeed, the study of developmental differences in suggestibility must be informed by an understanding of why these effects occur, so that more specific questions can be asked about potential developmental differences in the various factors that contribute to these effects. It is only by understanding how children differ from adults in terms of these underlying mechanisms that we will be able to predict when developmental differences in suggestibility will occur. Perhaps then we will be able to devise test situations that minimize inaccuracies.

Some understanding of why misinformation effects occur has been attained in research with adults. Most of the research to date has been concerned with determining whether misinformation phenomena are due to memory impairment, that is, with exploring the possibility that inaccuracies in testimony occur because misleading suggestions impair witness' ability to remember original details. One of the most important insights we have gained from research on the memory impairment issue is that distortions in the witness' testimony are not necessarily due to distortions in the witness' memory for the original event. What subjects report they remember about a witnessed event is influenced by a variety of factors other than the memory record gleaned from the original perceptual experience. In particular, the subject's performance in a memory test situation is likely to be influenced by what the witness remembers from postevent inputs and by guessing, in addition to what the subject can remember from the original event. Furthermore, there are a number of social variables (e.g., the credibility of the misleading source, pressures to conform to the suggestion) that will heavily influence performance in these test situations.

To the extent that memory is in fact distinct from testimony, it is important to distinguish between the suggestibility of memory and the suggestibility of testimony. The suggestibility of memory refers to changes in what the subject remembers about the original event caused by misleading suggestions, the suggestibility of testimony refers to changes in what the subject reports about a witnessed event caused by misleading suggestions. As we have seen, changes in testimony can be influenced by factors other than what the subject remembers. Furthermore, we can also distinguish between two ways in which memory might be said to be suggestible, each depending on what subjects have stored in memory at the time they are misled. At one level there is the possibility that misleading suggestions will change the subjects' ability to remember information about the original event that the subject has in memory. This possiblity is what we have referred to as the memory impairment hypothesis. Research with adults has failed to uncover any evidence for this type of suggestibility in adults, and the research presented here found no evidence of this suggestibility in children (however, see Ceci et al., Chapter 5, this volume, for a description of data to the contrary).

A second possible way in which memory might be suggestible involves subject-witnesses who have forgotten some aspect of the witnessed event, and therefore have no memory to contradict the misleading information. The memories of these subjects would be suggestible if misleading suggestions change what they remember about the original event, that is, if the subject now thinks he or she remembers seeing the misleading information. It is important to note that this is a possibility that has not yet been addressed in the eyewitness memory literature. There is ample evidence that these subjects will report the misleading information with confidence (as evidenced by performance in the traditional test conditions). What is not clear is whether these subjects merely believe the information to be true because it was provided by a credible source, or whether they in fact now remember the misleading information as part of the original witnessed experience. It is entirely possible that some subjects believe the suggestion was part of the original event, even though they know full well they do not remember seeing it. Some preliminary data collected in my laboratory suggest that, even though subjects report the misleading information with confidence, they nevertheless know they did not see the misleading information as part of the original event. More research is clearly needed to determine whether adults' memory is suggestible in this way. More importantly, this is one type of suggestibility that needs to be investigated from a developmental perspective.

Research on the role of memory in misinformation phenomena has also called attention to the fact that the information a witness reports will depend to a large extent on the characteristics of the test situation. This is especially apparent when the performance of both adults and children on the Modified Test is compared to their performance on the Original Test. Misled subjects' poor performance on the Original Test masks the fact that their ability to remember the original event is in fact not impaired. The interaction of test environemnt with memory performance is a critically important issue in evaluating developmental differences in suggestibility. Not only is it important to know how children differ from adults under various test situations, but there is also the more practical concern of knowing what test situations lead to the most accurate testimony in both children and adults.

Progress in our understanding of suggestibility in children is critically dependent on advances in our understanding of misinformation phenomena in adults. These advances will in turn depend on continued attention to the development of methodologies that allow us to examine separately the different factors contributing to these effects. At this time we do not have a complete understanding of misinformation phenomena, though we have made some progress toward that end. For example, we now have some understanding of the role memory impairment plays in misinformation effects. However, a number of questions remain unanswered. For example, how is the misleading information represented in memory? How well can people distinguish between different sources of information acquired about an event? Furthermore, because misinformation effects are not simple memory phenomena, more research is needed on the social variables that influence the occurrence of these phenomena. These and other questions deserve further attention in the adult literature, for they potentially bear on the future direction of research on development differences in suggestibility.

Nevertheless, our current understanding of the mechanisms underlying misinformation phenomena in adults can and should be used to guide the study of suggestibility in children. An understanding of misinformation phenomena in adults can provide the framework for asking a number of more specific questions about the factors contributing to the suggestibility of children's testimony. From specific questions we should be able to get clear answers about developmental differences in the factors that produce suggestibility effects. To date, much of the research on misinformation phenomena in adults has focused on understanding the role of memory in suggestibility phenomena. To the extent that we now understand the contribution of memory to these phenomena in adults, we can begin to assess the role of memory in the suggestibility of children.

Acknowledgment. I thank Stephen B. Fountain for insightful comments on an earlier draft of this manuscript.

References

Bach, M. J., & Underwood, B. J. (1970). Developmental changes in memory attribution. *Journal of Education Psychology, 61*, 292–296.

Bekerian, D. A., & Bowers, J. M. (1983). Eyewitness testimony: Were we misled? *Journal of Experimental Psychology: Learning, Memory, & Cognition, 9*, 139–145.

Belmont, J. D., & Butterfield, E. C. (1969). The relations of short-term memory to development and intelligence. In L. P. Lipsitt & H. W. Reese (Eds.), *Advances in child development and behavior* (Vol. 4, pp. 30-82). New York: Academic Press.

Bowers, J. M., & Bekerian, D. A. (1984). When will postevent information distort eyewitness testimony? *Journal of Applied Psychology, 69*, 466–472.

Brown, A. L. (1973). Judgments of recency for long sequences of pictures: The absence of a developmental trend. *Journal of Experimental Child Psychology, 15*, 473–481.

Brown, A. L. (1979). Theories of memory and the problem of development: Activity, growth and knowledge. In L. Cermak & F. I. M. Craik (Eds.), *Levels of processing in memory*. Hillsdale, NJ: Erlbaum.

Brown, A. L., & Campione, J. C. (1972). Recognition memory for perceptually similar pictures in preschool children. *Journal of Experimental Psychology, 95*, 55–62.

Brown, A. L., & Scott, M. S. (1971). Recognition memory for pictures in preschool children. *Journal of Experimental Child Psychology, 11*, 401–402.

Chi, M. T. H. (1976). Short-term memory limitations in children: Capacity or processing deficits? *Memory & Cognition, 4*, 559–572.

Christiaansen, R. E., & Ochalek, K. (1983). Editing misleading information from memory: Evidence for the coexistence of original and postevent information. *Memory & Cognition, 11*, 467–475.

Christiaansen, R. E., Sweeney, J. D., & Ochalek, K. (1983). Influencing eyewitness descriptions. *Law and Human Behavior, 7*, 59–65.

Clifford, B. R., & Hollin, C. R. (1981). Effects of the type of incident and number of perpetrators on eyewitness memory. *Journal of Applied Psychology, 66*, 364–370.

Cohen, R. L., & Harnick, M. A. (1980). The susceptibility of child witnesses to suggestion. *Law and Human Behavior, 4*, 201–210.

Corsini, D. A., Jacobus, K. A., & Leonard, D. S. (1969). Recognition memory of preschool children for pictures and words. *Psychonomic Science, 16*, 192–193.

Crowder, R. G. (1976). *Principles of learning and memory*. Hillsdale, NJ: Erlbaum.

Dodd, D. H., & Bradshaw, J. M. (1980). Leading questions and memory: Pragmatic constraints. *Journal of Verbal Learning and Verbal Behavior, 21*, 207–219.

Duncan, E. M., Whitney, P., & Kunen, S. (1982). Integration of visual and verbal information in children's memory. *Child Development, 83*, 1215–1223.

Emmerich, H. J., & Ackerman, B. P. (1978). Development differences in recall: Encoding or retrieval? *Journal of Experimental Child Psychology, 25*, 514–525.

Fajnsztein-Pollack, G. (1973). A developmental study of decay rate in long-term memory. *Journal of Experimental Child Psychology, 16*, 225–235.

Goodman, G. S. (1980). Picture memory: How the action schema affects retention. *Cognitive Psychology, 12*, 473–495.

Goodman, G. S. (1984). Children's testimony in historical perspective. *Journal of Social Issues, 40*(2), 9–31.

Hasher, L., & Thomas, H. (1973). A developmental study of retention. *Developmental Psychology, 9*, 281.

Johnson, M. K., & Foley, M. A. (1984). Differentiating fact from fantasy: The reliability of children's memory. *Journal of Social Issues, 40*(2), 33–50.

Keppel, G. (1968). Retroactive and proactive inhibition. In T. R. Dixon & D. L. Horton (Eds.), *Verbal behavior and general behavior theory.* Englewood Cliffs, NJ: Prentice-Hall.

Kobasigawa, A. (1974). Utilization of retrieval cues by children in recall. *Child Development, 45,* 127–134.

Loftus, E. F. (1975). Leading questions and the eyewitness report. *Cognitive Psychology, 7,* 560–572.

Loftus, E. F. (1977). Shifting human color memory. *Memory & Cognition, 5,* 696–699.

Loftus, E. F. (1978). Reconstructive memory processes in eyewitness testimony. In B. D. Sales (Ed.), *Perspectives in law and psychology.* New York: Plenum.

Loftus, E. F. (1979a). *Eyewitness testimony.* Cambridge, MA: Harvard University Press.

Loftus, E. F. (1979b). The malleability of human memory. *American Scientist, 67,* 312–320.

Loftus, E. F., & Davies, G. M. (1984). Distortions in the memory of children. *Journal of Social Issues, 40*(2), 51–67.

Loftus, E. F., & Loftus, G. (1980). On the permanence of stored information in the human brain. *American Psychologist, 35,* 409–420.

Loftus, E. F., Miller, D. G., & Burns, H. J. (1978). Semantic integration of verbal information into visual memory. *Journal of Experimenal Psychology: Human Learning and Memory, 4,* 19–31.

Loftus, E. F., & Palmer, J. C. (1974). Reconstruction of automobile destruction: An example of the interaction between language and memory. *Journal of Verbal Learning and Verbal Behavior, 13,* 585–589.

Loftus, E. F., & Zanni, G. (1975). Eyewitness testimony: The influence of the wording of a question. *Bulletin of the Psychonomic Society, 5,* 86–88.

Marin, B. V., Holmes, D. L., Guth, M., & Kovak, P. (1979). The potential of children as eyewitnesses. *Law and Human Behavior, 3,* 295–305.

McCloskey, M., & Zaragoza, M. (1985). Misleading postevent information and memory for events: Arguments and evidence against memory impairment hypotheses. *Journal of Experimental Psychology: General, 114,* 1–16.

Melton, G. B. (1981). Children's competency to testify. *Law and Human Behavior, 5,* 73–85.

Nelson, K. E. (1971). Memory development in children: Evidence from nonverbal tasks. *Psychonomic Science, 25,* 346–348.

Paris, S. G., & Upton, L. R. (1976). Children's memory for inferential relationships in prose. *Child Development, 47,* 660–668.

Perlmutter, M., & Myers, N. A. (1974). Recognition memory development in 2- to 4-year olds. *Development Psychology, 10,* 447–450.

Perlmutter, M., & Myers, N. A. (1975). Young children's coding and storage of visual and verbal material. *Child Development, 46,* 215–219.

Perlmutter, M., & Myers, N. A. (1976). Recognition memory in preschool children. *Developmental Psychology, 12,* 271–272.

Perlmutter, M., & Ricks, M. (1979). Recall in preschool children. *Journal of Experimental Child Psychology, 27,* 423–436.

Ritter, K., Kaprove, B. H., Fitch, J. P., & Flavell, J. (1973). The development of retrieval strategies in young children. *Cognitive Psychology, 5,* 310–321.

Rogoff, B., Newcombe, N., & Kagan, J. (1974). Planfulness and recognition memory. *Child Development*, *45*, 872–977.

Thomas, R. V. (1956). The problem of the child witness. *Wyoming Law Review*, *10*, 214–222.

Weinberg, H., Wadsworth, J., & Baron, R. (1983). Demand and the impact of leading questions on eyewitness testimony. *Memory & Cognition*, *11*, 101–104.

Yarmey, A. D. (1979). *The psychology of eyewitness testimony*. New York: Free Press.

Zaragoza, M. S., McCloskey, M., & Jamis, M. (1987). Misleading postevent information and recall of the original event: Further evidence against the memory impairment hypothesis. *Journal of Experimental Psychology: Learning, Memory, & Cognition*, *13*, 36–44.

5
Age Differences in Suggestibility: Narrowing the Uncertainties

STEPHEN J. CECI, DAVID F. ROSS, and MICHAEL P. TOGLIA

In the late seventeenth century the village of Salem, Massachusetts was gripped with what, in retrospect, seems like a series of strange and inexplicable events. During a three-month period in 1691, twenty-one citizens of Salem were accused, tried, and found guilty of practicing witchcraft and sorcery. The accused spanned all ages, social classes, and sexes. All but one were sentenced to death.

There is nothing inherently strange *or* inexplicable in being accused or found guilty of practicing witchcraft. Indeed, the news stories concerning sexual abuse cases in California, which appeared while we were writing this chapter (during the summer of 1985), were replete with charges of witchcraft by the children of at least a dozen defendants. These children tell harrowing tales of parental involvement in bestiality, sacrifice, and torture. But the trials in Salem were unique in the history of American jurisprudence. They represented the first time that children were called upon to testify in criminal cases. As a precedent for their use of children's testimony against witches, the elders of Salem actually cited the case of the Squire of Warboys, in England in 1593. In that case a number of children provided various types of evidence against a woman accused of being a witch; the most extraordinary form of evidence was the children's hysterical fits whenever the accused would recite certain words (Seth, 1967).

In each of the trials at Salem the key eyewitness testimony was provided by a child. The so-called "circle girls," aged between 5 and 12 years, testified to having observed adult defendants doing such things as transforming themselves into black cats, flying into pastures on a broomstick, and appearing "in the spirit" alongside apparitions of the deceased. In hindsight, the children's eyewitness testimony seems most incredible. In many of the cases, though not all, the defendants adamantly denied the children's charges, but to no avail (Seth, 1969). From the surviving records of those troubling times, we are able to piece together a picture of a village in which mass hysteria "electrified" young children's imagination, prompting them to reconstruct events in a wholly biased manner, based upon adults' suggestions. Parents and elders in the village wittingly and unwittingly "suggested" scenarios to the children, and the children's later testimony frequently incorporated elements from these scenarios. For example, it was known that the circle girls had met regularly with a woman from the Caribbean

Islands who was experienced in witchcraft. She was a vicar's wife, and she filled the girls' minds with images of witchcraft. Often the children of accused witches were themselves taken into custody and intensively questioned for long periods of time about their parents' acts of witchcraft (Seth, 1967, 1969). These children, too, knew the folklore and superstition that surrounded witchery. Not surprisingly, after such experiences many of them provided damning evidence against their parents. Consider the case of Martha Carrier, a woman executed on the basis of testimony from her four children. The children were taken into custody at the time of their mother's arrest, and one was also accused of witchcraft himself. Her daughter Sara (aged 8) offered the following answers to the magistrate's questions, following an indeterminate period of private questioning by him (Upham, 1867):

M: "But you said you saw a cat once: what did that say to you?
S: "It said it would tear me in pieces, if I would not set my hand on the book (swear an oath to the devil)."
M: "How did you afflict folks?"
S: "I pinched them."

Being asked whether she went in her body or spirit, she said in her spirit. She said her mother "carried her thither to afflict."

M: "How did your mother carry you when she was in prison?"
S: "She came like a black cat."
M: "How did you know it was your mother?"
S: "The cat told me so, that she was my mother. She said she afflicted the Phelps child last Saturday, and Elizabeth Johnson joined with her to do it." (p. 211)

Caught in a web of superstition and rural folklore, children in Salem, Massachusetts repeatedly reported having observed scenes that were highly improbable, except in the collective consciousness of Salem's elders. As the lore of the time included beliefs that the devil came to witches in the form of dark-colored animals, many of the children, upon being questioned about the prospect of such animals visiting in their homes, later testified that the animals came and spoke to them. It is thus easy to understand why so many of the Salem child witnesses testified to having spoken to black or brown dogs, black cats, or dark-colored rabbits. This was part of the lore that children probably knew, and, even if they did not, the pretrial questioning by elders probably created strong expectations about such matters.

Since the time of the Salem trials, psychologists and jurists have addressed the issue of the credibility of children's eyewitness memory on numerous occasions. A complete review of this literature is beyond the scope of this chapter, as accounts can be found elsewhere (Ceci, Ross, & Toglia, in press; Goodman, 1984). But it is noteworthy that there has not been a consensus on this issue. Binet (1900), Stern (1910), Pear and Wyatt (1914), Varendonck (1911), Messerschmidt (1933), and others argued forcefully, though often with flimsy or nonexistent data, that children's memories were too unreliable and susceptible to distortion to be admitted into evidence in criminal cases. Strong negative biases on the part of some of these researchers calls into question their conclusions. Other researchers disputed this claim, arguing that children were no less reliable than adults and were possibly even more reliable (Ceci et al., in press). Until fairly recently, the evidence supporting both sides of this argument has not been of the caliber to result in any firm conclusions. No empirically adequate database exists to forge scientific conclusions or public policy.

During the last decade there have been several attempts to reconsider this issue of children's reliability, and the results are quite mixed. Loftus and Davies (1984) reviewed four recent studies of the reliability of children's memory and concluded that, although there was adequate evidence for the position that children spontaneously recalled less about events than adults, there was not unequivocal evidence to indicate that what they did spontaneously recall was more "suggestible." Of the four studies, two found age differences in the suggestibility of children, and two failed to find such a trend.

This uncertainty about the suggestibility of children's memory sets the stage for our own research program. We explored this issue in a series of four experiments. In this chapter we shall describe our methods concisely, report the results of each study's most important points, and discuss the implications of these results for psycholegal researchers as well as policy makers. The complete archival account of these data can be found in Ceci et al., (in press), though the conclusions discussed here are largely unique to this chapter.

Experiment 1

In the first experiment we approached the prospect of children's susceptibility to misleading postevent information in a straightforward manner. We presented a story to children between the ages of 3 and 12 years, then one day later we biased half of them at random by suggesting that several plausible, yet nonexistent, details had been part of the story, and, finally, we tested the children's recognition memory for the original story 3 days after its presentation. The story was a simple narrative about a little girl's first day at school. Her name was Loren. In her haste to get ready for school, Loren had eaten her eggs too quickly. As a result, she developed a stomachache. The story was presented orally to 186 children in groups of 10-20. The children were attending a summer camp. The story was accompanied by black-and-white drawings that illustrated each of its major clauses. It took 3 to 4 minutes to present.

One day after hearing the story the children were interviewed individually by one of the experimenters. For half of them, it was suggested during the interview that Loren had eaten her *cereal* (as opposed to *eggs*) too fast and as a result developed a *headache* (as opposed to *stomachache*). The children in the control group also were interviewed individually about the story but were not given misleading information. Three days after hearing the story, they were given a forced-choice recognition test. All children were tested individually. They were asked to carefully compare two pictures of Loren, eating eggs in one and cereal in the other, and indicate which one actually appeared in the original story. The pictures were identical in all respects other than the eggs versus cereal. Children were also asked to pick which of two pictures, one of Loren with a headache and one of her with a stomachache, appeared in the original story.

The results of primary interest are the accuracy rates of children between the ages of 3 and 12 years. In the control condition, all children did very well. Accuracy ranged from 84% for the 3-year-olds to 95% for the 12-year-olds. There were no statistically reliable differences over the age range among these control (nonbiased) children. The experimental children, however, *did* differ as a function of age, with 3-year-olds recognizing significantly fewer original pictures (37%) than 12-year-olds (84%). A significant Age × Condition interaction seemed to imply that vulnerability to misleading postevent information was substantially greater for the youngest children. Two cautions should be noted, however. First, accuracy for the original details peaked around the ages 7 to 9 years. Children at this age were already fairly resistant to misleading postevent information. Second, it was not clear to us whether the 3-year-olds were actually more suggestible than older children or whether they were simply more accommodating. In other words, it could be argued that the youngest children were especially eager to please adults. After all, adults who had read the story to them subsequently had indicated that Loren had a headache and had eaten cereal. Lacking a motive as to why adults would deliberately mislead them, the younger children may have complied with their perceptions of these adults' wishes. Adults may invoke more demands for conformity among young children than older ones. The second experiment was undertaken to explore these possibilities a bit further.

Experiment 2

To assess the tendency of children to conform to their perceptions of adults' wishes, we replicated the first experiment with one important change. Instead of having the same adults who presented the story also subsequently suggest an incorrect scenario, another child was trained to do this. The child, a 7-year-old boy, interviewed the children individually on the day following the presentation of the story and suggested the erroneous information that Loren had eaten cereal and developed a headache. All other details of the first experiment remained unchanged.

The data in Table 5.1 show the results of this manipulation. As can be seen, the use of a 7-year-old child to present the misleading information did not bias children nearly as much as when an adult presented the erroneous information. They improved from 37% accuracy when an adult suggested erroneous details (Experiment 1) to 53% when a child made the same suggestions. Clearly, the youngest children demonstrated a sensitivity to the age of the manipulator and a desire to conform to their perceptions of an adult authority figure's expectations. ("Authority" is used here in the sense of either being perceived by the children

TABLE 5.1. Mean percentages of preschoolers' recognition accuracy across Experiments 1 and 2, as a function of age of questioner and condition.

	Condition	
Age of questioner	Biased	Unbiased
Adult	37	74
Child	53	72

as a powerful adult figure who, like most adults, is capable of controlling rewards and punishments or else an authority figure in the sense of being the person who sometimes read the story, therefore in the best position to know what it contained.) Having a youngster provide the misleading information suggests that *some* of the youngest children's poor performance in Experiment 1 was owing to their desire to conform to an adult's wishes, either because of some demand characteristic ("authority") or simply because they remembered the correct information but did not possess sufficient confidence in it to override the adult's suggestion. As already mentioned, they had no reason to suspect the adult was deliberately misleading them when he provided the erroneous postevent information. Even if the details of the original story were still vividly clear to the children, the youngest ones may have opted to choose the erroneous information because they believed the adult knew better than they, given he was sometimes the same person who had read the story. The third experiment was designed to separate these competing hypotheses. Specifically, we asked whether young children's susceptibility to misleading information resulted from a desire to conform to an adult's expectations or from a lack of confidence in their own accurate recollections.

Before turning to the third experiment, however, another aspect of the data from Experiment 2 should be noted. Although the use of a 7-year-old boy to present the misleading information was effective in the sense that children's performance improved over what it had been when an adult presented the misleading information, their performance was still significantly worse than both the older children's and, even more importantly, peers who were not exposed to misleading information. Even after one controls for the age of the "misleader," young children remained somewhat "suggestible" as compared to the control group. Using a 7-year-old improved their resistance to the misleading information (from 37% accuracy to 53%), but they still fared worse than control group peers, whose accuracy was nearly 72%. Thus, the age of the misleader, although important in accounting for some of the preschoolers' error variance, cannot explain all of it.

Experiment 3

The basic approach in this experiment was similar to that of the first two experiments, with a story being read to the children, followed one day later by a 7-year-old boy providing erroneous information. This was followed several days later by recognition test. A different story was used and a slightly different procedure was employed to examine children's willingness to abandon what might be vividly clear memories on their part in favor of the suggested erroneous information because of a lack of confidence. The modification was based on McCloskey and Zaragoza's (1985) claim that prior reports of adult suggestibility were seriously confounded because of the methodology employed in those experiments. In particular, McCloskey and Zaragoza suggested that adults who had been presented misleading information following an event, and later asked to select between the original information and the misleading information, were likely to select the misleading information at a greater than chance rate because they should select it 50% of the time (assuming a forced-choice, two-stimulus array) when they have completely forgotten the original information, that is, when guessing. But they also should select the misleading information occasionally, even when they remember the original information because of a lack of confidence in their memory. After all, they had no reason to distrust the erroneous information. McCloskey and Zaragoza (1985) carried out a series of experiments in which subjects were asked to choose either between (a) the original information and the erroneously suggested information or (b) the original information and new, not previously suggested, information. In addition, McCloskey and Zaragoza included a standard control group that had not been subjected to any misleading postevent information but were asked to choose between the original information and what was for the other two groups the suggested or new information. Thus the control group performance vis-à-vis the other two groups permits an assessment of the inherent distractibility of various distractors.

In the story in Experiment 3, a boy went on his first airplane ride as a birthday present. The flight in a small, single-engine plane was scary, with a storm occurring, then subsiding, during the flight. The pilot and the boy were unworried, though. They chatted and drank juice during the storm. The story contained two major clauses that were manipulated: one dealing with the type of juice the boy drank, and one describing the color of his cap. One third of the children were randomly assigned to the *control* condition. They were presented the story, were interviewed but not given any erroneous information, and later were asked to choose between the original juice and cap and their foils. The second group, called the *replication* condition, received the same type of erroneous information that occurred in the first two experiments. They were shown a boy wearing a red cap in the story, and later were told he had been wearing a blue one. Their test consisted of choosing between the red and blue cap. The third group, called the *modified* condition, received erroneous information but were given a choice between the original information and new information. For example, the boy was depicted as wearing a red cap in the original story, and later these subjects were told he had worn a blue cap. The test for this condition consisted of choosing between the original red cap and a new green cap. The logic behind this manipulation is that, if the subjects' memories were actually distorted by the presentation of the erroneous postevent information, then a sizable proportion of the *modified* condition subjects should choose the green cap because the presentation of the erroneous information should have distorted the trace of the original memory. Whenever the original trace is lost, subjects should choose the new information (e.g., the green cap) about 50% of the time. Also, if subjects do in fact remember that the original cap was red and not blue, as had been suggested, there is no demand characteristic operating to conform with the experimenter's wishes, as the blue cap is not a possible choice, only red versus green.

The results of this experiment were straightforward. The *replication* group performed almost identically to the misled groups in the first two experiments, giving us some confidence that this was indeed a replication of the first two experiments. Similarly, the *control* group behaved almost identically to the earlier control groups. The *modified* group, however, performed differently from the misled subjects. Their accuracy rate was significantly higher than the *replication* group, 71% versus 52%. This indicates that McCloskey and Zaragoza's (1985) argument has some merit. Some of the children's incorrect choices in the earlier experiments appear to have been the result of abandoning their accurate memories in favor of another's in whom they might have more confidence. Importantly, however, even after one controls for this effect statistically, these young children remain vulnerable to misleading postevent information. They still chose the new information (the green cap) significantly more often than the control subjects did. (The accuracy rate for the *control* group was 87%, whereas the *modified* group's accuracy rate was only 71%, $p < .01$). Although the demand characteristics involved here seem to be important, particularly the tendency of young children to relinquish their recollections in favor of another's even when they are accurate, the point is that they were still suggestible after controlling for this tendency. The McCloskey and Zaragoza procedure elevated their performance to some extent, but it did not elevate their performance to the *control* group level, as those authors had reported for their adult subjects.

Experiment 4

Before commenting on the significance of the above findings for both basic research and social policy, it is necessary to report the results of one final experiment. This last experiment was carried out to replicate Experiment 3 and to add three new design features. In this experiment we counterbalanced the critical stimuli that were used in the three treatment conditions to control for any effects that might have resulted from our choice of targets and distractors. One could argue, we reasoned, that young children's performance was not actually vulnerable to erroneous postevent information, but they simply found red and green more difficult to distinguish than red and blue. (Or they found apple juice and orange juice more difficult to distinguish than apple juice and grape juice.) In Experiment 3 we had not controlled for this potential source of variance because we had done so in the earlier experiments and found that it did not account for any of the observed differences. But the story and pictorial stimuli used in Experiment 3 were not the same as those in the earlier experiments so we thought that it would be best to address it in view of the potential relevance of the results to criminal justice workers.

The second design feature added to Experiment 4 was a set of questions that assessed subjects' memories for *accurate* information provided by the 7-year-old misleader as well as for the erroneous information he supplied. The final addition was to add a group of college-aged subjects to serve as a comparison with the adult literature as well as to chart the developmental course of vulnerability to misleading postevent information.

A new story was used in this experiment because the stories used earlier were not thought to be appropriate for preschoolers as well as college-aged subjects. The new story described a carnival in which children were depicted eating one of three types of fruit (apples, bananas, grapes) and clowns were depicted with balloons of one of three colors (orange, blue, yellow). Within each age there were 18 stimulus combinations that allowed the assessment of any variance due to the particular stimulus combination and whether certain targets were more or less difficult to distinguish from their distractors than were others. All procedural details were identical to those employed in the first three experiments, save one. When the 7-year-old met with the college students to provide the misleading information, he did so in groups of 7 to 14 rather than individually, as was the case when young children were used. In addition to providing the misleading information, he provided accurate information about his name and home town. We later tested subjects' memory for this accurate information in order to determine whether the college subjects attended to the 7-year-old, given the group administration. This story lasted about 3 minutes and was accompanied by 12 line drawings that illustrated the main clauses.

Because performance levels were at ceiling for the adults, but not for the children, the data for the college students and the young children were analyzed separately. The results for the children were as follows: None of the various stimulus combinations differed significantly from the others, nor did they interact with the *condition* variable. The same pattern of results that had been obtained in Experiment 3 were once again evident, with *control* group children performing at 88% accuracy in Experiment 4 versus 87% in Experiment 3. Furthermore, young children's recognition memory was significantly impaired by the presentation of misleading postevent information, but this effect could not be accounted for on the basis of McCloskey and Zaragoza's (1985) methodological criticisms of the findings reported in the adult literature. The manipulation suggested by these authors (i.e., the *modified* procedure) *was* shown to be effective in these experiments, however. The fact that subjects' performance in the *modified* condition (72%) was superior to that in the *replication* (46%) condition suggests that some of the demand characteristics mentioned by McCloskey and Zaragoza were operative in producing memory degradations in preschoolers in our earlier experiments. But the fact remains that preschoolers in this experiment were still vulnerable to misleading information when these factors were statistically controlled.

College students' performance in Experiment 4 was substantially better than the preschoolers' in two out of the three conditions. The only condition in which the groups were comparable was the *control* group. This result is similar to that obtained in the first experiment. In that experiment the control group performance had nearly reached the ceiling by the age of 8 years (95%). In this experiment the college students and preschoolers were both nearly at ceiling again. In the case of college students, recognition performance was at or near ceiling in all three conditions across all stimulus combinations, whereas for the preschoolers the *replication* and *modified* condition led to significant reductions in accuracy. College students also were reasonably proficient at recognizing the accurate information provided by the 7-year-old misleader, remembering 80% of the misleader's name and home town. Interestingly, preschoolers were somewhat more accurate in recognizing the child's name and home town. This strikes us as an important finding because it suggests that age differences in vulnerability to misleading postevent information may originate in young children's inability to detect and/or to protect against incoming information that is incongruent with stored representations of events. In contrast, older children and adults are more adept at detecting and/or protecting the contents of stored traces from degradation due to new information. One suspects that these differences are a manifestation of the larger age differences in metamnemonic awareness (Schneider, 1984).

One final aspect of these data requires comment. Unlike those of McCloskey and Zaragoza (1985), our college subjects did not appear to do better in the *modified* condition than in the *replication* condition. The reason is that the task was sufficiently easy for them and performance was near ceiling in the *replication* condition. This is probably an inescapable requirement of trying to make our stimulus materials suitable over such a wide age range. This result should not be construed, however, as disconfirming either of McCloskey and Zaragoza's (1985) arguments; nor should they be invoked as evidence in favor of or against the repeated findings of Loftus and her colleagues that adults are also vulnerable to the effects of misleading postevent information. Our procedures render our position in this dispute equivocal, although it is to be noted that several colleagues who have used different procedures from those used here have also observed young children to be quite "suggestible" (see Goodman, Aman, & Hirschman, Chapter 1, this volume; King & Yuille, Chapter 2, this volume).

However, one consideration in the context of McCloskey and Zaragoza's (1985) procedure has not received attention. This is the "all-or-none" way in which they forged their distinction between the *modified* and *replication* or *biased* conditions. Implicit in their reasoning is the supposition that postevent suggestions either have no effect at all on subsequent efforts to retrieve the original memory trace or that any effects that are observed are the result of demand characteristics. Yet, it is possible to conceptualize the memory performance of subjects in these experiments in terms of a continuous "trace strength" model rather than an "all-or-none" approach. According to the former model, subjects may have strong, weak, or nonexistent memory traces for an original event, and

they may also have strong, weak, or nonexistent traces for the postevent suggestion. If their memory is equally strong for the original event and for the postevent
information, this could create a suggestibility effect in the traditional (biased)
condition. (This is because a pair of equally strong traces may create a retrieval
decision problem.) If both traces are equally strong, the subject *may* face the
prospect of not being able to discern the actual trace, and hence guess between the
original and the suggested information at a 50% rate. If, however, the postevent
trace is weaker than the original trace, then the rate of choosing the original trace
would be greater than chance. Finally, if the trace for the postevent information
is nonexistent and the original trace is strong, then subjects always would be
expected to select the original trace.

The above reasoning can be extended to cover all the conditions shown in Table
5.2. The table depicts the percentages of accurate recognition predicted for each
combination of original trace strength for the event (e.g., a *hammer*), the trace
strength for the biased postevent information (e.g., a *screwdriver*), and the new
information that has not been previously seen or suggested (e.g., *pliers*). These

TABLE 5.2. Predictions of recognition performance based on a trace-strength model.

Group	Trace strength		Choice in recognition	
	Hammer	Screwdriver		
Traditional	Strong	Strong	Guess hammer	(50%)
(Biased)		Weak	Hammer	(75%)
		None	Hammer	(100%)
Control	Strong	N/A	Hammer	(100%)
Modified	Strong	Strong	Hammer	(100%)
		Weak	Hammer	(100%)
		None	Hammer	(100%)
Traditional	Weak	Strong	Hammer	(25%)
(Biased)		Weak	Guess hammer	(50%)
		None	Hammer	(100%)
Control	Weak	N/A	Hammer most of time	(85%)*
Modified	Weak	Strong	Hammer	(75%)*
		Weak	Hammer	(60%)*
		None	Hammer most of time	(85%)*
Traditional	None	Stong	Hammer	(0%)
(Biased)		Weak	Hammer	(0%)
		None	Guess hammer	(50%)
Control	None	N/A	Guess hammer	(50%)
Modified	None	Strong	Guess hammer	(50%)
		Weak	Guess hammer	(50%)
		None	Guess hammer	(50%)

Note. Trace strengths: original: hammer; biased: screwdriver; new: pliers (see text).
*Asterisks indicate guestimates.

percentages are "guestimates," especially in those conditions that are asterisked. It is possible to conceive of alternate percentages, but a full discussion of these alternatives would carry us beyond the scope of this chapter. All the percentages must be confirmed by empirical means, and we are in the process of doing this. The important point for this discussion is to acknowledge the possibility that, under some conditions, the use of the *modified* condition would obscure the coexistence of a memory trace for the postevent information because it does not permit the subject to choose between a weak trace for the original information and a strong trace for the postevent information. If the subject's choice is, say, between a weak original trace and a nonexistent new trace, the original trace will be chosen most of the time. (On the basis of theoretical considerations, we have hypothesized that the actual range should extend from 60 to 85%, but these are crude estimations and need empirical confirmation.) However, if the choice is between a weak original trace and a strong postevent trace, then we anticipate that subjects will usually choose the postevent trace.

The McCloskey and Zaragoza modification does not permit the assessment of the above possibility, in that it assumes that the difference between the traditional (*biased*) condition and their *modified* condition is owing to the superiority of the latter as an index of the subject's memory. As can be seen from Table 5.2, this may be an unwarranted assumption. We hope to provide experimental tests of the predictions made in Table 5.2 in the near future by manipulating variables known to influence trace strength (e.g., length of retention interval, stimulus salience, number of repetitions). Along with data on recognition accuracy as a function of retention interval, number of repetitions, and salience in the story, we plan to record subjects' reaction times to affirm the experimental stimuli—as a convergent measure of trace strength (i.e., strong traces are expected to be affirmed faster than weak ones). Conceptualizing memory in terms of the strength of a trace may go a long way toward explaining many real-world aspects of eyewitness memory, such as the "unconscious transference effect" (Loftus, 1976) or the "vague familiarity effect" (Ross & Ceci, 1984), wherein witnesses are faced with the task of discriminating between an observed assailant and someone previously seen in the same context but who cannot be confidently identified. It could also help us understand under what conditions witnesses would choose someone from a lineup or photo parade who was not the actual assailant but someone whom they had nevertheless seen in the past.

Conclusions

What is one to make of these findings in view of the recent and not-so-recent history of research on children's "suggestibility"? One thing seems clear to us: preschoolers *do* appear more likely to incorporate erroneous postevent information into their subsequent recollections than older children. The reason for their enhanced suggestibility is not clear; we have ruled out several variables as the primary causes of age differences in suggestibiity, but we have not yet discovered a single dominant variable. It may be that some combination of the variables we have studied along with some that we have not studied will yield an adequate account of children's heightened vulnerability to distortion. One variable that suggests itself as a candidate is *metamemory* (e.g., Schneider, 1984). Preschoolers' memory may be more suggestible than older subjects' because they either fail to detect erroneous information or else fail to take the necessary mental actions to combat erroneous information when they do detect it.

In terms of social policy, our findings have less relevance than may appear at first glance. They do not allow one to argue with any certainty that a preschooler's account of an event is distorted merely because it can be demonstrated that someone suggested information during postevent (but pretrial) questioning. Even though preschoolers' memories were more suggestible than older children's and adults', a substantial proportion of them did manage to avoid succumbing to the detrimental effects of the misleading information. Before psychologists confidently can testify at children's competency hearings, it is necessary to learn more about the factors that are responsible for the individual differences that were observed in each of the experiments reported here. In our efforts to extend basic research to the legal arena, it is well worth remembering that developmental psychology is a relativistic science, not an absolutistic one. Our goal as expert witnesses should be to engender in judges and jurors a respect for the sheer mental unrest of children's memories in everyday settings that are frequently accompanied by high levels of stress, leading questions, and transparent adult expectations (Ceci & Bronfenbrenner, 1985). Under such circumstances preschoolers' recollections need to be critically evaluated to determine the likelihood of distortion. We believe that, in the majority of cases, children's recollections will prove to be accurate. Although it is not possible to develop our findings into broad, overarching cautions that serve to discredit the average child's testimony, it should be possible to "tilt" the odds in favor of rejecting children's erroneous testimony while simultaneously appreciating that the majority of children's recollections will prove to be accurate.

Finally, the experiments reported in this chapter were aimed at assessing the degree of suggestibility of preschoolers. The first experiment showed that preschoolers' memories were more problematic than older childrens'. The next three experiments helped determine the basis of their inferior performance. To some extent the methodological issues addressed in Experiments 2 through 4 are of "academic" interest only. The poor performance of preschoolers is not alleviated simply by identifying their basis. In an actual adjudicatory context, a child may be interviewed by numerous persons (e.g., social workers, attorneys, policy, parents, judge, teachers, peers) following an act of domestic violence or suspected sexual molestation. If erroneous information is introduced during such interviews, it may resurface in the form of the child's reconstruction of the events, *if* the choice presented to the child is between the misleading information and the original information (e.g., between the actual perpetrator of a molestation and someone who was erroneously suggested to have been the perpetrator). Our efforts at reducing children's erroneous performance in the last three experiments demonstrate that conditions can be created to minimize these errors, but in an actual crime and its subsequent investigation the child will often be faced with the type of choices faced by the children in the first two experiments, that is, between the original information and the erroneously suggested information. There is frequently little likelihood of asking the child to choose between the original information and new, not previously suggested, information. Such manipulations, though important for research purposes, may tend to overestimate younger children's performance in actual settings.

References

Binet, A. (1900). *La suggestibilitè*. Paris: Schleicher Frères.

Ceci, S. J. & Bronfenbrenner, U. (1985). "Don't forget to take the cupcakes out of the oven": Memory, strategic time-monitoring, and context. *Child Development, 56,* 152–164.

Ceci, S. J., Ross, D. F., & Toglia, M. P. (in press). Suggestibility of children's memory: Psycho-legal implications. *Journal of Experimental Psychology: General.*

Goodman, G. (1984). Children's testimony in historical perspective. *Journal of Social Issues, 40,* 9–31.

Loftus, E. (1976). Unconscious transference in eyewitness identification. *Law and Psychology Review, 2,* 93–98.

Loftus, E., & Davies, G. (1984). Distortions in the memory of children. *Journal of Social Issues, 40,* 51–67.

McCloskey, M., & Zaragoza, M. (1985). Misleading postevent information and memory for events: Arguments and evidence against memory impairment hypothesis. *Journal of Experimental Psychology: General, 114,* 1–16.

Messerschmidt, R. (1933). The suggestibility of boys and girls between the ages of six and sixteen. *Journal of Genetic Psychology, 43,* 422–437.

Pear, T., & Wyatt, S. (1914). The testimony of normal and mentally defective children. *British Journal of Psychology, 3,* 388–419.

Ross, D., & Ceci, S. J. (1984). *Effects of vague familiarity on recognition accuracy: More on factors implicated in eyewitness reports.* Paper presented at the Eastern Psychological Association meeting, Baltimore, MD. April.

Schneider, W. (1984). Developmental trends in the metamemory-memory behavior relationship: An integrative review. In D. Forest-Pressley, G. MacKinnon, & T. G. Waller (Eds.), *Cognition, metamemory, and human performance* Vol. 1 (pp. 57-109). New York: Academic Press.

Seth, D. (1967). *Stories of great witch trials*. Boston: Arthur & Butler.

Seth, D. (1969). *Chidlren against witches*. New York: Taplinger.

Stern, W. (1910). Abstracts of lectures on the psychology of testimony and on the study of individuality. *American Journal of Psychology, 21,* 270–282.

Upham, C. W. (1867). *Salem witchcraft; with an account of Salem Village*. Boston: Wiggin & Cunt.

Varendonck, J. (1911). Les témoignages d'enfants dans procès retentissant. *Archives de Psychologie, 11,* 129–171.

6
Reality Monitoring and Suggestibility: Children's Ability to Discriminate Among Memories From Different Sources

D. STEPHEN LINDSAY and MARCIA K. JOHNSON

Throughout the relatively brief period since the invention of the modern Romantic concept of childhood in the nineteenth century (Aries, 1962, cited in Kessen, 1979), and throughout the even briefer history of the science of psychology, the idea of young children serving as eyewitnesses in courts of law has run counter to our notions of children's capabilities (Goodman, 1984). Now, in the mid-1980s, children's competency as eyewitnesses has become an important issue, as children more and more frequently are the victims of reported crimes and as psychologists become increasingly concerned with conducting research and constructing theory within "ecologically valid" contexts and constraints (e.g., Bahrick & Karis, 1982; Bronfenbrenner, 1977; Neisser, 1976, 1982, 1985).

Giving accurate testimony demands many cognitive abilities, any or all of which may develop with age. A partial list of such abilities includes perceiving and comprehending the initial event, retaining representations of one's perception of the event, understanding questions about the event, retrieving relevant information, and discriminating between memories of one's perception of the event itself and memories from other sources of information pertaining to the event. This chapter focuses on theories and evidence concerning the last of these: developments in children's abilities to discriminate the sources of their experiences and memories. Specifically, we are interested in two general classes of discriminations that can influence the accuracy of eyewitness testimony: (a) discriminations between memories of perceived and imagined events and (b) discriminations between different external sources of memories pertaining to the same event.

When a person witnesses an event, mulls it over in his or her mind, and hears other people talk about it, he or she stores information about the event from all three sources. If later asked to recall the event as it was witnessed, such a person must discriminate memories of the event itself from memories of his or her ruminations and from memories of what other people said about the event. Discriminating memories of largely externally derived experiences (e.g., the initial perception of the event) from memories of largely internal experiences (the ruminations) has been termed "reality monitoring" (Johnson & Raye, 1981). In this chapter, discriminating between memories derived from different external sources (e.g., the initial perception of an event and what others said about it) will be termed "external-source monitoring" (Johnson, 1987).

In the following pages, we will first discuss some of the theoretical and empirical work that bears on the development of reality monitoring. Then we will turn to the development of external-source monitoring, focusing particularly on the role of source monitoring in suggestibility. We will present three major arguments: (a) developmental theory suggests that preschool-age children should be less accurate in their reality monitoring and external-source monitoring attributions than older children and adults; (b) eyewitnesses' susceptibility to misleading suggestions, which is often described in terms of disruptions of memory for the original information, may instead be accounted for in terms of erroneous source monitoring attributions; and (c) the small number of empirical studies to date indicate that 6-year-old children show a deficit in some types of source attributions but not in others. We also indicate some potential directions for further work on children's ability to discriminate among memories from different sources.

Reality Monitoring

Many philosophers (e.g., Hume, 1739/1962; James, 1890/1983; Locke, 1689/1965; Reid, 1764/1975) and psychologists (e.g., Cameron, 1963; Freud, 1895/1966, 1925/1961; Horowitz, 1978; Perky, 1910; Segal, 1970) have been interested in how people discriminate externally derived (perceptual) experiences from internal experiences. Locke (1689/1965) did not discuss this issue as a problem, but he may well have created it; for Locke, the word "idea" referred to both sensations and reflections. Hume (1739/1962) took exception to this lack of differentiation ("I [would] rather restore the word 'idea' to its original sense, from which Mr. Locke has perverted it.") (p. 177), and argued that sensations and reflections are different phenomena. Hume suggested that the two are differentiated primarily in terms of their strength or vividness. James (1890/1983) made a similar argument, whereas other philosophers (e.g., Reid, 1764/1975) claimed that perceptions and images are qualitatively different from one another.

For the most part, interest has focused on "reality testing," the process of distinguishing present perceptions from present imaginations and recollections. As Johnson and Raye (1981) argued, however, people face an analogous (but harder) problem when they retrieve memories of experiences. Johnson and Raye termed the processes involved in discriminating memories of perceptually derived experiences from memories of internal experiences "reality monitoring."

Johnson and Raye proposed that there are characteristic differences between memories of externally derived events and memories of internally generated events, and that reality-monitoring decisions are made on the basis of a few general dimensions along which the two types of memories vary. Johnson and Raye argued that, in general, memories of externally derived experiences include more contextual information (the "where" and "when" of an event), more sensory attributes, and more detail than memories of internal experiences. On the other hand, because perception is characteristically more "automatic" than thought or imagination (Hasher & Zacks, 1979; Posner & Snyder, 1975), Johnson and Raye suggested that memories of externally derived experiences usually include fewer indications of cognitive operations active at the time of the experience.

In the model Johnson and Raye proposed, most reality-monitoring decisions are made by a "fast-guess" procedure (e.g., Atkinson & Juola, 1973) on the basis of the characteristics mentioned above. That is, memories with lots of sensory vividness and semantic and contextual detail, and relatively few indications of cognitive operations, will tend to be classified as memories of perceived events. Memories that are not vivid and lack detail and contextual information, but include indications of many cognitive operations, will tend to be classified as memories of imagined events. Most of the time, we do not make such decisions consciously—we recall an experience from our past and "simply know" that it is a memory of an event that actually happened, or a memory of an event that we fantasized or thought about. If, however, a particular memory cannot confidently be classified as perceptual or imaginal by the fast-guess procedure, more extended reasoning processes may be performed. These include examination of the content of the memory and its relation to other knowledge and various biases based on the beliefs people have about memory phenomena (i.e., metamemory).

The studies of reality monitoring in adults have been reviewed elsewhere (e.g., Johnson, 1985, 1987; Johnson & Raye, 1981) and will only be mentioned briefly here. In general, the results have supported Johnson and Raye's model of reality monitoring. Memories of externally derived experiences do seem to have more sensory, spatial, and temporal information than memories of internal experiences, and people use the amount of such information associated with a memory when they make reality monitoring decisions (Johnson, 1985; Johnson, Raye, Foley, & Kim, 1982; Schooler, Gerhard, & Loftus, 1986; Suengas & Johnson, 1985, 1986). People have more difficulty discriminating between memories if both are of internal events or both are of externally derived events than if one is of an internal event and the other is of an externally derived event (Foley, Johnson, & Raye, 1983; Raye & Johnson, 1980). Confusions between memories of internal and externally derived events occur more frequently when the internal events are especially vivid (Johnson, Raye, Wang, & Taylor, 1979), share many sensory qualities with the externally derived events (Johnson, Foley, & Leach, in preparation), or involve relatively few cognitive operations (Johnson, Kahan, & Raye, 1984; Johnson, Raye, Foley, & Foley, 1981).

How good are children at reality monitoring? According to a long tradition of theorizing in child development, young children should be relatively poor at reality monitoring. In the following sections, we will briefly discuss the theories of Freud and Piaget as they relate to this issue, and attempt to summarize the views of more modern researchers. We have focused on Freud and Piaget both because of the tremendous impact they have had on developmental theory and because of the direct relevance of their work to reality monitoring. We will also review and critique our research on the development of reality monitoring in children.

Freud

At a general level of analysis, Freudian theory (e.g., 1917/1964; 1933/1964; see Miller, 1983, for a helpful overview) describes development as the gradual emergence of the ego and "secondary-process" or rational/practical thought to dominance over and control of the id and "primary-process" or irrational/fantastical thought. The newborn is said to be ruled by the id, that is, by impatient gratification-seeking in accordance with the pleasure principle. According to Freud (e.g., 1911/1958), the first mental images are hallucinations of gratification, the products of primary-process thought. The id cannot directly distinguish between the subjective and the real, and, when its needs are not met in reality, it uses primary-process thinking to hallucinate fulfillment.

With the development of the ego and secondary-process thought, infants begin to be able to use reasoned, practical behaviors to satisfy their needs and desires. Through reality testing, the child eventually comes to abandon the pleasure principle and adhere to the reality principle. This is a gradual process, however, and throughout the first 6 or 7 years of life rational thought often fails to mediate successfully between the demands of the id and the constraints of reality. Further, young children are said to progress through a series of sexually charged conflicts concerning their bodies and their relationships with their parents. Consequently, the id and its fantasies were claimed to often dominate the mental life of the young child.

Although Freud (e.g., 1908/1959, pp. 143–144, 1917/1964, pp. 371–372) did not claim that preschool-age children believe their fantasies are real, he did suggest that their proclivity for fantasy reduces young children's ability to be accurate and reliable (Freud, 1909/1955):

The untrustworthiness of the assertions of children is due to the predominance of their imagination, just as the untrustworthiness of the assertions of grown-up people is due to the predominance of their prejudices. (pp. 102-103)

One interpretation of Freud's writings on this subject is that he believed that preschool-age children are aware of the unreality of their fantasies when they are engaged in them, but are prone to confuse memories of fantasies with memories of reality. That is, preschool-age children may have mastered reality *testing* but not reality *monitoring*.

Freud specifically discussed what is here referred to as reality monitoring in the context of his "seduction theory." In the course of analysis, Freud's patients frequently described traumatic sexual experiences that they recalled from their early childhood. Early in his career, Freud (1896/1962) believed that these reports were veridical and that he had uncovered the primary cause of neurotic disorders among Victorian women: A frighteningly high percentage of young girls were sexually abused by adults—most often by their fathers. Freud named this the "seduction theory."[1] Freud later decided that his patients' reports were often memories of childhood fantasies, rather than memories of actual childhood experiences (e.g., Freud, 1906/1953, cited in footnote to Freud, 1933/1964, pp. 120–121). This new interpretation was extremely important for the development of psychoanalytic theory, in which the young child is invested with both sexual/aggressive drives and with a tendency to satisfy those desires through fantasy. Masson (1984) has criticized Freud's decision to attribute his patients' reports of sexual abuse to fantasy, as well as the psychoanalytic establishment's continued avowal of that position. The controversial nature of this issue and its central importance in psychoanalytic theory is apparent in Anna Freud's comment that "Keeping up the seduction theory would mean to abandon the . . . whole importance of phantasy life, conscious or unconscious phantasy. In fact, I think there would have been no psychoanalysis afterwards" (Masson, 1984, p. 59). Today, with some authorities estimating that as many as 25% of the women in this country were sexually abused as children (Finkelhor, 1984; Sedney & Brooks, 1984), it is no wonder that both seduction theory and psychoanalysis in general are being critically reevaluated. (See Malcolm, 1984, and Tavris, 1984, for reviews of Masson's work.)

In summary, Freudian theory suggests that the mental life of the infant and preschool-age child is strongly influenced by wish-fulfilling fantasies, and that young children may confuse fantasized and actual experience. By extension, then, Freudian theory implies that young children should be more prone to erroneous reality-monitoring attributions than are older children and adults.

Piaget

Piaget's work on developmental theory is vast and complex. We will discuss four areas within Piagetian theory that are particularly relevant to the issue of children's reality monitoring: egocentrism, fantasy, mental imagery, and memory.

EGOCENTRISM

Piaget described development as a gradual process of decentration. Piaget (e.g., 1927/1977) maintained that the newborn has no sense of him- or herself as a particular object in a universe of other objects, and therefore cannot separate self from not-self. The infant is said to be "solipsistic" in the sense that, being unable to differentiate self and not-self, he or she unwittingly assimilates external reality to the self and projects his or her feelings and desires onto the world. With development and through acting on the environment and adjusting his or her actions to the characteristics of the things acted upon, the infant gradually

---

[1]Freud's name for this theory seems as ill-chosen as Piaget's term "egocentrism." Masson (1984, p. 34) argues that Freud did *not* mean to imply that children invite sexual abuse.

develops a world view in which the self and other objects are differentiated from one another.

Although the 2-year-old is not said to be "solipsistic," Piaget claimed that the differentiation between self and not-self is still far from complete at the end of infancy. Piaget contended that preschool children are profoundly egocentric. While understanding that he or she is an object among a universe of objects, the 2- to 6-year-old child persists in projecting his or her thoughts, feelings, and desires onto external reality and, at the same time, objectifying his or her thoughts and feelings. Preschool-age children consequently have difficulty distinguishing internally generated and externally derived experiences: "So long as thought has not become conscious of itself, it is prey to perpetual confusions between objective and subjective" (Piaget, 1926/1983, p. 34).

FANTASY

Piaget (1937/1954; 1945/1962; Piaget & Inhelder, 1966/1969) did not concur with Freud's claim that newborns hallucinate. For Piaget, the ability to mentally represent nonpresent objects develops only toward the end of infancy (1½ to 2 years) and remains rather limited until the age of 7 or 8 years. Hence the experience of the newborn, according to Piaget, is devoid of fantasy. It is only at the end of infancy, when the child gains representational skills and begins to engage in symbolic or pretend play, that fantasy becomes an important part of the child's repertoire.

Piaget (1945/1962; Piaget & Inhelder, 1966/1969) viewed symbolic play as "pure assimilation" of reality to the needs and desires of the self. That is, in play the child assimilates reality to his or her schemata, without being constrained by the objective nature of the materials played with. Thus, a simple block of wood may be assimilated to a "toy car scheme." Play is said to provide the child with new ways to exercise schemata and master reality (as in practice play), on the one hand, and to allow him or her to distort and refashion reality according to his or her desires, on the other. For Piaget, the distortion of reality is the hallmark of symbolic play. (See Bretherton, 1984, for a critique of Piaget's approach to symbolic play.)

In terms of reality testing, the crucial question concerning children's make-believe play is "Does the child believe that the pretense is real?" Piaget suggested that it is only until the age of 3 or 4 years that children genuinely believe in their pretend play, and even then it is not really a matter of positive belief: The 2- to 4-year-old child simply "does not consider whether its ludic [play] symbols are real or not" (1945/1962, p. 168). By the age of 3, the child has "detected a shade of difference between . . . what is true and what is simply imagined," but "when he is in the presence of one it seems to him the only true one. . . . In consequence, these two planes, that of play and that of sensuous observation, are very different for the child from what they are for us, and, in particular, they are less distinct" (Piaget, 1924/1972, pp. 246–247). Thus, children were said to have difficulty separating fact and fantasy throughout the preoperational period:

The child's mind is full of these "ludistic" [pretend play] tendencies up to the age of 7–8, which means that before that age it is extremely difficult for him to distinguish between fabulation and truth. (p. 202)

IMAGERY

The child's perception of self-generated mental images is also relevant to the issue of reality testing and subsequent reality monitoring. Piaget argued that mental images are derived from "internalized imitations" rather than from perception. Imitation, the approximate copying of a model, is an important development in Piagetian theory. As in his treatment of play, Piaget approached imitation as an indication of developing representational and operational skills (see, e.g., Piaget, 1936/1953). When a child imitates a model, he or she accommodates schemes of action in order to fit his or her posture and movements to those of the model. The child gradually develops the ability to perform such "imitations" internally by manipulating figural mental representations, or symbols, that stand for the object.

Piaget classified perception, imitation, and imagery as "figurative" aspects of knowing, in contrast to "operative" aspects of knowing. Figurative thought is that which represents states or appearances (more or less accurate "pictures" of the world), whereas operational thought represents operations upon and transformations of reality. Piaget's primary interest, of course, was in the development of logicomathematical operations, and his main concern in discussing figurative thought was to argue that it is *not* the origin of operational intelligence. According to Piaget (e.g., Piaget & Inhelder, 1963/1969, 1966/1969), developments in figurative thought (e.g., mental imagery) are dependent on and follow from developments in operational thought. Thus, children's mental imagery, like their logical thought, remains quite limited until the development of "concrete operations" (fully internalized logical processes characterized by reversibility and closure) at around 7 years of age: "The mental images of the child at the preoperative level are almost exclusively static" (Piaget & Inhelder, 1966/1969, p. 71). If, as Piaget contends, children under age 7 are unable to freely manipulate mental images, it follows that they may be unable to engage in purely mental fantasies, unaided by actions and props. That is, it may be the case that children under 7 years cannot spontaneously fantasize complex scenarios without acting them out in some way.

As with play, the central issue regarding mental imagery in the present context concerns the child's ability to distinguish between image and reality. Although Piaget (1926/1983) suggested that the ability to distinguish the two develops quite early, he also contended that children are nonetheless prone to confuse image and reality until the development of formal operations (10 or 11 years).

Memory

Consistent with the general nature of his approach to cognitive development, Piaget (Piaget & Inhelder, 1968/1973) described memory as a dynamic process guided by intelligence rather than as a passive storehouse. Piaget theorized that there are two distinct but interactive kinds of memory. "Memory in the broad sense" refers to the schemata of intelligence in general, whereas "memory in the strict sense" refers to the preservation of specific experiences. The nature of one's memory for specific situations, objects, or actions is determined by the nature of the schemata involved in comprehending the initial information and in reconstructing the initial experience in memory. Thus, a given situation might be remembered differently by younger and older children because children of different ages would not have understood the situation in the same way. Likewise, a child's memory for a given situation or event may change in interesting ways as the child develops and his or her schemata change.

For example, Piaget and Inhelder (1968/1973) found that some children's reconstructions of an array of sticks ordered by increasing length were more accurate after a delay of several months than they were one week after the child initially viewed the array. Piaget and Inhelder argued that the improvement in the children's reconstructions reflected the fact that they had developed a general understanding of seriation during the extended delay period. Although Piaget and Inhelder's (1968/1973) demonstrations of memory improvements with long delays have not been consistently replicated (Liben, 1977), the general idea that memory and intelligence are interdependent is both intuitively appealing and well supported (e.g., Chi, 1978; Meacham, 1977).

Our claim that source monitoring is an active decision-making process performed during retrieval is compatible with Piaget's approach to memory: One aspect of reconstructing a memory involves determining the source of the original experience. Indeed, Piaget (1945/1962, pp. 187–188) reported a very vivid, but false, memory of an attempt to kidnap him when he was a young child. It turned out that the memory was based on a story he had heard as a child, and the visual images of the event that he remembered were actually fantasy images based on the story.

Piaget's approach to memory, in which memory "in the strict sense" is interdependent with world knowledge and ways of thinking, is also compatible with the idea that reality-monitoring changes with age. As we discussed above, Piaget (e.g., 1924/1972, 1926/1983, 1945/1962) argued that as children develop they come to differentiate fact and fantasy more clearly and consistently in their ongoing experience. If memory for specific events is determined by the intelligence that apprehends those events, it follows that memories of perceived and imagined events come to be more discriminable, and more consistently differentiated at recall, as the child develops. Thus, Piaget's theory, by extension, implies that children under 7 or 8 years of age are more likely to make reality-monitoring errors than are older children. It also follows that a child who misattributes the origin of a memory at one age (e.g., mistakes a memory of a fantasy as a memory of an actual experience) may later attribute the memory to the correct source.

SUMMARY

According to Piaget, young children do not clearly and consistently differentiate between the subjective and the objective until the age of 7 or 8 years. Further,

Piaget maintained that the nature of the child's memories of specific events is determined by the nature of his or her developing understanding of the world. Based on these ideas, one would expect a developmental trend in reality monitoring: Young children should have more difficulty discriminating between memories of actual and imagined events.

Current Views

Although Freud's ideas about children raised considerable controversy, we are not aware of any rigorous empirical tests of his claims regarding hallucinatory satisfaction in infancy or sexual fantasies in early childhood. This is in large measure because these claims are inherently difficult to test. It is fair to say, however, that most modern researchers in cognitive development have rejected the notion of infantile hallucination (see Miller, 1983, pp. 153–158).

Whereas Freud's theories have resisted experimental study, Piaget's claims have precipitated a large number of empirical investigations. Many cognitive developmentalists today believe that Piaget exaggerated the egocentrism of children between 3 and 7 years of age (e.g., Donaldson, 1978; Flavell, 1977). There is evidence indicating that children as young as 3 years are, under some conditions, able to appreciate the differences between their perspective and that of another person (e.g., Maratsos, 1973; Marvin, Greenberg, & Mossler, 1976; Whitehurst & Sonnenschein, 1978). It is important to note, however, that young children do demonstrate egocentric thinking under some conditions (e.g., Glucksberg, Krauss, & Higgins, 1975).[2] Thus, although it now appears that children are not as egocentric as Piaget suggested, they are still often said to be less able than adults to clearly and consistently separate subjective and objective aspects of their experiences.

From Sully (1895/1896) to Singer (1973), psychologists have described the preschooler as a being enchanted by fantasy and make-believe play. In the last two decades, the study of children's play has become a field in its own right. Much of this literature has concerned the development of social and communicative skills involved in shared play. Modern cognitive developmentalists have also emphasized the dynamic, creative role of make-believe play in the development of cognition. Bretherton (1984), for example, has argued that "the ability to create symbolic alternatives to reality and to play with that ability is as deeply a part of human experience as the ability to construct an adapted model of everyday reality" (p. 38). The consensus seems to be that fantasizing is a remarkable cognitive ability that gradually develops from around 18 months through at least the early school years. During that period, the content of symbolic play evolves from

---

[2]Earlier, we discussed Piagetian egocentricism in the general sense of the inability to separate the objective from the subjective. Most recent empirical work, however, has focused on developments in the ability to appreciate the differences between one's own perspective and that of another person. For Piaget (e.g., 1926/1983) the inability to take another's point of view was simply one aspect of egocentrism in the general sense.

enactments of everyday schemata (e.g., pretending to go to sleep) to far-flung flights of imaginative fancy.

Very little experimental research to date has focused specifically on children's ability to distinguish reality and fantasy. Those studies that have been published report developmental improvements in the ability to separate fact and fancy (Lottan, 1967; Morrison & Gardner, 1978; Scarlett & Wolf, 1979; Taylor & Howell, 1973; also see Winner & Gardner, 1979). Developmental trends have also been found in related work on the development of the ability to distinguish between the actual and apparent characteristics of stimuli (e.g., the color of a white piece of paper placed under a blue transparency) (e.g., Flavell, Flavell, & Green, 1983; Kohlberg, 1968). In general, the current view is that, between the ages of 3 and 6 or 7 years, children's grasp of the distinction between pretend and not-pretend develops from an implicit and tenuous separation to a consciously apprehended, but still violable, dichotomy (e.g., Bretherton, 1984; Scarlett & Wolf, 1979; Winner & Gardner, 1979). Even the 2-year-old never *really* attempts to eat a pretend cookie, yet considerably older children sometimes have trouble separating reality and pretense, especially when the content of the pretense is emotionally charged (Bretherton, 1984).

In summary, although both Freud's and Piaget's claims have been challenged, current research nonetheless suggests that young children should be more prone to failures of reality testing than older children or adults. Fantasy and make-believe appear to be important parts of the young child's mental life, and young children are said to be less likely than older children to clearly and consistently differentiate fact and fantasy.

Implications for Children's Reality Monitoring

The theoretical and empirical work reviewed above suggests that reality and fantasy commingle in children's minds more than in adults'. In this section, we will discuss the implications of these views for children's reality monitoring.

If children do not differentiate ongoing fact and fantasy as clearly as adults do, their memories of these two kinds of experiences might not differ from one another in the ways that adults' memories do (i.e., sensory vividness, contextual and semantic detail, cognitive operations). Thus, the characteristic differences that adults use to discriminate between memories of imagined and perceived events might not differentiate the two in children's memories, simply because the two kinds of experiences themselves do not differ along those dimensions.[3] Alternatively, it might be that children's experiences (and their memories) of imagined and perceived events do characteristically differ along the same dimensions as

---

[3]This idea is consistent with Kosslyn's (1978) hypothesis that young children tend to think in images, whereas adults more often think in abstract propositions. Assuming that images are more similar to percepts than are propositions, it follows that the thoughts and percepts of young children should be more similar to one another (and hence less discriminable) than the thoughts and percepts of adults.

adults', but children do not know that these attributes provide reliable cues to the differentiation of actual and imagined events. That is, children may lack the metamemory assumptions that adults have. This idea is consistent both with the claim that children lack a conceptual grasp of the distinction between fantasy and reality and with the suggestion made by Flavell et al. (1983) that children are less prone than adults to reflect upon and evaluate their memories and are "less cognizant of and attentive to the source and nature of their [mental] representations" (p. 117).

If children do not have a conscious understanding of the distinction between actual and imagined events, they may simply not even think of dichotomizing their memories into those that refer to actual and to imaginal experiences. That is, it may be the case that preschool children do not actively belive that actual and imagined events are equally real, but, rather, that they do not actively draw the distinction between the two as sharply and consistently as older children and adults (cf. Sugarman, in press). There is evidence that children have some understanding of the distinction between fact and fantasy from a fairly young age (5 or 6 years) (e.g., Kohlberg, 1968). It is possible, however, that children might have some understanding of the distinction, but not know that it is pertinent, when one is asked to recall an event.

In our review of developmental theory, we have focused on children's ability to differentiate fact and fantasy in their ongoing experience. We should note, however, that even if preschool-age children differentiate actual and imagined events perfectly in their ongoing experience, they may nonetheless be prone to reality-monitoring failures. After all, adults who initially know the reality status of events sometimes make erroneous reality-monitoring attributions, and the factors that have been shown to increase the likelihood of reality-monitoring errors in adults (e.g., ease and vividness of imagining) may well be more characteristic of children's fantasy than of adults'.

Johnson and Raye (1981) hypothesized that when adults are unable to make reality-monitoring decisions solely on the basis of the attributes that characteristically differentiate memories of actual and imagined events, they use higher mental processes involving the semantic content of the memory and its relation to their general world knowledge to make the decision. Limitations in children's world knowledge or abstract reasoning skills may limit their ability to use this strategy. Johnson and Raye also proposed that adults use metamnemonic decision biases when making reality-monitoring decisions (e.g., the belief that memories of actual events are "stronger" than memories of imagined events). Young children may lack such metamnemonic knowledge.

In summary, there are a number of reasonable hypotheses that suggest that children should be more likcly than adults to make erroneous reality-monitoring attributions. Coupled with the claim that children spend a great deal of their time immersed in fantasy (e.g., Winner & Gardner, 1979), these hypotheses suggest that children may make inaccurate reality-monitoring attributions quite often in their daily lives.

Empirical Investigations of Children's Reality Monitoring

Empirical investigations of children's reality monitoring have only recently begun. We have started with relatively constrained laboratory-type experiments and are gradually moving to broader, more realistic procedures. In this section, the published research on children's reality monitoring is summarized and critiqued, and some of our current projects are briefly discussed.

If people sometimes confuse memories of perceived and imagined experiences, then their estimates of the number of times a particular event occurred may be affected by the number of times that event was imagined as well as by the number of times it actually occurred. Johnson, Taylor, and Raye (1977) found support for this hypothesis with adult subjects: Estimates of the number of times an item had been presented increased with the number of times that item had been imagined. If children are more likely than adults to make reality-monitoring misattributions, their frequency estimates should be even more affected by the number of times an event was imagined. In the first published experiment concerning children's reality monitoring, Johnson, Raye, Hasher, & Chromiak (1979) asked 8-, 10-, and 12-year-old children and adults to look at pictures of common objects on some sets of trials and, on other sets of trials, to form mental images of some of the same pictures. Over the course of the procedure, each picture was shown once, twice, or three times and imagined once, three times, or not at all. Repetitions of items occurred across, not within, blocks of trials, and each picture was shown at least once before the subject was asked to form an image of it.

Following this acquisition phase, the subjects were shown each picture and asked to estimate how many times they had actually seen that picture during the experiment. Consistent with the earlier work with adults, the number of times an item was imaged affected subjects' estimates of how many times they had seen that item. Contrary to our expectations, however, no developmental trends appeared in the data: If anything, the children's frequency estimates were slightly *less* affected by the number of times the items were imaged.

There are two explanations for the lack of developmental trends in these data. First, it may be the case that reality monitoring simply does not develop beyond the age of 8 years. Second, the children's mental images of the items may have been less accurate or less detailed than those of the adults. In order for imaging trials to affect frequency estimates, each memory of an image must be accurate and vivid enough to be taken as a token of the type exemplified by the test stimulus. If children's images were less vivid or accurate, then they might show little evidence of reality-monitoring failures despite a general deficit in reality monitoring. Even if young children's spontaneous images are more vivid than adults', the images they form on demand in an experiment such as this might be less vivid or less accurate than adults, thus, a possible deficit in reality monitoring may have been masked by poor imagery.

Foley et al. (1983) used a different procedure and younger subjects to explore developmental changes in reality monitoring. In the first of two experiments,

6-, 9-, and 17-year-old subjects either said words and listened as another person said words (the Say-Listen condition) or said words and imagined themselves saying words (the Say-Think condition). Subsequently, subjects were given a surprise "identification-of-origin" test in which they were to indicate whether each test item was (a) a new word, (b) a word they had said, or (c) a word the other person had said (for subjects in the Say-Listen condition) or a word they had imagined themselves saying (for subjects in the Say-Think condition).

The reality-monitoring model proposed by Johnson and Raye (1981) suggests that it should be harder to determine whether a word was spoken or imagined (both self-generated) than to determine whether a word was spoken or heard (one self-generated and one other-generated). Saying and imagining saying a word share many common attributes, whereas hearing and saying a word are relatively distinct processes. The developmental literature suggests that young children should find it particularly difficult to discriminate between imagining saying and actually saying or hearing because young children are said to closely identify thought and speech (Piaget, 1926/1983). Because young children are said to have at least some grasp on the self-other distinction, developmental theory suggests that young children, like adults, should be more prone to confuse memories of saying and imagining saying than memories of saying and hearing. Finally, developmental theory also predicts that children in both conditions will perform more poorly than adults.

As predicted, subjects in the Say-Think condition made significantly more errors on the identification-of-origin test than did subjects in the Say-Listen condition. Moreover, the 6-year-olds in the Say-Think condition were significantly less accurate than the older subjects.[4] These findings suggest that 6-year-old children are as accurate as older children and young adults when asked to remember whether a test item was a word they had said themselves or one they had heard another person say, but they do not perform as well as older children when the discrimination is between having said and having imagined saying a word.

The second experiment reported in Foley et al. (1983) demonstrated that this selective deficit was not because of a general problem with discriminating imagined events from actual events. In the Think-Listen condition of Experiment 2, 6-year-olds were as accurate as 9-year-olds when deciding whether a test item was a word they had imagined themselves saying or one they had heard another person say. Children's performance in another condition of the same experiment suggests that the selective deficit observed among the 6-year-old subjects in the Say-Think condition was not due to a generally greater difficulty with separating memories from the same origin-class (i.e., discriminating between memories of self-generated events or between memories of other-generated events). The 6-year-olds performed no differently than the 9-year-olds in a Listen-Listen

---

[4]The interpretation of these data is somewhat complicated by the unexpected performance of the 9-year-old children: The 9-year-olds in the Say-Think condition performed slightly better than those in the Say-Listen condition (although the difference was not significant).

condition, in which subjects were asked to identify which of two other people had said each test word, although both age groups performed more poorly than subjects in the Say-Listen condition. The reality-monitoring model predicts that Say-Listen judgments should be easier than Listen-Listen judgments because the former requires a distinction between memories from two different classes (internal vs. external), whereas the latter is a within-class (external) judgment, and subjects must rely on specific details of the memory (e.g., sound of speaker's voice) to make the differentiation. For present purposes, the important point is that the performances of 6- and 9-year-olds in the Listen-Listen condition did not differ from one another. Thus, it is not the case that 6-year-olds' difficulty with the Say-Think condition was due to a general difficulty with discriminating between memories of the same origin class.

Two other developmental trends were observed in the Foley et al. (1983) study when they examined how subjects classified new test items that were misidentified as old items (i.e., false positives). When both 9- and 17-year-old subjects in the Say-Listen condition erroneously classified an item that had not been used in the acquisition phase as an old item, they significantly more often decided that it had been spoken by the other person than by themselves. Apparently, these subjects were demonstrating a response bias based on metamemory: Memories for self-generated events are generally "stronger" than memories for other-generated events. When subjects decide that a new word is an old word, their memory of the item is likely to be weak and uncertain, and they appear to decide "It must have been you, because I'd remember it more clearly if I had said it" (Johnson & Raye, 1981, discussed earlier evidence of this decision-making bias among adult subjects). The 6-year-old children in the Foley et al. study did not consistently show this decision-making bias.

The second developmental trend that emerged in the false positive data also concerned a decision-making bias. When 17-year-olds in the Say-Think condition erroneously classified a new test item as a word that had been used in the acquisition phase, they tended to indicate that the item had been imagined rather than said. Again, this decision-making bias probably represents metamemory: Memories of self-generated actions are generally "stronger" than memories of thoughts. Neither the 6-year-olds nor the 9-year-olds displayed this decision-making bias.

To summarize the findings of Foley et al. (1983), 6-year-old children were as accurate as older children when asked to judge (a) whether they or another person said a word, (b) whether they imagined themselves saying or heard another person say a word, or (c) which of two people had said a word. On the other hand, 6-year-olds were less accurate than older children when they attempted to determine whether a test word was one they actually said or one they only imagined themselves saying. The study also provided evidence for the development of two decision-making biases: If a memory is weak, it is probably a memory of a word another person said (if one is deciding whether the word was said by oneself or by someone else) or a memory of a word one imagined saying (if one is deciding whether one said or imagined saying the word). The 6-year-olds in these experiments did not consistently show either bias, and the 9-year-olds showed only the former, "It had to be you," bias. The 17-year-olds, on the other hand, evidenced both biases.

The studies reviewed thus far indicate that children are as accurate as adults at discriminating the origins of their memories, except when required to differentiate between having said a word and having imagined saying a word. That children should have particular difficulty discriminating between their own thoughts and their own actions is consistent with the idea that children have a tendency to confuse some kinds of imagined and actual events. Perhaps, however, this tendency is restricted to the task of discriminating thoughts and *words*. As mentioned above, Piaget posited a special relationship between thought and word among young children.

The findings of two experiments by Foley and Johnson (1985) indicate that children's tendency to confuse memories of doing with memories of imagining doing is not specific to words. In the first experiment, 6- and 9-year-old children and adults either (a) performed and watched another person perform simple actions (e.g., clapping, bending backward) (the Do-Watch condition), (b) watched two people perform simple actions (the Watch-Watch condition), or (c) performed and imagined themselves performing simple actions (the Do-Pretend condition). Children of both ages in the first two conditions scored as well as adults on an identification-of-origin test. Both 6- and 9-year-old children scored significantly more poorly than adults, however, when asked to determine whether they had actually performed or only imagined themselves performing an action.

Foley and Johnson (1985) also asked their subjects to simply recall the actions used in the acquisition phase. (This free-recall task was performed before the identification-of-origin task.) Earlier research (e.g., Johnson et al., 1981; Slamecka & Graf, 1978) demonstrated that adult subjects tend to recall more self-generated than other-generated words. Slamecka and Graf termed this phenomenon the "generation effect." Foley and Johnson (1985) found that the size of the generation effect increased with age. Indeed, the 6-year-old subjects did not evidence a generation effect at all. This finding is consistent with earlier findings (Foley et al., 1983; L. R. Johnson, Perlmutter, & Trabasso, 1979, Experiment 1; McFarland, Duncan, & Bruno, 1983) and is particularly interesting in light of the finding by Foley et al. (1983) that 6-year-old children do not use the "It had to be you, because I'd remember it more clearly if I had done it" decision bias. It may be that the reason 6-year-old children do not use this bias is simply that its premise is not valid: 6-year-olds' memories of self-generated actions may not be "stronger" than their memories of observed actions.

To summarize the work published to date, it appears that children as young as 6 years of age perform as well as adults when asked to determined the origin of a memory of an event, except when they must discriminate between memories of actions they imagined themselves doing and memories of actions they actually perform. The difficulty young children evidence when asked to separate memories of doing and imagining does not arise from a general tendency to confuse their imaginations with actual events. Nor does it reflect a general tendency to confuse memories of events that belong to the same origin class (i.e., self- or other-generated). Rather, the deficit appears to be specific to confusions between self-generated behaviors and imaginings of self-generated behaviors.

Critique of the Reality-Monitoring Research

There are three major limitations of these studies as they relate to eyewitness testimony. The first is the artificial nature of the stimulus materials and procedures. Whereas eyewitnesses are called upon to recall the actions of people performing complex and meaningful behaviors within the context of a richly structured physical and social environment, the studies to date have focused on relatively simple and decontextualized events.

We are currently conducting and planning studies of reality monitoring involving naturally occurring events and more realistic stimuli, settings, and procedures. One such study, concerning adults' memories for their dreams and for dreamlike narratives, has already been published (Johnson et al., 1984). We are presently investigating adults' memory for perceived and imagined "mini-events," coherent sequences of actions such as wrapping a package (Suengas & Johnson, 1985, 1986), and we hope to extend this paradigm to children soon. In another current project, young children both hide and imagine themselves hiding an attractive toy in each of several differently furnished rooms. The child hides each toy in one place and imagines hiding it in another. Following a delay period, the child is simply asked to retrieve the hidden objects, and the locations the child searches are noted. We are finding, among other things, that 4- to 8-year-old children sometimes look for the toys in locations in which they only imagined hiding them. We are also conducting studies that include measures of the qualitative aspects of memories for actual and imagined events and self-report measures of subjects' insights into the characteristics of their memories and their cognitive styles. Few data on children have yet been gathered in any of these experiments, so they will not be discussed here. The important point is that reality-monitoring processes involving memories of complex, naturalistic experiences can be studied systematically.

The second major shortcoming of the reality-monitoring work reviewed above is more an omission than a failing, but it is an omission that is directly relevant to the issue of children's legal testimony. The young children in our studies have been less accurate than adults only when the subject was the actor in both the actual and the imagined events (i.e., the Say-Think and Do-Pretend conditions). It may be that younger children are less accurate at reality monitoring than older children and adults whenever the actor is the same in the actual and the imagined events. That is, although children are as accurate as adults when asked to discriminate between memories of actions they imagined themselves performing and memories of actions they observed another person performing (as in the Think-Listen condition of Foley et al., 1983, Experiment 2), they may have more difficulty when asked to discriminate between memories of what they imagined another person doing and what they observed that same person doing. Adults sometimes confuse memories of what they imagined another person doing with memories of what that person actually did (Johnson et al., in preparation). Children may be more likely to make such errors. Research investigating this question is under way in our laboratory.

The third major limitation of the research reviewed above—and perhaps the most important—concerns what subjects do when asked to imagine an event. Instructions to imagine an event may produce mentation that is qualitatively different from spontaneous fantasizing. Certainly the affective and motivational properties of the two differ markedly, and intuition suggests that spontaneous fantasies are often much more vivid and rich than images produced on demand. Moreover, people may more often *believe* in their spontaneous fantasies, if only in some limited way and only during the time that they are actually producing them. Real, spontaneous fantasies are also likely to be repeatedly re-created, perhaps because they are often emotionally charged and involving. Finally, spontaneous fantasies may involve fewer effortful cognitive operations than do images produced on demand (cf. Durso & Johnson, 1980; Johnson et al., 1984). In general, memories that are vivid and compelling, frequently rehearsed and richly elaborated, and that contain little evidence of effortful cognitive operations are experienced as more "real" than other memories (see Johnson, 1987). Thus, both children and adults may more often confuse fact and fancy in memory when the latter was spontaneously generated. On the other hand, reality monitoring might actually be better if both the actual and imagined events were more richly detailed and realistic. Our stimuli have consisted of decontextualized pictures, words, and movements that were arbitrarily assigned to different sources. It is possible that the richer the memory, the greater the opportunity to use extended reasoning to identify its source (but children may be less able to take advantage of this opportunity).

We are currently trying to devise procedures that would allow us to study reality-monitoring decisions involving spontaneous fantasies. One idea is to provide children with an array of unstructured toys (e.g., blocks, tubes) and observe their free-play behavior. Both casual observations and the literature on symbolic play indicate that many of the children will play with such objects as if they were other kinds of toys (e.g., a block might serve as a toy car). By observing children's imaginative play and later questioning them about the attributes of the objects they used, we may at least begin to probe the development of reality-monitoring processes involving memories of spontaneous fantasies and naturally occurring events.

Source Monitoring and Eyewitness Suggestibility

Discriminating between memories of actual and imagined events may be viewed as one aspect of a more general problem in memory: discriminating between memories on the basis of their origins (Johnson, 1987). To reiterate the example we used at the beginning of the section on reality monitoring, when a person witnesses an event and then thinks about it and hears or reads about it, he or she stores information from all three sources. We have referred to discriminations between memories of perceived and imagined events as reality monitoring. We will refer to discriminations between memories from different external sources as "external-source monitoring." This section briefly discusses some evidence regarding the development of external-source monitoring, focusing on children's susceptibility to misleading postevent information.

Most of the developmental studies of reality monitoring described in the preceding section included external-source monitoring conditions as controls (Foley et al., 1983; Foley & Johnson, 1985). For example, in the first experiment reported by Foley et al. (1983), subjects in one condition listened as two people took turns saying words, and were later tested on their ability to determine which person had said which words. No significant age trends emerged in the external-source monitoring data in any of these experiments. Moreover, subjects in all age groups (6-, 9-, and 17-year-olds and adults) performed surprisingly well on these tasks (ranging from 71 to 97% correct on identification-of-origin tests). (It should be noted, however, that both children and adults generally performed better when separating self-generated from other-generated events than when separating different other-generated events.)

Thus, it appears that children as young as 6 years are quite good at retaining and using information about the origin of memories of external events, at least in this type of procedure. To whatever extent these findings can be generalized to real-world situations, we would expect that children can be as accurate as adults when asked to report "who did what." These tasks, however, are fundamentally different from the external-source montoring problems facing the eyewitness who has been exposed to information about an event from other sources after witnessing the event. Whereas the subjects in our studies were asked to determine the origin of memories for discrete events (except for Johnson et al., 1979), the eyewitness is often called upon to separate different memories that all pertain to the same event. For example, a child in one of our studies may have been asked which of two people had spoken the word "car." In court, on the other hand, a child may be asked (implicitly) to separate memories of seeing a particular car from memories of fantasies, conversations, previous interrogations, and so on, all of which included reference to that same car.

The problem of separating memories of witnessing an event from memories of other sources of information pertaining to the same event has most often been discussed in terms of "suggestibility." Research on eyewitness suggestibility has a long history, dating at least from the late nineteenth century (see Goodman, 1984). The standard procedure is to expose subjects to an event (by staging, videotaping, or photographing one), then provide some sort of misleading information about some of the details of the event (in a written summary of the event or in the phrasing of leading questions). For example, in the studies reported in Loftus, Miller, and Burns (1978), subjects watched a series of slides that depicted an accident involving a red Datsun and a pedestrian. At one point, the car was shown approaching an intersection at which there was either a stop sign (for half the subjects) or a yield sign (for the remaining subjects). Later, the subjects were asked "Did another car pass the red Datsun while it was stopped at the stop sign?" For those subjects who had seen the slide with a yield sign at the intersection, this question contained misleading postevent information. Subjects were later asked to indicate, on a forced-choice recognition test, whether the intersection had been marked with a stop sign or a yield sign. In this particular experiment, as many as 80% of the subjects (adults) were affected by the misleading postevent information. Generally, investigators have found that subjects are extremely susceptible to misleading postevent information (see Loftus, 1979; Wells & Loftus, 1984).

Are children more susceptible to suggestion than adults? There is surprisingly little rigorous empirical evidence on the issue. Loftus and Davies (1984; see also Johnson & Foley, 1984) reviewed five experiments on children's suggestibility. No systematic relationship between age and suggestibility has been consistently documented. Some studies (e.g., Cohen & Harnick, 1980; Dale, Loftus, & Rathbun, 1978; Murray, 1983) have found that suggestibility decreases with age, but others (e.g., Duncan, Whitney, & Kunen, 1982; Marin, Holmes, Guth, & Kovac, 1979) have found no systematic change with age. Loftus and Davies suggested that whether or not children are more susceptible to suggestion than adults depends upon the interaction of age with other factors, such as attention, comprehension, and interest. This volume includes several interesting investigations of developmental changes in suggestibility (Ceci, Ross, & Toglia, Chapter 5; Goodman, Aman, & Hirschman, Chapter 1; King & Yuille, Chapter 2; Saywitz, Chapter 3; Zaragoza, Chapter 4). All but Zaragoza's chapter report evidence for a decrease in suggestibility with age, although the effect is usually small.

What cognitive processes mediate suggestibility? Predictions for developmental changes in susceptibility to suggestion depend to a large extent on the explanation of the basic phenomenon itself. Loftus (e.g., 1979) has argued that misleading postevent information "overwrites" or replaces the memory for the original information. Other researchers (e.g., Bekerian & Bowers, 1983; Christiaansen & Ochalek, 1983) suggest that misleading postevent information does not overwrite memory for the original information, but rather reduces the probability that it will be retrieved. Recently, McCloskey and Zaragoza (1985a, 1985b; see also Zaragoza, Chapter 4, this volume) have claimed that postevent information does not affect memory for the original information at all.

McCloskey and Zaragoza presented a persuasive case to the effect that all of the evidence for eyewitness suggestibility can be explained in terms of (a) nonretention of the original information, (b) capitulation to demand characteristics, and (c) decisions made by the subject to the effect that the misleading postevent information is more reliable than his or her memory of the original information. McCloskey and Zaragoza argued that it is inappropriate to speak of "overwriting" or loss of availability in subjects who, for reasons unconnected with the manipulation, did not have the original information in memory when the misleading postevent information was presented: Such subjects are simply gaining new information about the original event. As long as some subjects "spontaneously" fail to retain the original information, then the misled group will perform worse than the control group on the recognition test. This is because subjects in the misled condition who failed to retain the original information but retained the postevent information could use it to guide their test selections, whereas those subjects in the control condition who failed to retain the original information would simply have to guess on the test. Because it is known that some subjects do spontaneously fail to retain the original information, McCloskey and Zaragoza concluded that the procedure Loftus and other researchers have used cannot provide unambiguous evidence about the effects of misleading postevent information on memories of earlier information.

McCloskey and Zaragoza proposed a new test for suggestibility studies. If the overwriting hypothesis is correct and memory for the original information (e.g., STOP SIGN) is totally overwritten by the misleading postevent information (e.g., YIELD SIGN), then the subject should be at a complete loss and should have to guess when asked to choose between STOP SIGN and, for example, CAUTION SIGN. That is, if the memory for the original item is overwritten when the misleading postevent information is presented, subjects should perform at chance level when later asked to choose between the original item and a completely new item. In six experiments using this new testing procedure, McCloskey and Zaragoza found that misled subjects, who presumably should have been guessing more often because the original information had been "overwritten," did not choose the new option more often than control subjects who were not misled. McCloskey and Zaragoza concluded that "misleading postevent information has no effect on memory for the original event" (1985a, p. 1).

Ceci et al. (Chapter 5, this volume) report two developmental studies (Experiments 3 and 4) in which McCloskey and Zaragoza's procedure was used in addition to the traditional Loftus procedure. Misled children in the Loftus procedure chose items consistent with the original information significantly less often than control subjects (46% as opposed to 88% correct).[5] The misled children in the McCloskey and Zaragoza procedure selected items consistent with the original information significantly more often than did the subjects in the traditional Loftus procedure (72% as opposed to 46% correct), but still significantly less often than the controls (72% as opposed to 88% correct). This latter comparison is the strongest evidence to date in favor of the idea that misleading postevent information can render the original information inaccessible (but see Zaragoza, Chapter 4, this volume).

Ceci et al. conclude that, because the performance of subjects who were in the McCloskey and Zaragoza procedure was better than that of those in the traditional procedure, "some of the demand characteristics mentioned by McCloskey and Zaragoza were operative in producing memory degradations" (p. 86). We would like to suggest that at least part of the difference between the performances of subjects in the two conditions may reflect failures in external-source monitoring rather than demand characteristics or other nonmnemonic phenomena. McCloskey and Zaragoza's procedure cannot assess failures of external-source

---

[5]These data are from Experiment 4. Experiment 3 yielded comparable results.

monitoring. That is, only subjects in the Loftus procedure were given an opportunity to misattribute their memories of the misleading postevent information to the original source. Misleading information may not increase the number of subjects who do not remember the old information, but it may produce subjects who mistakenly believe that the source of the misleading information was the original event. Such misattributions are memory effects, and we can only see them when the suggested information is an option on the test.[6]

Why would subjects who received a misleading suggestion later make erroneous external-source monitoring attributions and choose the suggested item instead of the original item on the Loftus test? We propose that external-source monitoring, like reality monitoring, is a decision-making process performed when memories are accessed. Thus, if a subject recognizes the postevent information instead of (or as well as) the original information, he or she may erroneously attribute it to the original source. The aspects of a memory that allow a subject to recognize a test item as something that was presented earlier in the experiment are not necessarily the same aspects that allow a subject to determine the specific origin of the item (Johnson, 1985; Johnson & Raye, 1981; Kahan & Johnson, 1984). There are several potential reasons subjects might be led to mistakenly identify the postevent information as being from the original source, depending on the criteria they use to make the attribution. For example, if subjects' judgments are influenced by the relative familiarity of the items, the suggested item might seem more like part of the original event than the original item because of its relatively greater recency and salience or because (as McCloskey and Zaragoza suggest) the original item was not encoded or retained at all. For the same reasons, subjects might think the postevent information was from the original source if their judgments are influenced by the relative "strength" or clarity of their memories of the items (see Ceci et al., Chapter 5, this volume, for a related point). We should note, however, that misattributions require more than a "strong" trace of the postevent information. Having a strong and clear memory of the suggested item would not necessarily lead one to misattribute its source.

For analytic purposes, we have discussed reality monitoring and external-source monitoring as distinct phenomena. In practice, however, the two may overlap. For example, subjects may generate visual images of items referred to in misleading postevent information. Such subjects may later be faced with a reality-monitoring problem: discriminating between their memory of the original information and their memory of the image they constructed when the narrative was read.

Schooler et al. (1986) have recently reported several studies in which the nature of memories for suggested misinformation is discussed in terms of John-

---

[6]It is possible that external-source monitoring failures also explain the effect Ceci et al. observed among subjects who took the McCloskey and Zaragoza test. During the test, some subjects in the McCloskey and Zaragoza condition might spontaneously recall the misleading postevent information and believe that it is the correct answer to the question that is being asked. Such subjects might respond haphazardly to the item because they believe that neither alternative is correct.

son and Raye's (1981) reality-monitoring model. Although Schooler et al. do not explicitly propose substituting a source-monitoring explanation for an overwriting explanation of suggestibility effects, they do acknowledge that reality-monitoring failures may play an important role in suggestibility. Schooler et al. found that subjects' descriptions of items suggested in the misleading postevent information systematically differed from their descriptions of items that were actually in the original source: the former were longer and included more verbal hedges, more references to cognitive operations, and fewer references to sensory and contextual details than the latter. Consistent with the Johnson and Raye model, these researchers concluded that memories for suggested and observed information differ in characteristic ways, and that subjects who misattribute the misleading postevent information to the original source may have failed to note or use those differences.

The explanations for external-source monitoring misattributions mentioned above do not require that memory of the original event is directly affected by the misleading postevent information. Another interesting possibility is that misleading postevent information impairs aspects of subjects' memory of the original item in such a way that accurate external-source monitoring becomes more difficult. As we mentioned above, McCloskey and Zaragoza (1985a, 1985b) have concluded that misleading postevent information does not impair memory for the original information because misled subjects tested with the McCloskey and Zaragoza procedure perform as well as control subjects. This conclusion does not necessarily follow from their findings. As long as subjects have some memory of the original item, they should choose it over the completely new item with which it is paired on the McCloskey and Zaragoza test. People are extremely sensitive to differences between items presented once and items presented not at all (e.g., Hintzman, 1969). Thus, misleading postevent information could substantially reduce the retrievability of various aspects of memory for the original information without affecting performance on the McCloskey and Zaragoza test, provided it did not reduce retrievability below the (presumably minimal) threshold necessary to choose between the original item and the new item. Therefore, although McCloskey and Zaragoza's findings constitute strong evidence against the overwriting explanation of suggestibility effects, they do not demonstrate that misleading postevent information has no effect on memory for the original information.

Whether or not misleading postevent information has any effect on subjects' ability to remember the original information, we believe that suggestibility procedures do lead subjects to erroneously attribute postevent information to the original event. The conditions under which people are likely to make erroneous source attributions remain to be specified, as do any developmental differences in external-source monitoring.

We have begun to explore the source-monitoring interpretation of suggestibility effects. In one study, as in the traditional procedure, subjects will view a film of a complex event and then read a narrative recapitulation in which some details have been altered, added, and deleted. Later, some subjects will perform a recognition test in which they will be asked only to discriminate information present in either the film or the narrative from new information. Other subjects will perform an identification-of-origin test in which they will be asked to judge whether each test item was (a) in the film, (b) in the narrative, (c) in both the film and in the narrative, or (d) in neither the film nor the narrative. We anticipate that subjects will sometimes confuse the two sources of information, and that these confusions will be at least partially independent of subjects' ability to correctly recognize both the original and the postevent information. This study will be especially interesting developmentally because the identification-of-origin test eliminates demand characteristics and because we will be able to compare the results with those found in previous developmental studies that included external-source monitoring conditions.

In summary, suggestibility is not yet understood. The theoretical intererpretation of suggestion effects in adults is not clear, and the results of studies of developmental trends in susceptibility to suggestion have been inconsistent. We believe that at least some suggestibility effects are due to failures of source monitoring, and at this point our research does not suggest developmental improvements in external-source monitoring beyond 6 years of age (Johnson & Foley, 1984). On the other hand, both developmental theory (e.g., Piaget's) and the findings of most of the suggestibility studies included in this volume suggest that children are more susceptible to misleading postevent information than are adults. The extent to which such developmental trends (if they indeed exist) reflect greater susceptibility to overwriting, greater susceptibility to source confusions, or greater susceptibility to demand characteristics and other social factors remains to be sorted out.

Summary and Conclusions

This chapter has focused on the development of the ability to make two kinds of discriminations that must often be made when one attempts to accurately recount one's memories of an event: (a) separating memories of the event itself from memories of thoughts, dreams, and fantasies about the event (reality monitoring) and (b) separating memories of the event itself from memories of information about the event gathered from other sources (external-source monitoring).

Johnson and Raye (1981) proposed that reality-monitoring discriminations are made via a decision-making process. According to the reality-monitoring model, memories of perceptually derived experiences are distinguished from memories of internal experiences on the basis of a few dimensions along which the two characteristically differ, or on the basis of other available knowledge. The same sort of model may be extended to describe the processes involved in distinguishing between memories that were drawn from different external origins but pertain to the same event. That is, suggestibility effects (and related intrusions) may be viewed as failures to discriminate accurately between memories from different sources. Whereas reality-monitoring decisions may be made on the basis of the quantity of particular dimensions encoded as part of the memory (e.g., the amount of sensory detail), external-source monitoring decisions must typically involve evaluating the content of certain aspects of the memories. The more similar the memories produced by two sources the more difficult external-source monitoring should be. Furthermore, external-source monitoring should reflect reasoning, prior knowledge, and metamemory assumptions. For example, subjects might believe that pictures produce more lasting memories than words and consequently mistakenly decide that postevent information was part of the original event because they remember it.

Developments in the ability to monitor the origin of information take place in the context of general memory development. We believe that memory development is best considered in terms of knowledge development rather than in terms of increases in memory capacity or trace duration (Chi, 1978; Piaget & Inhelder, 1968/1973). By "knowledge development" we mean to refer both to changes in *what* is known and to changes in *how* things are known. Memory is an inseparable aspect of the developing child as an intellective, emotive, social being. Thus, the kinds of tasks on which children of different ages will demonstrate adult-like levels of recall and source monitoring will be determined by developments in their motivations, interests, and social knowledge as well as by developments in more purely "cognitive" capabilities and strategies. (See Meacham's 1977 review of Soviet research on memory development for related arguments.)

Among a great many other abilities, the "skills" required to provide accurate eyewitness testimony develop during childhood. Sometime between birth and adulthood, children develop new ways of (a) attending to and comprehending events, (b) encoding, retrieving, and communicating memories of events, and (c) understanding and participating in the sociocognitive interactions involved in communicating one's memories to others in various social contexts. Each of these constitutes a vastly complex set of skills and abilities, and all develop in interaction with one another.

At one level of analysis, reality monitoring and external-source monitoring can be viewed as subparts of the retrieval component of the skill domains mentioned above. That is, one of the problems involved in retrieving particular memories is separating them from other memories that pertain to the same subject. Thus, reality monitoring and external-source monitoring may be viewed as processes that reduce intrusions due to interference effects. At a more general level of analysis, however, reality monitoring and external-source monitoring reflect very broad, conceptual attitudes and beliefs that cut across all three of the domains mentioned above (event comprehension, memory, and social knowledge). Children's apprehension of the distinctions between self and other and between reality and fantasy plays a major role in influencing the way they perceive (and subsequently remember) events in the world around them, and their understanding of the social and practical importance of these distinctions may affect their performance as eyewitnesses.

The theories of Freud and Piaget, along with the ideas generated by the reality-monitoring framework and findings from empirical studies of children's memory, offer many intriguing (but not necessarily consistent) hypotheses about the nature of children's minds, and many points of departure for future research. For example, what are the characteristics of children's imaginations? Piagetian theory (e.g., Piaget & Inhelder, 1966/1969) suggests that children under 7 years of age should not be particularly adept at purely mental fantasy, unaided by props and actions, and Freudian theory (e.g., 1933/1964) suggests that the content of children's fantasies changes with age in systematic ways. Are there important differences between spontaneous and guided imaginations, and do these have implications for developments in source monitoring? Are there developmental differences in the amount of confusion between perceived and imagined events depending on who is the agent of the action (self, familiar other, unfamiliar other), or depending on the complexity of the event? Are there ways of improving source monitoring, either through instructions or training? We have emphasized the decision-making aspects of source monitoring, but such judgment processes presuppose concepts and contrasts such as self-other, real-imagined, and Source A-Source B. Before children use the fact that different classes of memories differ in characteristic ways, they must first have some idea that one would want to distinguish between those classes. How and when do children come to appreciate the necessity of discriminating the origin of information?

The complexity and difficulty of reality-monitoring and external-source-monitoring decision making may be particularly great in the case of children who have been physically or emotionally victimized. What goes on in the mind of such a child before and during testimony? It is hard to imagine a question that more insistently demands an integration of many different approaches because cognitive, psychodynamic, social, and sociological factors are all involved. The intention and ability to categorize the origin of one's experiences and memories in various ways is a fundamental part of children's development in all of these domains.

Acknowledgments. We would like to thank the editors of this volume and Ed Casey, David Goldstein, Roger Kreuz, Marion Perlmutter, Carol Raye, Andrea Rusnock, and Susan Sugarman for their insightful comments and helpful suggestions concerning previous versions of this chapter.

References

Atkinson, R. C., & Juola, J. F. (1973). Factors influencing speed and accuracy of word recognition. In S. Kornblum (Ed.), *Attention and performance* (Vol. 4, pp. 583–612). New York: Academic Press.

Bahrick, H. P., & Karis, D. (1982). Long-term ecological memory. In D. R. Puff (Ed.), *Handbook of research methods in human memory and cognition* (pp. 427–465). New York: Academic Press.

Bekerian, D. A., & Bowers, J. M. (1983). Eyewitness testimony: Were we misled? *Journal of Experimental Psychology: Learning, Memory, and Cognition, 9*, 139–145.

Bretherton, I. (1984). Representing the social world in symbolic play: Reality and fantasy. In I. Bretherton (Ed.), *Symbolic play: The development of social understanding* (pp. 3–41). New York: Academic Press.

Bronfenbrenner, U. (1977). Toward an experimental psychology of human development. *American Psychologist, 32*, 513–531.

Cameron, N. (1963). *Personality development and psychology: A dynamic approach*. Boston: Houghton Mifflin.

Chi, M. T. H. (1978). Knowledge structures and memory development. In R. S. Siegler (Ed.), *Children's thinking: What develops?* (pp. 73–96). Hillsdale, NJ: Erlbaum.

Christiaansen, R. E., & Ochalek, K. (1983). Editing misleading information from memory: Evidence for the coexistence of original and post-event information. *Memory and Cognition, 11*, 467–475.

Cohen, R. L., & Harnick, M. A. (1980). The susceptibility of child witnesses to suggestion. *Law and Human Behavior, 4*, 201–210.

Dale, P. S., Loftus, E. F., & Rathbun, L. (1978). The influence of the form of the question on the eyewitness testimony of preschool children. *Journal of Psycholinguistical Research, 7*, 269–277.

Donaldson, M. (1978). *Children's thinking*. New York: Norton.

Duncan, E. M., Whitney, P., & Kunen, S. (1982). Integration of visual and verbal information in children's memories. *Child Development, 53*, 1215–1223.

Durso, F. T., & Johnson, M. K. (1980). The effects of orienting tasks on recognition, recall, and modality confusion of pictures and words. *Journal of Verbal Learning and Verbal Behavior, 19*, 416–429.

Finkelhor, D. (1984). *Child sexual abuse*. New York: Free Press.

Flavell, J. H. (1977). *Cognitive development*. Englewood Cliffs, NJ: Prentice-Hall.

Flavell, J. H., Flavell, E. R., & Green, F. L. (1983). Development of the appearance-reality distinction. *Cognitive Psychology, 15*, 95–120.

Foley, M. A., & Johnson, M. K. (1985). Confusions between memories for performed and imagined actions: A developmental comparison. *Child Development, 56*, 1145–1155.

Foley, M. A., Johnson, M. K., & Raye, C. L. (1983). Age-related changes in confusions between memories for thoughts and memories for speech. *Child Development, 54*, 51–60.

Freud, S. (1955). Two case histories. In J. Strachey (Ed. and Trans.), *The standard edition of the complete psychological works of Sigmund Freud* (Vol. 10). London: Hogarth Press. (Original work published 1909).

Freud, S. (1958). Two principles of mental functioning. In J. Strachey (Ed. and Trans.), *The standard edition of the complete psychological works of Sigmund Freud* (Vol. 12, pp. 218–226). London: Hogarth Press. (Original work published 1911).

Freud, S. (1959). Creative writers and day-dreaming. In J. Strachey (Ed. and Trans.), *The standard edition of the complete psychological works of Sigmund Freud* (Vol. 9, pp. 143–153). London: Hogarth Press. (Original work published 1908).

Freud, S. (1961). Negation. In J. Strachey (Ed. and Trans.), *The standard edition of the complete psychological works of Sigmund Freud* (Vol. 19, pp. 235–239). London: Hogarth Press. (Original work published 1925).

Freud, S. (1962). Heredity and the aetiology of the neuroses. In J. Strachey (Ed. and Trans.), *The standard edition of the complete psychological works of Sigmund Freud* (Vol. 3, pp. 143–156). London: Hogarth Press. (Original work published 1896).

Freud, S. (1964). Introductory lectures on psycho-analysis. In J. Strachey (Ed. and Trans.), *The standard edition of the complete psychological works of Sigmund Freud* (Vols. 15 & 16). London: Hogarth Press. (Original work published 1917).

Freud, S. (1964). New introductory lectures on psycho-analysis. In J. Strachey (Ed. and Trans.), *The standard edition of the complete psychological works of Sigmund Freud* (Vol. 22, pp. 5-182). London: Hogarth Press. (Original work published 1933).

Freud, S. (1966). Project for a scientific psychology. In J. Strachey (Ed. and Trans.), *The standard edition of the complete psychological works of Sigmund Freud* (Vol. 1, pp. 295-397). London: Hogarth Press. (Original work published 1895).

Glucksberg, S., Krauss, R. M., & Higgins, T. (1975). The development of communication skills in children. In F. Horowitz (Ed.), *Review of child development research* (Vol. 4). Chicago: University of Chicago Press.

Goodman, G. S. (1984). Children's testimony in historical perspective. *Journal of Social Issues, 40,* 9-32.

Hasher, L., & Zacks, R. T. (1979). Automatic and effortful processes in memory. *Journal of Experimental Psychology: General, 108,* 356-388.

Hintzman, D. L. (1969). Apparent frequency as a function of frequency and the spacing of repetitions. *Journal of Experimental Psychology, 80,* 139-145.

Horowitz, M. J. (1978). *Image formation and cognition.* New York: Appleton-Century-Crofts.

Hume, D. (1962). *A treatise on human nature.* New York: Collier Books. (Original work published 1739).

James, W. (1983). *The principles of psychology.* Cambridge, MA: Harvard University Press. (Original work published 1890).

Johnson, L. R., Perlmutter, M., & Trabasso, T. (1979). The leg bone is connected to the knee bone: Children's representation of body parts in memory, drawing, and language. *Child Development, 50,* 1192-1202.

Johnson, M. K. (1985). The origin of memories. In P. C. Kendall (Ed.), *Advances in cognitive behavioral research and therapy* (Vol. 4, pp. 1-27). New York: Academic Press.

Johnson, M. K. (1987). Discriminating the origin of information. In T. F. Oltmanns & B. A. Maher (Eds.), *Delusional beliefs: Interdisciplinary perspectives.* New York: Wiley.

Johnson, M. K., & Foley, M. A. (1984). Differentiating fact from fantasy: The reliability of children's memory. *Journal of Social Issues, 40,* 33-50.

Johnson, M. K., Foley, M. A., & Leach, K. (in preparation). The consequences for memory of imagining in another person's voice.

Johnson, M. K., Kahan, T., & Raye, C. L. (1984). Dreams and reality monitoring. *Journal of Experimental Psychology: General, 113,* 329-343.

Johnson, M. K., & Raye, C. L. (1981). Reality monitoring. *Psychological Review, 88,* 67-85.

Johnson, M. K., Raye, C. L., Foley, H. J., & Foley, M. A. (1981). Cognitive operations and decision bias in reality monitoring. *American Journal of Psychology, 94,* 37-64.

Johnson, M. K., Raye, C. L., Foley, M. A., & Kim, J. (1982). Pictures and images: Spatial and temporal information compared. *Bulletin of the Psychonomic Society, 14,* 23-26.

Johnson, M. K., Raye, C. L., Hasher, L., & Chromiak, W. (1979). Are there developmental differences in reality monitoring? *Journal of Experimental Child Psychology, 27,* 120-128.

Johnson, M. K., Raye, C. L., Wang, A., & Taylor, T. H. (1979). Fact and fantasy: The roles of accuracy and variability in confusing imaginations with perceptual experiences. *Journal of Experimental Psychology: Human Learning and Memory, 5*, 229–240.

Johnson, M. K., Taylor, T. H., & Raye, C. L. (1977). Fact and fantasy: The effect of internally-generated events on the apparent frequency of externally-generated events. *Memory and Cognition, 5*, 116–122.

Kahan, T. L., & Johnson, M. K. (1984, April). *Memory for seen and imagined rotations of alphanumeric characters*. Paper presented at the annual meeting of the Eastern Psychological Association, Baltimore.

Kessen, W. (1979). The American child and other cultural inventions. *American Psychologist, 34*, 815–820.

Kohlberg, L. (1968). Cognitive stages and preschool education. In J. L. Frost (Ed.), *Early childhood education rediscovered*. New York: Holt, Rinehart & Winston.

Kosslyn, S. (1978). The representational-developmental hypothesis. In P. A. Ornstein (Ed.), *Memory development in children* (pp. 157–189). Hillsdale, NJ: Erlbaum.

Liben, L. S. (1977). Memory in the context of cognitive development: A Piagetian approach. In R. V. Kail Jr. & J. W. Hagen (Eds.), *Perspectives on the development of memory and cognition*, (pp. 297–331). Hillsdale, NJ: Erlbaum.

Locke, J. (1965). *An essay concerning human understanding*. London: Collier-Macmillan Ltd. (Original work published 1689).

Loftus, E. F. (1979). *Eyewitness testimony*. Cambridge, MA: Harvard University Press.

Loftus, E. F., & Davies, G. M. (1984). Distortions in the memory of children. *Journal of Social Issues, 40*, 51–67.

Loftus, E. F., Miller, D. G., & Burns, H. J. (1978). Semantic integration of verbal information into a visual memory. *Journal of Experimental Psychology: Human Learning and Memory, 4*, 19–31.

Lottan, S. (1967). The ability of children to distinguish between the "make believe" and the "real" in children's literature. *Journal of Educational Thought, 1*, 25–33.

Malcolm, J. (1984). *In the Freud archives*. New York: Knopf.

Maratsos, M. P. (1973). Nonegocentric communication abilities in preschool children. *Child Development, 44*, 697–700.

Marin, B. V., Holmes, D. L., Guth, M., & Kovac, P. (1979). The potential of children as eyewitnesses. *Law and Human Behavior, 3*, 295–305.

Marvin, R. S., Greenberg, M. T., & Mossler, D. G. (1976). The early development of perceptual perspective taking: Distinguishing among multiple perspectives. *Child Development, 47*, 511–514.

Masson, J. M. (1984, February). Freud and the seduction theory. *The Atlantic Monthly*, 33–60.

McCloskey, M., & Zaragoza, M. (1985a). Misleading postevent information and memory for events: Arguments and evidence against memory impairment hypotheses. *Journal of Experimental Psychology: General, 114*, 1–16.

McCloskey, M., & Zaragoza, M. (1985b). Postevent information and memory: Reply to Loftus, Schooler, and Wagenaar. *Journal of Experimental Psychology: General, 114*, 381–387.

McFarland, C. E., Duncan, E., & Bruno, J. M. (1983). Developmental aspects of the generation effect. *Journal of Experimental Child Psychology, 36*, 413–428.

Meacham, J. A. (1977). Soviet investigations of memory development. In R. V. Kail Jr. & J. W. Hagen (Eds.), *Perspectives on the development of memory and cognition* (pp. 273–295). Hillsdale, NJ: Erlbaum.

Miller, P. H. (1983). *Theories of developmental psychology*. New York: W. H. Freeman.

Morrison, P., & Gardner, H. (1978). Dragons and dinosaurs: The child's capacity to differentiate fantasy from reality. *Child Development, 49*, 642–648.

Murray, S. (1983). *The effect of postevent information on children's memory for an illustrated story.* Unpublished paper, Aberdeen University, Scotland.

Neisser, U. (1976). *Cognition and reality.* New York: W. H. Freeman.

Neisser, U. (1982). Memory: What are the important questions? In U. Neisser (Ed.), *Memory observed* (pp. 3–19). New York: W. H. Freeman.

Neisser, U. (1985). Toward an ecologically oriented cognitive science. In T. M. Shlechter & M. P. Toglia (Eds.), *New directions in cognitive science* (pp. 17–32). Norwood, NJ: Ablex.

Perky, C. W. (1910). An experimental study of imagination. *American Journal of Psychology, 21*, 422–452.

Piaget, J. (1953). *The origins of intelligence in the child* (M. Cook, Trans.). London: Routledge & Kegan Paul. (Original work published in 1936).

Piaget, J. (1954). *The construction of reality in the child* (M. Cook, Trans.). New York: Basic Books. (Original work published 1937).

Piaget, J. (1962). *Play, dreams and imitation in childhood* (C. Gattegno & F. M. Hodgson, Trans.). New York: Norton. (Original work published 1945).

Piaget, J. (1972). *Judgment and reasoning in the child* (M. Warden, Trans.). Totawa, NJ: Littlefield, Adams. (Original work published 1924).

Piaget, J. (1977). The first year of life of the child (H. E. Gruber & J. J. Voneche, Trans.). In H. E. Gruber & J. J. Voneche (Eds.), *The essential Piaget* (pp. 198–214). (Original work published 1927).

Piaget, J. (1983). *The child's conception of the world* (J. Tomlinson & A. Tomlinson, Trans.). Totowa, NJ: Towman & Allanheld. (Original work published 1926).

Piaget, J., & Inhelder, B. (1969). Mental images. In P. Fraisse & J. Piaget (Eds.), *Experimental psychology: Its scope and method* (Vol. 7, pp. 85–143) (T. Surridge, Trans.). (Original work published 1963).

Piaget, J., & Inhelder, B. (1969). *The psychology of the child* (H. Weaver, Trans.). New York: Basic Books. (Original work published 1966).

Piaget, J., & Inhelder, B. (1973). *Memory and intelligence* (A. J. Pomerans, Trans.). London: Routledge and Kegan Paul. (Original work published 1968).

Posner, M. I., & Snyder, C. R. R. (1975). Attention and cognitive control. In R. L. Solso (Ed.), *Information processing and cognition: The Loyola Symposium* (pp. 55–85). Hillsdale, NJ: Erlbaum.

Raye, C. L., & Johnson, M. K. (1980). Reality monitoring vs. discrimination between external sources. *Bulletin of the Psychonomic Society, 15*, 405–408.

Reid, T. (1975). An inquiring into the human mind, on the principles of common sense. In K. Lehrer & R. E. Beanblossom (Eds.), *Thomas Reid's inquiry and essays.* Indianapolis, IN: Bobbs Merrill. (Original work published 1764).

Scarlett, W. G., & Wolf, D. (1979). When it's only make-believe: The construction of a boundary between fantasy and reality in storytelling. *New Directions for Child Development, 6*, 29–40.

Schooler, J. W., Gerhard, D., & Loftus, E. F. (1986). Qualities of the unreal. *Journal of Experimental Psychology: Learning, Memory, and Cognition, 12*, 171–181.

Sedney, M. A., & Brooks, B. (1984). Factors associated with history of childhood sexual experience in a non-clinical female population. *Journal of the American Academy of Child Psychiatry, 23*, 215–218.

Segal, S. J. (1970). Imagery and reality: Can they be distinguished? In W. Keup (Ed.), *Origin and mechanisms of hallucinations* (pp. 103–113). New York: Plenum.

Singer, J. L. (Ed.). (1973). *The child's world of make-believe: Experimental studies of imaginative play.* New York: Academic Press.

Slamecka, N. J., & Graf, P. (1978). The generation effect: Delineation of a phenomenon. *Journal of Experimental Psychology: Human Learning and Memory, 4,* 592–604.

Suengas, A. G., & Johnson, M. K. (1985, March). *Effects of rehearsal of perceived and imagined autobiographical memories.* Paper presented at the meeting of the Eastern Psychological Association, New York.

Suengas, A. G., & Johnson, M. K. (1986, April). *Memory effects of thinking about perceived and imagined complex events.* Paper presented at the meeting of the Eastern Psychological Association, New York.

Sugarman, S. (in press). The priority of description in developmental psychology.

Sully, J. (1896). *Studies of childhood.* New York: Appleton. (Original work published 1895).

Tavris, C. (1984, March). The hundred-year cover-up: How Freud betrayed women. *Ms. Magazine,* 78–80.

Taylor, B. J., & Howell, R. J. (1973). The ability of three-, four-, and five-year-old children to distinguish fantasy from reality. *Journal of Genetic Psychology, 122,* 315–318.

Wells, G. L., & Loftus, E. F. (Eds.). (1984). *Eyewitness testimony: Psychological perspectives.* New York: Cambridge University Press.

Whitehurst, G., & Sonnenshein, S. (1978). The development of communication: Attribute variation leads to contrast failure. *Journal of Experimental Child Psychology, 25,* 454–490.

Winner, E., & Gardner, H. (1979). Editor's notes: Investigations of the imaginative realm. *New Directions for Child Development, 6,* vii–xii.

7
The Impact of Naturally Occurring Stress on Children's Memory[1]

Douglas P. Peters

Since the mid-1970s there has been a tremendous growth in eyewitness research. One estimate indicates that over 85% of the entire eyewitness literature has been published since 1978 (Wells & Loftus, 1984). Numerous findings of forensic import to criminal investigators and courts of law have been generated by modern eyewitness researchers. Although psychologists, among others, have learned a great deal about the influence of various factors on adults' eyewitness memory, very little is known about their effect on children's memory. This is indeed unfortunate because many children observe and are victims in criminal proceedings. Children are increasingly being called upon by courts to provide their recollection of events they previously witnessed (Beach, 1983), especially if they are the only witness to a crime. In some cases today children as young as 3 or 4 years of age are testifying in criminal proceedings, for example, the McMartin Preschool trial of sexual abuse in Los Angeles, California, which has received nationwide publicity.

Of the relatively few studies that have examined the child witness, almost all have been conducted in laboratory settings in which films, pictures, or stories are presented (for recent reviews, see Chance & Goldstein, 1984; Yarmey, 1984). Then, following a period of time, the child's memory of the original stimuli is evaluated. With this procedure, the influence of such variables as postevent suggestion has been examined. Yet, there is growing concern that such an approach may be lacking in ecological validity, for example, the to-be-remembered material may not capture children's attention to the degree that actual real-life events do and may not be retained as well as events that are personally meaningful (see Brown, 1979; Ceci & Bronfenbrenner, 1985; Goodman, 1984; Nelson, Fivush, Hudson, & Lucariello, 1983; Perlmutter, 1980). Clifford (1979) asserts that studies such as these employing laboratory memory paradigms differ in a number of important respects from situations that actual eyewitnesses are likely to encounter. Identification of faces, for example, in the laboratory has often

[1]A shorter version of this paper was presented for the symposium, Current Trends in Evaluating Children's Memory for Witnessed Events, at the 1985 annual meeting of the American Psychological Association, Los Angeles, California.

involved procedures where the subjects are forewarned and know what is expected of them. These subjects are evaluated in a positive cognitive set encompassing maximally efficient processing and encoding strategies that may not accurately reflect those strategies employed in real-life witnessing situations, which are generally characterized as dynamic, rapid, unexpected, and of sudden onset and offset. Traditional memory studies may tell us how well faces can be remembered under ideal conditions, but this is not a very forensically relevant question when one considers the actual conditions surrounding witnessed events.

It has become clear that, in several cases of eyewitness research, laboratory findings are at odds with results from simulation studies attempting to create realistic eyewitness events. For example, laboratory studies of face recognition indicate that accuracy increases, whereas false positives (saying that a face had previously been presented when in fact it had not) decrease with age up to about 12 to 14 years. Age-related differences have not been found, however, in more realistic simulation studies. Here, all subjects—adults, adolescents, and children—show comparable levels of eyewitness performance, which is typically quite poor (Chance & Goldstein, 1984). Many laboratory-based investigations of voice memory have examined earwitnesses under optimal conditions of hearing and testing and have reported overall identification accuracies of 60 to 70% correct detection (Bull & Clifford, 1984). But when subjects are unsuspecting participants in staged events, their ability to recognize a previously heard voice is greatly diminished, sometimes even to chance levels of accuracy (Clifford & Denot, 1982; Clifford & Fleming, in press). Examples such as these certainly underscore the problem of ecological validity facing the growing body of witness "facts" that are based mainly on laboratory findings.

Another area of recent concern has been the lack of research focused on the issue of children's emotional reactions in viewing or experiencing crime, especially those with a high degree of personal impact, such as sexual abuse, assault, or homicide. Studies with adults examining the influence of stress on eyewitness memory have produced somewhat equivocal results with only about half of the reports suggesting a decrease in eyewitness accuracy as a function of increased amounts of arousal or stress (see Deffenbacher, 1983, for a review). Deffenbacher argues, though, that if you really examine only those studies that have employed forensically relevant (i.e., high) levels of arousal, those appearing most appropriate to criminal situations involving rape, assault, homicide, robbery, and so on, the picture is irrefutably clear—higher arousal levels are associated with lowered eyewitness accuracy.

Perhaps it is not surprising that there seems to be some confusion among judges, defense attorneys, prosecutors, and laypersons regarding the impact of stress on the reliability of eyewitness testimony. Based, in part, on the fact that United States judges typically do not allow expert testimony concerning the harmful effects of high arousal on information processing and memory, Deffenbacher (1983) suggests that criminal court judges commonly hold the view that high-stress levels can facilitate the accuracy of memory. If an expert witness were to state the opposite opinion in court, the trial judge might invoke Rule 403 of the *Federal Rules of Evidence* (1975) to exclude evidence that, in the judge's mind, wastes time, confuses the issues, and misleads the jury, that is, it goes against common knowledge. In a survey of 235 trial attorneys, Brigham (1981) reported that 82% of criminal defense lawyers believed that high arousal leads to poorer facial recognition, but 47% of the prosecutors sampled held the opposite view. Hastie's (1980) study of jury deliberations using six-person mock juries who viewed reenactments of an actual armed-robbery trial found that "stress" was discussed in the context of *aiding* the eyewitness' accuracy in 10 of the 11 juries. These findings are contrasted with those of Deffenbacher and Loftus (1982). Their data from four different samples of laypeople indicated that never more than 25% of the respondents believed that extreme stress experienced by a crime victim would facilitate recall of criminal acts, and only 5% of those who had had criminal trial jury experience over the prior 5 years held a positive view about stress and memory.

If stress and arousal experienced by an adult during an event can, in fact, impair eyewitness memory (Deffenbacher, 1983; Loftus, 1979; Woocher, 1977), are children similarly affected, or, as some might intuit, do they provide less accurate testimony following traumatic, very stressful events? This is of course an empirical question. (One should keep in mind that counter to simple intuition, several studies have found adult-child differences in recall and recognition with children being superior, e.g., Chi, 1978; Lindberg, 1980; Neisser, 1979.) Unfortunately, as of now we do not have the necessary body of data to address this question adequately. Experimental studies with adult witnesses have manipulated arousal by using electric shock (Brigham, Maas, Snyder, & Spaulding, 1982), loud noise (Clifford & Hollin, 1981; Giesbrecht, 1979), and films depicting violent events, for example, a robbery victim held at gunpoint and beaten on the head, with considerable bleeding as a result (Sussman & Sugarman, 1972); a young boy brutally shot in the face during a bank holdup (Loftus & Burns, 1981). For obvious ethical reasons it would be undesirable to subject young children to these stressful situations in order to evaluate the impact of arousal on eyewitness memory.

The research I will present in this chapter was, in part, a response to the issues raised above. Specifically, it represents a first attempt to address the issue of stress and children's memory in an ethically and ecologically sound manner. Young children's memory was examined (i.e., the ability to remember faces and voices and details of the built environment) in the context of a naturally occurring, meaningful event that has been known to produce high levels of fear or anxiety in many children and adults—namely, a trip to the dentist (Kleinknecht, Klepac, & Alexander, 1973; Lautch, 1971). It has been estimated that the fear of dentistry and the attending avoidance of professional dental care is significantly widespread to pose a serious health problem for thousands of people living in the United States (Freidson & Feldman, 1958; Kleinknecht et al., 1973).

Method

Subjects

With the cooperation of seven male dentists working in four different cities in Minnesota and North Dakota, a total of 71 children, ranging in ages from 3 to 8 years, were studied; 38 of the children were female and 33 were male. The only subject restriction was that the child could not have had more than one previous visit to the participating dentist. We felt this restriction was necessary so that we could make generalizations about children's identification of strangers. There was no restriction on what type of appointment the children had with their dentist. As it turned out, 68 of the appointments (96%) were for dental checkups or teeth cleaning. Of the remaining three subjects, one 4-year-old came in to see what a dentist looked like and to talk with him, one 7-year-old had his teeth measured for braces, and one 8-year-old had cavities filled.

The dentists and their assistants or hygienists each individually recorded the total amount of time they were physically present with each subject. The collective data indicated that the average time the children spent in the presence of the dentist and his assistant or hygienist was approximately equal, 13 and 15 minutes, respectively. Subsequent analyses found no significant relationship between exposure time for the dentist and the child's age ($r = .07, p > .05$) and a significant, but a trivial negative correlation between exposure time for the dental assistant/hygienist and the age of the subject ($r = -.14, p < .05$). It appears that younger children were getting neither more nor less attention (in terms of personal contact) than older children visiting the dentist.

Design and Procedure

When parents of a child who qualified for our study arrived for the child's appointment, the dentist's receptionist handed them a sheet of paper that briefly described the study and requested their participation. Those who consented were asked not to inform their children about the ongoing study. At the end of the child's dental appointment, his or her parent and the dentist (consulting with his assistant or hygienist) made independent anxiety ratings of the child's dental visit on a 9-point Likert scale with 9 = "extremely anxious," 5 = "moderately anxious," and 1 = "not anxious at all." The interrater agreement between parents and dentists on anxiety scores for the children was significant and fairly high ($r = .72, p < .05$). We combined these two ratings into one overall anxiety score for each child's dental visit.

The parents were contacted by telephone to establish times for visiting their children at home for memory tests following their child's trip to the dentist. For the first home visit, which lasted an average of 16 minutes, the children were seen either shortly after their dental appointment, 24–48 hours later ($n = 34$), or following a longer retention interval of 3 to 4 weeks ($n = 37$). The subjects in the comfort of their homes were all given face and voice recognition tests of (a) their dentist, and (b) the dental assistant or hygienist who saw them. Recognition tests consisted of photo and voice lineups with five choices to select from. For all recognition tests, including those yet to be described, the subjects were told that the target may or may not be in the lineup. In fact, half of the subjects for both retention intervals were given blank (target-absent) lineups where a foil substituted for the target. For each recognition test in this study, for example, the dentist and dental assistant/hygienist, a new random assignment was made to determine which subjects would receive the target-present or target-absent lineup condition. After being presented with a particular lineup, subjects were asked to indicate whether or not the target was present and, if present, to make an identification from the choice alternatives. Subjects were also given an option of saying they had "no idea" when they felt they would simply be guessing. In all target-present conditions the target appeared in the fourth lineup position, which, for practical reasons, was the easiest way to present targets. This fixed-position procedure has also been used successfully by other psycholegal researchers (e.g., Kassin, 1984; Sanders, 1984). Of course, if subjects had a strong response bias for or against the fourth position in a lineup, the results would be unreliable. Fortunately, statistical analyses indicated the absence of any significant positional responding.

Using a group of children approximately equal in age to those of the dental subjects, the functional size (Wells, Leippe, & Ostrom, 1979) of the lineups (voice and face) was calculated by determining the value N/D, where N = the number of nonwitnesses, each making a lineup selection based on a gross description of the target, and D = the number of nonwitnesses who pick the target. The closer the functional size is to the actual number of people in the lineup, the fairer the lineup is presumed to be, that is, the target becomes less distinguishable from others appearing in the lineup—at least in terms of general characteristics. The functional size of the lineups (voice and face) ranged from 3.8 to 5, with an overall mean of 4.5 for faces and 4.7 for voices.

For face recognition, subjects were presented with a photospread that consisted of five color portrait photographs (5 in. × 7 in.). The targets and foils were matched with respect to age, hair color and length, and the presence of facial hair and eyeglasses. In the voice-recognition task, target (dentist and dental assistant or hygienist) and foil voices had no speech impediments, and all were free of noticeable ethnicity or accent. Also, differences in pitch were controlled, for example, if the dentist had a high-pitched voice, so did his foils. Five voice-choices were presented over a stereocassette player for each subject. The speech samples consisted of 9 and 8 sentences totaling 62 and 57 words for the dentist and assistant/hygienist lineups, respectively. For these two lineups, subjects heard voice samples that lasted an average of 22 and 20 seconds, respectively. The subjects could hear the lineup a second time if they wished.

The subjects were also given a third recognition test to see if they could remember more peripheral details of their dental visit. They were asked to identify their dentist's room from a five-room color photospread. In this case lineup foils were pictures of other dentists' rooms. Again, half the subjects viewed lineups in which the target was not present. Figure 7.1 displays some of the room photos that were shown to our subjects. No attempt was made to match room characteristics. It is doubtful whether this would have even been possible.

Following each recognition test, all subjects were asked to indicate how confident they were of their choice on a 5-point rating scale, with 1 = "not at all sure" and 5 = "absolutely sure." For the younger children, as each point on the confidence scale was described, the researcher varied the distance between his hands to indicate the concept of magnitude underlying each rating point, for example,

FIGURE 7.1. Examples of dental room photos used in recognition tests.

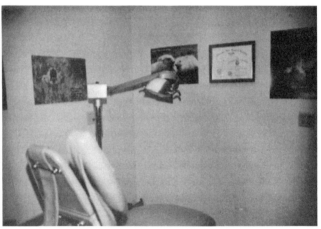

FIGURE 7.1. *Continued.*

his hands were almost touching for a rating of "1" and fully extended apart for a "5" rating. We felt that this procedure was useful in helping several of the youngest subjects, ages 3 to 4 years, understand the meaning of the confidence scale.

A second series of memory tests were given to the subjects by a *new* researcher either 24 to 48 hours ($n = 34$) or 3 to 4 weeks ($n = 37$) following the first visit to their home. As in the case of the first home visit, none of the children was forewarned about the memory tests. This time subjects were asked to identify the face and voice of the *first* researcher (the one who had originally tested them) from photo and voice lineups and again to indicate their level of confidence. As was the case for the first testing period, approximately half of the subjects here, for both retention intervals, received blank (target-absent) lineups. In addition, parents, the first researcher, and the second researcher made independent ratings of the child's anxiety during the home visits, using the 9-point anxiety scale described earlier. The interrater agreement on anxiety scores was significant (*ps* < .05) and relatively high for parents and the first researcher (*r* = .78) and parents and the second researcher (*r* = .68). We averaged these sets of scores to arrive at a composite anxiety rating for (a) the first visit to the subject's home and (b) the second visit to the subject's home.

In summary, subjects of this study were randomly assigned to one of four conditions within a 2 (short vs. long delay for first home visit) by 2 (short vs. long delay for second home visit) factorial design. Thus 16 subjects received the short-short delay combination, 19 subjects were given the long-long delay condition, and the remaining two groups were comprised of 18 subjects each. (One subject assigned to the short-short delay condition had to be reassigned to the long-long delay condition because of a scheduling conflict.) In addition, subject age was balanced across the four experimental conditions with the largest mean difference in group age being 0.6 years (5.9 vs. 5.3 years).

Results and Discussion

Anxiety Ratings

As previously mentioned, the overall amount of time the children spent in the presence of the dentist, the assistant/hygienist, and the researcher was approximately equal. Given similar exposure times, would subjects recognize faces and voices to an equal degree from the dental setting versus home setting? If subjects experienced more stress and displayed more anxiety during the dental visit than in the comfort of their own home, then memory differences across settings might be attributed to this factor. However, since memory tests were administered at two different times, differences in anxiety levels across testing sessions could be used to explain any resulting memory differences—for there is evidence to suggest that stress at time of *identification*, as well as during the initial observation, can lead to less accurate performance (Dent & Stephenson, 1979). If our subjects were significantly more relaxed, less anxious during the second home visit (perhaps because of some desensitization—a researcher visiting their home had become a more familiar event), then the better recognition of the researcher (second testing at home) versus the dentists (first testing period at home) could be due to this factor and not to stress during the original observation and encoding. Fortunately, this was not the case. The overall mean anxiety rating for the dental visit was 5.8, compared to 4.2 for the first home visit and 4.6 for the second home visit. On the 9-point anxiety scale, a rating of 5 indicates the subject was "moderately anxious," and a rating of 3 indicates "slightly anxious." Mean anxiety scores for subjects receiving target-present versus target-absent lineups for dental vs. home (first visit) ratings were 5.6, 6.0, 4.1, and 4.3, respectively. Although the differences in anxiety ratings were not as great as we had anticipated, especially considering the literature on dental phobias, statistically the dental versus home differences were reliable (*ps* < .05), whereas differences in rated anxiety for the two home visits were not ($p > .05$). Having determined this, let us now turn our attention to the recognition results.

Photo Recognition

Although subjects had, numerically, better photo-recognition scores following the short (24 hr) versus the long (3 to 4 weeks) retention interval (i.e., identification accuracy decreased and false identification increased with the longer retention interval) for both home visit testing periods, the effect was not statistically significant, with the largest obtained difference in correct and false identification across retention intervals being 13% and 11%, respectively.

The photo-recognition data for the dentist, dental assistant or hygienist, dental room, and researcher have been collapsed across retention intervals and are presented in Table 7.1 as a function of target-presence or target-absence in the lineup. In Table 7.2 we see the proportions of correct response (i.e., correct identification when target is in the lineup or correct nonidentification when target is absent from the lineup), false identification, false nonidentification (only possible for target present lineups), and "no idea" given for each of the different target lineups. The proportions listed for the first three responses are based on the total

TABLE 7.1. Photo recognition as a function of target presence in a lineup.

Photo recognition		Lineup condition	
		Target present	Target absent
Dentist	Correct response	43% (15)	26% (9)
	False ID	40% (14)	74% (25)
	False non-ID	17% (6)	—
	No idea	3% (1)	3% (1)
Assistant/hygienist	Correct response	64% (23)	22% (7)
	False ID	33% (12)	78% (25)
	False non-ID	3% (1)	—
	No idea	0% (0)	9% (3)
Dental room	Correct response	53% (19)	35% (12)
	False ID	31% (11)	65% (22)
	False non-ID	16% (6)	—
	No idea	0% (0)	3% (1)
Researcher	Correct response	71% (25)	30% (10)
	False ID	20% (7)	70% (23)
	False non-ID	9% (3)	—
	No idea	3% (1)	6% (2)

Note: Frequencies in parenthesis.

TABLE 7.2. Overall effect of lineup condition with target data (dentist, assistant/hygienist, dental room and researcher) combined.

Photo choice	Lineup condition	
	Target present	Target absent
Correct response	58% (82)	29% (38)
False ID	31% (44)	71% (95)
False non-ID	11% (16)	—
No idea	1% (2)	5% (7)

Note: Frequencies in parentheses.

number who made a *choice* in the sample, that is, they either selected a photo or stated that the target was not in the lineup. In computing the "no idea" proportion, the total sample size for each condition was used.

It is quite clear from Table 7.1 that, in the Target-Present condition, subjects could correctly identify the target at a greater than chance level (chance = 20% correct), especially when the target was the dental assistant/hygienist or researcher (64 and 71% correct ID). It is also apparent that when the subjects were given blank lineups (Target Absent), their recognition performance suffered greatly, with false identifications ranging from 65% to 78%.

Table 7.2 presents the overall effect of Lineup Condition (Target Present vs. Target Absent) with target data (dentist, assistant/hygienist, room and researcher) combined. Analyses indicated that subjects who viewed target-present lineups made significantly more correct responses than subjects given blank lineups (58% vs. 29%). Furthermore, false identifications rose significantly going from 31% to 71% when blank lineups were used. Even though the children were told that the targets may not be in the lineups, it seems that they had great difficulty in withholding a selection. If anything, this certainly illustrates the need for blank lineups in eyewitness research. As others have pointed out (Malpass & Devine, 1984; Wells, 1984), examining identification accuracy only when the target is present is of limited forensic value.

Effects of Stress

Turning back to Table 7.1, the data here are somewhat equivocal with respect to the issue of stress and eyewitness memory. If subjects experienced more stress in the dental office than in their own home, as the anxiety ratings indicated, and if stress does impair memory, then we might expect to see differences in recognition accuracy for the dental versus home visit. However, in only one comparison of photo-recognition levels did the *less* stressful setting (home visit by the researcher) yield superior ($p < .05$) recognition scores, that is, correct identification when target was present in the lineup (researcher ID = 71% vs. dentist ID = 43%). Other comparisons did not produce significant differences between dental visit and the home visit recognitions. In some respects though, the dentist versus researcher recognition is perhaps the most relevant comparison for it examines recognition memory of male faces in both settings (all male dentists and a male researcher). Thus, the to-be-remembered targets are relatively similar as opposed to the other recognition comparisons involving female (assistants/hygienists) versus male (researcher) and dental room versus male (researcher) recognition.

Anxiety ratings for the two to-be-remembered settings, the dental office and the first home visit were weakly, but significantly, related ($r = .16, p < .05$). A child who was seen as very nervous and anxious during the dental appointment might just as likely have been calm and relaxed during the researcher's visit to his or her home. It would appear that situational anxiety, and not trait anxiety, is what was being observed in this study. Several past investigators have reported finding detrimental effects of high state anxiety, trait anxiety, or neuroticism on eyewitness accuracy (Buckhout, Alper, Chern, Silverberg, & Slomovits, 1974; Mueller, Bailis, & Goldstein, 1979; Nowicki, Winograd & Millard, 1979; Siegel & Loftus, 1978; Zanni & Offermann, 1978).

In the present investigation we did find several significant correlations ($ps < .05$) between rated anxiety and recognition accuracy, but they were only for target-present lineup conditions, and the magnitude of the correlations were rather meager. For recognition of dentists, anxiety was negatively related to correct identification ($r = -.32$) and positively related to false identifications ($r = .21$). For recognition of assistants/hygienists anxiety correlated with correct identification ($r = -.24$) and false identification ($r = .23$). So the picture emerging here seems to be that the more anxiety a child experienced during the dental visit the less accurate he or she was in identifying the male or female target, and the greater the likelihood of false identification. One might wonder why similar findings for dental room recognition were not obtained, as there is some evidence suggesting that during heightened arousal or stress, a person's attention may narrow, thus excluding peripheral detail from memory (Johnson & Scott, 1976). In the context of sitting in a dental chair having your teeth cleaned, one's attention might certainly be focused on the hands of the hygienist or on dental tools she is using or even on her face. In this case, features of the room, such as wall hangings or pictures, color and shape of the room, lighting patterns and floor designs, may not be remembered as well as the central focus of attention, the hygienist. One could argue, though, that when a young child is stressed by having fingers and strange instruments thrust into his or her mouth for an uncomfortable period of time, he or she may intentionally redirect attention toward peripheral details as a coping strategy to reduce arousal level and to serve as a distraction. Perhaps that is what took place in this study and explains the absence of an accuracy-anxiety effect for dental room recognition.

One further comparison is worth mentioning with respect to the possible effects of dental anxiety on memory in this investigation. In a recently completed study of ours (Peters & Hagen, 1986), preschoolers (ages 3 to 6) saw and interacted with a stranger for approximately 10 minutes at their day-care center or nursery school and then received a gift (children's stickers), all in the presence of their teachers. Face recognition of the stranger (a male researcher) from a five-person photospread, following a 3-week passage of time, was significantly better than what we observed for the dentists of this study with the target-present lineups, for example, 59% versus 40% (3 to 4-week retention period) and 47% (24-hour retention period) correct identification. The children in the day-care study were generally very relaxed, appeared happy, and were eager to receive their gifts during the stranger's visit. Perhaps this lack of anxiety compared to the reported anxiety of the children visiting the dentist explains in part the difference found here in eyewitness accuracy. The face-recognition procedures were identical, none of the children in either study had advance warning about the memory tests, and they all came from similar populations.

Voice Recognition

There was no effect of retention interval on any of the response outcomes for any of the three target conditions (dentist, assistant/hygienist, and researcher). Table 7.3 presents the overall voice-recognition data with target conditions combined. Analyses of the target-present versus target-absent scores failed to yield any significant differences, a finding due to "floor effects" for the case of correct responses, resulting in a lack of variation.

Analyses of the voice-recognition data collapsed across retention intervals indicated that, in all comparisons of correct response (correct identification of target when in lineup or correct nonidentification—saying target not present for blank lineups), accuracy levels did not differ significantly from chance (20%). The absence of any reliable voice recognition following a 24–48-hour retention interval is consistent with findings from a recent study of adult earwitness memory. Clifford and Fleming (in press) conducted a field experiment in which unsuspecting shopkeepers and bank clerks were asked to identify the voice of a stooge who had interacted with them prior to the recognition tests. Correct identification went from 50% with immediate testing to chance following a 24 hour delay. However, another study of voice-identification accuracy with adults under *unprepared* conditions (Clifford & Denot, 1982) obtained 50%, 43%, and 9%

TABLE 7.3. Voice recognition with target data (dentist, assistant/hygienist, and researcher) combined.

Voice choice	Lineup condition	
	Target present	Target absent
Correct response	25% (17)	18% (12)
False ID	71% (48)	82% (56)
False non-ID	6% (4)	—
No idea	4% (3)	3% (2)

Note: Frequencies in parentheses.

(chance) correct recognition after delays of 1, 2, or 3 weeks, respectively. Subjects here were not as quickly impaired by recognition delays as those in the Clifford and Fleming (in press) study. Bull and Clifford (1984), in their review of the earwitness literature (almost all of which has come from laboratory settings making forensic generalizations difficult), concluded that delays in voice identification following initial exposure will reduce accuracy, but just how quickly and over what time scale remains unanswered. The data from the present study would suggest that young children cannot recognize a stranger's voice (one that was heard for at least five minutes during active conversation) following a 24- to 48-hour period. If future studies of earwitness memory in naturalistic settings report similar findings, the wisdom of accepting earwitness testimony (under similar circumstances) of young children should be seriously questioned.

Finally, there is the possibility that if the voice lineups we used were "too fair," that is, they contained very similar-sounding voices, voice recognition suffered as a result. Handkins and Cross (1985) have presented some recent evidence to suggest such a possibility. For six test sets in their study, a target voice was presented to the subjects, and then followed 10 seconds later by a five-voice lineup. Half the voice sets had voices very similar to one another and to the target; for the other half, the voices were quite dissimilar, as measured by the "Voice Profile Check List," which evaluates a number of speech charcteristics such as pitch, pitch variation, rate, rate variation, expression, enunciation, speaker's age, inflection, accent, tremor, pauses, nasality, and voice quality. Also, in half the sets used, the target voice was either present or absent. The results showed that for target-present lineups, more hits (66% vs. 52%) and fewer false identifications (18% vs. 37%) occurred when dissimilar voices comprised the lineup. Using dissimilar voices also produced better recognition performance for target-absent lineups, with more correct nonidentifications (46% vs. 28%) and fewer false identifications (18% vs. 37%). These findings are relevant for the present study because great care was taken to provide subjects with voices as similar sounding as possible for each lineup. (Approximately 80 voices were examined in constructing the lineups). It should be noted that increasing physical similarity between the target and foils in eyewitness lineups has a positive influence in helping to protect innocent suspects by spreading choices across lineup members (see Wells, 1984). It has no effect on the willingness of subjects to make an identification.

Age of Subject

PHOTO RECOGNITION

When subjects were blocked into three age groups, 3 to 4 years ($n = 19$), 5 to 6 years ($n = 32$), and 7 to 8 years ($n = 20$), a significant effect of age ($ps < .05$) on correct identification and false identification for recognition of researcher in the target-present condition was obtained. The oldest group was superior to the two younger ones (who did not differ from each other) on correct identification and false positives. Analyses of age differences for recognition of the dentist, assistant/hygienist, and dental room with target-present and target-absent lineups failed to yield any significant effects. Correlational analyses showed a somewhat similar pattern, whereby the age of the subject was only reliably ($ps < .05$) related to correct identification ($r = .31$) and false identification ($r = -.28$) for the target-present condition with the researcher as the target. All other correlations were nonsignificant. These results lend partial support to laboratory studies that have shown clear improvement in facial recognition for unfamiliar faces over the age range of 6 to 10 years (e.g., Blaney & Winograd, 1978; Diamond & Carey, 1977; Flin, 1980), and 5 to 14 years (Chance & Goldstein, 1984). Our study does extend the lower age level in developmental analyses of face recognition to include 3- and 4-year-olds.

At this time it is not clear why an age effect was only observed in the one condition, that is, researcher recognition with target-present lineup, although a floor effect may have prevented age effects from showing in the target-absent lineups. It is also possible that if the oldest group of subjects, the 7- to 8-year-olds, had experienced less stress or anxiety than the younger subjects during the first home visit when they saw the researcher, or during the second home visit when recognition tests for the researcher were administered, these anxiety differences could result in better eyewitness accuracy for the less stressed (at time of encoding and/or recall) older subjects. However, as we shall now see, these differences did not exist.

Anxiety Ratings

The three age groups did not significantly differ in any analyses of anxiety scores. Thus they all showed the same amount of anxiety *within* each visit: dentist appointment, first home visit, and second home visit. Correlational analyses revealed that age of subject was in one case (the dental visit) marginally related to anxiety scores ($r = -.15, p < .06$), but this single exception is to be expected on the basis of chance alone.

Voice Recognition

There is no age effect here for voice-recognition accuracy. Analyses failed to produce any significant age group (3 to 4, 5 to 6, 7 to 8 years) differences across all target and lineup conditions ($ps > .05$) partly due to floor effects. The voice-recognition tasks would seem to be very difficult for all ages of children tested.

Confidence Ratings

Are older children, with typically greater social, physical, and cognitive skills more confident in their memory abilities than younger children? Our data would suggest "no"—at least in the context of recognizing targets from photo lineups. The three age groups did not reliably differ when their averaged overall confidence scores were compared.

Sex of Subject

A few studies report female superiority in face (see Chance & Goldstein, 1984) and voice (see Bull & Clifford, 1984) recognition. Others suggest that this may turn into inferiority when stress occurs either at input or output (Clifford, 1979). We found no evidence of this to support either claim. There were no significant sex differences in any of the photo- or voice-recognition analyses among children in our age range of 3 to 8 years.

Interaction Effects

Statistical analyses failed to yield a significant age by retention interval, sex by retention interval, and sex by age interaction for any measure of photo- or voice-recognition accuracy.

Confidence-Accuracy Relationship

One important witness factor that can favorably bias jurors' impressions is confidence (Deffenbacher, 1980; Hovland, Janis & Kelley, 1953; Miller & Burgoon, 1982; Sealy & Wain, 1980; Wells, Ferguson, & Lindsay, 1981; Wells & Leippe, 1981). A confident witness is perceived as a credible witness. However, this intuitively appealing position is not supported by studies that are ecologically valid with respect to this issue (for a recent review of eyewitness confidence see Wells & Murray, 1984). Studies that have included both target-present and target-absent lineups or have simulated realistic events for unsuspecting subjects have, collectively, shown that eyewitness confidence is not a forensically useful predictor of eyewitness accuracy. The results of this study also support such a conclusion. The photo-recognition data produced only two instances where the overall confidence-accuracy relationship was significant, that is, recognition of assistant/hygienist ($r = .16, p < .05$) and researcher ($r = .19, p < .05$). As has been the case in many earlier studies, the magnitude of the correlations are so low here as to make them relatively useless in any forensic sense. Analyses examining the overall confidence-accuracy relationship for voice-recognition failed to produce any reliable correlations, which is unusual for earwitness research (see Clifford, 1980). However, prior studies of voice-recognition have almost always failed to include target-absent (blank) lineups and, as Wells and Murray (1984) point out, this often inflates confidence-accuracy estimate and severely limits any meaningful generalizations about confidence-accuracy relationships for real-world events.

Conclusions and Future Directions

The reader should bear in mind that when evaluating and comparing studies of stress it is always important to note how the stress construct is defined and measured. One of the major conceptual difficulties within the stress field has been the lack of convergence between psychological and physiological perspectives of stress (Selye, 1975). In our study we used a 9-point rating scale of anxiety to measure stress levels. This was mostly done for practical reasons—it was non-invasive as well as easy to administer and score, which are important considerations when you are working with young children in field settings. Future researchers who anticipate studying arousal effects on young children's eyewitness memory might want to consider getting concurrent measures of stress and arousal. Not only would this allow for "conceptual replication," but it could also increase the likelihood of getting at least one sensitive measure in your study. Presently, two assessment techniques seem promising. One is the Preschool Observation Scale of Anxiety (POSAR), which employs an observational methodology for recording 25 well-defined behavioral indicates of anxiety, including physical complaints, desire to leave, expressions of fear or worry, crying, screams, whimpering, trembling voice, stuttering, whispering, silence to questions, nail-biting, lip-licking, sucking or chewing objects, lip contortions, trembling lips, gratuitous hand movements near parts of body, gratuitous leg and foot movements, and trunk contortions. Initial findings suggest that it may provide a way of evaluating situationally induced anxiety in children who are too young to accurately give verbal reports of their emotional states (Glennon & Weisz, 1978). The other stress measure is a biochemical one (actually two) that has recently been used by McClelland (1982), McClelland, Davidson, Floor, and Saron (1980), and McClelland and Kirshnit (1984). Unlike getting urine or blood samples from young children, a difficult process at best, this approach is simpler and less intrusive. It simply involves taking saliva samples from subjects and having them analyzed for (a) salivary immunoglobin A (S-IgA), which is a measure of B-cell immune function—the body's first line of defense against viral infections that enter through the mouth and nose, and/or (b) salivary norepinephrine—a measure of sympathetic activation. Decreases in S-IgA and increases in salivary norepinephrine have been associated with a number of stress conditions, for example, taking a final examination or viewing a film depicting the sick and suffering of the world. The major drawbacks to this approach is the need for proper facilities and personnel to perform the chemical assays. This typically would require collaborative efforts with specialists in such fields as neuroendocrinology, immunology, or physiology. However, the increase in precision of measurement as well as conceptual linkage to established theories of stress might offset the costs of this procedure.

As stated at the beginning of this chapter, the major focus of our study was to learn more about the effects of stress on children's ability to function as accurate witnesses. The research activity in this area has been very limited. Our approach in addressing this increasingly important psycholegal topic has been to work first from the real-world environment, where stress occurs naturally for children. (Most likely laboratory simulations will eventually follow in a series of converging studies utilizing different settings, material, and designs.) We believed that a child's trip to the dentist could provide us with (a) a natural setting having personal significance for the subject and (b) desired levels of the ethically sensitive variable—stress. Our results indicated that the children were more anxious in the dental environment, as compared to the home setting, but did not differ in rated anxiety during the two periods of recognition tests given at home. Thus it was possible to evaluate the effects of stress at time of initial observation without the confounding effects of stress at recall being present. Some of the present results suggest a negative effect of stress or anxiety on recognition memory, but this outcome was observed in only one test case, recognition of dentist versus researcher, whereas two out of three photo-recognition, and all comparison tests of voice recognition, failed to show a significant stress effect. The voice-recognition results are not that surprising when one realizes that the memory tasks were so difficult that subjects showed essentially chance responding. Any possible stress effects would be masked by this. On the other hand, the absence of a stress effect in two thirds of the relevant photo-recognition tests is more problematic and remains unresolved at this time. Our study would certainly have made a stronger test case for stress effects if our sample of subjects had experienced higher levels of anxiety during their dental visit, for example, ratings toward the upper end of the scale ("very anxious" or "extremely anxious") instead of those around the middle ("moderately anxious"), as correlations are sensitive to range. Also, if 95% of our subjects had come to their dentist for cavities to be filled instead of dental exams and teeth cleaning, perhaps much more anxiety would have been seen.

Given the clinical reports and retrospective accounts of children who have been traumatized by crimes (e.g., Pynoos & Eth, 1984; Terr, 1981) the levels of stress our subjects received during their dental visit could not be considered equivalent to what children would experience as a witness to and/or victim of violent crimes such as homicide or sexual molestation or assault. In order to study in natural settings these high levels of stress in children, it is going to take a certain degree of creativity and perseverance on the part of the researcher. Certain situations that may at first glance appear highly anxiety provoking for children, for example, opening night for their first school play, should be pretested in order to realistically evaluate the degree of stress involved. The search for ecologically valid analogs of eyewitness conditions that exist when children are exposed to traumatic events may prove to be quite a difficult undertaking. Nevertheless, the attempt should be made to develop more realistic eyewitness simulations with children, especially since the laws affecting child witnesses are undergoing revision and the courts need hard data from ecologically valid studies of children as witnesses.

Acknowledgment. I would like to extend my thanks to Foster Fitz, Dean Quigley, and Sharon Hagen for their valuable help during the data collection phase of this research.

References

Beach, B. H. (1983, January 31). Out of the mouthes of babes. *Time*, p. 43.
Blaney, R. L., & Winograd, E. (1978). Developmental differences in children's recognition memory for faces. *Developmental Psychology, 14*, 441–442.

Brigham, J. C. (1981). The accuracy of eyewitness evidence: How do attorneys see it? *Florida Bar Journal, 55*, 714–721.

Brigham, J. C., Maas, A., Snyder, L. D., & Spaulding, K. (1982). Accuracy of eyewitness identifications in a field setting. *Journal of Personality and Social Psychology, 42*, 673–681.

Brown, A. L. (1979). Theories of memory and the problem of development: Activity, growth, and knowledge. In L. Cermak & F. I. M. Craik (Eds.), *Levels of processing in memory.* Hillsdale, NJ: Erlbaum.

Buckhout, R., Alper, A., Chern, S., Silverberg, G., & Slomovits, M. (1974). Determinants of eyewitness performance on lineup. *Bulletin of the Psychonomic Society, 4*, 191–192.

Bull, R., & Clifford, B. R. (1984). Earwitness voice recognition accuracy. In G. L. Wells & E. F. Loftus (Eds.), *Eyewitness testimony.* New York: Cambridge University Press.

Ceci, S. J., & Bronfenbrenner, U. (1985). Don't forget to take the cupcakes out of the oven: Prospective memory, strategic time-monitoring, and context. *Child Development, 56(1)*, 152–164.

Chance, J. E., & Goldstein, A. G. (1984). Face-recognition memory: Implications for children's eyewitness testimony. *Journal of Social Issues, 40(2)*, 69–85.

Chi, M. T. H. (1978). Short-term memory limitations in children: Capacity or processing deficits? *Memory and Cognition, 4*, 559–572.

Clifford, B. R. (1979). A critique of eyewitness research. In M. Greeneberg, P. Morris, and R. Sykes (Eds.), Practical Aspects of Memory. London: Academic Press, pp. 199–209.

Clifford, B. R., & Denot, H. (1982). *Visual and verbal testimony and identification under conditions of stress.* Unpublished manuscript, North East London Polytechnic.

Clifford, B. R., & Fleming, W. (in press). Face and voice identification in a field setting. *Journal of Applied Social Psychology.*

Clifford, B. R., & Hollin C. (1981). Effects of the type of incident and the number of perpetrators on eyewitness memory. *Journal of Applied Psychology, 66*, 364–370.

Deffenbacher, K. (1980). Eyewitness accuracy and confidence: Can we infer anything about their relationship? *Law and Human Behavior, 4*, 243–260.

Deffenbacher, K. (1983). The influence of arousal on reliability of testimony. In B. R. Clifford & S. Lloyd-Bostock (Eds.), *Evaluating witness evidence.* Chichester, England: Wiley.

Deffenbacher, K., & Loftus, E. (1982). Do jurors share common understanding concerning eyewitness behavior? *Law and Human Behavior, 6*, 15–30.

Dent, H. R., & Stephenson, G. M. (1979). An experimental study of the effectiveness of different techniques of questioning child witnesses. *British Journal of Social and Clinical Psychology, 18*, 41–51.

Diamond, R., & Carey, S. (1977). Developmental changes in the representation of faces. *Journal of Experimental Child Psychology, 23*, 1–22.

Federal Rules of Evidence for United States and Magistrates (1975). St. Paul, Minn.: West.

Flin, R. H. (1980). Age effects in children's memory for unfamiliar faces. *Developmental Psychology, 16*, 373–374.

Freidson, E., & Feldman, J. J. (1958). The public looks at dental care. *Journal of American Dental Association, 57*, 325–335.

Giesbrecht, L. W. (1979). *The effects of arousal and depth of processing on facial recognition.* Doctoral dissertation, Florida State University, Tallahassee. *Dissertation Abstracts International, 40*, 4561-B. (University Microfilms No. 80-06, 257)

Glennon, B., & Weisz, J. R. (1978). An observational approach to the assessment of anxiety in young children. *Journal of Consulting and Clinical Psychology, 46,* 1246–1257.

Goodman, G. S. (1984). Children's testimony in historical perspective. *Journal of Social Issues, 40(2),* 9–31.

Handkins, R. E., & Cross, J. F. (1985, May). *Can a voice lineup be too fair?* Paper presented at Symposium on Forensic and Scientific Issues in Voice Recognition at the meeting of the Midwestern Psychological Association, Chicago, IL.

Hastie, R. (1980). *From eyewitness testimony to beyond reasonable doubt.* Unpublished manuscript, Howard University, Washington, DC.

Hovland, C. I., & Janis, I. L., & Kelley, H. H. (1953). *Communication and persuasion.* New Haven, CT: Yale University Press.

Johnson, C., & Scott, B. (1976, August). *Eyewitness testimony and suspect identification as a function of arousal, sex of witness, and scheduling of interrogation.* Paper presented at meeting of American Psychological Association, Washington, DC.

Kassin, S. M. (1984). Eyewitness identification: Victims versus bystanders. *Journal of Applied Social Psychology, 14,* 519–529.

Kleinknecht, R. A., Klepac, R. K., & Alexander, L. D. (1973). Origins and characteristics of fear of dentistry. *Journal of American Dental Association, 86,* 842–848.

Lautch, H. (1971). Dental phobia. *British Journal of Psychiatry, 73,* 212–218.

Lindberg, M. (1980). Is knowledge base development a necessary and sufficient condition for memory development? *Journal of Experimental Child Psychology, 30,* 401–410.

Loftus, E. F. (1979). *Eyewitness testimony.* Cambridge, MA: Harvard University Press.

Loftus, E. F., and Burns, T. W. (1981, November). *Mental shock can produce retrograde amnesia.* Paper presented at the meeting of the Psychonomic Society, Philadelphia.

Malpass, R. S., & Devine, P. G. (1984). Research on suggestion in lineups and photospreads. In G. L. Wells & E. F. Loftus (Eds.), *Eyewitness testimony.* New York: Cambridge University Press.

McClelland, D. C. (1982). The need for power, sympathetic activation and illness. *Motivation and Emotion, 6,* 31–41.

McClelland, D. C., Davidson, R. J., Floor, E., & Saron, C. (1980). Stressed power motivation, sympathetic activation, immune function and illness. *Journal of Human Stress, 6(2),* 11–9.

McClelland, D. C., & Kirshnit (1984). The effect of motivational arousal through films on salivary immune function. Unpublished paper: Harvard University, Department of Psychology and Social Relations.

Miller, G. R., & Burgoon, J. K. (1982). Factors affecting assessment of witness credibility. In N. L. Kerr & R. M. Bray (Eds.), *The psychology of the courtroom.* New York: Academic Press.

Mueller, J. H., Bailis, K. L., & Goldstein, A. G. (1979). Depth of processing and anxiety in facial recognition. *British Journal of Psychology, 70,* 511–515.

Neisser, U. (1979). The control of information pickup in selective looking. In A. D. Pick (Ed.), *Perception and its development: A tribute to Eleanor Gibson.* Hillsdale, NJ: Erlbaum.

Nelson, K., Fivush, R., Hudson, J., & Lucariello, J. (1983). Scripts and the development of memory. In M. T. H. Chi (Ed.), *Trends in memory development.* New York: Karger.

Nowicki, S., Winograd, E., and Millard, B. A. (1979). Memory for faces: A social learning analysis. *Journal of Research in Personality, 13,* 460–468.

Perlmutter, M. (Ed.). (1980). *Children's memory. New directions in child development.* San Francisco: Jossey-Bass.

Peters, D. P., & Hagen, S. (1986, August). *A stranger at daycare: Preschoolers' memory of physical contact, faces and voices*. Paper presented at the meeting of the Midwestern Psychological Association, Chicago.

Pynoos, R., & Eth, R. (1984). The child as witness to homicide. *Journal of Social Issues, 40(2)*, 87–108.

Sanders, G. S. (1984). Effects of context cues on eyewitness identification responses. *Journal of Applied Social Psychology, 14*, 386–397.

Sealy, A. P., & Wain, C. M. (1980). Person perception and juror's decisions. *Journal of Social & Clinical Psychology, 19*, 7–16.

Selye, H. (1975). Confusion and controversy in the stress field. *Journal of Human Stress, 1*, 37–44.

Siegel, J. M., & Loftus, E. F. (1978). Impact of anxiety and life stress upon eyewitness testimony. *Bulletin of the Psychonomic Society, 12*, 479–480.

Sussman, E. D., & Sugarman, R. C. (1972). The effect of certain distractions on identification by witnesses. In A. Zavala & J. J. Paley (Eds.), *Personal appearance identification*. Springfield, IL: Charles C Thomas.

Terr, L. (1981). Psychic trauma in children. *American Journal of Psychiatry, 138*, 14–19.

Wells, G. L. (1984). The psychology of lineup identifications. *Journal of Applied Social Psychology, 14(2)*, 89–103.

Wells, G. L., Ferguson, T. J., & Lindsay, R. C. L. (1981). The tractability of eyewitness confidence and its implications for triers of fact. *Journal of Applied Psychology, 66*, 688–696.

Wells, G. L., & Leippe, M. R. (1981). How do triers of fact infer the accuracy of eyewitness identifications? Memory for peripheral detail can be misleading. *Journal of Applied Psychology, 66*, 682–687.

Wells, G. L., Leippe, M. R., & Ostrom, T. M. (1979). Guidelines for empirically assessing the fairness of a lineup. *Law and Human Behavior, 3*, 285–293.

Wells, G. L., & Loftus, E. F. (1984). Eyewitness research: Then and now. In G. L. Wells & E. F. Loftus (Eds.), *Eyewitness testimony*. New York: Cambridge University Press.

Wells, G. L. & Murray, D. M. (1984). Eyewitness confidence. In G. L. Wells & E. F. Loftus (Eds.), *Eyewitness Testimony*. New York: Cambridge University Press.

Woocher, F. D. (1977). Did your eyes deceive you? Expert psychological testimony on the unreliability of eyewitness testimony. *Stanford Law Review, 29*, 969–1030.

Yarmey, A. D. (1984). Age as a factor in eyewitness memory. In G. L. Wells & E. F. Loftus (Eds.), *Eyewitness testimony*. New York: Cambridge University Press.

Zanni, G. R., & Offermann, J. T. (1978). Eyewitness testimony: An exploration of question wording upon recall as a function of neuroticism. *Perceptual and Motor Skills, 46*, 163–166.

8
The Child in the Eyes of the Jury: Assessing Mock Jurors' Perceptions of the Child Witness

DAVID F. ROSS, BETH S. MILLER, and PATRICIA B. MORAN

In many criminal cases involving sexual abuse, kidnapping, and domestic violence, a child is the sole eyewitness to the crime (Goodman, Golding, & Haith, 1984). Prosecutors are often hesitant to bring these cases to trial because of burdensome legal obstacles concerning child witnesses (Berliner & Barbieri, 1984). Recently, however, there have been several legal changes that are easing this burden. For instance, several states have abolished their rule regarding corroborating evidence (Goodman et al., 1984; Melton, 1984). This rule specifies that a child's testimony can be accepted in court only if it is supported by the testimony of an adult. The retraction of this rule may have a sizable impact on the number of crimes that are brought to trial. In 1983 there were 183 reported cases of sexual abuse in New York State. However, only one of these cases resulted in conviction. It is believed that the lack of corroborating evidence is one factor contributing to such low conviction rates (Berliner & Barbieri, 1984; Ceci, Ross, & Toglia, 1987).

In addition, several states have eliminated competency examinations for child witnesses and have adopted Rule 601 of the Federal Rules of Evidence; this ensures that a child cannot be deemed incompetent to testify simply as a function of his or her age (Goodman 1984). Under this rule, the jury itself is left to determine the child's competence. Other legal changes have been concerned with reducing the amount of stress involved when a young child testifies. Several states are no longer requiring the child to be present in the courtroom during his or her testimony (Berliner & Barbieri, 1984). Rather, the child's testimony is videotaped and then presented to the jury on a videomonitor. With these legal changes, the judicial system may observe a concomitant increase in the number of children who are providing testimony in court (Beach, 1983).

Therefore, it is important to determine the impact that a child's testimony will have on the jury deliberation process. Many legal scholars believe that eyewitness testimony, when given by an adult, is one of the most persuasive types of evidence that can be offered during a criminal court trial (Loftus, 1979). For example, a study with mock jurors (Loftus, 1974) found that subjects were much more likely to convict a defendant when circumstantial evidence provided by the prosecution was supported by adult eyewitness testimony (72% convict), than when the same circumstantial evidence was presented alone (18% convict). This conviction rate remained high (68%) even when the eyewitness was shown to be legally blind by the defense and therefore unable to clearly see the events being described. Perhaps one explanation for these findings is that adults consistently overestimate the accuracy of eyewitness performance (Brigham & Bothwell, 1983; Deffenbacher & Loftus, 1982; Lindsay, Wells, & Rumpel, 1981; Wells & Leippe, 1981; Yarmey & Jones, 1983). Thus it appears that adult eyewitness testimony is a salient factor that may influence the outcome of the jury deliberation process.

Although there has been a fair amount of research on the impact of adult eyewitness testimony, little is known about how jurors react to a *child* witness. Several important questions have only recently begun to be addressed. Specifically: Do jurors perceive children as credible witnesses? How much weight does a jury give to a child's testimony in the jury deliberation process? What factors do jurors use in making judgments about the credibility of a child witness? Will jurors in general perceive the testimony given by children to be inaccurate, highly suggestible, and unreliable, as compared to that given by an adult? In light of these questions, this chapter serves two purposes. First, we will review the most recent literature on jurors' perceptions and beliefs about the child witness. This will include a brief historical overview of how the child witness has been perceived by the scientific and legal community. Second, we will present the results of a recently completed experiment performed in our laboratory that bears directly on this issue, and we will suggest new directions for theory and research in this area.

Historical and Contemporary Views of the Child Witness

Historically, there has been a strong bias in the American legal system against relying on the eyewitness testimony of young children. This bias is owing, in part, to a large body of research, conducted around the turn of the twentieth century, that was designed specifically to investigate the malleability of children's memory through the use of suggestive questions (Binet, 1900; Stern, 1910). In a classic study, Varendonck (1911) illustrated the suggestibility of a group of 7-year-old children by asking them to describe the color of the beard belonging to one of the teachers in their school. He found that 84% of the children indicated a color, when in actuality the teacher *did not possess* a beard. As a result of this body of research, the scientific community came to the general conclusion that children are highly suggestible and unreliable as witnesses. For example, Baginsky (cited in Whipple, 1911, p. 308) argued that "children were the most dangerous of all witnesses and that their testimony should be excluded from court record wherever possible." Similarly, Ladamac (cited in Whipple, 1912, p. 266) surveyed the literature on eyewitness testimony and reported the following to the Congress of French Alienists and Neurologists "1) Error is a constant factor in testimony; so that even perfectly honest testimony deserves less credence than is commonly given it; 2) Any question that carries a suggestion should be avoided; in especial; children have a very slight resistance to suggestion."

Unfortunately, today highly publicized cases in the media help perpetuate this negative view of the child witness. For example, in January 1985, in Sacramento, California, five men were imprisoned after being charged by police authorities with being members of a satanic sex ring that employed a ritualized sacrifice of children. The horrifying allegations involved the creation of a "snuff film" depicting the murder of three children. Two of the key witnesses for the prosecution were young girls, aged 9 and 10 years, both of whom claimed to have been raped by the defendants. However, gynecological examinations failed to find any evidence to support these claims. In addition, the children reported that these rapes had occurred in the basement of one of the defendant's homes, where they reported seeing human bones and skulls. Contrary to their testimony, the house, where the children alleged that these acts occurred, did not have a basement, nor were police investigators able to find any evidence of human remains. The prosecution was subsequently forced to drop the case when the two child witnesses admitted the accounts that they had given to police were false. The headlines that appeared in national newspapers the day after the children retracted their stories read, for example, "Abuse case against 5 Californians collapses after children recant" (1985).

Before jurors enter the courtroom, exposure to these types of highly publicized cases in the media may influence their assumptions about child witnesses. Once in the courtroom, other factors may contribute to the jurors' beliefs about the child as a witness. For example, Goodman et al. (1984) argue that judges often "warn jurors of children's limited abilities" in their predeliberation instructions to the jury (p. 148). In addition, Goodman et al. (1984) point out that lawyers may discredit child witnesses in their closing statements by "alluding to their presumed difficulties in differentiating fantasy from reality or their suggestibility" (p. 146). Thus many factors, both inside and outside of the courtroom, may help perpetuate the negative view of the child witness.

Unfortunately, there has been very little empirical research that focuses directly on jurors' attitudes or perceptions of the child witness. To our knowledge, there are only a few published studies on the topic.

Survey Studies

Yarmey and Jones (1983) asked subjects to estimate the eyewitness abilities of a hypothetical 8-year-old child (e.g., where the child is responding to questions from either police or a lawyer). The subjects include laypersons, college students, law students, psycholegal researchers, and legal professionals. The results revealed that, across these various groups of subjects, the child was viewed as an unreliable witness who was both vulnerable to manipulation by the questioner and unable to accurately answer the questions. Interestingly, 91% of the psycholegal researchers held these beliefs, in contrast to 69% of the laypersons.

Experimental Studies

Goodman, Golding, Helgeson, Haith and Michelli (1986) (see also Goodman et al., 1984) were the first to use an experimental approach to study mock-jurors' perceptions of child witnesses and the impact of a child's testimony on the jury deliberation process. In the first of three experiments, college students were given a written description of a fatal car-pedestrian accident. The description included the testimony of five witnesses, three presenting circumstantial evidence, an eyewitness (for the prosecution), and the defendant. The case involved a dispute between the defendant, who argued he was not at fault, and the eyewitness, who presented conflicting testimony.

All subjects in the study received the same written trial description except that the age of the eyewitness was varied. The description that the subjects received depicted the eyewitness as either 6, 10, or 30 years old. After having read the description, subjects were asked to rate the degree to which they believed the defendant was *guilty*, and how *credible* they found the testimony of *each* witness (e.g., how much they "valued and relied on" the testimony). In view of the fact that all aspects of the case were held constant, except for the *age of the eyewitness*, any variation in the guilt or credibility ratings among the three conditions can be attributed directly to this manipulation.

The results indicated that the 6-year-old witness was seen as less credible than the 10-year-old witness, who, in turn, was seen as less credible than the 30-year-old witness. However, the age-of-eyewitness manipulation did not affect the subject's perceptions of the guilt or innocence of the defendant.

A second experiment was conducted to determine whether the results of the first experiment involving vehicular homicide were generalizable to other cases, in particular, murder cases. The design of Experiment 2 was the same as that used in the first study. Subjects were given a written description of a murder trial involving the testimony of six witnesses, including one key eyewitness for the prosecution who was described to the subjects as either 6, 10, or 30 years of age.

In general, the results indicated a replication of the first experiment; there were no significant differences among the three age-of-eyewitness conditions on subjects' ratings of the guilt of the defendant. In addition, the 6-year-old was rated as significantly less credible than the 30-year-old witness. However, unlike the first experiment, the credibility ratings of the 10-year-old *were not* found to be significantly different from either the 6-year-old or the 30-year-old.

Finally, a third study was conducted to determine the external validity of the findings from Experiments 1 and 2. Although Experiment 3 employed the same age-of-eyewitness manipulation as the previous experiments, there were three major procedural changes. First, instead of using college students as subjects, a more representative sample of potential jurors was used. This is an important design feature because college students have been found to differ from other more heterogeneous samples on a variety of personality variables, such as conservatism

(Jurow, 1971) and authoritarianism (Berg & Vidmar, 1975; Mitchell & Byrne, 1973) that may be influential in the deliberation process (Field & Barnett, 1978).

The second procedural change was that the trial description was presented to the subjects not in written form, but in the form of a videotaped version of the trial. The third change was that, after making individual judgments of the guilt of the defendant and the credibility of the witnesses, subjects were assigned to 12-member juries and were asked to deliberate until they had reached a verdict. This design feature addressed another common criticism of jury-simulation research—the lack of jury deliberation. Many jury-simulation studies ask subjects to make individual decisions of guilt or innocence of the defendant, rather than using a group decision as the dependent measure (Weiton & Diamond, 1979).

These three design changes, allowed Goodman et al. (1986) to investigate the effects of three factors: (a) mode of presentation of trial information (written description versus videotape), (b) type of subject (college student versus a more heterogeneous sample), and (c) type of dependent measure employed (individual rating of guilt or innocence versus group deliberation outcome).

In general, the results of Experiment 3 were consistent with those of the first two experiments. There were no reliable differences as a function of age of the eyewitness in the subjects' individual (predeliberation) ratings of the guilt of the defendant, or in the jury deliberation outcomes. Again, the 6-year-old witness was seen as significantly less credible than the 30-year-old, whereas the credibility attributed to the 10-year-old *did not* differ from either of the other two conditions. A second analysis was done to determine the degree to which witness credibility is predictive of guilt. This analysis indicated that credibility of the 30-year-old eyewitness was a significant predictor of the subjects' guilt ratings. The credibility ratings of the 10-year-old eyewitness was "still relatively influential, but the 6-year-olds' credibility did not correlate with the degree-of-guilt ratings any more than did that of the other witnesses" (Goodman et al., 1986, p. 18). Finally, an analysis of the content of the deliberations (which were tape recorded) indicated that the number of negative comments made about the eyewitness increased as the age of the eyewitness decreased.

The picture that emerges from this series of experiments indicates that the age of the eyewitness may have a powerful impact on the perceived credibility of the witness, but it does not sway subject's decisions as to the guilt or innocence of the defendant. Combining the results of Goodman's experiments with the survey research by Yarmey and Jones (1983), one finds that the child witness is seen as less reliable in terms of remembering events, more suggestible and able to be manipulated on the stand, and, in general less credible as a witness than an adult.

In a recently completed study on this topic, conducted in our laboratory, a strikingly different picture emerged concerning mock-jurors' perceptions of the child witness. In this study college students watched a 50-minute videotape of a simulated court trial, based on an actual court transcript. There were three versions of the "trial," all of which were identical, except for the age of the key eyewitness for the prosecution. One third of the subjects were randomly assigned to each version in which the eyewitness was either an _8-year-old_, a _21-year-old_, or a _74-year-old male_. All other aspects of the videotapes were identical across conditions. In order to enhance the authenticity of the videotape, the respective roles of judge, prosecution, and defense, were played by an actual judge and two lawyers.

The particular circumstances of the case were as follows: the trial involved two witnesses (including the key eyewitness), and a woman charged with the possession of a large quantity of narcotics. Specifically, the defendant was caught with 12,000 dollars worth of cocaine in her apartment. She had been dating a previously convicted drug dealer, who testified in her favor under a grant of immunity, that the cocaine belonged to him. There was no question that the cocaine was in the defendant's apartment; rather, the issue was how it got there, and whether or not she was aware of its presence. The prosecution's case was based, in large part, on the testimony of the key eyewitness who alleged, contrary to the drug dealer's testimony, that the drug dealer did not enter the apartment with the cocaine. Thus, the prosecution argued that the cocaine must have been in the defendant's apartment the entire time, and that she must have known that such a large quantity of drugs was stored there. Throughout the trial the defense attempted to discredit the testimony of the eyewitness by questioning the accuracy of his memory.

The inclusion of a 74-year-old witness condition is important because the few extant studies have compared adults' perceptions of child witnesses, to witnesses who were described as 30-year-olds. It may be the case that 30-year-olds do not accurately represent adults of all ages. This raises questions such as: Are elderly witnesses perceived by jurors' as equally credible as young adults? How does the credibility of an elderly witness compare to that of a child? One could hypothesize than an elderly witness would be perceived as less credible than a young adult. Consistent with this view, Yarmey, Rashid, and Jones (cited in Yarmey, 1984, p. 149) found that mock-jurors viewed elderly witnesses as "ineffective, highly dependent, and personally unacceptable." Yarmey (1984) argues that this finding is due, in part, to a common stereotype of the elderly as "psychologically helpless and intellectually inferior. To the extent that this stereotype is held by judges and juries, the credibility of the elderly witness will be low." (Yarmey, 1984, pp. 49–50). Conversely, another possibility is that an elderly witness could be seen as more credible than either a child or a young adult because they are viewed as the "pillars of society"; they are people who have lived in the community for years and who have made their contributions. In general, they may be viewed as highly respectable, trustworthy, and credible figures. Given these two very different possibilities, including the "74-year-old" condition in the design was expected to provide new and interesting information about the influence of age on mock-jurors' perceptions of the credibility of eyewitnesses.

After viewing the videotape, subjects were asked to rate the degree of guilt or innocence of the defendant. In addition they were asked to rate each of the three witnesses that testified in the case (the two witnesses and the defendant), on a variety of dimensions, including witness accuracy, witness confidence, forcefulness, credibility, objectivity, consistency, manipulation by either the prosecution or defense attorneys, truthfulness, intelligence, attractiveness, trustworthiness, and so forth. Although many of these factors have been shown to influence jurors' impressions of adult witnesses (Deffenbacher, 1980; Goodman et al., 1984; Wells, Ferguson, & Lindsay, 1981), little is empirically known about the role that these factors play in jurors' perceptions of a child witness. Goodman et al. (1984) argue that many of these factors "would seem, if anything, to work to the child's disadvantage." (Goodman et al., 1984, pp. 145–146). For example, in relation to witness consistency, she argues that "often children answer questions too literally: A child may answer "no" to the question, "Were you in the man's house?", but "yes" to the question, "Were you in the man's apartment?" This inconsistency alone may be enough to undermine the child's believability" (Goodman et al., 1984, pp. 145–146).

The results of our experiment present a somewhat different picture than that described by Goodman. Specifically, the age of the eyewitness manipulation had no effect on subjects' ratings of the guilt or innocence of the defendant (replicating Goodman's finding), nor was an age effect found for witness credibility. That is, subjects viewed the testimony of the "8-year-old" as *equally* credible as compared to both the "21-year-old" and the "74-year-old" witness. However, the age of the eyewitness manipulation did have a reliable overall effect on many of the other variables as indicated by a Multivariate Analysis of Variance (MANOVA) performed across the dependent measures. In general, the child witness was viewed much more positively than the 21-year-old adult, and the ratings of the elderly witness were more similar to those found for the child witness, than those found for the 21-year-old witness. Specifically, subjects tended to view the child as more accurate, more forceful, more consistent, more truthful, more intelligent, and more confident, than the 21-year-old witness (*p* values ranging from .001 to .10). The ratings of the elderly witness tended not to differ from the child witness. Interestingly, there were no significant differences found for the variable concerned with manipulation by the prosecution or the defense attorneys. This finding is contrary to the research by Yarmey and Jones (1983), which indicated that adults tend to believe that child witnesses are easily manipulated by attorneys or law enforcement officials when being questioned.

How does one interpret these findings? How is it that a child witness can be viewed more positively than an adult witness, particularly when previous research suggests that adults believe child witnesses are highly suggestible and have limited memory capabilities? One possibility concerns a principle in social psychology referred to by Maccoby and Jacklin (1974) as a "perceptual adaptation hypothesis" or by Cook and Campbell (1979) as a "scaling effect" (see also Condry & Ross, 1985). Applying this principle to our data, the idea is that jurors interpret or evaluate the same stimuli, the testimony of the key eyewitness for the prosecution, using *different standards* depending upon the age of the witness (one standard is used for the adult and another for the child). For example, if an adult witness describes an event that is fairly complex and does so with a moderate level of detail, jurors may report that the witness is only average in terms of both intelligence and accuracy, because jurors expect such abilities from an adult witness. Thus, in the eyes of the jury, the witness does not appear to be *extremely* competent or to have a better than average memory. However, if a child witness gives the identical description (as occurred in this experiment), the jurors are likely to rate the child as being *extremely* intelligent and as having an *excellent* memory because they do not expect child witnesses to be able to remember and describe detailed events (Yarmey & Jones, 1983). Our data appear to suggest that the subjects in the 21-year-old condition may be judging the eyewitness in terms of what they would expect from a *young adult*, as compared to the subjects in the *"child"* condition, who judge or evaluate the eyewitness in terms of what they *expect from a child*. Thus, the application of two different standards of evaluation and judgment to the *same* stimuli results in different perceptions of the "child" and "21-year-old" witness. Since subjects' ratings of the "elderly" witness tended not to differ from those of the "child", this explanation also suggests that subjects' underlying beliefs about the elderly witness are similar to their beliefs about the child witness. This is supported by the literature cited above, which indicates that adults hold negative beliefs about the eyewitness capabilities of both children (Yarmey & Jones, 1983) and the elderly (Yarmey, Rashid, & Jones, 1981).

A second series of analyses was performed to determine to what degree, if any, eyewitness credibility ratings are related to subjects' ratings of the guilt or innocence of the defendant. Although there were no differences found among conditions in terms of eyewitness credibility, the degree to which these credibility ratings actually influenced subjects' guilt ratings might vary by condition. For example, a child could be seen as equally credible (likely to be believed, etc.) as an adult; however, in making the final judgment about the guilt or innocence of the defendant, subjects may elect not to weigh the testimony of the child heavily in their decision; rather they may choose to give more weight to the testimony of the other witnesses in the trial. (This is essentially the finding Goodman et al., 1984 reports; however, in her studies there were also significant differences in witness credibility across conditions.)

In order to further explore this possibility, three correlations were computed, one for each condition, between witness credibility and ratings of guilt. It should be the case, since the key eyewitness is for the prosecution, that higher levels of credibility are associated with more guilt. The results showed that in the child condition, the correlation was essentially zero, suggesting that the child's testimony was not weighed heavily in making the final decision of guilt. Rather, jurors apparently relied on other available evidence. However, in both the young adult and the elderly condition, there was a significant positive correlation between ratings of witness credibility and guilt. Therefore, it appears that subjects discounted the testimony when it was given by a child, but the same testimony, when given by an adult (either young or old), was weighed heavily.

These findings tell an interesting story. Although the child witness was viewed more positively than either the young adult or elderly witness, the child's testimony was not weighed heavily. It may be that *independent* of the positive impressions that jurors may form of a child witness, it is very difficult for them to convict a person on the basis of a child's testimony. Jurors simply may not place the same trust in the testimony of a child as they do an adult's testimony. For example, in a child sexual abuse case in Maryland, immediately after acquitting the defendant, a member of the jury said, "It's very difficult to put someone in prison for something so serious, based on a child's story" (Beach, 1983, p. 58). Thus it seems reasonable that the credibility of the child was unrelated to ratings of guilt.

Finally, a third analysis was done to examine the question: What is meant by witness credibility? This question has been of interest to psycholegal researchers since the early part of the century. For example, Wigmore (cited in Saks and Hastie, 1978, p. 165–166) outlines five components of witness credibility: (1) *witness accuracy* - the ability to accurately remember the events being described; (2) *objectivity* - the amount of personal or vested interest the witness has in the outcome of the case; (3) *character of the witness* - the temperament and behavior of the witness displayed on the stand (speech styles or forcefulness of responses, etc.); (4) *consistency of testimony* - the degree to which the witness makes conflicting statements; and (5) *corroboration* - the degree to which there is evidence to support the witness' testimony. The question of interest is whether these factors (with the exception of corroboration which was not assessed in the present study), as well as several others that are listed below, predict witness credibility in the same way across all three conditions of the experiment.

One hypothesis is that jurors rely on different sets of characteristics when forming impressions of witness credibility as a function of the age of the witness. For example, in the study reported here, mock jurors may have relied heavily on cognitive factors when evaluating the credibility of the "child" and "elderly" witnesses due to beliefs about their limited memory ability. That is, jurors may question the memory of children due to their presumed susceptibility to leading questions, and the elderly, since their memory ability is believed to fade with age. However, when evaluating the credibility of the "young adult," subjects may not be concerned with cognitive factors; rather social factors such as objectivity may become crucial. For example, in the present case, the key eyewitness for the prosecution was a friend of the defendant who was being charged with the possession of cocaine. The young adult may be viewed by jurors as more likely to be a peer and confidante of the defendant, and more likely to be a drug user himself, than either the child or elderly person. Thus the young adult witness may be seen by the jury as less trustworthy and/or objective.

In an attempt to determine whether the same factors predict witness credibility across the three conditions, simultaneous multiple regression analyses were performed. For each condition witness credibility was predicted from 10 factors: (1) witness accuracy, (2) confidence in testimony, (3) forcefulness of response, (4) consistency of testimony, (5) objectivity, (6-7) degree to which the witness was manipulated by the defense and prosecuting attorneys (two factors), (8) truthfulness of witness, (9) intelligence of witness, and (10) physical attractiveness. In the "child" condition five factors tended to predict witness credibility: (1) witness accuracy ($p = .02$), (2) truthfulness ($p = .02$), (3) intelligence ($p = .05$), (4) manipulation by the defense attorney ($p = .08$—marginal), and (5) attractiveness ($p = .10$—marginal). In the "21-year-old" condition, surprisingly, only one factor, truthfulness, was found to be a significant predictor of credibility ($p = .02$). Finally, in the "elderly" condition, four factors emerged as important predictors: (1) witness accuracy ($p = .03$), (2) manipulation by the prosecution ($p = .06$—marginal), (3) consistency ($p = .056$), and (4) attractiveness ($p = .02$). Thus, although the subjects' *general* ratings of witness credibility were equal across conditions, different factors were predictive of this credibility as a function of the age of the witness. In the "child" and "elderly" conditions, both cognitive (e.g., intelligence, witness accuracy) and social factors (e.g., truthfulness, manipulation by the attorneys) appear to be crucial in jurors' impressions of the witness. In contrast, truthfulness was the only factor that predicted the credibility of the young adult.

What is the Verdict on Jurors' Perceptions of the Child Witness?

Although there are a limited number of studies examining mock jurors' impressions of the child witness, several tentative statements can be made. First, age of witness appears to be an important and salient factor that influences mock jurors' impressions of a witness. Second, it does not, however, appear to influence jurors' judgments about the guilt or innocence of a defendant. When making a decision about the guilt of a defendant, mock jurors apparently rely on other available evidence. On these points, the findings presented by Goodman and those reported here, are in agreement.

However, before generalizing these findings, one needs to evaluate the content of the cases that were presented in these studies. It may be that factors such as the age of an eyewitness influence jurors' judgments of the defendant's guilt, only in ambiguous cases, where the evidence provided by the prosecution and defense is equally convincing (Goodman et al., 1984). In these types of cases, any biased judgment a juror makes as a function of the age of an eyewitness may sway the outcome or "tip the scales." Thus, one should consider the possibility that the cases used by Goodman and her colleagues, and the one used in the present study, may be *unambiguous* in that the evidence heavily favored either the prosecution or the defense. (Certainly, in the present study the evidence heavily favored the defense.) Manipulating the ambiguity of the evidence in the case would appear to be an important topic for future research.

Another issue concerns whether the age of an eyewitness affects jurors' perceptions of witness credibility. On this question, our findings conflict with Goodman's because we found no age differences in witness credibility. A possible explanation for the discrepancy is that witness credibility may be affected by the particular characteristics of the persons who play the witnesses in the videotape.

That is, one could argue that the child witness in our study was particularly "angelic" in appearance and thus made a very good impression on the mock jurors. Perhaps if another child played the part, he might not have been viewed as positively. We attempted to control these types of factors, in part, by obtaining actors for the eyewitness roles who we felt were equal and average in attractiveness. We also asked subjects to rate the attractiveness of the eyewitness and there were no reliable differences across the conditions. However, it remains very difficult to completely control these types of potentially confounding variables.

A more rigorous solution to this problem would be to create several videotape versions of *each* condition (child, young adult, elderly), so that the eyewitness roles are played by different characters. If the same results are found with different persons playing these roles, one could be more certain of the robustness of the results. Goodman has begun to address these types of issues by showing that the same results are obtained with different types of trial content, and when different means are used to present the trial information (videotape vs. written scripts.) Future researchers may be able to increase the consistency and external validity of their findings through the use of these types of procedures.

Another consideration for future research involves the types of models being investigated. The majority of research on this topic has used what is referred to as a "main effect" model. The typical study involves presenting to subjects trial information that varies in terms of the age of the key eyewitness. The investigator is primarily interested in looking for main effects of the age-of-witness manipulation on jurors' ratings of defendant guilt and witness credibility. Rarely are the interactive or moderating effects of other characteristics of an eyewitness investigated, such as sex, race, or physical attractiveness. There is a history of jury-simulation research showing that these types of factors are important in terms of jurors' reactions to a defendant (Saks & Hastie, 1978; Weiton & Diamond, 1979). The point is that research designs are needed that will more accurately reflect the full range of factors and situations that a juror is likely to experience in court.

In addition to examining the effects of other witness characteristics, this line of research should also incorporate *juror* characteristics in the model (e.g., age, sex, race). Perhaps one of the most important of these is the jurors' beliefs about the social and cognitive abilities of eyewitnesses of different ages. Unfortunately, individual studies have either surveyed adults' *beliefs* about age and eyewitness performance, or examined, experimentally, adults' *reactions* to eyewitnesses of various ages. What is needed is a unification of the two procedures. This should allow for a more precise prediction of whether or not a juror will react to a witness' age. Specifically, one could expect that the age of an eyewitness should only influence the judgments of jurors who believe that there are age differences in eyewitness performance.

In addition, future research should also address the issue of *how and in what manner,* jurors' beliefs about child witnesses influence judgments and impressions of witness credibility or competence. It appears that adults do believe that children are less competent as witnesses (Yarmey & Jones, 1983). However, this belief may result in two very different outcomes. Goodman et al.'s (1984; 1986) findings suggest a direct link between jurors' attitudes and perceptions of children. That is, Goodman's experiments show that children are perceived as less credible than adults. Conversely, our findings suggest a perceptual adaptation process, whereby a jurors' attitude that children are less credible than adults, may result in a child being perceived *more positively than an adult*. Thus, understanding what conditions produce these two very different processes, may provide an explanation for the conflicting results in this literature.

In sum, it appears that the development of any model designed to explain how jurors may respond to the age of an eyewitness, needs to examine at least three sets of factors: (1) characteristics of the eyewitness (age, race, sex, etc.), (2) characteristics of the juror (including beliefs about eyewitness performance), and (3) the ambiguity of the evidence in the case (i.e., the strength of the evidence presented by the prosecution and defense). The addition of these factors into the research design, would greatly expand our theoretical and practical understanding of how the age of an eyewitness influences mock jurors' perceptions of witness credibility and ratings of guilt. However, the extent to which these *individual* judgments influence the verdict made by a jury as a group, is another challenging question that remains to be addressed in future research.

References

Abuse case against 5 Californians collapses after children recant. (1985, Nov. 13, page 6A), *Grand Forks Herald*.

Beach, B. H. (1983, January 31). Out of the mouths of babes. *Time*, p. 58.

Berg, K. S., & Vidmar, N. (1975). Authoritarianism and recall of evidence about criminal behavior. *Journal of Personality and Social Psychology, 9*, 147–157.

Berliner, L., & Barbieri, M. K. (1984). The testimony of the child victim of sexual assault. *Journal of Social Issues, 40*, 124–139.

Binet, A. (1900). *La suggestibilité*. Paris: Schleicher Frères.

Brigham, J. C., & Bothwell, R. K. (1983). The ability of prospective jurors to estimate the accuracy of eyewitness identifications. *Law and Human Behavior, 7*, 19–30.

Ceci, S. J., Ross, D. F., & Toglia, M. P. (1987). Suggestibility of children's memory: Psycholegal implications. *Journal of Experimental Psychology: General*.

Condry, J. C., & Ross, D. F. (1985). Sex and aggression: The influence of gender label on the perception of aggression in children. *Child Development, 56*, 225–233.

Cook, T. D., & Campbell, D. T. (1979). *Quasi-experimentation: Design and analysis issues for field settings*. Chicago: Rand McNally.

Deffenbacher, K. A. (1980). Eyewitness accuracy and confidence: Can we infer anything about their relationship? *Law and Human Behavior, 4*, 243–260.

Deffenbacher, K. & Loftus, E. F. (1982). Do jurors share a common understanding concerning eyewitness behavior? *Law and Human Behavior, 6*, 15–30.

Field, H. S., & Barnett, N. J. (1978). Simulated jury trials: Students vs. "real" people as jurors. *Journal of Social Psychology, 104*, 287–293.

Goodman, G. S. (1984). Childrens testimony in historical perspective. *Journal of Social Issues, 40*(2), 9–31.

Goodman, G. S., Golding, J. M., & Haith, M. (1984). Jurors' reactions to child witnesses. *Journal of Social Issues*, *40*, 139–153.

Goodman, G. S., Golding, J. M., Helgson, V., Haith, M. M. & Michelli, J. (1986). When a child takes the stand: Jurors' perceptions of children's eyewitness testimony. *Law and Human Behavior.*

Jurow, G. L. (1971). New data on the effect of a "death-qualified" jury on the guilt determination process. *Harvard Law Review*, *84*, 567–611.

Lindsay, R. C. L., Wells, G. L., & Rumpel, C. (1981). Can people detect eyewitness identification accuracy within and between situations? *Journal of Applied Psychology*, *66*, 79–89.

Loftus, E. (1974, August). Reconstructing memory: The incredible eyewitness. *Psychology Today*, pp. 116–119.

Loftus, E. (1979). *Eyewitness testimony.* Cambridge, MA: Harvard University Press.

Maccoby, E. M., & Jacklin, C. N. (1974). *The psychology of sex differences.* Stanford, CA: Stanford University Press.

Melton, G. B. (1984). Child witnesses and the First Amendment: A psycholegal dilemma. *Journal of Social Issues*, *40*, 109–125.

Mitchell, H. E., & Byrne, D. (1973). The defendant's dilemma: Effects of juror attitudes and authoritarianism on judicial decisions. *Journal of Personality and Social Psychology*, *25*, 123–129.

Saks, M. J., & Hastie, R. (1978). *Social psychology in court.* New York: Van Nostrand Reinhold.

Stern, W. (1910). Abstracts of lectures on the psychology of testimony and on the study of individuality. *American Journal of Psychology*, *21*, 270–282.

Varendonck, J. (1911). Les témoignages d'enfants dans un procès retentissant. *Archives de Psychologie*, *11*, 129–171.

Weiten, W., & Diamond, S. S. (1979). A critical review of the jury simulation paradigm. *Law and Human Behavior*, *3*, 71–93.

Wells, G. L., Ferguson, T. J., & Lindsay, R. C. L. (1981). The tractability of eyewitness confidence and its implications for triers of fact. *Journal of Applied Psychology*, *66*, 688–696.

Wells, G. L., Leippe, M. R. (1981). How do triers of fact infer the accuracy of eyewitness identifications? Memory for peripheral detail can be misleading. *Journal of Applied Psychology*, *66*, 682–687.

Wells, G. L., & Lindsay, R. C. L. (1983). How do people infer the accuracy of eyewitness memory? Studies of performance and a metamemory analysis. In S. M. A. Lloyd-Bostock & B. R. Clifford (Eds.), *Evaluating witness evidence: Recent psychological research and new perspectives.* Chichester, England: Wiley.

Whipple, G. M. (1911). The psychology of testimony. *Psychological Bulletin*, *8*, 307–309.

Whipple, G. M. (1912). Psychology of testimony and report. *Psychological Bulletin*, *9*, 264–269.

Yarmey, A. D. (1984). Age as a factor in eyewitness memory. In G. L. Wells & E. F. Loftus (Eds.), *Eyewitness testimony.* New York: Cambridge University Press.

Yarmey, A. D., & Jones, H. P. T. (1983). Is the psychology of eyewitness identification a matter of common sense? In S. M. A. Lloyd-Bostock & B. R. Clifford (Eds.), *Evaluating witness evidence: Recent psychological research and new perspectives.* Chichester, England: Wiley.

Yarmey, A. D., Rashid, S., & Jones, H. P. T. (1981). *Attitudes of elderly and young adults toward jurors.* Unpublished manuscript, University of Guelph, Ontario.

9
Children on the Witness Stand: A Communication/Persuasion Analysis of Jurors' Reactions to Child Witnesses

MICHAEL R. LEIPPE and ANN ROMANCZYK

Eyewitnesses are pivotal participants in criminal cases, and psychological research on eyewitness memory is therefore of potentially enormous practical value. Yet juries ultimately decide those cases that reach the courtroom. Research may (indeed does) yield insights about factors that influence memory and about the accuracy rates that typify a given witnessing-identification context, but an important question always remains: Do jurors take these factors into account when evaluating an eyewitness report? Put simply, how do jurors perceive and evaluate eyewitness testimony? Despite some claims to the contrary (e.g., McCloskey & Egeth, 1983), the growing research on this issue suggests that jurors' reliance on eyewitness testimony in deciding guilt is greater than research findings merit. Jurors in laboratory studies, for example, have been found to overbelieve eyewitness identifications (Brigham & Bothwell, 1983; Lindsay, Wells, & Rumpel, 1981), rely too heavily on their impressions of eyewitness confidence (Lindsay et al., 1981; Wells, Lindsay, & Tousignant, 1980), and be misled by witness memory for trivial details when judging face-recognition accuracy (Wells & Leippe, 1981). In short, jurors' perceptions of adult eyewitness memory and memory-relevant influences may, at least in part, be based on inaccurate stereotypes and assumptions. An important role of psychological research is to identify where and to what extent jurors' conceptions of eyewitness memory differ from the research-derived "facts" of eyewitness memory. In turn, methods of educating jurors (e.g., through pretrial instructions) might be developed.

The gaps between the memory capabilities of child witnesses and jurors' assessments of these capabilities may be particularly wide and possibly in the opposite direction of what is typically seen with adult witnesses. Child eyewitnesses, that is, may be underbelieved rather than overbelieved. Goodman (1984), for example, has noted that much of the early twentieth century work purportedly demonstrating that children's memories are decidedly unreliable may have reflected stereotypes of children held by the research psychologists themselves. In contemporary times, the criminal justice system continues to be skeptical about children's memory skills, judging by competency standards that generally require children younger than 14 years to undergo a judicial inquiry to demonstrate their competence (cf. Stafford, 1962). Finally, at least one recent survey suggests that both laypeople and (even more so) eyewitness researchers regard a young child's testimony as highly susceptible to suggestion (Yarmey & Jones, 1983). Thus, adults may indeed have stereotypes about children's memories, as well as about their social characteristics (such as suggestibility and sincerity) and communication skills (such as cogency and organization of oral presentations).

This chapter deals with how adult jurors perceive and evaluate the memorial accounts of children in the context of deciding the guilt of a criminal defendant. We will, in essence, address the issue of how the credibility and probative impact of an eyewitness account is affected by the fact that the eyewitness is a child. Since very little empirical research has directly examined this topic, much of our theoretical discussion will draw from the somewhat more extensive literature on juror reactions to adult testimony and from the social psychological study of communication, persuasion, and social cognition.

Testimony as a Persuasion Process

Eyewitness testimony can be seen as a one-way communication that travels from the witness (source) to the jury (audience). The witness, in a sense, is an influence agent, attempting to persuade or convince the juror of his or her account of the what and who of a criminal event (cf. Saks & Hastie, 1978). Persuasion researchers have found that source characteristics, such as expertise and attractiveness, can influence belief change among message recipients (cf. Kelman, 1961; McGuire, 1969) often by affecting the way recipients process the message (Hass, 1981). Recipients, for example may feel less compelled to covertly counterargue a message delivered by an expert source (Hass 1981; Petty, Cacioppo, & Goldman, 1981), whereas their attention may be distracted from message details by a source who is highly attractive or particularly adept at using nonverbal cues (Chaiken & Eagly, 1983). At the same time, characteristics of the recipient, such as a negative stereotype about the source or a vested interest in the belief the message attacks, may exert equally powerful influences on how the message is processed. Recipients, for instance, may selectively attend to aspects of the message (Kleinhesselink & Edwards, 1975) or the source (Nisbett & Wilson, 1977) that support their stereotypes or prior beliefs, or selectively interpret message information in a belief-preserving manner (Lord, Ross, & Lepper, 1979).

These few illustrations suggest that an account of how jurors react to child witnesses should address three basic sets of questions. First, how do jurors *typically* evaluate the message of an eyewitness? That is, what criteria do jurors use to judge the verity of eyewitness testimony? Second, what *source* attributes do children possess, both in terms of their age alone and in terms of their delivery of testimony, that might affect juror perceptions of them and the way jurors process their testimony? Third, do jurors, or at least a substantial percentage of jurors, carry stereotypes or beliefs about children's memories, honesty, and suggestibility that might affect their criterial evaluation of childrens' testimony? If so what are these effects?

Jurors' Assessment of the Quality of Eyewitness Testimony

Contemporary approaches to persuasion (e.g., Chaiken, 1980; Petty & Cacioppo, 1986) recognize that belief change via communication can come about in two general ways. Communication recipients may take a peripheral or heuristic route, in which they forego careful analysis of message content and rely instead on some peripheral cue such as source credibility to decide whether or not they should agree with the message. Alternatively, recipients may take a central or systematic route, characterized by careful appraisal of the message itself. This latter route is typically taken when the message is personally relevant or important to the recipient (Petty & Cacioppo, 1986). Most jurors no doubt recognize the gravity of their task and accordingly attempt to systematically and carefully analyze the content of an eyewitness report.

But what are the criteria against which jurors evaluate eyewitness testimony? What deems a witness persuasive or unpersuasive? Wells and Lindsay (1983) have suggested that people rely on at least three types of information when judging the likely accuracy of another's memory report: (1) *witnessing conditions* such as duration of exposure to and visibility of the memory stimulus; (2) the *consistency* of the memorial report, both within the focal witness's account and in relation to the reports of other witnesses; and (3) *response-bias* information, or signals that suggest whether the witness is applying a suitably high threshold in deciding what he or she remembers (e.g., the witness's confidence and his or her willingness to report certain memory failures). According to Wells and Lindsay, jurors will believe the eyewitness account if they are satisfied that (a) witnessing conditions were generally sufficient for acquisition of a strong memory trace, (b) the trace is specifically strong for the particular witness judging by its internal consistency and agreement with other evidence, and (c) the witness is applying the proper threshold in willingness to report the memory trace.

Source Characteristics of the Child Eyewitness

Given the foregoing judgment criteria, how might judgments be influenced by the fact that the source of testimony is a child? Figure 9.1 portrays a communication/persuasion model of the various ways child-status might have an influence on the processing that leads ultimately to belief or disbelief in the eyewitness. Children may have unique characteristics as communication sources that affect *how* and *to what extent* the criterial evaluation proceeds. Moreover, these characteristics may emanate from the child (e.g., age-related communication styles) or be

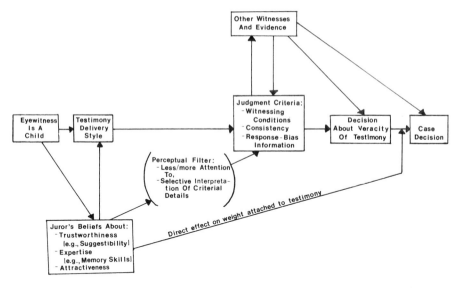

FIGURE 9.1. A communication/persuasion model of jurors' reactions to child eyewitnesses.

more in the minds of the juror-recipient (e.g., stereotypes about children's trustworthiness or memory "expertise").

Source Effects That Are a Consequence of How Children Are Perceived

Other things being equal, at least three characteristics of sources may affect the persuasive impact of the messages they deliver. Sources perceived as *expert* generally are more persuasive than inexpert sources (e.g., Aronson, Turner, & Carlsmith, 1963), as are sources perceived as *trustworthy* (e.g., Eagly, Wood, & Chaiken, 1978) and *attractive* (e.g., Chaiken, 1979) relative to their untrustworthy and unattractive counterparts. Each of these source traits may map onto possible stereotypes of children. If the courts require a demonstration of young children's competence, they apparently view these children as apt to be less expert memory sources than adults. If survey respondents worry about childrens' suggestibility, they are apt to distrust children's responses to a "suggesting" lawyer. Perhaps more remotely, finally, if current cultural traditions dictate that "young is beautiful," adults may find youngsters attractive.

A (MODEST) SURVEY

Although the courts seem skeptical of young children's credibility as witnesses, and those who research children's memory occasionally discuss their findings in terms of some presumed reigning conception of children, little is really known about whether adults in general actually have strong stereotypes about children along witness/source-relevant dimensions. Accordingly, we conducted a small survey in which adults were asked to compare children to adults on several memorial, cognitive, and social dimensions. Respondents included members of a Long Island PTA group ($n = 18$) and college students at a private Long Island university ($n = 8$). The first part of the survey was restricted to perceptions of "5- to 9-year-old children," an age group we suspected is young enough to be stereo-typed, yet reasonably likely to "pass" a competency test and be allowed to give courtroom testimony. Respondents rated this age group in relation to adults on (a) ability to remember details of events, (b) ability to recognize faces seen once or twice, (c) suggestibility to adults, (d) suggestibility to peers, (e) sincerity when communicating to an adult authority figure, and (f) consistency in action and conversation. All ratings were made on a 5-point scale (e.g., for suggestibility, 1 = much less suggestible than adults, 2 = less . . . , 3 = about as . . . , 4 = more . . . , 5 = much more . . .).

The results of this part of the survey are presented in Table 9.1. As can be seen, the majority of respondents saw 5- to 9-year-old children as more suggestible than adults when the influence agent is an adult, a finding consistent with those of Yarmey and Jones (1983). Children were also widely perceived as more sin-cere than adults. Somewhat surprisingly, however, there was no dominant ten-dency to see children as inferior in memory skills or as less consistent. On these dimensions, a good many respondents saw children as *superior* to adults, while numerous others perceived children as inferior. It is interesting to note that this widespread disagreement among our respondents concurs with similar disagree-ment by memory researchers. For example, conclusions of inferiority (e.g., Chance & Goldstein, 1984; Yarmey, 1984) and of equality (Marin, Holmes, Guth, & Kovac, 1979; Melton, 1981) of face-recognition skills among young chil-dren relative to adults can be found in the literature.

TABLE 9.1. Percentage of ratings of 5- to 9-year-old children's characteristics in compari-son to those of adults among Survey 1 respondents ($N = 26$).

Rated characteristic	Worse/ much worse	About the same	Better/ much better
Ability to remember details	31	27	42
Ability to recognize faces	19	39	42
	Less/ much less	About as	More/ much more
Suggestibility (to adults)*	15	8	77
Suggestibility (to age peers)	19	35	46
Sincerity*	0	12	88
Consistency in action and conversation	42	23	35

Note: An asterisk beside a characteristic indicates that the Goodness-Of-Fit test of proportions was significant at $p = .05$. Each test contrasted the obtained proportions across categories against the null expectation of equal proportions in each category.

In a second section of the survey, respondents were asked to indicate the age at which they believed a child becomes "equal to an adult" on numerous cognitive dimensions. Respondents gave an average age of 11.42 years for when children typically can resist adult suggestion as readily as an adult. An average of 11.03 years was given as the age at which children would be just as believable as adults as an "eyewitness in a criminal court case." These ages fall in the middle of the range of ages (10 to 14 years) that various states set as the minimum age of presumed competency to testify.

A SECOND SURVEY

To gain additional insight into how people generally perceive children's memory, we employed a survey procedure previously used by Brigham and Bothwell (1983). These investigators had prospective jurors in a Florida community read the method-section descriptions corresponding to a specific experimental condition of two published "staged-crime" studies of eyewitness identification. After reading each description, respondents estimated how many of 100 witnesses correctly identified the "criminal." Brigham and Bothwell found that, for both cases, the percentage of accurate identifications was dramatically and significantly overestimated (70.6% vs. 12.5% and 60.0% vs. 31.8%).

In our survey, we used a well-known study by Marin et al. (1979) as our stimulus scenario. In this study, an angry encounter between the experimenter and an intruder was staged for the benefit of individually tested subjects in four age groups: kindergartners and first-graders, third- and fourth-graders, seventh- and eighth-graders, and college students. The encounter lasted about 15 seconds, during which the intruder was in full view of the subject. Afterward, subjects answered 20 recall questions about the intruder and then attempted to identify the intruder from a 6-person photo array. Marin et al. found no significant age differences on either the recall or identification task (although young children recalled less on a *free* recall task).

We described the incident and memory tasks of Marin et al. to college students in a large introductory psychology class, varying only the age of the "witness" (the four age groups studied by Marin et al.) in the scenarios we presented (in booklet form). Students were told there were 100 "witnesses" in the experiment they read about, and that their task was to estimate (a) the number of recall questions (out of 20) the "typical" witness answered correctly (the questions were listed in the booklet) and (b) how many witnesses correctly identified the target person. Their estimates in comparison to Marin et al.'s actual results are presented in Table 9.2. In sharp contrast to Brigham & Bothwell's results, our subjects rather consistently *under*estimated both recall and recognition across all witness age groups.[1] Of more immediate concern, though, is whether estimates

---

[1]Interestingly, our college student respondents appeared to have little cognizance of the concept of chance. As the 20 questions were all of the yes-no variety, actual witnesses would have answered, on the average, 50% correctly by chance alone. Yet it can be seen in Table 9.2 that the mean estimates for the four witness age groups ranged from well

TABLE 9.2. Results of Survey 2.

Dependent variable	Age of witness			
	Kindergarten/ first grade	Third/ fourth grade	Seventh/ eighth grade	College student
Recall (mean percent of 20 questions correct)				
Actual results of Marin et al. (1979)	71.5	73.5	77.5	74.5
Survey respondents' mean estimates	38.3	43.9	54.1	50.0
Face recognition (percent accurate)				
Actual results of Marin et al. (1979)	54.0	45.5	75.0	54.0
Survey respondents' mean estimates	48.2	42.6	52.4	40.0
(Survey n)	(18)	(19)	(17)	(18)

themselves varied across age groups. Analyses of variance on the recall and recognition estimates revealed no age differences on recognition accuracy, consistent with the results of Marin et al. Witness age, however, did significantly affect estimates of recall. As seen in Table 9.2, the older the witness, the higher the estimated recall accuracy, up to the grades 7 to 8 group, for which the estimate was about the same as that for the college group. Thus, our young adult respondents tended to view recall skills as (a) inferior among young children and (b) tied to development so as to improve through the elementary school years.

These results appear at first glance to be inconsistent with the results of our first survey, in which young children were not generally seen as less able to remember details of witnessed events. The inconsistency cannot be explained by the fact that most respondents in the first survey were older adults (PTA parents), whereas the second survey's respondents were all college students. In the first survey, neither the older adults nor the college students evidenced a stereotypical belief about children's recall skills.[2] More likely, the inconsistency can be traced to a difference between the survey questions themselves. Whereas the first survey asked a very general question that did not describe a specific event-to-be-remembered, the second survey meticulously described the witnessed event. In the latter case, it was made clear that the observed event was a brief and stressful one-time encounter with a stranger. In this very "eyewitnesslike" situation, a stereotypical belief in age differences in memory emerges.

In summary, our two survey studies suggest that elementary school children are perceived by adults as more suggestible and more prone to recall (but not

below to just barely above 50%. Because this failure to account for chance was a constant across the four age conditions, it does not invalidate the observed age trend in respondents' estimates.

[2]Indeed, the responses of PTA members and college students were very similar overall in the first survey.

recognition) errors than adults. On the other hand, these children are perceived as more sincere than adults. Finally, a fair percentage of adults may believe 5- to 9-year-olds are less consistent than adults, but just as many may not share this belief.

Young children, then, do seem to have certain source attributes in the minds of many would-be jurors. They "score low" on certain aspects of trustworthiness (i.e., high suggestibility) and expertise (i.e, poor memory for specific details of witnessed events). In turn, as indicated in Figure 9.1, these perceived source attributes might (a) *directly* affect jurors' acceptance of the tesimony and/or (b) affect acceptance through their influence on how the testimony is perceived and interpreted.

DIRECT EFFECTS

In Figure 9.1, a final judgment about the veracity of a child witness's testimony is seen as an input that, along with judgments about other evidence, influences the ultimate decision of guilt or innocence. One way in which *all* the evidence is combined into a decision regarding guilt may be the integration process described by Anderson (1974; Kaplan & Kemmerick, 1974). Integration theory holds that each piece of evidence is independently evaluated along an incriminating-exonerating dimension and weighted by its subjective importance. In turn, all evidence is integrated, typically through weighted averaging, into a subjective probability of guilt. From this perspective, the major effect of a preconceived, source-relevant belief about the child would be on the weight or importance attached to the child's testimony. Thus, if children are seen as poorer rememberers (lower expertise) or, as our survey especially suggests, highly suggestible (lower trustworthiness), their testimony will receive a lower weight in the jurors' decision-making calculus. Importantly, this would be so even if jurors evaluate the testimony itself as if they were blind to the witness's age, taking the same criterial attributes into account and to the same degree for both children and adult witnesses. Moreover, the child witness would have less ultimate influence (vis-à-vis the adult witness) whether the independent evaluation of his or her testimony suggested it was likely to be accurate or inaccurate.

MEDIATED (PROCESSING) EFFECTS

Research inspired by cognitive approaches to persuasion (e.g., Eagly & Chaiken, 1984; Petty & Cacioppo, 1986) suggests that, to the extent that child-status has source implications, source effects are more likely to manifest themselves in the ways jurors *process the child's testimony itself* rather than solely in the weight attached to already evaluated testimony. A preconceived belief about children as memory sources, that is, may work as a "filter" (see Figure 9.1) that affects amount of attention to testimony, interpretation of judgment criteria-relevant details of testimony, degree of reliance on other evidence presented in the course of the trial, and even interpretation of the other evidence.

Attention

Earlier we noted that recipients of persuasive messages may either heuristically or systematically process a message. The latter involves close attention to message content and probably characterizes the typical juror strategy. Source characteristics, however, are known to influence the *relative* amount of systematic processing recipients engage in. Most relevant to the present topic, for example, is the work of Eagly and her colleagues (Eagly, Chaiken, & Wood, 1981; Wood & Eagly, 1981), which found that untrustworthy sources (i.e., communicators who advocate a position consistent with their vested interests) command closer attention to, and greater subsequent comprehension of, their messages. Apparently, recipients need to "decide for themselves" whether the advocated position is meritorious or prompted solely by the communicator's self-interest. An analogous situation may exist when jurors doubt the trustworthiness of a key child witness. Their doubt may compel them to examine the child's testimony especially closely and perhaps more critically. It may also compel them to more closely examine other evidence as well (Goodman, Golding, & Haith, 1984). Below, we report a study designed, in part, to assess whether this heightened reliance on other evidence occurs.

It should be noted, though, that persuasion research suggests also the other possibility: that jurors will pay *less* attention to a child's testimony. Trials involve massive amounts of information, and jurors, consciously or unconsciously, may search for any subjectively reliable shortcuts that ease their information-processing burden. For some jurors, the heuristic, "don't trust a child's word on memory matters," may be sufficiently believed to be invoked. In turn, the heuristic may be used to decide (indeed, prejudge) the child's believability, thus precluding systematic processing of the child's message. Presumably, such a response will typify only adults with the strongest and most rigid child stereotypes (who, in turn, probably seldom become jurors to the extent they communicate their stereotypes during the voir dire).

Evaluation on Criterial Dimensions

Jurors very probably apply similar criteria when judging the memory accuracy of adults and children. But they may (a) demand greater amounts of criterion-relevant information and (b) see different factors as relevant to a criterion when the witness is a child. The first of these possibilities may characterize application of the witnessing-conditions criterion. For jurors who perceive children's memories as generally poorer, less durable, or more malleable, the subjective minimum conditions jurors consider sufficient for forming an accurate memory trace may be higher for children than for adult witnesses. These jurors, then, may require more optimal witnessing conditions before they trust the child's testimony. Alternatively, or in addition, jurors may tend to forego heavy reliance on the witnessing-conditions criterion when the witness is a child. This is because, as Wells and Lindsay (1983) have noted, jurors' judgments of witnessing conditions may be self-based. That is, jurors may discern the apparent witnessing conditions and ask themselves: "Would I have remembered the criminal's face under those conditions?" Clearly, when the witness is a child, self-based referencing is more difficult because the juror is not a child and cannot readily take the child's perspective. Of course, experience with children (e.g., parenthood, teaching) may make this task easier, or at least more likely to be attempted in the form of "Given what my children's memories seem to be like, would they have remembered?"

Jurors might also require greater consistency between the focal eyewitness account and other evidence when the focal witness is a child. That is, if children are seen as prone to memory failure, greater corroboration will be sought by jurors. Indeed, jurors who view children this way might be especially vigilant in their search for between-witness disagreements, noticing inconsistencies that would go unnoticed if the focal witness was adult. Such vigilance is akin to greater covert counterarguing of involving communications delivered by a low-credibility source (Hass, 1981) and the selective attention to belief-supporting message details on the part of already biased recipients (Kleinhesselink & Edwards, 1975).

In the case of within-witness consistency, a similar vigilance effect may arise among stereotype-holding jurors, given that a fair percentage of our survey respondents reported viewing children as less consistent than adults in behavior and conversation. Interestingly, though, quite an opposite effect could also be plausibly predicted. If young children's communications are *expected* to be characterized by numerous inconsistencies, some jurors may *discount* at least noncrucial inconsistencies (e.g., those regarding extrafacial characteristics or situational details) as uninformative. That is, they may view these inconsistencies more as a natural result of childhood limitations in communication and details-memory than as diagnostic of whether, say, the child really does recognize the defendant's face. In the second experiment described below, we examined which of these opposing relationships, if either, is apt to be correct.

Response-bias information may also enjoy differential attention and interpretation as a function of witness age. Relevant here is the possibility that, among jurors who see children as highly deferent to authority, a response bias toward giving answers that the child believes will please adult authority figures (e.g., the lawyer, parents, police) will be suspected. These jurors may selectively notice evidence of such a bias in a child's testimony, or, via their suspicion, require stronger "proof" of memory accuracy from a child's as opposed to an adult's testimony.

Source Effects That Are a Consequence of How Children Behave in Court

In Figure 9.1, connections are drawn between the perceived source characteristics of the child and what we will call the child's testimony-delivery style, and between delivery style and the criteria jurors use to decide on memory veracity. The first connection points up that, as we have noted, presumed characteristics of children may compel jurors to be especially attentive to the particular way the child communicates his or her story. Expectations, of course, often direct attention to expectation-confirming aspects of behavior (Ross, 1977; Snyder & Swann, 1978). The second connection, however, suggests that the actual communication styles of children may influence jurors' judgments along the very criterial dimensions we have discussed, in particular consistency and response-bias.

Consistency

Both developmental psychologists and psycholegal scholars (e.g., Austin, Ruble, & Trabasso, 1977; Goodman et al., 1984; Melton, 1981) have observed that children, especially younger ones, have some difficulty reporting lengthy events in an internally consistent and logically sequential fashion. Their problems here may stem from omitting connecting events that they consider unimportant, from an insufficiently developed sense of time, or from difficulty expressing comparisons in adult language (e.g., "tall" in reference to oneself vs. in reference to other adults; "dark" in relative terms vs. too dark to see). Whatever the source of the inconsistencies, a great number of them would clearly affect jurors if they indeed use the consistency criterion. (As noted earlier, though, it is an empirical question whether a child's numerous inconsistencies reduce jurors' beliefs or whether jurors discount it as "expected of children.")

Response-Bias Information

Wells and Lindsay (1983) have suggested that jurors are more apt to believe a witness who appears confident, admits to some memory failure and so appears to be discriminating about his or her memory, and does not overly use verbal qualifiers (e.g., "I guess") that imply reconstructive or confabulative memory. Obviously, children might chronically differ from adults in these behaviors. Children are apt to project less confidence than adults (Goodman et al., 1984), especially in the threatening context of a courtroom appearance. Moreover, to the extent that young children will give less forceful presentations and need to be led somewhat by the lawyer, they may project still less confidence. However, caution is necessary in these speculations, since children have also been found to be unduly cocky about their memory (Flavell, 1979), at least outside the courtroom. Finally, though there is little direct evidence, it seems probable that, unless coached against such tendencies, children may more readily admit memory failures (which may enhance their credibility unless they overdo it) and use more verbal qualifiers such as, "I think . . . ," if only because children's language is typically less precise than adults' (which may lessen their credibility). Consistent with these speculations, Goodman et al. (1984) have suggested that children will typically deliver less guarded testimony, in a *powerless style* (e.g., Lind & O'Barr, 1978) characterized by qualified answers.

Indirect Effects of the Child Witness: Evaluating Other Evidence

In previous sections, it was suggested that jurors confronted with a child witness might rely more on other trial evidence and require greater sensitivity to inconsistencies between the child's testimony and other evidence. These potential outcomes are highly consistent with a more *general* effect of eyewitness testimony that has been suggested by Saunders, Vidmar, and Hewitt (1983; see also Leippe, 1985); namely, a tendency for the presence of an eyewitness to influence interpretation of *all* other trial information. To explain why even *discredited* witnesses often influence juries in mock-trial research, Saunders et al. argued that eyewitness testimony may *increase* the weight given to other *incriminating* evidence. In light of the foregoing discussion, it is, of course, not clear whether child eyewitnesses also have this "power." Indeed, the possibility of greater sensitivity to inconsistencies suggests the opposite. This issue is an additional focus of the investigations that follow.

Experiment 1: Child Eyewitnesses and the Quality of Other Evidence

In a seminal study of mock-jurors' reactions to child witnesses, Goodman et al. (1984) presented subject-jurors with a trial case in which the sole eyewitness, testifying for the prosecution, was either 6, 10, or 30 years old. The case was presented in the form of a written summary in one experiment, and as a video-taped simulation in a second experiment. In both cases, there was a small but *non*significant tendency for guilt ratings to be higher when the eyewitness was an adult. Child eyewitnesses, though, were rated as significantly less credible than the adult eyewitness. Moreover, when the eyewitness was a child, the credibility ratings of the child *and* the credibility ratings of other noneyewitness testifiers who made a statement during the trial were highly correlated with guilt judgments, whereas *only* the rated credibility of the eyewitness correlated with guilt judgments when the eyewitness was 30 years old. Goodman et al. suggested that, when the eyewitness is a child, the other evidence in the case is accorded greater importance.

   The present study was designed to test more firmly this notion, which we will call the *importance-displacement* hypothesis. If jurors weigh other evidence more heavily and perhaps attend to it more closely when the eyewitness is a child, the strength of that other evidence should be a stronger determinant of jurors' decisions when the eyewitness is a child then when he or she is an adult. For example, relative to a case involving a child eyewitness and mixed or ambiguous additional evidence, a case in which a child's eyewitness testimony is surrounded by strong evidence of guilt should evoke a sharply higher rate of guilty verdicts, whereas a case involving weak additional evidence should evoke sharply fewer guilty verdicts. On the other hand, if the eyewitness is an adult, the strength of surrounding evidence should have a less dramatic effect on guilty rates. Jurors should rely merely on the adult's eyewitness testimony. To test this hypothesis, we varied age of eyewitness and strength of evidence in a factorial study.

   Clearly, our theoretical discussion of children's testimony suggests other processes that might create a different set of reactions to the eyewitness in relation to other evidence. For example, jurors may simply give less credence to the child eyewitness and tend to employ a "don't trust anyone under 11" heuristic. This *heuristic hypothesis* would suggest a simple suppression of guilt rates when the eyewitness is a child, regardless of surrounding evidence. Another possibility stems from Saunders et al.'s suggestion that eyewitness testimony causes jurors to selectively place greater weight on other *incriminating* evidence. If child eyewitnesses *do not* have this effect, but rather compel jurors to cast a more critical glance at other incriminating evidence, we would expect strong noneyewitness evidence to more dramatically heighten guilt rates when the eyewitness is an adult than when the eyewitness is a child. We call this the *anti-selectivity* hypothesis.

METHOD

College students ($n = 12$ per condition) read a detailed summary of a robbery-murder case (adapted from Sue, Smith, & Caldwell, 1973) in which a grocer was shot and killed during a robbery of his store. The case summary included a description of the incident, the arrest, and the eyewitness identification, followed by a point-by-point summary of the prosecution's and the defense's case. The sole eyewitness was either the 6- or 10-year-old grandson of the victim, or his 30-year-old son. In addition, the incriminating value of seven additional pieces of evidence (testimony of witnesses to events preceding and following the crime, alibi, paraffin tests for gunpowder, and so on) was varied to create a strong, ambiguous, or weak case against the defendant. The defense's case attacked the single eyewitness's testimony, warning jurors not to rely on the memory of a child (or, in the adult eyewitness condition, a "single eyewitness"). Finally, a control group read an otherwise strong case that included *no* eyewitness. (This case was pursued on the basis of a verbal report delivered by the grocer shortly before he died.)

Subjects were instructed to read the case summaries as if they were jurors who would later deliberate with other jurors. After reading the case, the subject-jurors were asked to indicate the judgments they would communicate to other jurors at the outset of deliberation. These judgments were made individually, that is, without any discussion with other jurors. Specifically, subjects indicated whether, in their opinion, the defendant was guilty or not guilty ("undecided" was not allowed). Then, on 11-point scales, subjects rated their certainty in their verdict, the strength of the evidence against the defendant, and the credibility of the eyewitness, a second witness who interacted before the crime with a "suspicious-looking" man whose description fit the defendant, and a third witness who had a backside view of the criminal following the crime. Subjects were allowed to peruse the case summary while making these judgments.

RESULTS

As we would expect, case strength had a significant effect on strength-of-evidence ratings. The strong case was rated highest, $M = 8.31$, followed by the ambiguous case, $M = 7.50$, and, finally, the weak case, $M = 6.28$. In the no-eyewitness control condition, the mean was 7.50. Age-of-eyewitness had no effect on perceived strength of evidence.

Table 9.3 displays the percentage of subject-jurors in each condition who gave a guilty verdict. As suggested by Table 9.3, the percentage of guilty verdicts (analyzed by log-linear analysis) significantly increased overall as case-strength increased from weak to strong. No such overall strong effect on verdicts occurred for age-of-eyewitness. Rather, consistent with Goodman et al.'s results, there was a nonsignificant tendency for a higher percentage of guilty verdicts to be associated with an adult eyewitness, 66.7%, than with a 6-year-old, 47.2%, or 10-year-old, 52.8%, eyewitness. The true tale of this study, however, lies in the interaction of age-of-eyewitness and case strength. Table 9.3 shows that age made virtually no difference on verdicts when the case against the defendant was weak, a slight (but nonsignificant) difference when the case was ambiguous, and a large and significant difference when the case was strong. A significantly higher percentage of guilty verdicts were rendered for strong cases when the eyewitness was an adult, 100%, than when he was a child, 58.3%. Moreover, when the case was strong, only an adult made *any difference at all*. The 100% guilty rate in the adult-witness condition was significantly higher than the 66.7% observed in the no-eyewitness control condition, which, in turn, did not differ from the rates in the child-eyewitness conditions.

The only other reliable effects of age-of-eyewitness occurred on the ratings of the eyewitness's credibility. The adult eyewitness was rated most credible, $M = 8.06$, and the 6-year-old least credible, $M = 6.64$. Interestingly, ratings of the 10-year-old eyewitness, $M = 7.83$, were closer to those of the adult eyewitness. Correlational analyses failed to show the pattern observed by Goodman et al. In *each* of the age-of-eyewitness conditions, guilt judgments correlated significantly and similarly with ratings of the eyewitness', $rs = .57-.73$, and the other two witnesses', $rs = .285-.57$, credibility. One finding that does suggest Goodman et al.'s importance-displacement hypothesis, though, was revealed in a repeated-measures analysis of variance of credibility ratings, in which witness (the eyewitness, and each of the two other witnesses) was a 3-level repeated measure. Overall, the eyewitness was given greatest credibility, $M = 7.51$ vs. 6.81 and 6.61, but, as seen in Table 9.4, this difference was particularly pronounced when the eyewitness was an adult.

TABLE 9.3. Percent guilty decisions across court case conditions in Experiment 1.

Strength of prosecution's noneyewitness evidence	Age of primary witness			No-witness control
	6	10	30	
Strong	58.3	58.3	100.0	66.7
Ambiguous	50.0	58.3	75.0	
Weak	33.3	41.7	25.0	

Note: $n = 12$ in each condition.

TABLE 9.4. Mean judged credibility of the three prosecution witnesses in Experiment 1.

Witness	Age of primary witness		
	6	10	30
Primary witness to crime	6.63	7.83	8.05
Witness preceding crime	6.61	6.67	6.56
Witness following crime	6.61	7.39	6.44

Note: Ratings were made on an 11-point scale on which higher numbers indicate greater credibility. Each mean is based on 36 observations.

DISCUSSION

The results of the foregoing study suggest that the age of an eyewitness influences guilt judgments mainly when the case against the defendant is otherwise fairly strong. When the case was strong and the eyewitness was an adult, a guilty verdict was always given. When the eyewitness in a strong case was 6 or 10 years old, the guilty rate was no greater than when there was no eyewitness. On the other hand, age made little difference in guilt rates when the case was otherwise weak or ambiguous, a finding that replicates the absence of a significant age effect in Goodman et al.'s two experiments, in which the "other trial evidence was ambiguous" (p. 149).

This pattern of results is most consistent with the antiselectivity hypothesis derived from the work of Saunders et al. (1983). Specifically, adult eyewitnesses seem capable of casting a selective focus on the other incriminating evidence in a court case. Thus, when there is considerable incriminating evidence, the presence of an adult eyewitness is a powerful force in creating an impression of guilt among jurors. In contrast, when the eyewitness is a child, selective interpretation of incriminating evidence may not occur, presumably because, as Goodman et al.'s and our data show, children are seen as less credible witnesses and jurors continue to be doubtful. Jurors may turn their attention to other evidence in this case, as the importance-displacement hypothesis suggests, but they may do so with a critical look rather than a selectively favorable perspective.

Alternatively, selective interpretation may work the other way—from other evidence to eyewitness testimony—and more so for an adult than a child eyewitness. That is, recognition of strong noneyewitness evidence may heighten acceptance of adult eyewitness testimony but fail to dent the armor of suspicion toward children's testimony.

Why was there no advantage to the adult witness in the weak case and only a small, nonsignificant one in the mixed case? Possibly reality gets in the way of jurors' selective treatment of incriminating evidence. When other evidence is generally weak or very mixed in its implications, jurors' skepticism may be too strong to succumb to the selective perception described by Saunders et al. This reasoning is supported by recent empirical work (Leippe, 1985), showing that jurors carry more suspicion of eyewitness testimony in otherwise weak cases than previous investigations have given them credit for showing (e.g., Loftus, 1974). In any event, children may fare no worse than adults as testifiers in weak and mixed cases not because they command equal credibility, but because jurors regard *any* eyewitness testimony with a jaundiced view under these circumstances.

Experiment 2: Consistency and the Child Eyewitness

Experiment 2 focused, in part, on how the amount of inconsistency in an eyewitness report influences mock-jurors' reactions to child and adult eyewitnesses. Earlier we noted that children may be less convincing on the witness stand because their stories contain more inconsistencies. We also noted, however, that a child witness' inconsistency may tend to be *overlooked* or *discounted* as uninformative. Because children may be expected to show some inconsistencies even if their memory is accurate, jurors may look elsewhere for diagnostic cues to accuracy. This analysis concurs with Kelley's (1972) discounting principle, which stipulates that if a behavior (i.e., inconsistency) has multiple possible causes (i.e., poor memory or a natural characteristic of childhood), any given cause tends to be discounted as *the* cause. Adults, however, may enjoy no such luxury if they are expected to be consistent when they are accurate. Accordingly, it is possible that inconsistency "damns" adults' testimony more than children's testimony.

A second focus of Experiment 2 was the effect of severity of the defendant's possible sentence. Research (Kerr, 1978) indicates that jurors require a greater preponderance of incriminating evidence when a sentence will be harsh. If this is so, and given that mock-jurors view children's testimony as less credible, any age differences in guilt rates should be especially large when the defendant faces especially heavy punishment. Mock-jurors should be very reluctant to convict on the basis of a child's word under these circumstances.

METHOD

College students ($n = 15$ per condition) read a case summary of a mugging and murder. A man was held up at knifepoint on a deserted street and ultimately stabbed to death in the ensuing struggle. The sole eyewitness was either a 6-, 10-, or 30-year-old male who observed the crime from his second-floor bedroom window. The case summary included, in sequence, (a) a summary description of the crime, (b) a transcript of the verbal report provided by the eyewitness to the police the night of the crime, (c) a description of the arrest and identification of a male suspect/defendant, (d) a description of the prosecution and defense evidence presented in court, (e) the defense's closing arguments, and (f) the prosecution's closing arguments. Inconsistency of eyewitness testimony was manipulated in terms of the contrast between what the eyewitness originally told the police and what he said in court. In response to police questioning, the eyewitness gave numerous statements about the criminal (e.g., clothing, height, age), the temporal sequence of events leading to the stabbing, and the witnessing conditions (e.g., temporal duration, lighting). In the low-inconsistency condition, the eyewitness appeared to contradict only *one* of these statements during courtroom testimony, whereas, in the high-inconsistency condition, he appeared to contradict *five* of the statements. In its closing arguments, the defense highlighted these inconsistencies (either one or five), noting that they cast great doubt on the accuracy of the testimony. The inconsistencies were noted as good reasons to avoid relying on the word of a small child (or "single eyewitness" in the 30-year-old conditions). The prosecution countered that the inconsistencies were understandable, given the childhood status of the witness (e.g., since the victim was only 5 ft. 4 in., the 5 ft. 9 in. criminal would look tall to a small child) or, in the adult-eyewitness conditions, given the fact that the inconsistencies dealt with a peripheral aspect of the event/criminal. In any case, the prosecution concluded, what really mattered was the confident *facial* identification made by the eyewitness.

Before reading the case, and again before making a judgment, subjects were informed either that, if found guilty, the defendant faced a 5- to 7-year sentence with possible parole after 2 years (light sentence), or that he faced a life sentence with no parole (heavy sentence). Subjects individually responded to the same relevant dependent measures used in Experiment 1.

RESULTS

None of the independent variables had any significant effects on verdicts. Guilty rates were 76.7%, 76.7%, and 78.3% in the 6-, 10-, and 30-year-old eyewitness conditions, respectively. Nonsignificantly fewer guilty verdicts were delivered in the high-inconsistency condition, 73.3%, than in the low-inconsistency condition, 81.1%.

The inconsistency of the witness's testimony, though, did have reliable effects on two other dependent variables. Subject-jurors judged the evidence against the defendant as stronger when the witness' testimony included only one inconsistency, $M = 8.40$, as opposed to five inconsistencies, $M = 7.76$. They also judged the low-inconsistent eyewitness as more credible, $M = 8.36$, than the high-inconsistent eyewitness, $M = 7.68$. Most important for present purposes, the main effect of inconsistency on perceived witness credibility was qualified by a significant Consistency × Age interaction. Inconsistency had little or no effect on the perceived credibility of the 10-year-old ($M_{high} = 8.03$, $M_{low} = 7.97$) and the 30-year-old ($Ms = 7.87$ and 8.37) eyewitness. The high-inconsistent 6-year-old, however, was perceived as significantly less credible, $M = 7.13$, than the low-inconsistent 6-year-old, $M = 8.73$. Further analyses indicated that the credibility ascribed to the high-inconsistent 6-year-old was also significantly lower than that ascribed to the high-inconsisent 10-year-old and inconsistent 30-year-old taken together.

DISCUSSION

Numerous inconsistencies during the course of his testimony appeared to tarnish the credibility of a young child, but not of an older child or an adult. Thus, we can give a tentative nod of support to the hypothesis that jurors are particularly sensitive to a young child's inconsistency, and perhaps tend to take it as a confirmation that the child has questionable credibility.[3] Inconsistency on the part of 6-year-old children in any case, is not "excused."

Yet, despite its influence on credibility, inconsistency in testimony did not significantly affect the proportion of guilty verdicts delivered in the 6-year-old witness conditions. Indeed, guilt rates were insensitive to all of the manipulations, including age, of Experiment 2. We can offer three speculations about these nil effects. First, it can be observed that, despite some reliable differences in perceived eyewitness credibility across conditions, mean credibility judgments were relatively high for all of the experimental cases, always exceeding 7 on an 11-point scale. Perhaps only some minimum level of perceived credibility of the sole eyewitness is necessary to compel a guilty decision when, as in the present case (but unlike Experiment 1) the eyewitness is the only really major source of evidence. Jurors may tend to judge guilty whenever they see the dominating evidence as "reasonably believable," particularly because research suggests that not all jurors suitably understand the reasonable-*doubt* standard (Ellison & Buckhout, 1981).

A second reason for the nil effects on guilt rates may be the fairly convincing case made by the prosecution. In an actual trial, the prosecuting attorney would almost certainly respond to a defense tactic of highlighting the eyewitness' inconsistencies. Thus, we built this rebuttal into the case summaries mock-jurors read. By downplaying the importance of the inconsistencies (whether there were many or few), and noting how they were "understandable" when the eyewitness was a child, the prosecution's closing arguments may have been more successful than we anticipated in removing any doubts the inconsistencies *and* the eyewitness' age created among jurors about the accuracy of the eyewitness' facial identification.

Finally, it is noteworthy that, in the adult-witness conditions, the overall guilt rate was 78.3%, which is similar to the 75.0% rate for the ambiguous case of Experiment 1. For that case, as in the present study, there was no age effect. As suggested by the antiselectivity hypothesis we applied to the results of Experiment 1, it may only be in particularly strong cases, containing considerable incriminating evidence beyond the eyewitness testimony, that age differences favoring adult witnesses emerge. The cases in Experiment 2 included little

---

[3]An additional possibility is that exceptionally little inconsistency on the part of a 6-year-old is taken as evidence that the child is extraordinarily credible because such consistency might be unexpected for a young child. We are reluctant to consider this hypothesis at this point because, although the differences are in the appropriate direction, the age differences within the low-inconsistency condition were not significant.

extraeyewitness evidence and therefore afforded little opportunity for selective interpretation of case material guided uniquely by belief in the *adult's* testimony.

Conclusions and Implications

The survey and experimental research presented in this chapter only scratches the surface of the interesting, complex, and practically important issue of how jurors react to child witnesess. We hope this issue will attract extensive empirical attention in the near future. It is with this hope in mind that we believe the communication/persuasion model is a fruitful way of approaching the potential differences between how jurors evaluate children's testimony and how they evaluate the testimony of adult witnesess. Indeed, given the similarities between courtroom testimony and the more traditional persuasion contexts studied by social psychologists, the fairly well-developed attitude-change theories currently active in social psychology may serve as a productive point of departure for the study of testimony in general. In the specific case of child witnesses, we have argued that children either have, or are perceived as having, source attributes that are known to influence audience receptivity to a source's communication. To the extent children are seen as less trustworthy or less expert memory sources, the communication/persuasion model predicts systematic effects on jurors' attention to and interpretation of the information contained in a child's eyewitness testimony.

At the same time, even though youth may be correlated with well-researched source attributes, it is also a unique attribute in and of itself. Surprisingly little is known at this time about child-to-adult influence outside the nuclear family. The courtroom, as well, is a unique persuasion context, with multiple communicators, multiple sources of information, and a decision task that necessarily reduces to a dichotomous choice for the jury. Thus, the topic of jurors' reactions to children's testimony is particularly complex, given the wide variety of important variables that have few analogs outside the courtroom and about which, therefore, behavioral scientists have little advance insight.

Findings-to-Date

Our survey results suggest that elementary schoolchildren are perceived by adults as rather highly susceptible to adult suggestion and as less adept or complete at recalling details of once-witnessed events. Rightly or wrongly, adults do not share a belief that young schoolchildren have poorer face-recognition skills than adults. Given the small and probably nonrepresentative samples we employed, these findings must be considered tentative. There is a great need for replication with larger, systematic surveys, both to enhance understanding about children's performance in the courtroom and to learn about adult perceptions of children in general—an outcome that could prove important in many ways, including in regard to child-rearing practices, theories of socialization processes, and so on.

The results of the two experiments underscore the fact that witness age does not have simple, clear-cut effects on juror judgments. In neither study did we observe a significant main effect on judgments of guilt for witness age, an outcome that is consistent with Goodman et al.'s results. Age only affected guilt judgments when the case against the defendant was particularly strong (Experiment 1). Here child eyewitnesses secured fewer guilty decisions than did a 30-year-old witness, possibly because a child's testimony does not prompt a perceptual set through which jurors selectively interpret other, more equivocal evidence as incriminating.

Like Goodman et al., we did observe rather consistent effects of age on the perceived credibility of the eyewitness. These effects, though, were mainly limited to the 6-year-old eyewitnesses, who were perceived as less credible than the adult eyewitness. Ten-year-olds tended to receive credibility ratings that were only slightly below those of the adult. This suggests two important questions for future research. First, what is the age at which a child eyewitness is functionally equivalent to an adult eyewitness? Second, under what conditions do the subtle, but often-observed, effects of age on credibility judgments have a meaningful influence on the outcome of a court case? Most likely, there are many situations in which even small doubts about a child's credibility could turn a verdict. One possibility is that such doubts could become magnified during juror deliberation through a process of group polarization (cf. Myers & Lamm, 1976).

Beyond Simulations

Both of the experiments reported in this chapter were laboratory simulations that fall somewhat short of closely reproducing an actual trial case. Our mock-jurors, for example, *read* a case summary and did not deliberate. Obviously, experiments with greater realism should also be done. Nevertheless, we believe simulation studies like ours are especially useful in the early stages of research on topics as novel as the present one. As Monahan and Loftus (1982) have noted, laboratory simulations are best-suited for theory-testing, an endeavor that is highly appropriate when the researcher is breaking ground on a not-yet-well-researched topic. If support for a theory or model such as the communication/persuasion approach is found, a framework is established for asking (and answering!) ever more specific questions with applied relevance. In turn, large-scale, highly realistic (and usually expensive) simulation studies as well as field and archival research can be designed, executed, and guided by clear empirical hypotheses. One of the most satisfying results of this chapter would be the stimulation of such an empirical journey toward further understanding how child eyewitnesses influence triers of fact.

Acknowledgments. The authors thank Ruth Meshejian and the other parents of Herricks (Long Island) Middle School P.T.A. for their helpful participation in Survey 1.

References

Anderson, N. H. (1974). Cognitive algebra. In L. Berkowitz (Ed.), *Advances in experimental social psychology* (Vol. 7). New York: Academic Press.

Aronson, E., Turner, J. A., & Carlsmith, J. M. (1963). Communicator credibility and communication discrepancy as determinants of opinion change. *Journal of Abnormal and Social Psychology, 67*, 31–36.

Austin, V. D., Ruble, D. N., & Trabasso, T. (1977). Recall and order effects as factors in children's moral judgments. *Child Development, 48*, 470–474.

Brigham, J. C., & Bothwell, R. K. (1983). The ability of prospective jurors to estimate the accuracy of eyewitness identifications. *Law and Human Behavior, 7*, 19–30.

Chaiken, S. (1979). Communicator physical attractiveness and persuasion. *Journal of Personality and Social Psychology, 37*, 1387–1397.

Chaiken, S. (1980). Heuristic versus systematic information processing and the use of source versus message cues in persuasion. *Journal of Personality and Social Psychology, 39*, 752–766.

Chaiken, S., & Eagly, A. H. (1983). Communication modality as a determinant of persuasion: The role of communicator salience. *Journal of Personality and Social Psychology, 45*, 241–256.

Chance, J. E., & Goldstein, A. G. (1984). Face-recognition memory: Implications for children's eyewitness testimony. *Journal of Social Issues, 40*, 69–86.

Eagly, A. H., & Chaiken, S. (1984). Cognitive theories of persuasion. In L. Berkowitz (Ed.), *Advances in experimental social psychology* (Vol. 17). New York: Academic Press.

Eagly, A. H., Chaiken, S., & Wood, W. (1981). An attribution analysis of persuasion. In J. H. Harvey, W. J. Ickes, & R. F. Kidd (Eds.), *New directions in attribution research* (Vol. 3). Hillsdale, NJ: Erlbaum.

Eagly, A. H., Wood, W., & Chaiken, S. (1978). Causal inferences about communicators and their effect on opinion change. *Journal of Personality and Social Psychology, 36*, 424–435.

Ellison, K. W., & Buckhout, R. (1981). *Social psychology of the criminal justice system.* Monterey, CA: Brooks/Cole.

Flavell, J. H. (1979). Metacognition and cognitive monitoring: A new area of cognitive-developmental inquiry. *American Psychologist, 34*, 906–911.

Goodman, G. S. (1984). Children's testimony in historical perspective. *Journal of Social Issues, 40*, 9–32.

Goodman, G. S., Golding, J. M., & Haith, M. M. (1984). Jurors' reactions to child witnesses. *Journal of Social Issues, 40*, 139–156.

Hass, R. G. (1981). Effects of source characteristics on cognitive responses and persuasion. In R. E. Petty, T. M. Ostrom, & T. C. Brock (Eds.), *Cognitive responses in persuasion*. Hillsdale, NJ: Erlbaum.

Kaplan, M. F., & Kemmerick, G. D. (1974). Juror judgment as information integration: Combining evidential and nonevidential information. *Journal of Personality and Social Psychology, 30*, 493–499.

Kelley, H. H. (1972). Attribution in social interaction. In E. E. Jones, D. E. Kanouse, H. H. Kelley, R. E. Nisbett, S. Valins, & B. Weiner (Eds.), *Attribution: Perceiving the causes of behavior.* Morristown, NJ: General Learning Press.

Kelman, H. C. (1961). Processes of opinion change. *Public Opinion Quarterly, 25*, 57–78.

Kerr, N. L. (1978). Severity of prescribed penalty and mock jurors' verdicts. *Journal of Personality and Social Psychology, 36*, 1431–1442.

Kleinhesselink, R. R., & Edwards, R. E. (1975). Seeking and avoiding belief discrepant information as a function of its perceived refutability. *Journal of Personality and Social Psychology, 31*, 787–790.

Leippe, M. R. (1985). The influence of eyewitness nonidentifications on mock-jurors' judgments of a court case. *Journal of Applied Social Psychology, 15*, 656–672.

Lind, E. A., & O'Barr, W. M. (1978). The social significance of speech in the courtroom. In H. Giles & R. St. Clair (Eds.), *Language and social psychology*. Oxford, England: Blackwell.

Lindsay, R. C. L., Wells, G. L., & Rumpel, C. (1981). Can people detect eyewitness identification accuracy within and between situations? *Journal of Applied Psychology, 66*, 79–89.

Loftus, E. F. (1974, December). The incredible eyewitness. *Psychology Today*, 116–119.

Lord, C. G., Ross, L., & Lepper, M. R. (1979). Biased assimilation and attitude polarization: The effects of prior theories on subsequently considered evidence. *Journal of Personality and Social Psychology, 37*, 2098–2109.

Marin, B. V., Holmes, D. L., Guth, M., & Kovac, P. (1979). The potential of children as eyewitnesses: A comparison of children and adults on eyewitness tasks. *Law and Human Behavior, 3*, 295–306.

McCloskey, M., & Egeth, H. E. (1983). Eyewitness identification: What can a psychologist tell a jury? *American Psychologist, 38*, 330–334.

McGuire, W. J. (1969). The nature of attitudes and attitude change. In G. Lindsay & E. Aronson (Eds.), *The handbook of social psychology* (2nd ed., Vol. 3). Reading, MA: Addison-Wesley.

Melton, G. B. (1981). Children's competency to testify. *Law and Human Behavior, 5*, 73–85.

Monahan, J., & Loftus, E. F. (1982). The psychology of law. *Annual Review of Psychology, 33*, 441–475.

Myers, D. G., & Lamm, H. (1976). The group polarization phenomenon. *Psychological Bulletin, 83*, 602–627.

Nisbett, R. E., & Wilson, T. D. (1977). The halo effect: Evidence for unconscious alteration of judgments. *Journal of Personality and Social Psychology, 35*, 250–256.

Petty, R. E., & Cacioppo, J. T. (1986). The elaboration likelihood model of persuasion. In L. Berkowitz (Ed.), *Advances in experimental social psychology* (Vol. 19). New York: Academic Press.

Petty, R. E., Cacioppo, J. T., & Goldman, R. (1981). Personal involvement as a determinant of argument-based persuasion. *Journal of Personality and Social Psychology, 41*, 847–855.

Ross, L. (1977). The intuitive psychologist and his shortcomings: Distortions in the attribution process. In L. Berkowitz (Ed.), *Advances in experimental social psychology* (Vol. 10). New York: Academic Press.

Saks, M. J., & Hastie, R. (1978). *Social Psychology in court*. New York: Van Nostrand Reinhold.

Saunders, P. M., Vidmar, N., & Hewitt, E. C. (1983). Eyewitness testimony and the discrediting effect. In S. M. A. Lloyd-Bostock & B. R. Clifford (Eds.), *Evaluating witness evidence: Recent psychological research and new perspectives*. Chichester, England: Wiley.

Snyder, M., & Swann, W. B., Jr. (1978). Hypothesis testing in social interaction. *Journal of Personality and Social Psychology, 36*, 1202–1212.

Stafford, C. F. (1962). The child as a witness. *Washington Law Review, 37*, 303–324.

Sue, S., Smith, R. E., & Caldwell, C. (1973). Effects of inadmissable evidence on the decisions of simulated jurors: A moral dilemma. *Journal of Applied Social Psychology, 3*, 345–353.

Wells, G. L., & Leippe, M. R. (1981). How do triers of fact infer the accuracy of eyewitness identification? Using memory for detail can be misleading. *Journal of Applied Psychology, 66*, 682–687.

Wells, G. L., & Lindsay, R. C. L. (1983). How do people infer the accuracy of eyewitness memory? Studies of performance and a metamemory analysis. In S. M. A. Lloyd-Bostock & B. R. Clifford (Eds.), *Evaluating witness evidence: Recent psychological research and new perspectives*. Chichester, England: Wiley.

Wells, G. L., Lindsay, R. C. L., & Tousignant, J. P. (1980). Effects of expert psychological advice on human performance in judging the validity of eyewitness testimony. *Law and Human Behavior, 4*, 275–285.

Wood, W., & Eagly, A. H. (1981). Stages in the analysis of persuasive messages: The role of causal attributions and message comprehension. *Journal of Personality and Social Psychology, 40*, 246–259.

Yarmey, A. D. (1984). Age as a factor in eyewitness memory. In G. L. Wells & E. F. Loftus (Eds.), *Eyewitness testimony: Psychological perspectives*. New York: Cambridge University Press.

Yarmey, A. D., & Jones, H. P. T. (1983). Is the psychology of eyewitness identification a matter of common sense? In S. M. A. Lloyd-Bostock & B. R. Clifford (Eds.), *Evaluating witness evidence: Recent psychological research and new perspectives*. Chichester, England: Wiley.

10
The Memory of Children

CAROL B. COLE and ELIZABETH F. LOFTUS

On the evening of March 2, 1984 in Hawaii, a 3-year-old girl (we will call her Katie) complained to her mother that she had been burned on her leg. Katie's mother, thinking it was a mosquito bite, did not inspect the leg. Later that evening, Katie seemed to be inexplicably upset; she refused to be alone with her father, had nightmares, and screamed during the night. The following morning, the child talked of mosquito bites on her legs, but, when questioned by her mother, she eventually said the "bites" were burns from a gunlike device. After probing, Katie described a man who had abducted her from her preschool the previous day, had taken her to a house and photographed her, hugged her, and kissed her while she was naked. The man, she said, also burned her with fire from a gunlike device. Katie mentioned that a girlfriend from her preschool may also have been at the house.

The next day, Katie was interviewed by two police detectives, a social worker, and a physician, who also physically examined her. The first police officer to interview Katie described her as "drifting" and "fabricating"; she did not report having been sexually abused. During a later interview with a social worker, with the aid of anatomically correct dolls, the child revealed that she had been sexually abused and raped by her abductor. However, the results of the physical examination yielded no evidence of penetration.

The following day, Katie's parents took her for a drive in an attempt to have her identify the house to which she had been abducted. No house was identified, but during the course of the drive the child mentioned that the family's realtor, who had taken the family on similar drives to look at houses, had been at the house. At the time the parents did not interpret their daughter's statement to mean that the realtor had been her abductor. Later the same day, they took their child to the home of the girlfriend ("Jane") who, according to Katie, had been abducted with her two days earlier. Jane, who was 4 years old at the time, had so far reported only that a man may have taken her from preschool on the day in question, but he took her to McDonald's or Sea Life Park. After overhearing some of her friend's story about the abduction, Jane began to agree with allegations of abduction and sexual abuse.

In late March, Katie identified her abductor as the family's real estate agent. Both she and Jane picked his photograph from a lineup. However, several people in the man's office remembered having seen him at about the time the children reported having been abducted. Finally, the two girls reported that a third child, a 5-year-old boy, had also been abducted and abused sexually. But the boy claimed never to have been taken from the school.

Over the next several months, parents, physicians, attorneys, and the prosecutor's office questioned both children about the incident more than 30 times. The children also received psychotherapy to deal with the abuse.

In January 1986, the defense moved to disqualify the two girls as witnesses. The defense argued that the girls "learned" that the incident had occurred through the coercive questioning of many adults. Moreover, they claimed the girls could not separate fantasy from reality, and now believe that the abuse occurred and therefore behave as if they were abused. The judge granted the motion.

The Hawaii case highlights many of the issues arising when children become witnesses. Could children fabricate an entire incident, as the defense claimed occurred in the Hawaii case? If so, how can we detect such fabrication? When a troubling or illegal incident has in fact occurred, how accurately can children remember and report its details? Do children remember less than adults, and are their memories less trustworthy? Are they more likely than adults to make a false identification? How do they report their recollections of events to others? Are there ways in which we can improve the accuracy of children's reports?

The Hawaii case also brings us quickly to another issue, namely the malleability of children's memory. We know that the recollections of adults can be distorted by new information (Loftus, 1979). Are children more susceptible to leading questions and misinformation than adults? A deep concern on the part of the judge in Hawaii about suggestibility and memory distortion was the basis for the decision to disqualify the children. The judge disqualified the children as witnesses because the methods by which they had been questioned led to serious doubts as to their ability to report their own personal recollection of the events. His decision was based in part on the testimony of a clinical psychologist, who reviewed the case and stated that ". . . each child has been subjected to layers and layers of interviews, questions, examinations, etc., which were fraught with textbook examples of poor interview technique", and ". . . there was a 4:1 ratio of highly pressurized/coercive questions from adults to unpressurized responses from children in the taped interviews." (Unpublished opinion, Judge Klein, January 15, 1986).

In the Hawaii case, the defense attorneys implied that these preschoolers were so suggestible as to be unable to separate fantasy from reality, and that none of the "remembered" events ever occurred. The judge concluded that, "The questioning process utilized by layers of adults to understand and organize the information attributable to (Katie and Jane) concerning the 'incident' has served to create an 'experience' which both (girls) merely learned." This is clearly taking the suggestibility issue a step farther. To say that a person's memory for an event has been distorted does not imply that no aspect of the event is remembered correctly or that the entire event was fabricated. In this case, the children were disqualified because it was believed that it would be impossible to glean an accurate reporting of the incident from them; this is, of course, not equivalent to a ruling that the incident never took place. When adults provide eyewitness testimony, we may question their ability to accurately report what they have seen and the extent to which their memories may have been distorted, but we do not routinely suggest that they are fabricating entire incidents, such as a rape, robbery, or accidents. More often, it is suggested that an adult misperceived or misremembered some detail or mistakenly identified the wrong perpetrator. When a child is involved, however, his or her entire story is sometimes considered suspect, as it was in the Hawaii case.

Should we be more reluctant to believe what children tell us? Unfortunately, there are few empirical studies of total fabrication of events, false reports, or the development of the ability to distinguish fact from fantasy. This problem is particularly difficult to study in the case of child molestation because often the child and the offender are the only witnesses, and there may be no corroborating evidence. We know of no substantial evidence to support the notion that children frequently fabricate such events. In fact, the preliminary report of one recent study suggests that, although fabrication does occur, it is quite rare (Jones, 1985). In this study of all cases reported to the Denver Department of Social Services Sexual Abuse Team in 1983, 8% were fictitious. Only 2% of the reports initiated by children were considered to be fictitious; all of these children were teenage girls who had histories of prior sexual abuse. Moreover, we know that such molestation does in fact occur because children's reports of sexual abuse are often supported by admission by offenders or other evidence (Berliner & Barbieri, 1984). Two challenges for future research are to determine the incidence of false reporting by children, and to provide guidelines for detecting false reports.

Although the question of false reporting is an important one in the area of children's testimony, we believe it is beyond the scope of this chapter. We will therefore limit our discussion to the questions concerning the memory of children. In summary, the issues upon which we shall focus are (a) the accuracy of children's memories for events and their ability to report these events, (b) their ability to identify people they have seen previously, and (c) the malleability of their memories. Many of the chapters in this volume constitute important contributions to our understanding of these issues. Three of the chapters are important additions to this literature because they examine children's memory for real-life events (Goodman, Aman, & Hirschman, Chapter 1; King & Yuille, Chapter 2; Peters, Chapter 7). Three of the chapters provide some excellent insight into the components of suggestibility and the complexity of the concept (Ceci, Ross, & Toglia, Chapter 5; Saywitz, Chapter 3; Zaragoza, Chapter 4). Two of the studies are among few developmental studies to include preschool-age children (Ceci et al., Chapter 5; Goodman et al., Chapter 1). Several studies described in this volume examine the development of face recognition ability and point out some of the special problems children may have with this task in an eyewitness situation (Goodman et al.; King & Yuille; Peters). In the following sections, we discuss these findings and attempt to integrate them with our previous knowledge of children's memory. Many of these studies provide data bearing on more than one of the three areas to be discussed (children's memory for events, suggestibility, and face recognition). The relevant findings of each will be presented and discussed in the appropriate sections.

Children's Memory for Events

The bulk of what we know about memory development comes from laboratory studies of deliberate memory tasks. These studies have shown that sophistication in the use of memory skills such as rehearsal, use of mental imagery, and semantic organization increases steadily with age (e.g., Brown, 1979; Brown, Bransford, Ferrara, & Campione, 1983). Although this approach to studying children's memory may be relevant, it is somewhat removed from the question at hand. In assessing children's competence to provide testimony, we are interested in their ability to remember and report real-life events. In many cases, the events occur without prior knowledge that something is about to take place which should be remembered. Thus we draw from literature that involves more realistic stimuli. This literature includes studies that assess children's memories for simulated eyewitness situations, several of which are presented in this volume. It also includes a handful of more naturalistic studies that describe children's memories for naturally occurring events in their lives.

Simulated Events

The laboratory studies of children's eyewitness memory differ in a number of important ways that can make the findings difficult to compare. One of the key factors is the ecological validity of the design. Studies that employ narratives or audiotapes are less ecologically valid than those involving films of real-life events, which in turn are less true to life than those in which the child witnesses a staged event or participates in an activity. The content of the stimuli also varies and may differ with respect to interest level across age groups. These studies also vary with respect to exposure time and retention intervals, age range of subjects, and methods of assessing memory performance. Nevertheless, some consistent findings have emerged from these studies.

FREE RECALL

One of the most stable findings is that children spontaneously recall less than adults. For example, Goodman, Aman, and Hirschman (Chapter 1, this volume), in a study involving an arm-movement game, found that 3-year-olds recalled less about the event than did 6-year-olds, who in turn recalled less than the adults.

Similarly, King and Yuille (Chapter 2, this volume) found that younger children (ages 5 to 9) provided reliably less information than older children (ages 11 to 17) during free recall of two witnessed events. Marin, Holmes, Guth, and Kovac (1979) also found that free recall for an observed event increased with age in a sample of kindergarten-though-college students, approaching adult levels in seventh- and eighth-graders. Taken together, these studies suggest that the amount of information provided in a free recall report of a previously experienced event increases steadily until preadolescence, at which time it reaches adult levels.

Interestingly, these investigators and others have found that, although children recall less, their free recall is often not less accurate than that of adults. This seems to be true even when inaccuracies have been introduced during questioning prior to free recall. For example, Goodman et al. (Chapter 1) employed a paradigm in which children and adults participated in an arm-movement game with a man, and returned several days later for questioning. They were first asked a series of objective and leading questions and were then asked to recall what had happened. Even though the children had been more likely to go along with the suggested information during the questioning phase of the study, they were no more likely than adults to include this information in their subsequent free reports. In fact, suggested information rarely appeared in the free reports of any of the subjects in both this work and in the work of King and Yuille (Chapter 2).

Several studies have yielded interesting findings regarding the types of errors made in free recall (Goodman et al., Chapter 1, this volume; Marin et al., 1979; Saywitz, Chapter 3, this volume). Subjects in the Marin et al. (1979) study ranged in age from 5 to 22 years, and each observed a staged argument between two experimenters. Either 10 or 30 minutes later, they freely recalled the argument. Surprisingly, subjects of all ages recalled more following a longer delay. As mentioned earlier, the number of items correctly recalled increased with age. However, the number of *incorrect* items mentioned also increased with age. One difficulty in interpreting this finding is that the increase in incorrect items mentioned may be an artifact of the increase in overall information provided. That is, we might expect that as more items are mentioned, the absolute number of incorrect items will increase, but that the proportion of incorrect to correct information would remain about the same. In fact, Marin et al. found that, although the *number* of items incorrectly mentioned increases steadily with age, when analyzed in terms of percent of total recall the results are less clear. Approximately 3% of the items "recalled" by the 5- to 6-year-olds were incorrect, compared to 12% for the 8- to 9-year-olds, 8% for the 12- to 13-year-olds, and 10% for the college students. The youngest children clearly introduced fewer inaccurate details, but the proportion of correct to incorrect information seems to be roughly equivalent for the 8- to 22-year-olds.

Saywitz (Chapter 3, this volume) presented children with an audiotaped story about a theft, followed by both objective and suggestive questioning and a free recall task. Children in her study ranged in age from 8 to 15 years. Free-recall protocols were coded with respect to accurate and inaccurate recall, with inaccurately reported information further characterized as either a distortion of the original event or an addition of extraneous information. In keeping with the earlier studies, the 8-year-olds recalled less than the 11- to 15-year-olds. Moreover, there were no age differences in distortions of previously presented material, although the data suggested a trend toward younger children incorporating less suggested information into their reports. However, the youngest children in this study did include more extraneous information than did the older children. Saywitz describes these additions as less constrained by the actual stimuli than are the distortions; that is, they tended to involve exaggerations and blatantly false contradictions. She suggests that they may therefore be easier to detect as inaccurate.

In contrast, Goodman et al. found that although the children and adults in their study were equally likely (or, more accurately, equally unlikely) to incorporate suggested information into their narrative accounts of the event, the adults were significantly more likely to report expected but nonexperienced information. This type of information might be more difficult to tag as inaccurate because it is likely to seem plausible and consistent with the rest of the story.

Taken together, these studies suggest that when asked to give an account of an event, children under the age of 11 or 12 years will spontaneously provide less information than adults, but that the information provided will be equally accurate. When errors do occur, they are likely to be of a different variety for children than adults. Children up to the age of 6 are less likely to provide inaccurate information during free recall. Eight- to nine-year-old children are most likely to add extraneous and perhaps less plausible information to their accounts, whereas adults are most susceptible to errors of inference.

Another robust finding of the memory literature is that the memory of both children and adults is most accurate during free recall (Loftus & Davies, 1984). However, both children and adults remember more on recognition tasks than on free-recall tasks (e.g., Saywitz, Chapter 3, this volume). In addition, it is usually the case in an eyewitness situation that the witness will be asked specific questions about the event. Because young children tend to provide very little information spontaneously, they may be asked even more questions in this situation than would an adult in an effort to obtain a complete account.

CUED RECALL AND RECOGNITION

The most common method of cued recall is direct questioning regarding the event of interest. There have been several recent efforts to examine the accuracy of cued recall in children. As with the studies of free recall, these findings are difficult to compare because of the differences with respect to age range of subjects, type of stimulus used, and exposure time and retention interval. They also vary in the methods used to assess recall. Questions may be asked in either a yes/no or true/false format, a short answer format (e.g., What color was the man's hair?) or a multiple choice format. The multiple choice format is not common in real-life eyewitness situations, except in the case of a photo or in vivo lineup, which will be discussed in a later section. Nevertheless, the multiple choice format has been employed in some laboratory studies of children's memory for events. Finally, both questions and answers may be presented in either verbal or written form.

Several studies of cued recall and recognition have suggested that even very young children can sometimes be as accurate as adults in providing information about previously observed events. Ceci et al. (Chapter 5, this volume) presented 3- to 12-year-old children with stories accompanied by line drawings. Three days later, the children were presented with pairs of drawings, one of which had been part of the original story and one which differed in some respect. Unbiased 3-year-olds were as accurate as the 12-year-olds in their recognition of the drawings (84% accuracy for the younger children compared to 95% accuracy for the older group). In the Marin et al. (1979) study described above, 5-year-olds were as accurate as college students in answering yes/no questions about a staged argument between two experimenters following a 10- or 30-minute and a 2-week delay. Overall, the subjects answered about 74% of the questions correctly, with group averages of approximately 71, 73, 77, and 74% for the kindergarten and first grade, third and fourth grade, seventh and eighth grade, and college students, respectively. The authors reported a response bias to say "no" in 41% of the subjects. Finally, Saywitz (Chatper 3, this volume) presented 8- to 15-year-olds with an audiotaped description of a crime, and tested their memories immediately and following a 5-day delay. Children were asked true/false questions regarding the crime, and there were no differences among the age groups with respect to percent correct recognition. Overall, the children were accurate 70% of the time. These studies encompass a variety of stimuli (audiotape, picture/story, live event), age groups (3 years to adult), and assessment methods (yes/no or true/false questions, multiple choice with pictures). While no age differences were found, the results suggest that subjects of all ages are better at recognizing visual stimuli than they are at answering yes/no questions about previously observed events.

In contrast, a number of studies have found age differences in the ability to respond correctly to questions about past experiences. For example, Goodman et al. (Chapter 1, this volume) describe three studies in which children participated in some event and were then asked a series of questions to assess their memory for the event. Unfortunately, the authors do not describe the nature of the questions (yes/no, multiple choice, or short answer). In the first study, 3-year-olds, 6-year-olds, and adults participated in an arm-movement game with a man, and after a 4- to 5-day delay were questioned about that experience. In this study, the performance of the 3-year-olds was reliably worse, whereas the 6-year-olds were as accurate as the adults. In the second study, a small group of 3- to 7-year-olds either had their blood drawn or had a design placed on their arms. In both conditions, the younger children again answered fewer questions correctly than did the older ones. Because of the small number of subjects, age-group comparisons could not be made. A third study was similar in that children received inoculations and were later tested for memory of the event. In this study, 5- to 6-year-olds answered more questions correctly, and 3- to 4-year-olds showed a decline in memory performance when a longer delay was imposed.

One interesting finding to emerge concerns the type of information that the children remembered best. Across age groups, the children were better at remembering information about actions (86%) than descriptive information about a person or the room (60 and 64%, respectively). This is an important piece of information for several reasons. Many studies of children's memory and suggestibility for events focus on children's ability to recall some specific detail of the event. A favorite type of question seems to be either the color of, or the presence/absence of some article of clothing, such as a hat, shoes, or watch. This finding of greater accuracy for actions than descriptions suggests that the level of performance observed in description studies may underestimate the ability of children to recall action information. Further research should clearly specify the type of information being sought. We may find that children are reasonably accurate with respect to certain types of information but not others.

The results summarized thus far suggest that while preschoolers may be at a disadvantage in some types of cued recall situations, children as young as six can be relatively accurate in recognizing or recalling information. In contrast, Cohen and Harnick (1980) showed 8- to 12-year-old children and college students films of petty crimes, and found that 8- to 9-year-olds correctly recalled fewer items than did 11- to 12-year-olds and college students, both immediately following the film and again one week later. Immediately following the viewing of the film, subjects were asked a series of yes/no and short answer questions. The 8- to 9-year-olds were only about 50% accurate, compared to 73 and 82% for the older groups The latter were not significantly different. One week later, questions were presented in a multiple choice format. Performance improved for all three groups, but was still worse for the younger children. They now selected the correct response 75% of the time, compared to 85 and 95% for the older subjects.

Taken together some consistent findings emerge from these studies. It appears that all age groups perform best when asked to select the correct response from an array of two or more choices. Unfortunately, such a forced choice situation may not occur very often in an actual eyewitness situation. Subjects of all ages appear to do less well with a short answer or true/false format, which one is more likely to experience in real life. Marin et al.'s finding of a negative response bias may indicate that uncertainty about one's memory for a fact may lead to denial of the fact. However, in a forced choice format the subjects may assume that one of the choices is correct, and consequently select the correct answer with some confidence. In other words, if asked, "Was the woman wearing a hat?," a subject who is uncertain may say "no." But if asked, "Was the woman wearing a hat or a scarf?," the subject may be more likely to select the correct response. When the stimulus is a picture and recognition is assessed by means of a forced choice paradigm, it seems that preschoolers are as accurate as adults.

In general, the findings are less consistent with respect to age differences in the ability to answer yes/no or short-answer questions. This ability is well-developed by the age of 5 or 6 (Goodman et al., Chapter 1, this volume; Marin et al., 1979),

186 Carol B. Cole and Elizabeth F. Loftus

and may be close to adult levels by the age of eight (Saywitz, Chapter 3, this volume). Why, then, were Cohen and Harnick's 8-year-olds performing less well than older children and adults? It is possible that the films used by these authors are less interesting to the children than some of the other stimuli. However, it is difficult to imagine that they are less interesting than the audiotaped descriptions of crimes used by Saywitz, who did not find a performance decrement for this age group. One possibility is that the audiotape task is easier for all subjects because any relevant information is described; there are fewer demands on the subject to select the details or activity on which to focus. For example, suppose a recognition question has to do with the presence or absence of headwear on the perpetrator of the crime. In an audiotape presentation, that detail must have been specifically described in the initial presentation. In contrast, if the same information is conveyed visually in a film, a subject may or may not attend to that detail. In addition, in the audiotape paradigm, the original stimulus and the memory assessment are presented in the same mode—that is, verbally. The film presents information visually, but the memory assessment is presented verbally and requires a verbal response. Unfortunately, Saywitz does not present the accuracy levels of her subjects, so that a direct comparison of the difficulty of these two tasks cannot be made.

Naturalistic Studies

Of the laboratory studies discussed above, the methods employed by Marin et al. and Goodman et al. are closest to an eyewitness situation that might occur in real life. These studies suggest that children as young as 5 years can be as accurate as adults in providing information about recently observed or experienced events, but that preschoolers provide less accurate accounts. Thus far, Goodman et al. are the only researchers to include children as young as 3 years in a simulation study of verbally reported memory of an event. However, the results of three recent lines of research are useful in furthering our understanding of the very young child's memory for events and his or her ability to relate these events to others. It should be noted here that some innovative naturalistic procedures including preschoolers have been employed by Goodman et al. (Chapter 1, this volume), who studied children's memories for having their blood drawn, and Peters (Chapter 7, this volume), who questioned children following a visit to the dentist. The results of these studies are discussed in detail in several other sections of the chapter, as they provide data that seem particularly relevant to the discussions of free versus cued recall, suggestibility, and face recognition.

Todd and Perlmutter (1980) observed 12 children between the ages of 35 and 50 months during play sessions in their homes. They were particularly interested in information provided by the children that was evidence of memory for some event. The information was classified as either memory for a specific event, memory for a recurrent event, or generalized information. The authors found that specific events were related by the use of the past tense, and the children provided information about actions in a particular context, localized in time. Recurrent events were often related by combining information about a number of specific events without indication that the events were separate. Generalized information was related by the use of the present tense and dissociated from a particular point in time. In other words, children talk about different kinds of events in different ways.

In this research, the spontaneous communication of a memory was almost always triggered by some discernible external cue, usually something in conversation (24%) or an object (17%). Spontaneously mentioned events tended to be about common occurrences in the child's life, and were somewhat more frequent for the 4-year-olds (56%) than for the 3-year-olds (45%). The remaining memories resulted from direct questions from the experimenter, and tended to be about less common occurrences. Finally, children provided more information per question about an event for which they had initiated the retrieval process.

With respect to the specific events, the younger children required somewhat more probing in order to communicate as many details as the older children. In terms of content, the majority of information provided by the children was about what occurred (27%) and about the people involved (21%). In the "what occurred" category, 60% of the information described actions. This fits nicely with Goodman et al.'s finding that children were more accurate in their memories for action versus descriptive details. The remaining memory units consisted primarily of details, objects, and location, with infrequently mentioned aspects of the events, including temporal, abstract, and causal information. The children also occasionally mentioned nonoccurrences, that is, violations of expectency; this type of information decreased with age.

Accuracy of the children's reports was assessed by the parents. In terms of global occurrence of the events, parents were confident that 3% of the episodes had not occurred, and were uncertain about another 10%. According to parent report, the detailed information provided by the children was very accurate. When errors were mde, they tended to involve misperception of some event by the child, or inaccuracies with respect to time and location. Parents were also asked whether an event had been "rehearsed," that is whether the child had previously discussed it with the parent. This is an important factor in questioning a child who has witnessed an event, as we saw in the case of the two Hawaii preschoolers. These authors found that to a point, children provided more information about events that had been previously rehearsed. However, frequently rehearsed episodes resulted in a decrease in the amount of information communicated during the play sessions. Unfortunately, no data were presented regarding differential accuracy of information for rehearsed versus nonrehearsed episodes.

A commonly held belief about young children is that they do not remember events over a very long period of time. The children in Todd and Perlmutter's (1980) study reported events that had occurred anywhere from less than one month to over one year previously. The average time lag for the 3-year-olds was 7.7 months, and 14.5 months for the 4-year-olds. There was no decrease in the accuracy of the memories over time.

Nelson and Ross (1980) studied the memories of younger children, ages 21 to 27 months, by teaching their mothers to keep diaries of evidence of memories over a 3-month period. The memories were approximately equally divided between novel situations, people, objects and activities, and recurrent stimuli. The majority of memories were either recollections of some aspect of an event or the location of an important person or object. The 27-month-old children most often recalled some aspect of an event, whereas the 21-month-olds more often recalled location information. The majority of the memories of the 24-month-olds were equally divided between these types. While the majority of the events recalled had occurred within 3 months (80%), there was a time lag of up to 6 months for the younger children, and up to 1 year for the 27-month-olds.

For these younger children, 80% of the memories were cued by either the location where an event had occurred or by seeing an object or person associated with the remembered event. Whereas the use of location and object/person cues occurred equally for the children over 2 years, location was by far the most common cue for the younger toddlers. Only 5% of these memories were cued by verbalizations of another person, suggesting that the effectiveness of such cues increases dramatically by age 3 years (Todd & Perlmutter, 1980). There was no evidence for uncued, or spontaneous, memories in these children.

The salience of location and object or person cues in eliciting memories from these children is highly relevant to the issue of child testimony. In a similar vein, a recent study by Price (1984) demonstrated the usefulness of props in maximizing narrative detail in the accounts of 4-year-olds, and of placing 2½-year-old children back in the original location to improve their recall of an event. By 5 years of age, the children in Price's study did as well with verbal prompts as with toy props. Research with adults has also sometimes demonstrated increased accuracy when the original environment is reinstated (e.g., Malpass & Devine, 1981).

In the Hawaii case, and in many other cases of child sexual abuse, children have been unable to describe their molestation in words but have demonstrated what occurred using anatomically correct dolls. The defendant's attorneys argued that the fact that the 3-year-old did not report having been sexually abused until she was presented with the dolls suggests that the abuse never occurred. While we can never know for sure what happened in the Hawaii case, the results of the naturalistic studies and of Price's work do not lend support to this argument. On the contrary, when the children in Price's study used the toy props, not a single child's account or reenactment contained elements of fantasy. Because the use of anatomically correct dolls in the assessment of child sexual abuse is now widespread, there is a need for research specifically aimed at providing normative information about how children play with these dolls, and whether they do, in fact, stimulate sex-related fantasy play. In a recent study using a small number of subjects, Jampole (1986) found that sexually abused children were significantly more likely than nonabused children to engage in sexual play behavior with the dolls.

Nelson and Ross (1980) have also used a somewhat more structured approach to study children's memories for specific versus general instances of recurrent events. General memories were tapped by asking the child a question like,"What happens when you have a snack at school?." Specific memories were tapped by asking, "What happened yesterday when you had a snack at school?." Children were also asked to tell about something special that had happened to them, such as a trip to the zoo. The children were 3 and 5 years of age. When asked to report a specific episode of a recurrent event, they reported significantly less information than when asked to tell about the general case. Responses to the general case were framed in general terms, using the present tense. The past tense was used only for specific cases, although the present tense was also used in this condition from 10 to 50% of the time. In addition, their memories appeared to be highly generalized. That is, infrequent or atypical actions (particular) were much less frequently included in their reports than usual actions (standard). Particular actions occurred four times as often in the specific condition, but standard instances were much more frequently given even in this condition.

Children in both age groups were able to give relatively long and specific reports about novel events, although this task seemed to be more difficult for a few of the 3-year-olds. An event had to be truly novel to be remembered in specific terms. Special events that occur infrequently but are not truly novel, such as birthday parties, could not be retrieved in specific terms.

Nelson and Ross (1980) have used the term "scripts" to describe children's memories for recurrent events. They suggest that the more experience a child has with a given activity or event, the less the child will be able to describe a specific instance of that event. This finding has clear implications in cases in which a child is asked to testify about a recurrent event such as repeated abuse of him- or herself or of a parent, friend, or sibling. It may be unrealistic to expect a child to provide an account of distinct episodes, anchored in time. Unfortunately, this is often what the legal system asks the child to do in such a situation.

In summary, these naturalistic studies of memory for events in young children suggest that even very young children can remember past events. Children under the age of 2 years have been shown to recall events that occurred 6 months ago. Children over two have been shown to recall events occurring a year or more ago. However, the communication of such memories is rarely spontaneous. In toddlers these "reports" are almost exclusively cued by location or by some object or person associated with the event. By the age of 3 years, verbal cues become more effective in eliciting information, but objects and other cues are still primarily responsible for eliciting information about prior experiences. The information that is provided tends to be relatively accurate, particularly with regard to actions. Children are most likely to make errors locating events in time, and it is particularly difficult for them to distinguish among specific instances of recurrent events. It also appears that returning a toddler to the location of an event, or providing props for a preschool child can be an effective way to elicit more information about the event, and there is no concrete evidence thus far that these tools elicit fantasy material.

Although it seems we cannot expect young children to provide us with the coherent, detailed, chronological accounts of events that we would often like, they can provide some valuable information. The challenging task for professionals in this field is to learn how this information can be obtained while minimizing the risk of introducing inaccuracies to a child's report. For example, in questioning preschoolers about what happens when they eat lunch at school, Nelson (1978) found that when asked for information they did not have (e.g., where the lunch came from), some children gave a response which seemed to come from similar scripts (e.g., mother and daddy buy it), rather than saying they did not know. In the Hawaii case, the judge believed that the children's memories had been irreparably distorted by the questioning of many adults over a long period of time, such that it would be impossible to ever learn from them what had actually taken place.

Suggestibility in Memory

Suggestibility refers to the extent to which individuals can be made to believe events occurred that did not, or that details were different in some way than they really were. The concern in a legal situation is that when witnesses are questioned by a number of people, what they report may be a blend of information they have experienced and new information provided or constructed during the course of questioning. Loftus (1979) reviewed several studies in which adults are presented with a film of an event and are subsequently asked a series of questions about the event. In these studies, some of the questions provided the subject with misleading information, typically to suggest the existence of an object that was not originally present. These studies showed that subjects who have been exposed to misleading information were more likely to later "recall" having seen the nonexistent object. Other studies have shown that suggested information can also transform a recollection. For example, subjects who have seen a film in which there was a yield sign later report having seen a stop sign when this information was suggested during questioning. It has also been found that memories are more vulnerable to suggestion when the initial memory has been weakened over time.

This line of research suggests that susceptibility to misleading information is a problem in the eyewitness testimony of adults. In the absence of empirical support, it has been a commonly held belief for at least seven decades that children are highly suggestible, much more so than adults (Varendonck, 1911). Is it the case that children are more vulnerable to leading questions and postevent information than adults?

As it turns out, studying age trends in suggestibility is more complicated than it might seem. Loftus and Davies (1984) have suggested several possible reasons that we might expect to find age differences in suggestibility. The adult literature indicates that weaker memories are more susceptible to suggestion, and there is good evidence that young children remember fewer details of previously experienced events than do adults. These memory differences may be due to differences in the facility with which the original information is encoded into memory, in some aspect of the retention stage, or in the retrieval process. If children initially encode less information, and there is good evidence to suggest that they do, then the resulting memory representations are likely to be less rich and

therefore more susceptible to postevent input. It may be that childr
decay more rapidly, and are therefore more vulnerable to sugge
there is good evidence that children have greater difficulty than a
ing information from long-term memory (Brown, 1979; Chi, 1⁰
1980). New information, such as information provided by sugg
ing, could be more accessible than the original information, which couiu ...
lead to greater susceptibility to suggestive misinformation.

On the other hand, the incorporation of new information requires information-processing. Sometimes it involves the generation of inferences that go beyond what is explicitly stated, which may lead to the creation of inaccurate memories. If children are less likely to generate inferences spontaneously, or are less efficient at integrating information, then we would expect them to be less suggestible than adults. In other words, if children do not process postevent inputs as efficiently, they would be less influenced by them.

There is evidence that a higher interest level or greater knowledge base are somehow protective against misleading information. In a study of suggestibility in men and women, women were more accurate and more resistant to suggestions about female-oriented details, whereas men were more accurate and more resistant to suggestions about male-oriented details (Powers, Andriks, & Loftus, 1979). It is possible that children are also less suggestible to certain kinds of information than others, and that they might outperform adults in recalling such items.

The study of age trends in suggestibility is relatively new, but the paradigm used in several recent studies is similar to that used in adult work. Subjects of various ages are exposed to some event and are subsequently asked a series of questions, some of which contain misleading information. The subjects are then tested for the degree to which their memory for the original event has been distorted by incorporation of the inferred information. Numerous problems exist in studying suggestibility in children because it involves a combination of cognitive, social, and situational factors. One problem is that children may fail to demonstrate suggestibility because they do not make the appropriate semantic inferences from the postevent material. In essence, the attempted manipulation would be unsuccessful, and the misleading information would not be encoded. In this case, suggestibility might be underestimated. On the other hand, children may be more likely to go along with what an adult says, even though the actual memory representation remains unchanged (as seen in part in Experiment 2 by Ceci et al., Chapter 5, this volume). In this case, suggestibility might be overestimated. At this point, the results of the existing studies are mixed and often difficult to interpret.

A relatively early study investigating suggestibility in children (Dale, Loftus, & Rathbun, 1978) demonstrated that leading questions can have an impact on children as young as 4 to 5 years of age. They showed short film clips to these children and then questioned them as to the content of the film. Some of the questions were congruent with the content of the film, while others presented misleading information. For suggested objects or events that had not actually been present in the film, the children were significantly more likely to answer "yes" to a question posed in the form, "Did you see *the* . . ." as opposed to, "Did you see *a* . . ." . Similar, though weaker effects were observed for the use of "Did you see *some* . . ." versus "Did you see *any* . . ." . However, when the object or event had actually figured in the film, there was no effect of the form of the question on the number of subjects responding positively, and accuracy in these cases was fairly good (73-90%). In addition, the authors noted that where positive effects were observed, they were quite small in absolute terms. When the children were later asked to provide a free recall account of the film, a small percentage (4 out of 32 children; 13%) spontaneously mentioned an object which had been suggested in the postevent questioning. These results indicate that young children may be sensitive to relatively subtle semantic inferences, but provide no direct comparison with older children or adults.

Marin et al. (1979) conducted a study of juvenile testimony with subjects from 5 to 22 years of age. Each subject witnessed a live confrontation between two experimenters. Subjects were then asked to provide a free narrative account of the incident and to answer a number of questions, one of which included misleading information. The misleading question implied the presence of either a nonexistent object ("Was the package the man carried small?") or a nonexistent event ("Did the man slam the door as he closed it?"). Subjects were tested 2 weeks later to determine whether the postevent material was incorporated into their memories of the incident. As described in an earlier section, there were no age differences in accuracy of recall for the legitimate questions, with overall accuracy of 74%. Two weeks later, about half of the subjects in each age group gave false positive responses, giving answers consistent with the misleading information. No age differences in suggestibility were found. These data are consistent with those of Dale et al. (1978) in that children as young as 5 years were susceptible to verbally inferred information. However, they were no more suggestible than adults.

Two recent studies have suggested that when children's memory for an event is good, they may be even less susceptible to misleading information than are adults. Duncan, Whitney, and Kunen (1982) showed a cartoon slide sequence to subjects ranging in age from 6 years to adulthood. Subjects were then asked a series of questions, including (a) orthodox questions, such as, "When the bear appeared, where did it chase the man?," (b) questions including information consistent with the slides, such as "When the bear appeared and broke the man's spear, where did it chase the man?," and (c) questions including information inconsistent with the slides, such as "When the bear appeared and broke the man's fishing pole, where did it chase the man?." Susceptibility to the misleading information was later assessed by asking questions, such as "Were the men fishing when the bear appeared?."

Unlike Marin et al. (1979), these authors found that proficiency at answering the orthodox questions improved steadily with age. Several differences in methodology may account for this apparent discrepancy. Duncan et al. (1982) informed the subjects in advance that they would be asked some questions about the slides, so that purposeful memory skills such as rehearsal could be employed. We know that the sophistication and the use of such skills increases with age. Another difference in methodology is that the orthodox information questions in the Duncan et al. study were asked in a short-answer format, in contrast to the yes/no format used by Marin and her colleagues. The college students in the Duncan et al. study answered these questions with about 75% accuracy, which is equivalent to the performance of all the age groups in the Marin et al. study (kindergarten-through-college students). The youngest children in Duncan et al. were less accurate (48%).

In spite of these age differences in memory for the original event, Duncan et al. found that children and adults were equally influenced by postevent questions. However, they hypothesized that the generally lower overall accuracy of the younger subjects might have masked any real effects, so they analyzed the effects of the postevent information only for those instances where correct memory of the visual sequence was demonstrated. In this case, the younger subjects appeared to be less influenced by the misleading information than were the adults.

Duncan et al. employed a similar strategy in a second experiment, but this time memory change was assessed using a slide recognition task, rather than follow-up questions. In contrast to Ceci's findings with the recognition of drawings discussed earlier, recognition of the slides increased with age. The data were again partitioned on the basis of good memory for the original sequence, and again Duncan et al. found that the relative effect of the misleading questions was greatest among the older children and college students.

Saywitz (Chapter 3, this volume) presented 8- to 15-year-old subjects with an audiotape of a crime, and in a later questioning session included three questions with misleading information about a character in the story. In a test of recognition for the original story, Saywitz failed to find age differences in the proportion of questions answered correctly. There were also no significant age differences in the number of intrusions of previously suggested misleading information when subjects were asked to describe the character (although younger children were slightly less susceptible). In all, 14 of the 72 subjects (19%) produced the suggested information. It may be that this free-recall method of assessing the effects of suggested information underestimates the effect because the younger children report less information overall.

In contrast to the studies described above, several recent studies have demonstrated that younger children are more suggestible than older children and adults. One study (King & Yuille, Chapter 2, this volume) is similar to the Marin et al. (1979) study, in that the subjects were 6 to 17 years of age and they witnessed a real-life event. While the King and Yuille subjects waited alone in a room, a stranger entered and tended some plants. Subsequently, subjects were asked a series of questions about the event, two of which suggested erroneous but plausible inferences about the event. One involved a descriptive detail about the stranger (implying that he had worn a watch) and the other a detail of the action (that he had used scissors to remove a leaf; scissors had been present but the leaf was actually removed by hand). The 6- to 9-year-old children were more likely to agree with the misleading questions than were the older children, who were more likely to say that they had not noticed that particular detail.

Were the memory representations of the younger children more readily distorted than those of the 11- to 17-year-olds? Anecdotal information provided by King and Yuille suggests that factors other than vulnerability to postevent information must be considered. They report that several of the children who had agreed with the suggested information spontaneously informed them that they had "gone along" with the misleading suggestion because they thought it was the appropriate thing to do. For example, they really had no recollection of having seen a watch, and were aware that they were fabricating when they gave their responses. These spontaneous statements introduce the possibility that apparent age differences in suggestibility may be accounted for at least in part by social factors, such as demand characteristics, rather than differences in memory distortion.

In a similar study with 8- to 14-year-olds, King and Yuille (Chapter 2, this volume) demonstrated that the children could not be misled regarding details which had been highly salient and memorable. Children observed a staged bicycle theft and were asked leading questions about the thief's head- and footwear. Neither question had an effect on the subjects. Because several children spontaneously described the thief's shoes in great detail during free recall, King and Yuille concluded that they were highly salient to the children. This finding is consistent with the gender difference study (Powers et al., 1979) showing that a higher interest level or greater knowledge base can be protective against misleading information.

A study of suggestibility in subjects of 9 years, 12 years, and college-age undertaken by Cohen and Harnick (1980) also demonstrated that younger children were more influenced by leading questions. Subjects observed a short film depicting two petty crimes, and were immediately asked a series of questions about the film, half of which contained leading information (e.g., The young woman was carrying a newspaper when she entered the bus, wasn't she?). A multiple choice test was administered one week later to assess the degree to which suggested information had been incorporated into memory.

Cohen and Harnick found a significant increase in accuracy on the questionnaire for both orthodox questions and those containing postevent implied information. Twelve-year-olds and college students answered a higher proportion of the straightforward questions correctly and were more likely to disagree with the implications of the leading questions. Although the two older groups were more likely to resist previously suggested information, there was evidence that they were affected by the leading questions to some extent. Cohen and Harnick suggest that the younger children were more influenced by the leading questions because of their apparent inferior initial encoding of the film. Data were unavailable to determine if these younger children "went along" with the suggested information as some of the children in the King and Yuille study seem to have done.

The developmental studies discussed so far have consistently demonstrated that by the age of 10 or 11 years, children are no more vulnerable to suggestion than adults. However, the findings with respect to young school-age children (5 to 9 years) are less clear. In some studies these children appear to be less susceptible to leading information or at least no more susceptible, whereas in others they are significantly more affected. The results are quite difficult to interpret because there do not appear to be any methodological factors which consistently differentiate those studies that found age differences and those that failed to demonstrate such differences. These factors, which should theoretically have some impact on suggestibility, include interest level of the original stimulus, memory for the original stimulus, time delay between original presentation, presentation of suggested information, and assessment of suggestibility, and method of assessment.

Level of interest, knowledge base, and salience of an event or detail have been shown to influence the degree to which an individual is misled by postevent information. The studies that failed to find age differences or reported an advantage for young children employed a variety of stimuli, including audiotaped descriptions of crimes (Saywitz), cartoon slides (Duncan et al.), and a live argument between two adults (Marin et al.). Similarly, the studies demonstrating greater suggestibility in young children employed a film of a theft (Cohen & Harnick) and live events including a stranger tending plants and a bicycle theft (King & Yuille). There is no clear indication that one type of event is more interesting or less vulnerable to suggestion. In addition, two highly ecologically valid designs, employed by Marin et al. and by King and Yuille, produced different results.

Memory for the original event clearly plays a key role in susceptibility to suggested information. In two studies (Marin et al., 1979; Saywitz, Chapter 3, this volume), the youngest subjects were as accurate as the oldest in answering orthodox questions about the events, and these investigators failed to demonstrate age differences in suggestibility. In two other studies (King & Yuille, Chapter 2, this volume; Cohen & Harnick, 1980) there was an increase in recall with age, and the older children were better able to resist suggested information. However, Duncan et al. (1982) also found age differences in accuracy of recall, but failed to find the expected effect of age on suggestibility. In their study, younger children with good memories for the original stimulus were actually less suggestible than older subjects. Accuracy and richness of the original memory representation is clearly important, but the relationship between memory and suggestibility is not a simple one, and does not account for all of the age differences found.

The various studies also differ with respect to time intervals between the initial event, the suggestive information, and the final test. With adults, the interval between the event and suggestive information is critical, with longer intervals associated with greater influence. In other words, longer delays between event and postevent suggestion are more likely to increase vulnerability to memory change. Once again, the results of these studies do not provide a consistent picture. The longest delay between the original event and the introduction of suggested information was employed by Marin et al., who failed to find age differences in suggestibility. Three of the studies imposed delays of 5 days to 2 weeks between the introduction of suggested material and the final assessment. Two failed to find age differences (Saywitz; Marin et al.), while one clearly demonstrated age effects (Cohen & Harnick).

The method employed to assess recall and recognition has been shown to affect accuracy at all ages. Free recall is the most accurate, and in these studies it was fairly rare for misleading information to appear in narrative accounts. In the section on cued recall we concluded that subjects perform best when asked to select the correct response from an array of two or more choices. Subjects of all ages do less well with a short answer or true/false format. Interestingly, the one study that used a multiple choice format to assess suggestibility did find significant age differences (Cohen & Harnick). Researchers using the short answer or yes/no format obtained conflicting results.

The studies discussed thus far have not attempted to examine suggestibility in preschoolers. Three of the studies presented in this volume did include children as young as 3 years of age (Goodman et al., Chapter 1; Ceci et al., Chapter 5; Zaragoza, Chapter 4). Goodman et al. present the results of three studies. The first was designed to examine the types of information for which children might be most suggestible in addition to developmental changes in suggestibility. In this study, 3-year-olds, 6-year-olds, and adults participated in an arm-movement game with a man. After a 4- or 5-day delay, subjects were asked a series of questions about the event, including some leading questions. Overall, the children were more susceptible to suggested information. When information was categorized as central versus peripheral, the authors found that children were no more suggestible with respect to the central information. That is, the age differences were accounted for by the children's suggestibility regarding peripheral details of the event. Children were no more likely than adults to introduce suggested information into free-recall accounts. Goodman et al. also found that for all age groups, weaker memory for the event was associated with greater vulnerability to suggested information.

In a second study, Goodman et al. examined the effects of stress on children's memory for a real life event. Here, 3- to 7-year-old children either had their blood drawn (stress condition) or had a design placed on their arms (control condition). Children were questioned after a 3- to 4-day delay. Again, the authors found a correlation between age and suggestibility. Stress did not result in overall increases in suggestibility, but it did tend to focus the children's attention on central information. The authors conclude that stress may lead to a decrease in suggestibility for central information, but cause an increase in suggestibility for peripheral details.

In the third study, 3- to 6-year-old children received inoculations in a clinic, and were questioned about the event 3 to 4 days or 7 to 9 days later. The 5- to 6-year-olds showed greater resistance to misleading information than the 3- to 4-year-olds. All the children were more resistant to suggestions about the actions involved (75% accurate) and the nurse's appearance (76%) than to suggestions concerning characteristics of the room (57%).

Zaragoza (Chapter 4) presented 3- to 6-year-old children with a slide sequence taken from a children's storybook, and subsequently introduced misinformation about two of the slides during a verbal synopsis of the story. Following a 10-minute delay, children were presented with pairs of pictures, and were asked to identify the picture corresponding to the slide originally shown. Zaragoza employed two variations of the final memory test. The first was the traditional method used in this line of research; children were asked to choose between the original picture and one depicting the suggested information. The second method is a modified test, originally developed by McCloskey and Zaragoza (1985) in their work with adults. Children were asked to choose between the original picture and a new picture that included a detail not present in either the original stimulus or the suggested information. For example, if the original picture depicted a man holding a hammer and the verbal synopsis suggested he had been holding a screwdriver, the modified test included one picture with a hammer and one with a saw. The rationale of this modified design is to examine the extent to which a subject's memory for the original event was actually distorted by the suggested information. If the subject's memories were actually distorted by the introduction of misinformation (e.g., the man carried a screwdriver), such that the original trace is lost (hammer), then subjects should select the new information (saw) about 50% of the time—that is, at chance levels. If, on the other hand, the original trace does remain, there would be no demand factors operating to make the "wrong" choice by going along with the suggested information. In this case the subjects should be as accurate as they would be had no misinformation been introduced.

The children were tested on four pairs of pictures, two for which misinformation had been introduced and two for which neutral information had been provided in the synopsis (e.g., "tool"). The children assessed using the traditional test were significantly influenced by the misleading information. When misinformation had been introduced, they selected the original picture 54% of the time, in comparison to 77% accuracy in the absence of suggested information. In contrast, children in the modified test condition were equally accurate in the presence or absence of suggested information (69% and 70%, respectively). The results of a second study (Zaragoza, Chapter 4, this volume), in which the misinformation was presented twice during the synopsis, replicated the results of the first study. These findings suggest that when misinformation was introduced following the event, the original memory trace was not lost. Instead, the decrement in performance in the presence of suggested information appears to be accounted for by some other factor(s). Zaragoza suggests that demand factors account for some portion of the effect. Unfortunately, no comparisons of performance by age group are reported.

Finally, Ceci et al. (Chapter 5, this volume) examined suggestibility in subjects ranging in age from three years to adulthood, and their findings highlight the importance of demand characteristics in the questioning of young children. Subjects were told a simple story about a child, which was accompanied by drawings depicting the main action. Suggested information was presented 1 day later, and suggestibility was assessed following a 3-day delay, by means of a picture recognition task. The misleading questions pertained to relatively peripheral, descriptive details such as the color of an object or the type of food eaten. The younger children were more likely to select the picture containing the suggested information; by the age of 7, children were not as susceptible to this information. The age differences in suggestibility could not be accounted for by weaker memory in the younger children, because there were no age differences in accuracy of recognition for subjects who were not presented with misleading information.

One concern of Ceci et al. was to determine whether the apparently greater suggestibility of the young children might be the result of demand characteristics. They used the paradigm described above, but this time the misleading information was supplied by a 7-year-old child, and only young children served as subjects. This paradigm resulted in a significant decrease in suggestibility for the young children. In the first study, the 3-year-olds were only 37% accurate in recognizing the original pictures when suggestive information was provided by an adult. However, when it was provided by a child, it did not depress performance as much (accuracy = 53%). In both studies, a control group of 3-year-olds who were not presented with suggestive information were significantly more accurate than the experimental groups (accuracy = 84% in Experiment I).

In a third variation, Ceci et al. employed the modified test condition. Misleading information was again introduced by a child, but this time, the picture containing the suggested information was not offered as a choice during the final assessment procedure. For example, the original picture showed a boy wearing a red cap, and it was later suggested that the cap had been green. During the memory assessment, some of the children were asked to choose between a red cap and a blue one (modified condition), while others were shown a red cap and a green one (original condition).

The 3-year-olds in the modified test condition were 71% accurate in their selections, compared to 52% accuracy for the children in the original test condition. These findings provide excellent evidence that at least a portion of the apparently greater suggestibility in young children is actually the result of the demand characteristics of the situation. This implies that studies that fail to take such social factors into account will undoubtedly overestimate the effects of misleading information on children's memories. However, as Ceci et al. point out, demand characteristics do not account for all of the differences. Even when the misleading information was supplied by a child, thereby minimizing demand factors, and when the suggested information was not offered as a choice in the recognition task, the performance of the 3-year-olds was worse than the performance of their age peers who had received no misinformation (87%), and was also worse than the performance of the older children.

In a fourth experiment, Ceci et al. included an adult sample in the paradigm from Experiment III. They also had the 7-year-old misleader provide two pieces of accurate information to the subjects (his name and home town), in order to assess their attention to him. The results of this study were similar to the earlier findings. The preschoolers were most accurate in the control condition (no misleading information), and least accurate in the original test condition. The performance of the adult subjects was at or near ceiling levels for all three conditions; this was comparable to the 3-year-olds' for the control condition, but substantially better than their performance for the modified and original test conditions. Surprisingly, the preschoolers' memories were somewhat better for the accurate information provided by the misleader, when compared to the memories of the college students.

The finding that the performance of the subjects in the modified condition was worse than the performance of the subjects who did not receive misinformation seems inconsistent with Zaragoza's results. However, this apparent discrepancy may be explained at least in part by the way in which the data were analyzed in the two studies. Ceci et al. compared the performances of their subjects by age, and found that by the age of 7 years, children were fairly resistant to suggested information, even with the original test condition. It appears to have been only the 3-year-olds who were significantly influenced by suggested information, and for whom the test condition had a significant impact on accuracy. Zaragoza does not report age comparisons, instead averaging the performance of the 3- to 6-year-olds. It is possible that this methodology masked the suggestibility of the younger subjects.

Ceci et al. also mention an important factor which we have not yet discussed, namely, individual differences. They found that some of the preschoolers in their study successfully resisted the erroneous information, while others were greatly influenced. We know very little at this time about individual differences which may be associated with better memory or with vulnerability to suggested information.

Taken together, the results of these three lines of research suggest that children under 7 years of age are particularly vulnerable to misinformation regarding peripheral details of events, and this susceptibility to suggestion may be heightened in stressful situations. However, there is little evidence that they are more suggestible than adults with respect to the central aspects of an event. In addition, the demand characteristics of being given certain information by an adult, and even of being questioned by an adult are powerful components of suggestibility in young children.

Face Recognition Memory

Research on children's memory for faces has a history of using methodologies that are relatively removed from real-life events. It involves, for the most part, learning paradigms in which children are shown a set of face portraits for a short period of time. The children are subsequently presented with a large set of similar portraits which includes the original set, and are asked to identify the "familiar" faces. In a recent review of these studies, Chance and Goldstein (1984) concluded that they have shown almost unanimously that the rate of correct identifications increases with age, from about 35 to 40% accuracy at the kindergarten level to about 70 to 80% for 12- to 14-year-olds and adults. The tendency to make false identifications decreases with age. However, the one study that failed to demonstrate age differences was somewhat more true to life, in that subjects were not warned in advance that their memory would be tested, and there was an interference task between the presentation of the stimuli and the recognition test (Cross, Cross, & Daly, 1971).

Chance and Goldstein point to situational factors that may affect face-recognition memory, such as retention interval, familiarity, and disguises. In an eyewitness situation, the perpetrator may or may not be known to the child. If a crime is being committed, the perpetrator may have attempted to disguise himself, or may have either grown a beard or shaved in the interim between the crime and the identification procedure. Finally, the child may get only a brief glimpse of the person, or may view him over a more extended period of time, as in a case of sexual abuse. Chance and Goldstein conclude that recognition of *familiar* faces is quite good, even in children as young as 6 years, when the whole face can be clearly seen. Familiar faces seen under less optimal viewing conditions are also recognized, although not quite as well. Previously unfamiliar faces that were disguised and seen briefly are poorly recognized by children under the age of 10 years. They are better recognized by older children and adults; however, even adults have difficulty with some types of disguises, such as ones that alter facial features. Studies of face recognition in adults have demonstrated that longer retention intervals are associated with greater memory loss (see Chance & Goldstein, 1984, for a brief review). Comparable data are not yet available for children.

Although a clear developmental trend has been demonstrated in laboratory studies of face recognition memory, these findings cannot necessarily be generalized to more true-to-life eyewitness situations. In the standard recognition learning paradigm, subjects are generally forewarned about the impending memory test. They are given an opportunity to study the stimuli, and are then immediately presented with a recognition task. In contrast, an eyewitness situation generally occurs unexpectedly, and may be quite brief. The witness may not even be aware that something of significance has occurred. Such situations also differ with respect to the likelihood that the witness or victim will attend to the perpetrator's face, as well as the amount of time spent looking at the target. There may or may not be a long delay prior to an attempt to make an identification, and it is likely that some interference will occur in the interim. In addition, these events are often accompanied by some emotional response, such as fear, anxiety, or stress. This may be particularly true if the "witness" is also a victim.

As it turns out, face recognition in a more true-to-life eyewitness event is much more difficult for adults than the laboratory situation. In fact, performance in such simulation studies is typically quite poor, often at near chance levels (Goldstein, 1977). To date, there are only a handful of developmental studies of face-recognition memory in simulated eyewitness events, and the findings are inconsistent. As with the investigations of memory for events and suggestibility, the various studies are difficult to compare because of differences with respect to the ages of subjects, nature of the event, exposure time and retention interval, and method of assessment. However, some interesting findings are emerging.

One of the first attempts to examine age differences in face recognition using a simulation model was conducted by Marin et al. (1979). Subjects ranging in age from 5 years to college students observed an unexpected, brief argument between the experimenter and a confederate, and were subsequently presented with a 6-item photo array including a picture of the confederate. The recognition task was presented on two occasions: (1) following a 10 or 30 minute delay, during which an interference task was presented and (2) following a 2-week delay. Marin et al. found no significant effects of age, sex, or retention interval on accuracy of identifications. However, the results indicated a cubic trend, with the adolescents (13 to 14 years) outperforming both the younger subjects and the college students. The 5- to 6-year-olds were as accurate as the college students in this study (54%, compared to 75% accurate identifications for the 13- to 14-year-olds).

There is no reason to believe that face-recognition ability declines in young adulthood, so it seems reasonable to conclude that either situational factors, personal factors other than age, or some combination of the two, interact with age in this situation. Interestingly, although there were no main effects of sex on accuracy, there were large sex differences within two of the age groups. The adolescent girls were the most accurate, with 83% correctly identifying the male confederate; 67% of their male age peers made accurate identifications. The kindergarten girls' performance was comparable to the adolescent males (67%), while only 41% of the kindergarten boys made the correct identification. It may be that girls are simply better at this task, or it may be that 5- to 6-year-old girls and teenage girls are more interested in a male stranger and perhaps would spend more time looking at him. It is also possible that adults are more socialized to look away during a confrontation between two other adults. A replication of this study with a female confederate, or one that measured looking behavior, might improve our understanding of how such factors interact.

Goodman et al. (Chapter 1, this volume) also failed to find a steady increase with age in accuracy on a face-recognition task. In this study 3- and 6-year-old children and adults participated in an arm-movement game with a strange adult (male). This study differed from the Marin et al. study in several important ways. The social interaction was less unexpected, and subjects were exposed to the "target" for 5 minutes rather than 15 seconds. In addition, subjects were not asked to make an identification until 4 to 5 days following the event. The recognition test was a five-photo array including a picture of the experimenter. This task was apparently easier than the one posed by Marin et al. because the 6-year-olds were significantly more accurate than the adults, with correct identification rates of 93% and 75%, respectively. The 3-year-olds in this study were the least successful in their attempts to identify the photograph of the experimenter, with only 38% making the correct choice.

Goodman et al. reported three important results that were not examined by Marin et al. The first is the rate of false identifications made by the subjects. In a real-life eyewitness situation, we hope that a victim or witness will be able to identify the criminal, but we are also greatly concerned about the risk of false accusations. An accurate identification may result in the "bringing to justice" of one who has committed a crime, and may protect other potential victims from the repetition of such crimes by that individual. On the other hand, the inability of an eyewitness to make an identification may mean that a criminal goes free, and may lead to the commission of further criminal acts. However, a false identification has by far the most tragic result, because not only does the true criminal go free, but an innocent party suffers injustly, even if he or she is eventually acquitted. It seems to us that our greatest concern in the use of children as eyewitnesses should arise not if we find that they are less able to make a correct identification (an error of omission), but if we find that they are more likely to make a false identification (an error of commission).

Goodman et al. found that the age differences in false identifications paralleled those for correct identifications. The 3-year-olds made more false identifications than the older children and adults, and the 6-year-olds were least likely to make an erroneous identification.

Goodman et al. also measured the amount of time subjects spent looking at the experimenter. The 3-year-olds, who were least able to identify the experimenter, spent the least time looking at him during the interaction. Unfortunately, Goodman et al. do not tell us whether the 6-year-olds spent more time looking at the target than did the adults, so that the relationship between "looking time" and accuracy of identification is not entirely clear. It makes sense that more time spent "studying" a stimulus will result in a better memory for it, but why would we expect subjects of a certain age to spend more or less time looking at an individual? The Marin et al. findings suggest that the sex of the observer may play a role, and there may be an interaction between the age and sex of the observer and the age and sex of the target. Unfortunately, no sex differences are reported by Goodman et al.

In addition to the personal factors of age and sex, it is likely that certain situational factors also influence looking behavior. Goodman et al. report that the 3-year-olds were the most anxious, so much so that five of them refused to go into a room alone with a strange man. Unfortunately, it is unclear from their report whether these children were able to participate in the study (e.g., with a parent in the room), were replaced by less anxious 3-year-olds, or were simply not included in the analyses, thereby reducing the number of subjects in that age group. It is therefore difficult to hypothesize on the basis of these results about the effects, if any, of anxiety on face-recognition memory. However, it may be that anxiety decreases attention in some situations, thereby impairing an individual's ability to make an accurate identification.

The second study described by Goodman et al. (Chapter 1, this volume) was designed specifically to examine the effects of stress on eyewitness performance. Subjects were a small group of 3- to 7-year-old children who were seen in a clinic to have their blood drawn (stress condition) and a similar group of children who were brought to the same clinic, but had a design placed on their arms instead of the blood test (neutral condition). Recognition of the laboratory technician was assessed 3 to 4 days later by means of a six-item photograph array. Although the highly stressed children remembered significantly more central information than did the nonstressed children when they were asked objective questions about the event, there were no differences between these two groups with respect to accuracy of face recognition.

In their third study, Goodman et al. (Chapter 1, this volume) compared the face-recognition memory of 3- to 4-year-olds and 5- to 6-year-olds who came to a clinic for inoculations. Following a 3- to 4-day or 7- to 9-day delay, children were shown a six-item photo lineup and asked to identify the nurse who administered the shot. In contrast to the first study, there were no age differences in the rate of correct identifications over a 3- to 4-day delay (50% and 54% correct identifications for the younger and older groups, respectively). However, the performance of the younger group dropped to chance levels following a 7- to 9-day delay, but there was no effect of delay on the performance of the older children. The 3- to 4-year-olds made more false identifications than the 5- to 6-year-olds, although this difference was not significant.

Peters (Chapter 7, this volume) also made use of a naturally occurring stressful event to examine the effects of anxiety on children's face-recognition ability. Subjects, ranging from 3 to 8 years old, were asked to make eyewitness identifications regarding two events. The first event—a rather stressful one—was the child's first or second visit to the dentist. Following a 1- to 2-day delay or a 3- to 4-week delay, children were visited in their homes by a male experimenter who presented them with three 5-item photo lineups—one for the dentist (male), one for the dental assistant (female), and one for the dentist's office. Either 1 to 2 days or 3 to 4 weeks following this home visit, a second experimenter came to the home and asked the child to identify the first experimenter from a 5-item photo lineup. The purpose of this second visit was to assess face-recognition memory when the event (the first home visit) was believed to have been nonstressful. Exposure times were quite long in comparison to other face-recognition studies, with means of 13.4 minutes for the dentist, 15.5 minutes for the dental assistant, and 16.2 minutes for the experimenter.

Not surprisingly, the children were more anxious during the visit to the dentist than they were when visited at home by the experimenter. However, they were only moderately anxious in the first situation, and were somewhat anxious during the home visit as well. Nevertheless, anxiety (rated by dentists and parents) was negatively correlated with accuracy on the face recognition task. The 3- to 6-year-olds were more anxious than the 7- to 8-year-olds, and made fewer correct identifications and more false identifications. In addition, children were significantly better at recognizing the experimenter (71% accuracy) than the dentist

(43% accuracy), suggesting that anxiety impaired performance on the face-recognition task. In contrast, however, the children were just as accurate in their identification of the female dental assistant (64%) as they were for the experimenter, suggesting that anxiety alone cannot account for differences in accuracy. In addition, while Goodman et al. (Chapter 1, this volume) found that stress resulted in the narrowing of attention onto central information and away from peripheral details, Peters found the opposite. While anxiety impaired memory for the identification of central figures, it had no effect on memory for the room, which might be considered peripheral.

Surprisingly, these authors found no effect of retention interval on accuracy of face recognition. In addition, there were no sex differences, nor were there interaction effects for age and sex, as in the Marin et al. study.

In addition to manipulating anxiety, retention interval, and sex of the target, Peters introduced another important feature: half of the photo lineups were blank, that is, the target was not present. In true eyewitness situations, witnesses can be confronted with a lineup in which the target is absent, and the correct response would be to reject all of the choices. What do children do when faced with such a situation? From our discussion of cued recall we saw that children are less likely than adults to admit not knowing; rather, they tend to guess. Would children also do this in response to a blank lineup?

All children were told that the target might not be in the lineup. Nonetheless, it was rare for a child to make the correct response, that is, to reject the lineup, when it was blank. Overall, only 29% of the children rejected a blank lineup; 71% made false identifications from target-absent lineups, compared to 31% in the target-present condition. There were no age differences in response to target-absent lineups, and performance was equally poor for all three person targets (dentist, assistant, experimenter), in spite of significant differences in recognition when the target photographs were present. This suggests that even when memory for a face is good, a child may be prone to make a false identification when the correct choice is not offered.

Of the studies discussed so far, only Peters found a linear relationship between age and face-recognition memory, with 7- to 8-year-olds outperforming 3- to 6-year-olds. One study of King and Yuille (Chapter 2, this volume) found similar results. Here, 6- to 17-year-olds observed a stranger tending plants (the exposure time is not reported), and face-recognition memory was immediately assessed by means of an 8-item photo lineup. The 6-year-olds were less likely than the older children to correctly identify the target. In a second study, 8- to 14-year-old children observed a bicycle theft, and were again assessed immediately for recognition of the thief. This time, half of the lineups were blank. In the target-present condition, there were no age differences in face recognition, with 80% of the children in all age groups making the correct identification, and 10% in each group making false identifications.

In contrast, with a blank lineup, a significant effect of age was found. Of the 8- to 11-year-olds, 74% made a false identification when the target photo was not present (a level of performance close to that of the 3- to 8-year-olds in

Peters). In contrast, 36% of the 12- to 14-year-olds made this error, even though they were no more accurate in the target-present condition. Although the older children in this study did better than the younger ones when the correct choice was not offered, they still made more false identifications than when the target was present.

What do we make of these results? Three studies compared face recognition memory of children as young as 5 or 6 years of age and adults. Marin et al. found no age differences, King and Yuille found 6-year-olds to be less accurate than adults, and Goodman et al. found the 6-year-olds were more accurate than adults. Exposure times ranged from 15 seconds to 5 minutes, retention intervals from immediate to 2 weeks. In two cases the subjects were observers and in one they were participants. Two studies included 3-year-olds, and these children were consistently less accurate than older children and adults. The results of the two studies using blank lineups are more consistent and are quite alarming. Children from 3 to 11 years of age perform dismally in this situation, with both studies reporting false identification rates of approximately 71 to 74%. By 12 to 14 years, children are much more likely to correctly reject a blank lineup, but their performance is still worse than that of age peers receiving a target present lineup.

At present, the relationship between stress or anxiety and face-recognition memory is unclear, but there is some evidence that moderate levels of anxiety impair performance on this task. However, in a highly stressful, brief encounter, face recognition does not appear to be any worse than in a similar but less stressful interaction (Goodman et al., Chapter 1, this volume).

Conclusions

From the diverse set of studies discussed, several consistent findings have emerged with respect to children's memory for events. As with adults, free recall is more accurate than cued recall or recognition, but less information is provided during free recall. The amount of information provided during free recall increases with age, reaching adult levels by about 12 years of age. The information freely recalled by children tends to be as accurate as adult accounts. With respect to inaccuracies, children under 6 years of age are least likely to introduce inaccurate information into their accounts, while 8- to 9-year-olds are most likely to add extraneous, often implausible information, and adults seem to be most susceptible to errors of inference.

When memory is assessed by means of cued recall, subjects of all ages are more accurate with multiple choice questions than with either yes/no or short-answer questions. Most studies have found that the ability to answer true/false and short-answer questions is reasonably well-developed by the age of 5 or 6 years, and reaches adult levels by about 8 years. There is some evidence that errors of omission occur with greater frequency than errors of commission; that is, subjects are more likely to deny having seen or experienced an event than to falsely report an unexperienced detail. There is also some evidence that, at least for young children, memory for actions is better than memory for descriptive or peripheral details.

The results of the studies of malleability of memory in children are less clear cut. This small set of findings does not provide evidence that 10- to 11-year-old children are necessarily more suggestible than adults. The results for children in the 5- to 9-year age group are inconsistent, with some studies reporting greater susceptibility to suggestion, some reporting less susceptibility, and still others reporting no age differences. These inconsistencies are probably accounted for, at least in part, by an interaction among several factors, including interest level, memory for the event, and demand factors. There is evidence from anecdotal reports that at times children will "go along with" an experimenter's suggestion because they believe it is expected.

More work is needed to fully understand the issue of suggestibility in pre-schoolers. One study suggested that they may not be more suggestible for central aspects of an event, including action-related information. However, they were more susceptible than older children and adults to misinformation concerning peripheral, descriptive details. An interaction with stress may exist. Stress may cause a further focusing on central information, while leading to greater sug-gestibility for peripheral details (because the child's memory for these details is poorer).

The question of how suggested information affects a child's memory is not yet clear. It may serve to "fill in" where the original memory trace was weak, or it may actually distort an existing memory. It may have no impact on memory, but simply compel the child to report inaccurate information in an effort to please an adult. The evidence presented thus far suggests that all of these factors are in operation, particularly for preschoolers.

The area of greatest concern to us involves false identifications. The results are again inconsistent with respect to children 6 years old and older; at times they perform more poorly than older children and adults, and at times their perfor-mance has been shown to be superior (in a target-present test). Preschoolers, on the other hand, consistently make fewer correct identifications and more false identifications. Of particular concern is the finding that subjects of all ages are highly likely to make a false identification when the target stimulus (e.g., photo-graph) is absent, even when they are informed the picture may not be there. Although adults also perform poorly with target-absent tests, the performance of children up to 11 years of age is particularly dismal.

Most of the studies discussed in this chapter are applicable only to the memory of children for one-time, relatively brief occurrences involving a stranger. Only a few of the newer naturalistic studies of preschoolers are readily generalizable to recurrent events involving a person or persons known to the child, and the results of these studies are more optimistic. They suggest that very young chil-dren can provide reasonably accurate information concerning past events, and provide some guidelines for eliciting information from children at different ages. They also point to some of the limitations we can expect from young children with respect to the types of details they may be equipped to provide.

To complement basic research, further research efforts should continue to employ methodologies more closely approximating real-life situations, and should clearly specifiy the types of information sought. Because children of all ages can provide at least some information about previously experienced events, the challenge for researchers is to learn how we can elicit information that is maximally accurate. We need to learn more about the use of location and prop cues, and about methods of questioning children that would minimize demand characteristics. One possibility would be to develop programs for teaching children to admit to not knowing an answer, rather than guessing or going along with what they believe is expected. They should be routinely questioned about the source of their response; are they guessing, did someone else tell them, or do they remember that detail on their own? In the case of using photo or live lineups, it may be that children could be taught first to reject a blank lineup by being asked to identify themselves or the interviewer in a series of blank and target-present lineups.

In summary, there are clearly some special problems in the memory of children for events and in their reporting of these events. However, this should not imply that children are unfit to provide eyewitness testimony. The challenge to both psychologists and legal professionals is to expand our efforts to keep the baby without the bath water.

Acknowledgment. The writing of this chapter was supported in part by a grant from the National Institute of Mental Health.

References

Berliner, L., & Barbieri, M. K. (1984). The testimony of the child victim of sexual assault. *Journal of Social Issues, 40*(2), 125–137.

Brown, A. L. (1979). Theories of memory and the problem of development: Activity, growth and knowledge. In L. Cermak & F. I. M. Craik (Eds.), *Levels of processing in memory* (pp. 225–258). Hillsdale, NJ: Erlbaum.

Brown, A. L., Bransford, J. D., Ferrara, R. A., & Campione, J. C. (1983). Learning, remembering, and understanding. In J. H. Flavell & E. M. Markman (Eds.), *Handbook of child psychology* (Vol. 3, pp. 77–166). New York: Wiley.

Chance, J. E., & Goldstein, A. G. (1984). Face-recognition memory: Implications for children's eyewitness testimony. *Journal of Social Issues, 40*(2), 69–85.

Chi, M. T. H. (1976). Short-term memory limitations in children: Capacity or processing deficits? *Memory and Cognition, 4*, 201–210.

Cross, J. F., Cross, J., & Daly, J. (1971). Sex, race, age, and beauty as factors in recognition of faces. *Perception and Psychophysics, 10*, 393–396.

Dale, P. S., Loftus, E. F., & Rathbun, L. (1978). The influence of the form of the question on the eyewitness testimony of preschool children. *Journal of Psycholinguistic Research, 7*, 269–277.

Duncan, E. M., Whitney, P., & Kunen, S. (1982). Integration of visual and verbal information in chidlren's memories. *Child Development, 53*, 1215–1223.

Goldstein, A. G. (1977). The fallibility of the eyewitness: Psychological evidence. In B. D. Sales (Ed.), *Psychology in the legal process* (pp. 223–247). New York: Spectrum.

Goodman, G. S. (1980). Picture memory: How the action schema affects retention. *Cognitive Psychology, 12*, 77–94.

Jampole, L. (1986, May). *An assessment of the behavior of sexually abused and nonsexually abused children with anatomically correct dolls.* Paper presented the Fourth National Conference on Sexual Victimization of Children, New Orleans, LA.

Jones, D. P. H. (1985, November). *Reliable and fictitious accounts of sexual abuse in children.* Paper presented at the Seventh National Conference on Child Abuse and Neglect, Chicago, IL.

Loftus, E. F. (1979). *Eyewitness testimony.* Cambridge, MA: Harvard University Press.

Loftus, E. F., & Davies, G. M. (1984). Distortions in the memory of children. *Journal of Social Issues, 40*(2), 51–67.

Malpass, R., & Devine, P. G. (1981). Guided memory in eyewitness identification. *Journal of Applied Psychology, 66*, 343–350.

Marin, B. V., Holmes, D. L., Guth, M., & Kovac, P. (1979). The potential of children as eyewitnesses. *Law and Human Behavior, 3*, 295–305.

McCloskey, M., & Zaragoza, M. S. (1985). Misleading postevent information and memory for events: Arguments and evidence against memory impairment hypotheses. *Journal of Experimental Psychology: General, 114*, 1–16.

Nelson, K. (1978). How children represent knowledge of their world in and out of language: A preliminary report. In R. Siegler (Ed.), *Children's thinking: What develops?* (pp. 225–273). Hillsdale, NJ: Erlbaum.

Nelson, K., & Ross, G. (1980). The generalities and specifics of long-term memory in infants and young children. In M. Perlmutter (Ed.), *Chidlren's memory: New directions for child development, No. 10* (pp. 87–101). San Francisco: Jossey-Bass.

Powers, P. A., Andriks, J. L., & Loftus, E. F. (1979). Eyewitness accounts of females and males. *Journal of Applied Psychology, 64*, 339–347.

Price, D. (1984). *The development of children's comprehension of recurring episodes.* Unpublished doctoral dissertation, University of Denver, Colorado.

Todd, C., & Perlmutter, M. (1980). Reality recalled by preschool children. In M. Perlmutter (Ed.), *New directions for child development, No. 10* (pp. 69–85). San Francisco: Jossey-Bass.

Varendonck, J. (1911). Les témoignanes d'enfants dans un procès retentissant. *Archives de Psychologie, 11*, 129–171.

11
Getting Out of a Rut: Detours to Less Traveled Paths in Child-Witness Research[1]

GARY B. MELTON and ROSS A. THOMPSON

As public interest in child maltreatment (especially sexual abuse) has risen markedly in the past two or three years, so too has professional attention to the problem. Much of the professional discussion has focused on problems of children's interaction with the legal system. Especially acute issues arise from efforts to balance responses to children's purported vulnerability as eyewitnesses with constitutional guarantees of due process for the defendant and traditional reservations about the competency of children's testimony. Such issues have been addressed by numerous blue-ribbon groups: among them, the Attorney General's Task Force on Family Violence (1984), the Justice Department's (1984) national symposium on child molestation, the national symposium on child sexual abuse sponsored by the National Council of Juvenile and Family Court Judges in 1985, and the President's Task Force on Victims of Crime (1982). Congress (Missing Children's Assistance Act of 1984; Senate Subcommittee, 1984) has indicated a need for increased sensitivity to the needs of child victim/witnesses, and state legislatures have issued a plethora of new statutes governing children's testimony (Bulkley, 1985, 1986). The American Bar Association (1985) has adopted guidelines for "fair treatment" of child witnessess who allegedly have been abused.

Psychologists have contributed occasionally to the debate about policies and practices related to child witnesses (see especially Goodman's, 1984, symposium issue of the *Journal of Social Issues*; see also Melton, 1985, reporting Congressional testimony on behalf of the American Psychological Association and the Association for the Advancement of Psychology). Nonetheless, the problem has received remarkably little systematic attention from academic psychologists—or, for that matter, scholars of any discipline. At several national invited symposia, one of us (Melton) has found himself to be one of only two academicians. Indeed, researchers are matched only by defense attorneys in their underrepresentation at national symposia on sexual abuse.

---

[1]This chapter is based in part upon papers presented by the first author at the meeting of the American Psychology-Law Society in Tucson in March 1986 and the Fourth National Conference on the Sexual Victimization of Children in New Orleans in May 1986.

Two reasons occur to us for this conspicuous absence of research psychologists from this policy arena. First, the debate about the proper course of action concerning child victims has rested on a priori assumptions about children's vulnerability in the legal process and the effects of sexual abuse. For the most part, these assumptions have not been recognized as arguable and testable (Melton, in press b). Second, psychologists interested in studying children as witnesses typically have not focused on the most pressing psycholegal issues.

As reflected in this volume, most of the available research has focused on children's competency and credibility as witnesses. Our own early work on this topic (Melton, 1981a) arose from study of children's involvement as legal actors (see generally Melton, Koocher, & Saks, 1983), a topic which was essentially unresearched five years ago but is now one of the best developed areas of psycholegal scholarship about children (Melton, 1984b). Given the obvious relevance of research and theory on cognitive, social, and moral development, testimonial competence was a natural topic for psychological study. Moreover, as this volume illustrates, research on child witnesses has expanded with greater use of externally valid designs and of increasingly younger children as participants. Although the psychological literature on child witnesses was virtually nonexistent just a few years ago, knowledge now is sufficiently advanced to reach scholarly consensus about several dimensions of children's competence to testify.

Despite these salutary developments, we are concerned that child-witness research may be headed down the path that has led psycholegal researchers astray in other circumstances (cf. Monahan & Loftus, 1982). It is too easy to travel the road that leads "naturally" from one's training as a psychologist—simply to focus on children's cognition and memory because it fits easily with existing methods and knowledge. Although this path may be well traveled, it leads in the wrong direction. The research that would be most probative on the legal issues about child witnesses has yet to be undertaken. We intend in this chapter to provide a road map to new directions in child-witness research that might provide better guidance to policy makers.

Competency as an Interactive Construct

Child, Task, and Context

Children traditionally have been viewed as suspect eyewitnesses because of widely held perceptions that they are suggestible and can be easily manipulated, have difficulty distinguishing truth from fantasy, and are frequently uncooperative. This has resulted in a rebuttable common-law presumption that the testimony of children as a class is untrustworthy. Consequently, the research conducted by students of children's eyewitness testimony has focused on the variety of cognitive and memorial, communicative, and (less frequently) moral competencies that emerge with development, and their implications for the veracity of the eyewitness accounts of children at different ages. Like the legal debate over child competency, the perspective adopted by psycholegal researchers about children's credibility is largely age-graded: how does the quality of eye-witness testimony change as children grow older? Several themes have emerged in this small but growing literature, and each is reflected in the contributions to this volume.

MEMORY AND TASK DEMANDS

First, there has been considerable attention devoted to spontaneous errors or dis-tortions in the recollections of children at different ages. There is good reason to be concerned about the capacity of young children to produce a coherent, inter-nally consistent, and accurate account of events previously observed. The fact that preschoolers are poorer in free-recall ability, compared to older children and adults, is well documented (see reviews by Kail, 1984, and Perlmutter, 1986). In Chapter 2 of this volume, Saywitz found the same to be true of children's recall of crime stories. There are developmental changes in children's verbal production monitoring, and thus young children engage in less of the spontaneous self-monitoring of another's understanding, which results in a comprehensible, con-sistent communicative message (see, generally, Dickson, 1981; specifically, Asher, 1979; Robinson, 1981). There are also developmental changes in *compre-hension* monitoring, and thus younger children less frequently evaluate whether they have accurately understood another's message, instructions, or inquiries (Markman, 1977, 1979). Taken together, psychological research concerning cog-nitive and communicative skills relevant to eyewitness testimony seems to cast considerable doubt on the veracity of preschoolers' eyewitness accounts.

What is potentially misleading about this portrayal of developmental change, however, is that it masks the significant role that task demands play in young chil-dren's performance (see Ceci, Ross, & Toglia, Chapter 5, this volume; Gelman, 1978). For example, there is little change with age in children's recognition memory or in tasks where they are provided external cues to facilitate memory retrieval, and thus memory performance depends on the kind of memory skills required (Kail, 1984; Perlmutter, 1986). Consistent with this view, both Saywitz and Marin, Holmes, Guth, and Kovac (1979) found that, after hearing a story or witnessing an event, young children were just as accurate as older people when responding to true/false inquiries, even though their free recall was much poorer. Furthermore, in contrast to traditional views of the preschooler's misunderstand-ing of causal and temporal relations, researchers have now found that young children are sensitive to the temporal relations among events that occur in a logical, ordered sequence (Brown, 1976), can understand causality in familiar events (Berzonsky, 1971), and can appreciate others' viewpoints in simple situa-tions (Lempers, Flavell & Flavell, 1977; Shatz & Gelman, 1973). Although these competencies break down in the face of more complex task demands, it is clear that the requisite abilities can be manifested in simpler situations. In general, therefore, the emerging view of early cognitive and communicative development is that young children often perform inadequately in situations that are unfamil-iar to them or require complex reasoning, but they often perform at a level comparable to adults in simpler situations imposing fewer demands (Gelman, 1978; Perlmutter, 1986).

We think this perspective has profound implications for psycholegal analysis because it suggests that task demands may interact with the child's age in predicting the accuracy of eyewitness testimony. Very young children are more likely to produce a reliable account of events when specific, direct questions are posed, the temporal sequence of events is closely followed, external memory aids are used, and the questioner assumes responsibility for clarifying the child's understanding of inquiries and for clearing-up inconsistencies in the child's account. Conversely, the same children are likely to perform poorly when a global narrative of the account is solicited or the temporal order of events is violated. Furthermore, the child's familiarity and ease with the role of the examiner, the purpose of the inquiry, and the setting in which it occurs are also part of the context that is likely to be predictive of children's testimonial competency and credibility. Thus the prevailing emphasis on age-graded abilities in much of the current research on child eyewitnesses may be misguided because child (age) × task × context interactions are likely to be more informative than age alone in predicting competency and credibility.

Obviously, knowledge of the influence of task and contextual demands is a double-edged sword from the standpoint of trial strategy because it provides clues about how to undermine as well as bolster the accuracy of children's testimony. But this may not be a significant concern for several reasons. First, because cross-examination in trial occurs at the end of a long series of pretrial interviews during which the child's account is obtained and evaluated, the potential for strengthening a young child's credibility may occur largely before the trial begins. Indeed, a serious (and largely unexamined) concern with child eyewitnesses is with the potential for undermining eyewitness credibility through repeated interviews involving different investigators with varied agendae. Insofar as pretrial investigators remain sensitive to the influence of task demands on young children's accounting of events, they not only may obtain more reliable information but also may bolster (rather than undermine) the child's confident recall in cross-examination during trial. In addition, reducing the number of pretrial interviews, conducting them in a comfortable setting in the presence of a familiar caregiver, and using special aids to permit ease of recall are all likely to bolster the quality, credibility and consistency of the child's account during pretrial interviews as well as during the trial itself (Berliner & Barbieri, 1984). Second, it is also reasonable to expect judges and jury members to be sensitive to the efforts of a defense attorney to confuse and undermine a young child in court (although this remains an empirical question, and thus another detour to much-needed further research).

SUGGESTIBILITY AND THE NATURE OF THE EVENT

A second and related theme that has emerged in the research literature on child eyewitness testimony concerns children's susceptibility to suggestion. In this case, the concern is with the success of a rather deliberate effort by another to influence a child's recollection of events, rather than the naturally occurring distortions of the child's own memory. The chapters in this volume by King and Yuille (Chapter 2), Zaragoza (Chapter 4), Ceci, Ross, and Toglia (Chapter 5), and Goodman, Aman, and Hirschman (Chapter 1) all focus primarily on age differences in susceptibility to suggestion, as do most studies on this topic. Although results from this literature have been mixed, they suggest in general that younger children are more prone to misleading suggestion, especially from an authority, than are older children.

As several of the authors in this volume have noted, however, this conclusion must be qualified by the nature of the events to be recalled in the face of leading questions. For example, in most research the focus of misleading suggestion is on peripheral elements of the situation (e.g., did the boy have a red or blue cap?) rather than central elements (e.g., did the man have a knife?), though there are certainly exceptions to this claim. As Goodman and colleagues and King and Yuille point out, however, even though young children (and adults) are apt to be confused about peripheral information, young children are resistant to suggestion concerning information that is salient to them and that they know well. Central elements of a witnessed event are likely to fall into the latter category.

Studies in eyewitness suggestion have also varied in the *kind* of event to be recalled: whether it is directly witnessed by a child, for example, or indirectly perceived through a film or story narrative. The salience of direct experience would lead us to expect greater resistance to suggestion than when story narratives are recalled, and this is what the research findings to date seem to indicate. Marin and colleagues (1979), for example, found no developmental differences in children's responses to misleading questions concerning an event they had witnessed personally, even though it lasted only 15 seconds (see also Goodman et al., Chapter 1, this volume).

It appears, therefore, that young children's susceptibility to suggestion is also influenced by the nature of the task and the context in which it occurs. When an event is salient, is experienced directly, and is well understood, children are likely to be more resistant to misleading inquiries than when the child is unsure or uninterested in what occurred. This may derive, in fact, from the effects of event salience and interest on the quality of memory encoding (e.g., Renninger & Wozniak, 1985). Thus research about eyewitness suggestion may be misled by an exclusive focus on age-graded capacities to withstand misleading inquiries because characteristics of the task and situation may interact profoundly with child competencies.

This kind of child × task × context interaction is important to psycholegal analysis because the kinds of events that most frequently compel child-eyewitness testimony (e.g., child sexual abuse) entail the kinds of salient, frequently occurring experiences that are likely to be most resistant to misleading suggestion. Furthermore, when the witnessed event occurs in the context of regular routines with which the child is familiar, the child's scripted knowledge of these routines (Nelson, 1981) also may facilitate recall and resistance to suggestion. On the other hand, there is evidence indicating that memory for typical instances or scripted events is characterized by distortions because of both false recognition and recall intrusions errors (Bellezza & Bower, 1981, 1982; Graesser, Woll, Kowalski, & Smith, 1980). This is because typical, as opposed to atypical, events "fit" the script or regular routine. The extent to which scripts may aid recall and resistance to suggestion is a researchable question. However, one must be cautious in drawing conclusions given the current paucity of research data. One reason for such caution is Deffenbacher's (1983) argument that heightened arousal impairs rather than facilitates recall in adults, suggesting that the relationship between event salience and quality of recall may assume an inverted-U function in children. Regardless, it is apparent that a focus on age alone does not provide a complete account of children's susceptibility to misleading suggestion. The influences of event salience, the child's interest and level of arousal, and the elements of the event to be recalled (i.e., peripheral or central) must also be considered as they interact with the growth of age-related competencies (Loftus & Davies, 1984).

INDIVIDUAL DIFFERENCES IN CHILD COMPETENCE AND JUROR REACTIONS

A third focus of current research on children's eyewitness testimony concerns jurors' perceptions of the child witness. Inspired by the work of Goodman (see Goodman, Golding, & Haith, 1984), researchers like Ross, Miller, and Moran (Chapter 8, this volume) and Leippe and Romanczyk (Chapter 9, this volume) have evaluated the perceptions of adults in jury simulation tasks when faced with identical eyewitness accounts attributed either to a young child or to older persons. Generally speaking, they have found that the mere age of the eyewitness influenced jurors' perceptions of the quality and credibility of testimony, although this did not always directly contribute to a judgment concerning a defendant's guilt.

One important characteristic of these studies merits attention. By abstracting the age of the eyewitness from the quality of the testimony, these studies provide a somewhat limited perspective on jurors' overall perceptions of child eyewitnesses. As the foregoing review of research makes clear, child eyewitness testimony differs from that of adults not only in the *source* of the account, but also its *quality*. By controlling the quality of the account and only varying information about the source, these studies focus on a limited (perhaps unimportant) aspect of jurors' perceptions of the child eyewitness. Thus it is unsurprising that in such studies, jurors tend to differentially evaluate the *same* testimony when it is provided by a young child compared to an adult, because jurors have (reasonably) different expectations for the quality of the account that is likely to be provided in each case.

Such studies may be informative in a different way, however, by suggesting that *individual differences* in the quality of the accounts provided by young children may be more important than the age of the eyewitness per se. That is, if jurors expect relatively poor accounts from young children on the witness stand (cf. Yarmey & Jones, 1983), then a young eyewitness' inconsistent report may be discounted because it confirms this expectation (Leippe & Romancyzk, Chapter 9, this volume), while a strong account may be given greater weight because it violates the expectation (Ross et al., Chapter 8, this volume). In each case, it is juror expectations *in interaction with* the perceived quality of the child's testimony that may best account for how the child's report is likely to be weighed, and the nature of this interaction probably varies with eyewitnesses of different ages. This suggests that students of jurors' perceptions of child eyewitnesses should consider how individual differences in the quality of child reports interact with juror expectations in determining how influential the child's account is likely to be.

At present, we know very little about the determinants of individual differences in the quality of young children's eyewitness testimony. As suggested above, the quality and consistency of pretrial preparation is likely to significantly influence the coherence and internal consistency of a young child's account. "Status" characteristics of the child may also be influential, such as the child's socioeconomic background (e.g., quality and frequency of prior contact with legal authorities, linguistic style, conversational skills with unfamiliar adults), ethnic or racial group membership, breadth of prior social experiences (including out-of-home care), and other factors. The fact that the bases of individual differences in the quality of young children's eyewitness accounts is essentially "terra incognita" mandates greater attention to the nature of child (individual differences) × context (juror expectations) interactions in future studies of child competency in eyewitness testimony.

SUMMARY

In all, our argument is that in adopting a primarily psychologically based age-graded orientation to the study of children's eyewitness testimony, many researchers are missing most of the important policy-relevant issues meriting empirical study. Because age-graded skills are likely to interact profoundly with the nature of task demands and contextual features in children's performance, the issue of establishing age-graded parameters to children's competency to testify seems less important than establishing the features of the task and context that optimally support accurate, consistent reporting. From a policy analytic standpoint, the important questions meriting attention thus concern how to conduct pretrial interviews and courtroom examination in a manner that enhances a young child's repertorial skills, while maintaining appropriate concern for due process. Even young children (e.g., 4-year-olds) typically do have the capacity to respond to the demands of testimony, when questions are posed in a developmentally appropriate way.

The research that we have reviewed speaks more to children's *credibility* than their *competency*. Increasing the quality of child (and adult) witnesses' reports is a matter of concern at all phases of the legal process, not simply formal testimony. Similarly, even if a child's testimony is not so unreliable as to warrant outright exclusion (and, therefore, is competent), bolstering its probative value (and, therefore, its apparent credibility) still is desirable.

Whose Competency Matters?

Our discussion so far has focused on research that may be relevant to the development of procedures that will enhance the accuracy and credibility of children's testimony. The question of competency per se is relatively well settled because there is little reason to believe that children as a class are inherently untrustworthy. However, even if significant differences do exist between children and adults in their skills as witnesses, such findings respond to the wrong question. If not irrelevant to the usefulness of their testimony, children's skills per se are not especially important. The critical question is the competency of the *factfinder* (the judge or jury).

The presumption that children are incompetent to testify has always been rebuttable by a showing that the particular child in question possessed sufficiently great honesty, reality monitoring, and memory to provide testimony that would enhance justice (see, generally, Melton, 1981a). This finding was based on a wide-ranging voir dire (interview) of the child that probably lacks any significant validity. The current trend toward adoption of a presumption that *all* witnesses are competent (Federal Rule of Evidence 601) has not changed this process substantially. The presumption, although reversed, is still rebuttable.

Thus, even if the child's testimony is unreliable, the voir dire—itself of dubious validity (Goodman, 1986; Melton, 1981a)—will consume the time of the court. Therefore, as long as jurors are not misled by children's testimony (no matter how fragmented), justice will be served by its admission into evidence. As a matter of policy, we should be concerned not with children's competency per se, but instead their competency *in interaction with* that of the factfinder. Communicative skill is an attribute of speaker-listener pairs, not just the speaker. Given the linguistic competencies of children at various ages, will juries be significantly less capable of making accurate inferences about the reality being described than if they were listening to adult witnesses? Even if jurors are unable to make sense of part of what the child has to say, justice will be served (or at least not harmed) by admission of the testimony, if the factfinder is not misled toward an erroneous conviction. Although the factfinder's failure to comprehend a child's attempt to communicate that a crime did occur is indeed unfortunate, such an error is tolerable in a system of justice in which the defendant is presumed innocent. On the other hand, no matter what the relative competency of children to adults, exclusion of children's testimony would be desirable if juries were inclined to perceive legally relevant events in children's accounts that did not actually occur (or at least did not occur as the factfinder understood them to have happened).

JURORS' RESPONSES TO CHILDREN'S TESTIMONY

The available research on jurors' responses to children's testimony has focused on their attitudes and beliefs about children as witnesses or the degree to which they relied upon a child's testimony in rendering a verdict. These findings have sub-stantial implications for trial strategy but minimal relevance for legal policy. An attorney considering whether to put a child on the stand must make a judgment whether the testimony is likely to help the case. The attorney also needs to know if the jurors are apt to have prejudices about children's testimony that must be debunked and, if so, whether and how such change can be facilitated. Conversely, an attorney cross-examining a child can benefit from knowing attitudes and beliefs of jurors that can be built upon to discredit the witness.

The existing literature is relevant to evidentiary issues only insofar as the studies of the weight that jurors give to children's testimony provide some infor-mation about its prejudicial value. (Relevant evidence generally is admissible when its probative value exceeds its prejudicial value and its tendency to mislead or confuse; see Federal Rule of Evidence 403.) Data are lacking about the critical question: will jurors be misled by children's testimony?

CHILD-ADULT COMMUNICATION

Unfortunately, little research exists on child-adult communication to provide a basis even for speculation on this point. Nearly all the research on the growth of communication skills in children focuses on utterances to familiar adults, typi-cally the mother, and most concerns child abilities, not adult understanding (Shatz, 1983). This work cannot easily be generalized to communications with unfamiliar adults in any case because young children's language is often egocen-tric in quality, entailing reference to idiosyncratic events, objects or people in the child's prior experiences and often responding indirectly (if at all) to the other person's messages (cf. Asher, 1979). Because of these deficiencies in production and comprehension monitoring (see above), familiar adults like the mother can more easily comprehend a young child's utterances because of their greater understanding of the child's frame of reference and background experiences. They are also better acquainted with the child's phonological idiosyncracies and thus can better comprehend the spoken message. Thus, for example, Robinson (1981) has reported that only 9% of the utterances of preschoolers (age 3½ to 5½) were not understood adequately by familiar teachers. But lacking this knowledge, unfamiliar listeners are at a marked disadvantage in communicating with young children. Locke (1979), for example, found that naive adults had difficulty agreeing in their interpretations of what young children had spoken, and that their perceptions of child speech were significantly influenced by their expectations of what the child would say in certain situations. Thus there is rea-son to expect unfamiliar adults like jurors to have considerable difficulty under-standing the verbal communications of young children.

The question of whether jurors make proper inferences from children's tes-timony is not limited to adults' ability to determine the "deep structure" (under-lying meaning; see Chomsky, 1968) of children's verbalizations and the corresponding reality. Presumably such sociolinguistic vagaries become unim-portant if the words themselves are misunderstood. Preschoolers' speech often is riddled with misarticulations. Common experience tells us that adults often must look to adults familiar to a young child for translation of the child's speech or at least confirmation that the word the child uttered was what the unfamiliar adult thought that it was. Without such interpretation (perhaps even with it), the possibility that unfamiliar adults will err in encoding the child's words certainly must be entertained, particularly given that the context of interrogation and testimony may lead the listener to assume that the child's utterance was about a legally relevant event.

In evaluating a 3-year-old boy several weeks after he had been placed in foster care after having suffered bruises allegedly inflicted by his mother, one of us experienced a vivid demonstration of the potential for error in comprehending the speech of a young child and consequent risk of error in adjudication based on a child's statement. After the boy pointed out (correctly) places on his body where he had had bruises when he entered foster care, he was asked how he got them. All that he would say was what sounded like "Beat kids." However, in talking with him for an extended period of time in which the phrase was repeated several times, the possibility became evident that what the boy was really attempting to say was "Because." We were never able to confirm which word (or words) was intended by "be-kiz."

Young children typically will correct adult listeners who misinterpret their speech. For example, children whose misarticulated speech (e.g., "wing" instead of "ring") leads adult listeners to misunderstand the child usually will deny incorrect inferences from their phonology (e.g., responding negatively to "Did you say 'wing'?"; see Locke, 1979). However, they may be inconsistent in doing so. Five-year-olds who listened to tapes of their own speech often were confused about their own intent when the speech included phonemic substitutions that made words ambiguous (e.g., "wing" or misarticulated "ring"; see Locke & Kutz, 1975). Although a validity study of adults' interpretations of children's sounds may be impossible (how can we know what the child *really* meant to say), a reliability study should be possible. Related to the broader question of the accuracy of jurors' inferences from children's testimony, it should be possible to examine whether jurors are inclined to ignore or rely upon young child witnesses' ambiguous verbalizations (especially when unfamiliar adults cannot achieve reliability of perception).

Summary

In general, in arguing for a portrayal of competency as an interactive construct, we propose that the predominantly age-graded child-centered focus of current competency research misses many of the important policy-relevant issues concerning children's eyewitness testimony. From the child's standpoint, the competency and credibility of testimony must be addressed as a function of the complex interactions among age-graded child capabilities, elements of the memory and communicative task relevant to testifying, and components of the overall procedural context within which testimony occurs. But more importantly, the child's capabilities must be viewed interactively with jurors' capacities to make use of such testimony in developing an accurate interpretation of events. Clearly, a plethora of new research issues follows from such an interactive analysis, as outlined above.

What Else Do We Need to Know?

Children's Perceptions of the Legal System

The discussion thus far suggests the need for basic developmental research, but with questions framed with an eye toward their ultimate sociolegal relevance (cf. Bermant, 1982). Another example is the need for basic research on children's concepts of and attitudes toward the legal process. Personality research and theory strongly suggest that child witnesses will find the legal process (whether pretrial or trial procedures) to be less stressful and their performance as witnesses will be improved if they are prepared sufficiently for the experience—"inoculated" against stress (cf. Meichenbaum, 1977). However, we have little scientific basis for knowing *how* to prepare child witnesses for their involvement in the legal process. If caseworkers and other professionals are to prepare children adequately, they must know what children's expectancies, beliefs, and affective responses to the legal process are likely to be, in different specific contexts and among children of various ages. Such information also would be useful in shaping courtroom procedures. For example, knowledge of whether children commonly are reassured or frightened by uniformed bailiffs and robed judges would be helpful in determining the level of courtroom formality that is most desirable when children testify. Unfortunately, we lack even unsystematic data about most of these concepts.

That is not to say that we know nothing that is relevant; rather, what we do know provides little guidance, even by implication, for preparing child witnesses. Particularly in the context of study of children's competence (see, generally, Melton et al., 1983), knowledge has expanded about the development of some critical legal concepts—for example, rights (Melton, 1980) and law itself (Tapp & Kohlberg, 1971; Tapp & Levine, 1974). Generally, this literature on legal socialization suggests that, at some time in middle childhood, children begin to understand the social and moral underpinnings of law (e.g., fairness), but they do not begin to understand legal principles as basic to human dignity (and therefore irrevocable by authority) until adolescence, if at all. The rate of development of these concepts appears strongly linked to social class and experiences with entitlement (cf. Coles, 1977). However, studies of respondents in delinquency proceedings have shown that experience with the legal system per se does not increase sophistication about legal concepts and their application to one's own situation (Grisso, 1981). Skills and confidence in responding to the demands of the legal process are unlikely to develop "naturally," even when an older child is faced with sympathetic legal professionals. Rather, systematic instruction and preparation are required.

Although the legal socialization literature provides some clues about the pedagogical processes that are likely to facilitate law-related education (see, e.g., Tapp
& Melton, 1983), it tells us little about specific content that will help child
witnesses cope with the legal process. We lack knowledge about children's understanding of the roles of the various actors in the legal process and the nature
and purpose of various legal procedures. For example, Grisso (1983) concluded
a review of research on juveniles' responses to attorneys with the following
statement:

> The present research allows us to do little more than recommend that one cannot take for
> granted that juveniles understand an advocate lawyer's roles and functions. Asking
> juveniles to decide whether or not to waive counsel [in delinquency proceedings] often
> may be a meaningless procedure, and automatically providing counsel does not assure that
> juveniles will benefit. Our knowledge is nowhere close to allowing us to suggest what may
> be done about these problems, except to make vague recommendations regarding the edu-
> cation of both children and lawyers. (p. 145)

Knowledge about children's concepts of attorneys is essentially nonexistent for
early and middle childhood (Grisso & Lovinguth, 1982). Grisso (1981) did
find that adolescents facing delinquency charges had some notion of the purpose
of defense attorneys and the interchangeability of the terms "attorney" and
"lawyer." However, they were less likely than adult offenders to comprehend
attorney-client privilege and to perceive the proceedings as adversary rather than
inquisitorial. Perhaps as a result, small-scale studies of adolescents, primarily in
delinquency proceedings, have shown negative attitudes toward attorneys and
expectations that they will not be true advocates (see, for reviews, Grisso, 1983;
Grisso & Lovinguth, 1982). It should be noted, though, that adults also tend to
lack confidence in attorneys (Wilson, 1981).

Attempts to analogize these findings to child witnesses are almost purely
speculative. However, it is probable that even more confusion and antipathy
about attorneys exist for children in that context. A child who is a witness, but not
a party in litigation, is in effect unrepresented. We do not know whether the concept of representation is meaningful to preschool and elementary-school-age
children. Surely the relationship must be confusing, though, to a child who occasionally or even frequently meets with, or is confronted by, various attorneys,
none of whom really represents the child. This confusion is apt to be heightened
by both the abstract nature of the attorneys' tasks and the actual ambiguity of
their role. When attorneys themselves are unsure about the proper role of guardians ad litem in divorce or abuse/neglect proceedings (see, e.g., Bersoff,
1976–1977), it would be surprising to find that children are certain how to make
use of them, no matter what their general perceptions of attorneys are. Similar
ambiguity is likely to be attached to persons assuming new roles in the legal
process, such as advocates for child witnesses (see, e.g., American Bar Association, 1985, Guideline 3e). Children's understanding of the process also is apt to
be hampered by its complexity. For example, in cases of intrafamilial maltreat-

ment, proceedings may be simultaneous in various courts. The child's interaction with the legal system may be primarily through a child-protective worker, who may behave variously as prosecutor, law enforcement officer, judge, therapist, and witness.

Child witnesses' perceptions of the legal process also are likely to be affected by the diverse roles that they themselves experience. On one hand, they are witnesses bringing evidence before the court. On the other hand, a child witness often also is the focus of the legal proceeding. The issue at hand, at least in effect, may be with whom he or she will live. In research on actual child witnesses, care should be taken, therefore, to separate the effects of being a witness from those of the dispute itself.

In examining children's reactions to the process, attention should not be limited to the affective tone of their responses. Given the unpleasantness of the circumstances that compel exercise of the authority of the legal system, the serious and somewhat unpredictable consequences of testimony, and the evaluation of performance attached to the task of testimony, a lack of anxiety would be surprising, regardless of the age of the witness. However, distress, especially if transient, does not necessarily reflect dissatisfaction. The awesome nature of the courtroom and the adversaries of the procedure—the opportunity for all parties to have a say—may be more important subjectively than the discomfort experienced (see Melton & Lind, 1982; Thibaut & Walker, 1978). Over the long term, the child's perception of being treated fairly may be more significant than the level of anxiety experienced. In that regard, research is needed about children's understanding of the symbolism of the legal process—for example, the significance of trial by jury and confrontation of witnesses—and their perception of personal control within the process.

Regardless of the specific topic, studies of children's understanding of the legal process should take into account the reality of the social context. A perception of being ignored in the process may reflect actually being ignored. Descriptive studies are needed of how legal actors (e.g., prosecutors) actually relate to child witnesses. Research about situational variables affecting children's perception of the fairness of legal procedures and their own sense of empowerment by the law also would be useful both in the design of procedures and the preparation of children for involvement in the process as witnesses. At present, such studies are essentially nonexistent (see Grisso, 1983).

Effects of Legal Reforms

In the past three years, state legislatures have enacted a deluge of new statutes designed to protect child witnesses from the psychological harm purported to arise from testimony and/or to increase the probability that their testimony will be taken and admitted into evidence. Among the more popular provisions are special hearsay exceptions, testimony by closed-circuit television, limitations on the audience during testimony by a child victim, and admissibility of videotaped depositions. These reforms arguably intrude, at a minimum, upon the defendant's sixth amendment rights to a public trial and confrontation of witnesses and the public's first amendment right, through the press, to access to the trial process (Melton, 1981b). In view of the ubiquity and rapidity with which reforms are being enacted and the fundamental nature of the interests that they may affect, it is surprising that so little study has been made of whether reforms really are needed and, if so, whether they are effective. At present, knowledge is limited largely to anecdotal reports from four cities studied in a project for the National Institute of Justice (Whitcomb, Shapiro, & Stellwagon, 1985). No systematic time-series or cross-jurisdictional comparisons of the effects of new statutes are available.

Effects Upon Children

The need for procedural reforms has not been persuasively demonstrated. Because of plea bargaining and family-court options, most child victims do not testify in open court even in jurisdictions in which prosecutorial policy is to file criminal charges (Rogers, 1982; Whitcomb et al., 1985). Furthermore, clinical impressions suggest that many children experience testimony as empowering rather than traumatic (Berliner & Barbieri, 1984; Rogers, 1982). Prosecutors often believe that if children can withstand depositions or testimony under unusual procedures, they also can meet the challenge of live testimony under conventional rules of procedure (Whitcomb et al., 1985). Whitcomb et al. (1985) also found that courtroom audiences are rarely present and, when present, seldom are perceived to bother child witnesses.

Systematic data are unavailable about the effects of the various procedural reforms. However, Whitcomb et al. (1985) reported an impression from their surveys that the reforms are seldom being applied. The lack of application results from a combination of factors: a strategic preference for live testimony, a belief that testimony under conventional procedures is not substantially more stressful than testimony or deposition under unusual procedures, and a belief that negative side effects may result from some of the procedures. For example, a deposition actually may place the child at closer proximity to the defendant without protection of the child by a judge (Whitcomb et al., 1985). Two-way closed-circuit testimony may be stranger and more anxiety-provoking than conventional testimony, and it may diminish the child's understanding of expectations for testimony (Melton, in press a). Procedural and evidentiary deviations also create grounds for appeal that may actually keep the child in limbo for an extended period of time and even require new testimony in a retrial. Clearly, research is needed to determine the actual effects of the various reforms before legislatures enact other laws that either may be ineffective and divert attention from more helpful interventions, or that may exacerbate rather than diminish stress, at least for some children.

EFFECTS UPON THE FACTFINDER

Given the fundamental importance in Anglo-American justice of ensuring that criminal defendants are tried fairly and that they are not convicted erroneously, one must adopt a skeptical view toward trial procedures that may intrude upon the protections embedded in conventional procedure. Several of the unconventional procedures that some states have adopted in sex-abuse cases raise concerns that they may mislead the jury and deprive defendants of due process. Defense attorneys have suggested that juries may be unable to judge witnesses' credibility in some instances in which their testimony is presented over a television monitor, whether live testimony via closed circuit or a deposition recorded on videotape. For example, if a child responds to facial expressions of others in the courtroom, this information probably would be unavailable. Also, the camera operator might affect jurors' perceptions, even inadvertently, by choice of camera angle and shot (e.g., zooms and pans). More generally, the few studies available of effects of videotaping suggest that both the televised presentation itself and variations in such presentation (e.g., black-and-white vs. color) affect jurors' attention and their perceptions of witness credibility and attractiveness (Bermant & Jacoubovitch, 1975; Farmer et al., 1976; Miller, 1976). In the face of such evidence, plausible objections may be made to televised testimony on grounds of violation of the rights to trial by jury, due process, and a fair trial.

Concerns also have been raised about procedures in which the child witness is physically separated from the defendant, who watches the testimony on closed-circuit television or through a one-way mirror. Such procedures may violate the defendant's sixth amendment right to confrontation of witnesses (see *United States v. Benfield*, 1979) and his due-process right to self-representation (see *Faretta v. California*, 1975). More subtly, questions have arisen about the effects on jurors of observing that the defendant is not permitted to confront the child face to face, unlike other witnesses. Does the fact of compelled physical separation of the child from the defendant create inferences of his guilt and dangerousness (cf. Fontaine & Kiger, 1978)? If so, such separation, like shackling of the defendant or dressing him in prison garb, usually would violate due process (see *Estelle v. Williams*, 1976; *Illinois vs. Allen*, 1970). The possibility certainly merits empirical study (cf. *Holbrook v. Flynn*, 1986, p. 4318, note 4).

EFFECTS UPON PROSECUTORS

Research is also needed to determine the effects of various legal reforms on prosecutors' behavior. If unconventional procedures (e.g., testimony via closed-circuit television) are available, will prosecutors be more likely to prosecute cases involving victimization of children? If so, the state's interest in enhancing justice may warrant some modification of criminal procedure (see *Globe Newspaper Co. v. Superior Court*, 1982). Even if such a justification fails, however, a marked increase in prosecutions as a result of a change in procedure may be significant in analyzing its desirability. Thus, even if a procedural or evidentiary change makes no real difference in the stress child witnesses experience or the credibility that judges and juries ascribe to them, prosecutors' perception of a difference may change the proportion of cases tried.

Getting Off a Slippery Slope

Perhaps the most basic issue yet to be addressed systematically by scholars is *when* child witnesses are at risk. It is axiomatic in evidence law that every person's evidence is essential for justice (*United States v. Nixon*, 1973). Establishment of special procedures for testimony by child witnesses requires that such procedures be applied no more broadly than necessary to meet the compelling state interest in the prevention of harm to children, at least insofar as constitutionally recognized interests are adversely affected (*Globe Newspaper Co. v. Superior Court*, 1982; see Melton, 1984a). Two implications follow from this legal principle. First, justification of special procedures for child witnesses as a class or for some identifiable part of the class requires evidence that such witnesses are at substantially greater risk than other witnesses and that the procedure proposed is effective but no more drastic than necessary to protect them. It is not self-evident that child victims of sexual abuse, for example, are at substantially greater risk from testimony under conventional procedures than other child victims, child witnesses of violent offenses, adult victims of sexual offenses, or even witnesses in general. Second, even if a particular class is identifiably at risk, a case-by-case showing may be required that the particular witness is *especially* vulnerable and that he or she can be assisted only by a procedural innovation that adversely affects constitutional interests of the defendant or the public (*Globe Newspaper Co. v. Superior Court*, 1982). Therefore, attention should be given to individual differences in response to various legal procedures, both conventional and unusual, so that speculation about the effects in particular cases can at least be informed.

In that regard, several points are noteworthy. First, in view of the fact that data still are lacking about aggregate effects, research illuminating individual differences obviously is unavailable at present. Second, because so few children actually testify (and even fewer, of course, give testimony under unconventional procedures), data about individual differences in response to actual variations in courtroom conditions may take substantial time to gather. Third, particularly given the lack of data about similarly situated child witnesses, requests for use of extraordinary procedures typically will require clinical scrutiny of the child and, in effect, putting the witness on trial. The harm from intrusions on privacy may outweigh whatever benefits would result from the change in procedure. Fourth, although the current impetus for study of child witnesses emanates from concern about child victims, child witness research also should consider the other contexts in which children may be witnesses—e.g., disputes about their custody; delinquency and status offense proceedings in which they might testify in their own behalf; criminal and tort cases in which they are eyewitnesses but not victims. Information is needed about the effects of legal procedures in these contexts for their own sake as well as determination of the special issues in children's testimony in maltreatment cases.

Conclusions

The research reported in this volume has many commendable features. In particular, the general attention to both internal and external validity is impressive. The attention to preschool children is also useful, given the substantial frequency of reports of maltreatment of very young children and apparently increasing frequency of their testimony. However, we also wish to exhort caution about continuing to study younger and younger children. Besides the fact that such an inquiry ultimately is unnecessary, it may divert attention from general findings of competency among older preschoolers and school-age children.

Our major point, though, is that the emphasis on competency is misplaced. Given the strong evidence already present that children usually can handle testimony when faced with age-appropriate demands, attention should turn where, as a matter of legal policy, it probably should have been initially: jurors' ability to draw proper inferences from children's testimony. Much research also is needed about the effects of the various statutory reforms adopted in recent years.

Most important, the focus of inquiry and legislation should be moved from testimony. Insofar as the goal is to assist child witnesses in the legal process and to increase the value of their evidence, courtroom testimony is relatively insignificant, even for those children who ultimately do testify. Therefore, the most pressing agenda is to learn more about children's understanding of and attitudes toward the legal process and legal actors and the ways in which the process itself shapes such understanding and attitudes. In that context, and in the others mentioned, attention should be paid to individual and situational as well as developmental differences. Individual and developmental differences in cognitive and social abilities should be considered as they interact with task patterns and affect the process of interviewing children throughout an investigation, not just at trial.

References

American Bar Association. (1985). *Guidelines for the fair treatment of child witnesses in cases where child abuse is alleged.* Washington, DC: Author.

Asher, S. R. (1979). Referential communication. In G. J. Whitehurst & B. J. Zimmerman (Eds.), *The functions of language and cognition* (pp. 175–197). New York: Academic Press.

Attorney General's Task Force on Family Violence. (1984, September). *Final report.* Washington, DC: Author.

Bellezza, F. S., & Bower, G. H. (1981). The representational and processing characteristics of scripts. *Bulletin of the psychonomic Society, 18*, 1–4.

Bellezza, F. S., & Bower, G. H. (1982). Remembering script-based text. *Poetics, 11*, 1–23.

Berliner, L., & Barbieri, M. K. (1984). The testimony of the child victim of sexual assault. *Journal of Social Issues, 40*(2), 125–137.

Bermant, G. (1982). Justifying social science research in terms of social benefit. In T. L. Beauchamp, R. R. Faden, R. J. Wallace, Jr., & L. Walters (Eds.), *Ethical issues in social science research* (pp. 125–143). Baltimore: Johns Hopkins University Press.

Bermant, G., & Jacoubovitch, M. D. (1975). Fish out of water: A brief overview of social and psychological concerns about videotaped trials. *Hastings Law Journal, 26*, 999–1011.

Bersoff, D. N. (1976–1977). Representation for children in custody decisions: All that glitters is not *Gault. Journal of Family Law, 15*, 27–49.

Berzonsky, M. (1971). The role of familiarity in children's explanations of physical causality. *Child Development, 42*, 702–715.

Brown, A. L. (1976). The construction of temporal succession by preoperational children. In A. D. Pick (Ed.), *Minnesota Symposia on Child Psychology*, Vol. 10 (pp. 28–83). Minneapolis: University of Minnesota Press.

Bulkley, J. (1985). *State legislative reform efforts and suggested future policy directions to improve legal intervention in child sexual abuse cases.* Washington, DC: National Legal Resource Center for Child Advocacy and Protection, American Bar Association.

Bulkley, J. (1986, May). [Speaker]. In R. D. Matthews (Mod.), *New legislative approaches for prevention and intervention.* Symposium presented at the Fourth National Conference on the Sexual Victimization of Children, New Orleans.

Chomsky, N. (1968). *Language and mind.* New York: Harcourt, Brace, Jovanovich.

Coles, R. (1977). *Children in crisis: Vol. 5. Privileged ones.* Boston: Little, Brown.

Deffenbacher, K. A. (1983). The influence of arousal on reliability of testimony. In S. M. A. Lloyd-Bostock & B. R. Clifford (Eds.), *Evaluating witness evidence* (pp. 235–251). Chichester, England: Wiley.

Dickson, W. P. (Ed.). (1981). *Children's oral communication skills.* New York: Academic Press.

Estelle v. Williams, 425 U.S. 501 (1976).

Faretta v. California, 422 U.S. 806(1975).

Farmer, L. C., Williams, G. R., Lee, R. E., Cundick, B. P., Howell, R. J., & Rooker, C. K. (1976). Juror perceptions of trial testimony as a function of the method of presentation. In G. Bermant, C. Nemeth, & N. Vidmar (Eds.), *Psychology and the law: Research frontiers* (pp. 209–238). Lexington, MA: Lexington Books.

Fontaine, G., & Kiger, R. (1978). The effects of defendant dress and supervision on judgments of simulated jurors: An exploratory study. *Law and Human Behavior, 2*, 63–72.

Gelman, R. (1978). Cognitive development. *Annual Review of Psychology, 29*, 297–332.

Globe Newspaper Co. v. Superior Court, 457 U.S. 596 (1982).

Goodman, G. S. (1984). The child witness. *Journal of Social Issues, 40*(2), [Special issue].

Goodman, G. S. (1986, May). [Panel presentation]. In S. J. Awalt (Chair), *Assessing the credibility of the child victim/witness.* Symposium presented at the Fourth National Conference on the Sexual Victimization of Children, New Orleans.

Goodman, G. S., Golding, J. M., & Haith, M. M. (1984). Jurors' reactions to child witnesses. *Journal of Social Issues, 40*(2), 139–156.

Graesser, A. C., Woll, S. B., Kowalski, D. J., & Smith, D. A. (1980). Memory for typical and atypical actions in scripted activities. *Journal of Experimental Psychology: HLM*, *6*, 503–515.

Grisso, T. (1981). *Juveniles' waiver of rights: Legal and psychological competence*. New York: Plenum.

Grisso, T. (1983). Juveniles' consent in delinquency proceedings. In G. B. Melton, G. P. Koocher, & M. J. Saks (Eds.), *Children's competence to consent* (pp. 131–148). New York: Plenum.

Grisso, T., & Lovinguth, T. (1982). Lawyers and child clients: A call for research. In J. S. Henning (Ed.), *The rights of children: Legal and psychological perspectives* (pp. 215–232). Springfield, IL: Charles C Thomas.

Holbrook v. Flynn, 54 U.S.L.W. 4315 (U.S. Mar. 25, 1986).

Illinois v. Allen, 397 U.S. 337 (1970).

Justice Department. (1984, October). *Protecting our children: The fight against molestation. A national symposium*. Washington, DC: Author.

Kail, R. (1984). *The development of memory in children* (2nd ed.). New York: W. H. Freeman.

Lempers, J. S., Flavell, E. R., & Flavell, J. H. (1977). The development in very young children of tacit knowledge concerning visual perception. *Genetic Psychology Monographs*, *95*, 3–53.

Locke, J. L. (1979). The child's processing of phonology. In W. A. Collins (Ed.), *Minnesota Symposia on Child Psychology: Vol. 12. Children's language and communication* (pp. 83–119). Hillsdale, NJ: Erlbaum.

Locke, J. L., & Kutz, K. J. (1975). Memory for speech and speech for memory. *Journal of Speech and Hearing Research*, *18*, 176–191.

Loftus, E. F., & Davies, G. M. (1984). Distortions in the memory of children. *Journal of Social Issues*, *40*(2), 51–67.

Marin, B. V., Holmes, D. L., Guth, M., & Kovac, P. (1979). The potential of children as eyewitnesses: A comparison of children and adults on eyewitnesses tasks. *Law and Human Behavior*, *3*, 295–306.

Markman, E. (1977). Realizing that you don't understand: A preliminary investigation. *Child Development*, *48*, 986–992.

Markman, E. (1979). Realizing that you don't understand: Elementary school children's awareness of inconsistencies. *Child Development*, *50*, 643–655.

Meichenbaum, D. (1977). *Cognitive-behavior modification: An integrative approach*. New York: Plenum.

Melton, G. B. (1980). Children's concepts of their rights. *Journal of Clinical Child Psychology*, *9*, 186–190.

Melton, G. B. (1981a). Children's competency to testify. *Law and Human Behavior*, *5*, 73–85.

Melton, G. B. (1981b). Procedural reforms to protect child victim/witnesses in sex-offense proceedings. In J. Bulkley (Ed.), *Child sexual abuse and the law* (pp. 184–198). Washington, DC: American Bar Association.

Melton, G. B. (1984a). Child witnesses and the first amendment: A psycholegal dilemma. *Journal of Social Issues*, *40*, 291–305.

Melton, G. B. (1984b). Developmental psychology and the law: The state of the art. *Journal of Family Law*, *22*, 445–482.

Melton, G. B. (1985). Sexually abused children and the legal system: Some policy recommendations. *American Journal of Family Therapy*, *13*, 61–67.

Melton, G. B. (in press a). Children's testimony in cases of alleged sexual abuse. In M. Wolraich & D. K. Routh (Eds.), *Advances in developmental and behavioral pediatrics*. Greenwich, CT: JAI Press.

Melton, G. B. (in press b). The clashing of symbols: Prelude to child and family policy. *American Psychologist*.

Melton, G. B., Koocher, G. P., & Saks, M. J. (Eds.). (1983). *Children's competence to consent*. New York: Plenum.

Melton, G. B., & Lind, E. A. (1982). Procedural justice in family court: Does the adversary model make sense? In G. B. Melton (Ed.), *Legal reforms affecting child and youth services* (pp. 64–83). New York: Haworth Press.

Missing Children's Assistance Act of 1984, 98 Stat. 2125.

Miller, G. R. (1976). The effects of videotaped trial materials on juror response. In G. Berman, C. Nemeth, & N. Vidmar (Eds.), *Psychology and the law: Research frontiers* (pp. 185–208). Lexington, MA: Lexington Books.

Monahan, J., & Loftus, E. F. (1982). The psychology of law. *Annual Review of Psychology, 33*, 441–475.

Nelson, K. (1981). Social cognition in a script framework. In J. H. Flavell & L. Ross (Eds.), *Social cognitive development* (pp. 97–118). Cambridge, England: Cambridge University Press.

Perlmutter, M. (1986). A life-span view of memory. In P. B. Baltes, D. L. Featherman, & R. M. Lerner (Eds.), *Life-span development and behavior* (pp. 271–313). Hillsdale, NJ: Erlbaum.

President's Task Force on Victims of Crime. (1982, December). *Final report*. Washington, DC: Author.

Renninger, K. A., & Wozniak, R. H. (1985). Effect of interest on attentional shift, recognition, and recall in young children. *Developmental Psychology, 21*, 624–632.

Robinson, E. J. (1981). The child's understanding of inadequate messages and communicative failure: A problem of ignorance or egocentrism? In W. P. Dickson (Ed.), *Children's oral communication skills* (pp. 167–188). New York: Academic Press.

Rogers, C. M. (1982). Child sexual abuse and the courts: Preliminary findings. In J. Conte & D. A. Shore (Eds.), *Social work and child sexual abuse* (pp. 145–153). New York: Haworth Press.

Senate Subcommittee on Juvenile Justice. (1984, May 2 and 22). *Child sexual abuse victims in the courts*. Oversight hearings (Senate hearing 98-1207).

Shatz, M. (1983). Communication. In P. H. Mussen (Ed.), *Handbook of child psychology: Vol. 3. Cognitive development* (J. H. Flavell & E. M. Markman, Vol. Eds.). New York: Wiley.

Shatz, M., & Gelman, R. (1973). The development of communication skills. *Monographs of the Society for Research in Child Development, 38* (Serial No. 152).

Tapp, J. L., & Kohlberg, L. (1971). Developing senses of law and legal justice. *Journal of Social Issues, 27*(2), 65–91.

Tapp, J. L., & Levine, F. J. (1974). Legal socialization: Strategies for an ethical legality. *Stanford Law Review, 27,* 1–72.

Tapp, J. L., & Melton, G. B. (1983). Preparing children for decision making: Implications of legal socialization research. In G. B. Melton, G. P. Koocher, & M. J. Saks (Eds.), *Children's competence to consent* (pp. 215–233). New York: Plenum.

Thibaut, J., & Walker, L. (1978). A theory of procedure. *California Law Review, 66*, 541–566.

United States v. Benfield, 593 F.2d 815 (8th Cir. 1979).

United States v. Nixon, 418 U.S. 683 (1973).

Whitcomb, D., Shapiro, E. R., & Stellwagen, L. D. (1985). *When the victim is a child: Issues for judges and prosecutors*. Washington, DC: National Institute of Justice.

Wilson, K. (1981). Nebraskans, lawyers, and the law: A two-year analysis. *Nebraska Law Review, 60*, 101–140.

Yarmey, A. D., & Jones, H. P. T. (1983). Is the psychology of eyewitness identification a matter of common sense? In S. M. A. Lloyd-Bostock & B. R. Clifford (Eds.), *Evaluating witness evidence* (pp. 13–40). Chichester, England: Wiley.

12
Setting the Stage for Psychological Research on the Child Eyewitness

JOHN W. TURTLE and GARY L. WELLS

Although it is true that psychologists have shown an interest in the eyewitnessing capabilities of children throughout this century (e.g., Binet, 1900, 1911; Dauber, 1912; Marbe, 1913; Mehl, 1912; Stern, 1910, 1939), we argue that psychological research on the child eyewitness is nascent. With the exception of Binet's studies on suggestibility, which were somewhat narrow and restricted in focus, research on the child eyewitness did not receive systematic treatment until quite recently. The birth of systematic approaches to the study of child eyewitnesses in the 1980s probably is due to two primary factors: the rapid development of a psychological literature on eyewitness testimony in general (marked by books by Clifford & Bull, 1978; Loftus, 1979; Wells & Loftus, 1984; Yarmey, 1979) and the contemporary salience of children as victims of crime. The development of an eyewitness testimony literature within psychology has facilitated the study of child eyewitnesses by enhancing awareness of the fallibility of eyewitnesses, refining paradigms for experimentally investigating eyewitness variables, and opening the door to applying the research results (e.g., via expert testimony). The salience of the child eyewitness as a special concern has been motivated in part by the dramatic increase in awareness that children are vulnerable and frequent victims of crime—especially in the area of sexual assault. In light of the pressing need to further our understanding of children's testimony, this chapter outlines a number of psycholegal variables that require further investigation so that more information can be made available to those responsible for constructing a policy to handle the child-witness' testimony.

Before discussing these variables in detail, however, we first review the major findings of the preceding chapters. We note that some of the chapters can be grouped by their focus on similar topics, and we discuss some of the commonalities among the contributions. We then direct our attention to the question of whether age is a special variable in eyewitnessing or whether it simply is another in the long list of variables affecting eyewitness accuracy. We conclude that it is a special variable, largely because of its relationship to extramemorial factors. We then move to a discussion of the suitability of current experimental paradigms for testing the adequacy of child eyewitnesses, especially with regard to the form of testimony. We recommend that much more emphasis be placed on research directed at how children perform under conditions of direct- and cross-examination. We argue as well that the range of situations confronting child eye-witnesses greatly exceeds the range that we can expect to simulate in laboratory or field experiments, and therefore theory must play a large role in the child-eyewitness literature. Particularly fruitful in this regard is research on the development of metamemory. Finally, we discuss the role that eyewitness researchers might have in influencing judicial policy on child-eyewitness matters.

Overview of the Preceding Chapters

The contributors to this volume have provided information and insight to aid our understanding of some of the differences between children's and adults' eyewitness testimony. There were many chapters that can be grouped together on the basis of their common attention to popular, and sometimes controversial, research issues. Children's suggestibility to misleading information, for instance, was the focus of three chapters: Chapter 2 by Mary Ann King and John Yuille, Chapter 4 by Maria Zaragoza and Chapter 5 by Stephen Ceci, David Ross, and Michael Toglia. King and Yuille reported findings from two studies that appear to run counter to the predictions they made, based on the developmental literature: Younger children were most affected by misleading questions that required the witness to infer the presence of an object that was not actually seen originally, despite those authors' expectations that such inferences were less likely to be made by children than by adults. In addition, children were shown to be resistant to misleading information regarding details that were predicted to be less salient than others, but turned out to be of particular relevance to children (i.e., running shoes). King and Yuille went on to discuss a forensically relevant perspective on suggestibility and recommended three methods for improving interviews of child-witnesses.

Maria Zaragoza also contributed a chapter concerned with children's susceptibility to misleading information. Zaragoza's discussion is consistent with the argument she has proposed in conjunction with Michael McCloskey (McCloskey & Zaragoza, 1985); namely, that the misinformation effect is not the result of a memory impairment caused by misleading information, but instead results from a combination of social and methodological factors. The six experiments conducted by McCloskey and Zaragoza (1985) demonstrated that people who were exposed to misleading information were no more likely than controls to be inaccurate on a forced-choice recognition task when an alternative consistent with the misleading information was not present in the test. This suggests that the original memory was not affected by the misinformation. This procedure, in which the test phase presents participants with a novel item to accompany the slide consistent with the original information, is referred to as the Modified Test procedure. McCloskey and Zaragoza concluded that misleading information does not impair adults' memory for the original event, but that the nature of a typical experiment, using the Original Test procedure, influences adults who receive misleading information merely to choose the alternative in the test phase that is consistent with the misleading information. Zaragoza's recent studies, reported in the current volume, demonstrate that when an alternative consistent with the misleading information was not provided in the forced-choice recognition task, misled child-witnesses were no more likely to be inaccurate than were those children who did not receive misleading information. Zaragoza has concluded that, like adult eyewitnesses, misleading information does not impair the memory of child eyewitnesses. Zaragoza points out that there are likely to be a number of factors (other than memory impairment) that can affect the likelihood that misled witnesses will choose the alternative consistent with the misleading information in the Original Test procedure. She also makes an important distinction between eyewitness testimony and eyewitness memory, and suggests that researchers should appreciate the memory/testimony distinction when they design their experiments.

Last in our discussion of chapters that dealt with children's susceptibility to misleading information is the contribution by Ceci, Ross, and Toglia, in which they presented four studies designed to investigate some of the social and cognitive factors affecting suggestibility. After demonstrating a main effect for age, Ceci et al.'s research demonstrated that young children's high suggestibility can be accounted for, at least in part, by the fact that they are especially likely to conform to what they believe to be the expectations of the adult. This conclusion was based on a study in which a 7-year-old boy served as the source of the misleading information for child eyewitnesses. The results of that study showed that when the source was no longer an authority figure, the children were significantly less likely to incorporate the misleading information into their testimony regarding the to-be-remembered event.

In addition, in Experiments 3 and 4, Ceci et al. investigated the suitability of the Original Test procedure for assessing the impact of misleading post-event information (e.g., Loftus, Miller, & Burns, 1978) with respect to the Modified Test procedure introduced by McCloskey and Zaragoza (1985) and discussed by Zaragoza in this volume. Ceci et al. found that, although the Modified test procedure significantly reduced the effect of misleading questions, it did not eliminate the misleading-question effect. Ceci et al. contend that the "all-or-none" way in which McCloskey and Zaragoza have framed the distinction between the two procedures does not reflect the complexities of the situation faced by a participant-witness in a misleading information study. Ceci et al. argue that a witness' memory for the original event and/or the postevent information could be a continuous variable, the value of which is determined by a number of factors relating to memory strength, such as the length of the retention interval, stimulus salience, and the number of repetitions. Ceci et al. suggest that the investigation of the effect of these factors on eyewitness accuracy will determine whether the Modified Test procedure is really a superior test of witnesses' susceptibility to misleading information, or whether its use actually eliminates the detection of the coexistence of memories for both the original event and the postevent information.

Turning from the issue of suggestibility differences between children and adults, two other chapters dealt with the topic of stress and children's eyewitness memory: Are children susceptible to the expected deleterious effects on memory of a stressful to-be-remembered event? In Chapter 7 by Douglas Peters and also Chapter 1 by Gail Goodman, Christine Aman, and Jodi Hirschman, studies were described in which stress was operationalized in some naturalistic settings. Peters and Goodman et al. should be commended for their originality in managing to realize a stressful event for children while observing strict ethical considerations. Peters used scheduled visits to the dentist as the stressful event and reported that children in that condition were not significantly less accurate than controls on a thorough battery of subsequent memory tests (although he notes that more intense levels of stress remain to be investigated). Similarly, Goodman et al. used an apparently stressful venipuncture experience and reported that stress did not result in poorer memory performance overall, but that it did interact with the type of information about which the children were questioned; namely, children in the stressed condition had better recall than controls for central information, but were significantly less accurate in their ability to remember peripheral information.

Some chapters took a different approach to the child eyewitness issue, in that their concern was with mock-jurors' perceptions and evaluations of children's testimony. Michael Leippe and Ann Romanczyk (Chapter 9) drew extensively from the established literature in social psychology regarding the effects of source and situational variables on people's assessments of others' credibility. Partly on the basis of that review and on the results of their two studies, Leippe and Romanczyk concluded that very young eyewitnesses are rated as less credible by mock-jurors, but that this evaluation did not lead the jurors to alter their verdicts of guilt as a function of the age of the eyewitness in most cases.

In their investigation of jurors' reactions to child eyewitnesses, David Ross, Beth Miller, and Patricia Moran (Chapter 8) obtained credibility ratings that are somewhat inconsistent with those found by Lieppe and Romanczyk: Participants rated the alleged testimony of a very young eyewitness as being equally credible to that given by a young adult and an elderly eyewitness. Not only was there no difference among the groups with respect to credibility, but a subsequent analysis of other eyewitness attributes evaluated by the participants in the study indicated that the very young witness was actually viewed more positively than the young adult. Ross et al.'s findings are consistent with those obtained by Lieppe and Romanczyk on another measure, however, in that neither group found a significant relationship between mock-jurors' ratings of the child-witness's credibility and their subsequent ratings of the defendant's guilt. Ross et al. pointed out that the findings from the relatively small number of studies dealing with mock-jurors' perceptions of very young eyewitnesses are not yet at the stage at which general conclusions can be drawn. They note that personality and situational factors specific to a given study, or to an actual case, very likely have a major impact on the credence paid to the age of the witness. Consistent with our discussion in the next section regarding age as a special variable in eyewitness research, Ross et al. maintain that it may not be age per se that drives mock-jurors' perceptions of eyewitness testimony, but rather it is the accompanying traits and attributes associated with witnesses of different ages, and their relationship to specific situational factors, that determines how a witness will be viewed on the stand.

Last in our review of the contributions to this volume is a discussion of two chapters whose topics do not coincide with the common categories we have constructed so far. Karen Saywitz (Chapter 3) reported a well-designed, general investigation of children's eyewitness memory. Saywitz concluded that, although 8- and 9-year-olds tended to have less complete recall, more embellishments, and a higher variance of intrusions compared to the 11- and 12-year-old and 15- and 16-year-old groups, the youngest children did not differ from the older children in their percentage correct on the recognition tasks, the types of intrusions, or their susceptibility to misleading information. Furthermore, Saywitz pointed out an interesting finding: the ratio of distorted to accurate information during recall did not differ significantly across the three age groups.

D. Stephen Lindsay and Marcia Johnson (Chapter 6) discussed the development of children's ability to discriminate between real and imagined events and between different sources of information (that is, information from the original event versus information acquired after the to-be-remembered event has occurred). Much of Lindsay and Johnson's perspective is consistent with our discussion of metamemory development later in this chapter, namely, that the child's knowledge about his or her memory abilities and shortcomings is an integral variable that affects the accuracy and credibility of the child's testimony. In addition, the studies proposed by Lindsay and Johnson, in which children are asked to distinguish among the sources of various types of postevent information, have especially important potential. These studies should help to resolve the current controversy regarding the incorporation of misleading information, which pits the memorial impairment hypothesis (e.g., Loftus, 1979) against a host of extramemorial factors that almost certainly affect the likelihood that information inconsistent with the original event will be incorporated into a witness' testimony (e.g., McCloskey & Zaragoza, 1985).

The preceding chapters constitute an excellent overview of the current state of eyewitness research as it pertains to children. Contributions ranged from overall perspectives on general aspects of children's memory to detailed results and conclusions drawn from the researchers' laboratory and field experiments. We now move on to a discussion of a variable that has special status in this volume, then to the relative benefits of different research strategies, and finally to recommendations for the direction further research should follow.

Age as a Special Variable

Implicit in the contributions to this volume is the supposition that age is a special variable in eyewitnessing. It might prove instructive, however, to explore this supposition: Is age a special variable in eyewitnessing and, if so, why is it special?

The answer is not immediately obvious. It might be argued, for example, that age is a special variable because eyewitnesses who are under a particular age (e.g., 10 years) are especially prone to giving inaccurate eyewitness reports. However, the same claim could be made for numerous other variables, such as the duration of exposure to a witnessed event (e.g., less than 10 seconds duration vs. longer durations). Thus, the fact that age is related to eyewitness accuracy does not necessarily make it a special variable.

It could also be argued that age is a special variable because young children are especially vulnerable to outside influences such as police or parents (e.g., in the form of misleading questions), which, in turn, makes them questionable as independent sources of information. Again, however, the same could be said about many other variables such as exposure time (witnesses who have little time to process a stimulus are likely to be especially vulnerable to misleading questions) or delay between the event and the misleading question (Loftus et al. (1978) have demonstrated that the longer the delay the greater the impact of the false information). In fact, Ceci, Ross, and Toglia (Chapter 5, this volume) have indicated that their research will investigate the influence of variables like these on witnesses' susceptibility to misleading information. Thus, we argue, the fact that age is related to the impact of misleading information does not in itself make age a special variable.

It is clear, however, that the courts consider age to be a special variable. Many jurisdictions have exclusionary rules that disallow eyewitness testimony by those who are below a certain age (e.g., 8 years); virtually no jurisdiction would consider a rule that disallows eyewitness testimony on the basis of the eyewitness' status on some other variable (e.g., less than an 8-second exposure duration). It is true, of course, that there is a probabilistic nature to these other variables, such that some eyewitnesses who had less than an 8-second exposure, for instance, would have some accurate information to impart, and some of those whose exposure exceeded 8 seconds would provide some inaccurate information. But this is true of age as well. In fact, we believe that age is not a special variable for purposes of predicting or explaining variance in eyewitness memory accuracy. There are numerous other variables that alone or in combination may account for as much or more of the variance in the accuracy of eyewitness memory than does age.

In spite of the foregoing discussion, we argue that age *is* a special variable in eyewitnessing. However, its special status does not derive from the extent to which it relates to memory per se. Instead, age is a special eyewitness variable because of extramemorial considerations involved in the eyewitness testimony of children. For example, it makes sense to refer to a need to protect a child under 8 years of age from the trauma of reliving a negative event; it does not make sense to refer to the need to protect from trauma a person whose view of an event was less than 8 seconds. Similarly, it makes sense to question the extent to which a child under 8 years of age understands the meaning of an oath; it does not make sense to question the extent to which a witness understands the meaning of an oath simply because his view was less than 8 seconds.

The age of a witness is a special variable in another way, in that it relates to qualitative differences between children's and adults' testimony rather than to mere quantitative differences. For example, an 8- versus 30-second exposure to an event is likely to relate to the quantity of information in the witness' memory, whereas 8- versus 30-year-old eyewitnesses are likely to differ qualitatively in the type of information encoded, stored, and retrieved. This qualitative difference is exemplified in Chapter 3 by Karen Saywitz. By utilizing proven techniques from developmental research, Saywitz has provided a useful interpretation of qualitative, age-related differences in children's testimony and demonstrated that children's memories are best accessed by different routes in different situations and for different types of information. For instance, Saywitz concluded that children's abilities to utilize script and schema information, especially for personally relevant and repeated events, is competitive with that of adults and that much useful information can be obtained simply by rewording questions to make them similar to a schema or script with which the child is familiar.

Studies that are designed to investigate children's apparent specific memorial deficiencies are of doubtless value to the eyewitness literature. However, it is from studies and conclusions like Saywitz's, aimed at delineating the *patterns* of memorial and extramemorial development, as well as the relative strengths of children's memories at different ages, from which we stand to gain the most. Furthermore, the findings of such research are best suited for communicating to the legal system the factors that are most useful for determining the appropriateness of testimony delivered by children of various ages.

The Suitability of Current Paradigms

Given that the age of the eyewitness does deserve the special status it has enjoyed in the present volume, largely on the basis of its relationship to extramemorial factors and qualitative differences between children's and adults' testimony, we now turn to a discussion of the relative benefits and disadvantages of various experimental techniques with respect to their suitability for investigating children's eyewitness memory. Central to this discussion is the notion that research with children is especially susceptible to the criticism that laboratory studies are lacking in ecological validity and that findings from such research might not always generalize to the conditions faced by children in a real court setting. In this section we point out a number of ecologically valid variables that could be realized in controlled studies, with particular emphasis on the influence that an adversarial interviewer might have on a child's testimony. In spite of an increased interest in these ecologically valid studies, however, eyewitness researchers could never hope to simulate every possible set of circumstances involving children with which the courts will have to contend in the future. Indeed, this criticism forms the basis for our argument in the next section; we suggest that existent theory in the developmental literature be utilized by eyewitness researchers to fill in the gaps between the conditions that have been simulated in the laboratory and those encountered in actual cases.

Certainly, many eyewitness researchers are aware of the general need for their research to be applicable at some point in its development to the real-world situation it is supposed to be simulating in the laboratory. Especially relevant in this regard are Chapter 1 by Goodman, Aman, and Hirschman and Chapter 7 by Douglas Peters. As we have already mentioned, these authors managed to operationalize the concept of stress as a variable in eyewitnessing by conducting field experiments in which the stressful situation was unavoidable for the children (and was for the children's benefit, of course). Such research is of great value to the child-eyewitness literature; we applaud the innovativeness of those studies for their noninvasive techniques and encourage the development of that experimental paradigm.

A problematic aspect of the popular paradigms with respect to ecological validity is the appropriateness of using standard, controlled recognition tasks to assess children's eyewitness memory in the laboratory. In the majority of legal cases involving child eyewitnesses, recognition or identification accuracy is not a crucial issue in making the judgment of guilt or innocence. A lineup identification is not appropriate in the case of repeated sexual assault, for instance, especially if the accused assailant is a family member or has frequent encounters with the child, as is often true in such cases. Even more important is the fact that the typical forced-choice task employed in a recognition study does not capture the ecology of the lineup situation; in a lineup or photospread there are multiple options from which to choose and a no-choice alternative is always available. Studies that employ a forced-choice technique stand in stark contrast to the situation often faced by the child witness in which he or she must provide free narrative, oral testimony in court. As we discuss in the next section, one of the consistent findings across some of the preceding chapters is that children's relatively incomplete free recall is a characteristic of their testimony, which leaves them especially vulnerable to being viewed as inadequate witnesses. Perhaps more emphasis should be placed on investigating interview and narrative techniques appropriate to the courtroom situation that would improve the completeness of children's recall and minimize the tendency for jurors to view children as generally less credible witnesses.

Script and schema research has revealed that children's recall effectiveness is greatly enhanced when children are given the opportunity to relate the facts of an event in a form that allows them to employ personally relevant and situationally constant information (see Saywitz's results regarding children's use of these recall strategies). There are some especially traumatic cases, however, for which children's scripted recall might be insufficient to convince a judge or jury that the child's testimony is accurate and/or complete. By definition, a scripted account of an event is lacking in episodic details on matters such as times, dates, and locations to which jurors are instructed to attribute significant weight in deciding whether or not the child's testimony is accurate. Is it reasonable, therefore, to accept a child's story that includes vague, undated references to a relative's visits over the course of several years, during which the child has accused the relative of repeated sexual harassment or assault? If scripted testimony is deemed acceptable, despite its lack of episodic details, is the defense counsel left with a sufficient opportunity to disprove the child's story through the use of standard alibi or disconfirmation techniques to support the defendant's case? One of eyewitness researchers' main concerns, then, should be the need to develop acceptable retrieval techniques that maximize the accuracy and usefulness of children's testimony (much like the work by Geiselman, Fisher, MacKinnon, & Holland (1985) with adults), while, at the same time, ensuring the defendant's right to due process.

In experimental situations, child eyewitnesses typically are questioned by a supportive, friendly experimenter to whom they have been introduced previously. This gives us a relatively good indication of how child eyewitnesses might respond to police investigators, child-care workers, and direct examinations by attorneys. However, cross-examination by opposing counsel might elicit quite different reactions in young children. Although it is unlikely that opposing counsel would be explicitly hostile or aggressive in cross-examining a child eyewitness, it would be a mistake to assume that cross-examination would have an atmosphere of support or friendliness. How do young children react to opposing counsel? Do they become easily confused? Can they easily be made to appear inconsistent? The standard experiment with child eyewitnesses is not designed to examine this issue. If cross-examination creates special problems for children, and this can be demonstrated empirically, then perhaps we could argue for children to be questioned by a neutral party. Until we examine this question empirically, however, we cannot be certain about the degree to which young children are vulnerable to the adversarial nature of the trial situation.

One of the dominant characteristics of experiments involving child eyewitnesses is the use of environments and people who are unfamiliar to the children. Confederates of the experimenter or actors on a videotape typically serve as the to-be-recognized person and a psychological laboratory is the typical setting. This stands in contrast to what are frequently the people and settings in which children are victimized—commonly relatives, in-laws, babysitters, or friends of the family in the child's own home or a frequented location. In this sense, our paradigms might not be well suited for examining some of the issues that arise in common cases involving child eyewitnesses. In a similar vein, the first people to discover that a child has some eyewitness knowledge often are the child's parents or guardians. To what extent, if any, are parents or guardians more powerful agents of testimony distortion through the use of misleading questions than are unfamiliar questioners (such as police or child-care workers)? Again, the paradigms that currently are in wide use in child-eyewitnessing experiments do not capture these potentially important dimensions. Some recent work in our own laboratory, using adult witnesses, has been aimed at determining the effect of the witness's perception of the interviewer's credibility and its effect on the likelihood that the witness will incorporate misleading postevent information into his or her testimony regarding the event. Early indications from these studies suggest that the interviewer's credibility does influence the degree to which witnesses will report misleading information on a memory test. Although this research is somewhat removed from the issue of whether parents are more powerful agents of misleading question effects than are strangers, it highlights the importance of examining the impact of misleading information as it originates from some common sources, such as parents versus social workers versus police.

With respect to the discussion that follows in the next section, ascertaining children's abilities to distinguish between truth and fantasy is critical to any argument that supports the inclusion of children's testimony in court. As mentioned above, the idea that opposing counsel could destroy the testimony of a young child during cross-examination is perhaps more than just a remote possibility. Suppose, for example, that after relating a true event a young child is asked, "Did you imagine that all of this happened?" Many young children may be likely to answer "yes" to this question because they fail to distinguish between imagining an event that never happened and thinking about an event that in fact did take place. In Chapter 6, Lindsay and Johnson have expanded on this notion of "reality monitoring" and suggested that the distinction between fact and fantasy is a decision-making process; children of different ages may be more or less adept at making such a distinction, depending upon their understanding of a number of factors that require consideration, many of which were discussed in Lindsay and Johnson's chapter and in our subsequent section on basic research and theory. Finally, children's comprehension of the oath by which they swear to abide in court can easily vary from child to child. Research should be directed toward developing our understanding of the characteristics of the child that indicate his or her appreciation of the gravity of the situation in which the testimony is to be heard.

The Role of Basic Research and Theory

The preceding section outlined a number of possible shortcomings of the current experimental techniques in children's eyewitness testimony research and offered some recommendations to improve the ecological validity of such research. As we noted earlier, however, researchers cannot hope to mimic every possible real-life situation, so gaps will always exist in our repertoire of documented eye-witnessing conditions. In the case of the child eyewitness, though, we are for-tunate to have at our disposal an extensive body of developmental literature from which we can extract theory and results to aid our understanding of the child-witness' performance. Before turning to a discussion of that literature, however, it is constructive to abstract three consistent research findings regarding the differences between children and adult eyewitnesses that have been reported in the current volume.

First, there is a consensus that the information provided by children in their free reports is less complete than that provided by adults (e.g., Goodman, Aman,

& Hirschman, Chapter 1; Saywitz, Chapter 3). Goodman et al. reported that adults recalled over three times as many correct details from the original event, compared to 6-year-olds, who in turn recalled over six times as many details as their 3-year-old counterparts. Ironically, it is just this paucity of children's recall that can lead to an inordinate amount of subsequent questioning from various agents throughout the legal proceeding and hence to a greater exposure to possible misleading information. Unfortunately for the system, the second of the general conclusions drawn from the preceding chapters is that children suffer from a greater susceptibility to having their testimony distorted by such misleading information (Ceci et al., Chapter 5; Goodman et al, Chapter 1; King & Yuille, Chapter 2). The third general finding is that the ratio of recall intrusions to correct informatin does not differ significantly as a function of age (Goodman et al., Chapter 1; Saywitz, Chapter 3). This holds true for witnesses exposed to misleading information, as well; age differences in susceptibility to misleading information apparently are revealed only on recognition tasks, not on recall tasks.

These general findings are the result of extensive experimentation within a research domain specifically concerned with children's eyewitnessing. There are, however, some aspects of the basic literature in memory and cognitive development that may be quite relevant to the issue of children as eyewitnesses even if the paradigms giving rise to the findings are far removed from the eyewitness situation. For instance, we have already mentioned one generalization from the basic literature: Changes in memory as a function of age may be better described as qualitative changes than as quantitative changes. We argue that eyewitness research techniques using children, and the interpretation of the results from that research, could be improved and honed to the point at which the eyewitness and developmental literatures would benefit by incorporating relevant information from each line of research.

We offer a few observations from the basic literature on memory development in this section to demonstrate the ability of existing research findings to fill the gaps in the limited number of eyewitnessing conditions we can hope to simulate in the laboratory. Consider, for example, the research indicating that children's encoding strategies shift from perceptual to conceptual information in the early school years (Ackerman, 1981; Cramer, 1973; Melkman & Deutsch, 1977; Melkman, Tversky, & Baratz, 1981). This shift may be of vital importance for predicting and understanding the ways in which testimonial reports vary developmentally. Recall that King and Yuille (Chapter 2, this volume) made a prediction, based partly on a notion from the prose-comprehension literature (e.g., Paris, 1978), that younger children should be less likely than older children and adults to infer the presence of objects that actually were not contained in the originally witnessed event (i.e., children place relatively more emphasis on perceptual as opposed to conceptual information). Contrary to this prediction, however, King and Yuille found that 6 year-olds were significantly more likely to make the inaccurate inferences than were children in the 9 to 11 year old, and 16 to 17 year-old age ranges. For these age groups, then, the generalization that children move from emphasizing perceptual information ("databound") to conceptual information (inferences) is not supported. Investigation of the predicted effect with preschool children would help to refine our understanding of the influence of this perceptual-to-conceptual development on children's testimony.

In addition to the approach taken by King and Yuille, the importance of functional matches between encoding and retrieval operations (Flexser & Tulving, 1978; Tulving & Thomson, 1973; Watkins & Tulving, 1975; Wells & Hryciw, 1984) suggests that the perceptual focus of young children may restrict successful retrieval to a particular perceptual modality. At least for young children, cross-modal retrieval cues (e.g., pictures for words or vice versa) may be ineffective. Indeed, there is evidence that adults are more flexible in their use of retrieval cues than are children (Ceci & Howe, 1978; Hasher & Clifton, 1974).

A potentially important observation that may be relevant to how children's memories are tested is Nelson and Gruendel's (1981) argument that *scripts* constitute a basic form of event representation in young children. Scripts are a form of knowledge that is organized in terms of temporal and causal relationships between component acts (Nelson, 1983). In a similar vein, Mandler (1983) argued that young children's knowledge is organized schematically rather than categorically. This suggests that young children will have more difficulty retrieving information in a categorical form of interrogation than they will in a sequential form. This distinction is consistent with our earlier discussion regarding the advantages of obtaining narrative, oral testimony from children compared to the information obtained through the use of standard, controlled retrieval tasks.

Another important lesson from the basic literature on the develoment of memory in children is that, like adults, prior knowledge of a particular content area affects memory performance. As a result, when children have more detailed knowledge than do adults in a particular domain (e.g., cartoons and children's games), their levels of memory performance in that domain are elevated beyond that of adults (e.g., Chi, 1978; Lindberg, 1980). In itself, this observation regarding the role of content knowledge does not allow precise predictions about the situations giving rise to equal or superior performance of children relative to adults. It does suggest, however, that a child's testimony regarding familiar environments (e.g., the child's own neighborhood, bedroom, or playground) need not be considered untrustworthy on the basis of age per se.

There are eyewitness situations in which issues of limited processing capacity are relevant. For example, dynamic events sometimes tax the short-term memory system, and this has negative consequences for long-term memory and retrieval. Case, Kurland, and Goldberg (1982) proposed that short-term memory can be conceptualized in terms of *storage space* and *operating space*. Storage space is the amount of space an individual has for storing information, whereas operating space is the amount of space an individual has for performing mental operations. Case et al. (1982) argue that storage space increases developmentally, while operating space decreases developmentally, and total processing space is developmentally invariant. Bjorklund (1985) agrees with this analysis and proposes that it is due to processing becoming increasingly automatic with age (where automaticity is defined as relatively effortless, unintentional, and with little or no awareness, as in Shiffrin & Schneider, 1977). The increased automaticity presumably is due to the development of stronger mental associations among events, objects, and words, which reduces demands on operating space and frees up storage space, which, in turn, might aid long-term memory.

The developmental literature on metamemory is a useful perspective from which to further our understanding of the child's perception of a trial and his or her resultant testimony in court. Saywitz (Chapter 3) and Ceci et al. (Chapter 5) briefly touched on the issue, but decided not to detail the developmentalists' current conception of metamemory or provide comment on its relationship to the suggestibility, accuracy, and completeness of eyewitness testimony. A close examination of the metamemory literature (e.g., Flavell, 1977, Flavell & Wellman, 1977; Kail, 1979; Miller, 1983) reveals many conclusions that can be used to interpret experimental findings and some apparent controversies in the eyewitness literature, ranging from the confidence-accuracy relationship to the misinformation effect.

Miller (1983) describes metamemory as a subcategory of metacognition; that is, knowledge that a person has about factors that affect his or her information-processing efficiency and, concomitantly, ways in which such processing can be optimized. Metamemory, then, refers to the knowledge a person has about factors that affect his or her ability to encode, store, and retrieve information and the strategies by which these abilities are made maximally efficient.

Kail (1979) has provided a description of metamemory development from which it is possible to construct a framework to interpret the importance of the extramemorial factors we have been discussing to this point. Metamemory can be organized into three main areas: (1) awareness of the act that certain events are to be remembered, (2) awareness of one's personal memory limitations, and (3) awareness of contextual factors that can affect one's memory for an event. In a courtroom context it is important that the child be aware that his or her reason for being on the stand is to provide information from memory (as opposed to his or her imagination or external sources) regarding a specific event. Comments by Saywitz (Chapter 3) and by Lindsay and Johnson (Chapter 6) on reality monitoring in the current volume apply here: The child must realize that he or she is to report under oath the details of an event, about which he or she has privileged information, as opposed to a make-believe story, externally provided information, or fantasy.

Knowledge and verbalization of one's personal memory limitations has been discussed by Wells and Lindsay (1983) in the context of response-bias information—one of the cues used by jurors to infer the accuracy of an eyewitness' memory. As children develop, they come to realize that their memory capacity is limited and that people vary in their abilities to remember things accurately. It would be much to the child's advantage to know that adults are generally better at many memory tasks and that the child's memory is under especially careful scrutiny by the court. So, for example, it might be useful to ask the child about his or her knowledge regarding personal memory skills, deficiencies, and general observations to understand more about the child's competence to testify.

Finally, people come to realize that there are a number of task variables that can affect their ability to remember accurately an event or other person. Kail (1979) reports that as early as 6 years of age many children know that their familiarity with a to-be-remembered event is directly related to the accuracy of their memory for that event, and that the quantity of things to be remembered is inversely related to accuracy. Kail notes, however, that children at this age often are unable to appreciate the strategic effectiveness of using naturally occurring and arbitrary organizational cues to aid their memory accuracy.

The relationships between metamemory development and eyewitness issues has surfaced before. For example, Ceci et al. (Chapter 5, this volume) suggested that metamemory factors might be at work in the apparent discrepancy between their research findings and those discussed by Zaragoza (Chapter 4, this volume) using the Modified Test procedure to assess the influence of misleading information on testimony accuracy. Whether or not a witness knows that he or she has been provided with false information (Loftus's notion of "detectability") is obviously related to that witness' awareness of the factors that can limit his or her memory accuracy. In addition, the confidence-accuracy relationship for children might warrant especially cautious attention in light of the fact that very young children are less likely to know when their memories are apt to be wrong, because they are less sensitive to the factors that can limit memory accuracy.

The extent to which basic theoretical conceptualizations of memory development will influence our understanding, prediction, and control of the validity of children's eyewitness testimony is an open question. Our general argument is that, even though the paradigms of basic memory researchers are not of much relevance to eyewitness situations, the underlying, fundamental processes of memory development discovered in those paradigms cannot be ignored.

Policy Issues

Until recently, experimental psychologists in North America were safe in assuming that their research findings and conclusions would have little or no impact on judicial policy. We argue that this assumption is no longer true. Recent years have illustrated dramatic shifts in both psychology and the justice system, which have resulted in these two disciplines being interrelated. In psychology the shift has been toward ecologically valid experiments directed at the empirical assumptions underlying judicial policy. The explosive growth of an experimental eyewitness literature in the last decade (see Wells & Loftus, 1984, chap. 1) is indicative of the shift within psychology. Prominent legal scholars have also shifted, from a conclusion that eyewitness psychology has nothing to offer the legal system (e.g., Wigmore, 1909) to "expert psychological testimony probably is the best way for juries to learn about the unreliability of eyewitness testimony" (Frazzini, 1981,

p. 19). Judicial decisions up to and including the 1970s, dealing with eyewitness matters, cited no psychological research (e.g., major cases such as *Manson v. Braithwaite*, 1977; *Stovall v. Denno*, 1972; *Neil v. Biggers*, 1972). In recent years, scientific expert testimony is discussed routinely in major cases that hinge on eyewitness evidence, albeit not always in favor of allowing the expert testimony (e.g., see *State v. Chapple*, 1983; *United States v. Smith*, 1984). Virtually all major law journals have in recent years published reviews and commentaries on eyewitness psychology research (e.g., Frazzini, 1981 in *The Yale Review*; Woocher, 1977 in the *Stanford Law Review*) and psychologists have evaluated major court decisions based on empirical evidence from the eyewitness-psychology literature (e.g., Wells & Murray, 1983).

Given this recent state of affairs, it would be a mistake to assume that current psychological research, writings, and conclusions regarding the child eyewitness will not have an impact on judicial policy. The justice system is searching for an informed set of observations and arguments regarding the status of children as eyewitnesses and the present unfolding of a child-eyewitness literature in psychology is almost certain to receive attention. In this regard we must be careful that our writings in this area do not reflect a level of certainty that exceeds our actual knowledge. Policy makers are relatively distant from the actual research, rarely are familiar with the research methods, and often are not equipped to evaluate the research findings. The failure of those responsible for judicial policy to make meaningful discriminations between psychological studies is exemplified in the way that the United States Supreme Court handled the issue of jury size in *Colgrave v. Battin* (1973). In *Colgrave*, the Court cited four "recent" studies that concluded that jury size was of little consequence to the outcome of the case. The methodological flaws in these studies, however, were so serious that one expert concluded, "The quality of social science scholarship displayed in [the Court's] decisions would not win a passing grade in a high-school psychology class" (Saks, 1974, p. 18).

Judicial policy makers use psychological research much like a drunk uses a lamppost—more for support than for illumination. Because of the tendency to select studies that support their own prior position, a tendency exacerbated perhaps by the adversarial nature of the trial process, researchers should strive to insert appropriate caveats into their writings rather than assume these caveats to be understood. With respect to children's testimony, the failure to qualify many of the conclusions that one might be tempted to draw, on the basis of the existing literature, would be a failure to represent accurately the current state of the area. For example, Ceci, Ross, and Toglia (Chapter 5, this volume) have noted that, while it may be of interest to highlight the conditions in which children are apt to incorporate misleading information into their testimony, it is not the intent of researchers to discredit children's testimony overall. Ceci et al. point out that many of the children in their studies were able to resist the misleading information and that much of a child's testimony is likely to be correct in any given case.

The need for psychological researchers to include caveats along with their experimental findings extends beyond the specific case of children's testimony, as well. For example, although it is well understood by psychological researchers that statistical significance need not imply real-world importance, legal researchers who survey the psychological literature are not likely to make this distinction. Similarly, eyewitness researchers have an obligation to tell readers, some of whom will be influential in setting policy for a jurisdiction, that the methods used in their studies (e.g., a forced-choice recognition task) may be unlike the real-world situation that they are trying to simulate (narrative free recall or directed narration) and that the conclusions might not generalize to actual cases for that reason.

To the extent that researchers of children eyewitnesses are serious about providing meaningful information to policy makers, they must be prepared to abandon some of the ideas that, somewhat surprisingly, remain prevalent in the psychological literature. One such idea is that the square of a correlation (e.g., r^2 between age and memory) is a meaningful index of the degree to which the relationship is useful or predictive. The squared correlation and its family of "variance-accounted-for" measures (e.g., ω^2) are not meaningful indices of the usefulness or predictive utility of a two-variable relationship. These measures were devised for quite different purposes. As a simple illustration, consider a study in which 70% of adults were found to be accurate on an eyewitness task, whereas only 30% of 8-year-olds were accurate. Measures of the variance-accounted-for on accuracy by age (e.g., r^2) would yield a value of approximately 16%.[1] This estimate of variance-accounted-for is a profound underestimate of the predictive utility of age in this instance, for which we can say that adults were over two times more likely to be accurate than were the children. In other words, the variance-accounted-for notion can be irrelevant and misleading for real-world problems. Researchers in the area of child-eyewitnessing must remain alert to the distinction between procedures, methods, and statistics that were developed for basic research and those that are more appropriate to applied contexts. The measures of variance-accounted-for, as an example, remain useful as methods of scaling variables for purposes of comparing their *relative* impact, but not for purposes of describing the practical utility of variables.

Finally, we draw a distinction that has been somewhat useful in the adult eyewitness literature—a distinction between control variables and postdiction variables. Control (or system) variables refer to a class of variables that affect the accuracy or completeness of obtained eyewitness testimony and are under the influence of the justice system. Postdiction (or estimator) variables refer to a class of variables affecting the accuracy or completeness of eyewitness testimony that are not under the influence of the justice system (Wells, 1978). In the control category are such variables as the form of questioning, instructions on viewing

---

[1]This is because the population variance estimate when age is unknown is $(.5)(.5) = .25$ and when age is known is $(.7)(.3) = .21$. The absolute value of the increase in variance-accounted-for when age is known, therefore, is $.25 - .21 = .04$, and the percentage reduction is given by $.04 \div .25 = .16$ (see Rosenthal & Rubin, 1982, for a discussion of more meaningful alternatives to the "variance-accounted-for" measures).

lineups, minimizing retroactive interference, and so on. To the extent that research can establish procedural improvements on these control variables, the system can benefit from such research knowledge by trying to improve the accuracy and/or completeness of children's eyewitness reports. This stands in contrast to postdiction variables, which include the variable of age per se, stress at initial encoding, and so on. Although these postdiction variables also cause variation in the accuracy and/or completeness of eyewitness testimony, their applied or practical utility resides primarily in assessing or postdicting the accuracy of eyewitnesses (i.e., these conditions cannot be controlled in actual cases). Although we do not suggest that control variables inherently are more worthy of research efforts than are postdiction variables (obviously both are useful for our understanding of children's eyewitness capabilities) we believe that control or system variables relate to a more clearly defined practical goal. That practical goal is twofold: First, we need to discover control variables that can improve the accuracy and completeness of children's eyewitness reports under various levels and/or combinations of postdiction variables. Second, we need to communicate those findings to those people in the judicial system who might control those variables in actual cases. To the extent that this goal can be attained, it should facilitate the task faced by those actors in the judicial system who are responsible for evaluating the credibility of eyewitness reports.

References

Ackerman, B. P. (1981). Encoding specificity in the recall of pictures and words in children and adults. *Journal of Experimental Child Psychology, 31*, 193–211.

Binet, A. (1900). *La suggestibilité*. Paris: Schleicher Frères.

Binet, A. (1911). Le bilan de la psychologie en 1910. *Année psychologie, 17*, 5–11.

Bjorklund, D. F. (1985). Development of organization in children's memory. In C. J. Brainerd & M. Pressley (Eds.), *Basic processes in memory development*. New York: Springer-Verlag.

Case, R., Kurland, M., & Goldberg, J. (1982). Operational efficiency and the growth of short-term memory span. *Journal of Experimental Child Psychology, 33*, 386–404.

Ceci, S. J., & Howe, M. J. A. (1978). Age-related differences in free recall as a function of retrieval flexibility. *Journal of Experimental Child Psychology, 26*, 432–442.

Chi, M. T. H. (1978). Knowledge structure and memory development. In R. Siegler (Ed.), *Children's thinking: What develops?* Thirteenth Annual Carnegie Symposium on Cognition. Hillsdale, NJ: Erlbaum.

Clifford, B. R., & Bull, R. (1978). *The psychology of person perception*. London: Routledge & Kegan Paul.

Colgrave v. Battin, 413 U.S. 149 (1973).

Cramer, P. (1973). Evidence for a developmental shift in the basis for memory organization. *Journal of Experimental Child Psychology, 16*, 12–22.

Dauber, J. (1912). Die Gleichförmigkeit der psychischen Geschehens und die Zeugenaussagen. *Fortschritte der Psychologie, 1*, 83–131.

Flavell, J. H. (1977). *Cognitive development*. Englewood Cliffs, NJ: Prentice-Hall.

Flavell, J. H., & Wellman, H. M. (1977). Metamemory. In R. V. Kail & J. W. Hagen (Eds.), *Perspectives on the development of memory and cognition*. Hillsdale, NJ: Erlbaum.

Flexser, A. J., & Tulving, E. (1978). Retrieval independence in recognition and recall. *Psychological Review, 55*, 153–171.

Frazzini, S. F. (1981). Review of eyewitness testimony. *The Yale Review, 70*, 18–20.

Geiselman, E. R., Fisher, R. P., MacKinnon, D. P., & Holland, H. L. (1985). Eyewitness memory enhancement in the police interview: Cognitive retrieval mneumonics versus hypnosis. *Journal of Applied Psychology, 70*, 401–412.

Hasher, L., & Clifton, D. A. (1974). A developmental study of attribute coding in free recall. *Journal of Experimental Child Psychology, 17*, 332–346.

Kail, R. (1979). *The development of memory in children.* New York: W. H. Freeman.

Lindbergh, M. (1980). The role of knowledge structures in the ontogeny of learning. *Journal of Experimental Child Psychology, 30*, 401–410.

Loftus, E. F. (1979). *Eyewitness testimony.* Cambridge, MA: Harvard University.

Loftus, E. F., Miller, D. G., & Burns, H. J. (1978). Semantic integration of verbal information into a visual memory. *Journal of Experimental Psychology: Human Learning and Memory, 4*, 19–31.

Mandler, J. M. (1983). Representation. In Vol. 3, *Cognitive development.* P. Masson (Ed.), *Carmichael's manual of child psychology*: (J. H. Flavell & E. M. Markman, Vol. Eds.) New York: Wiley.

Manson v. Braithwaite, 432 U.S. 98, 97 S.Ct. 2243 (1977).

Marbe, K. (1913). Psychologische Gutachten zum Prozess wegen des Mullheimer Eisenbahnunglücks. *Fortschritte der Psychologie, 1*, 339–374.

McCloskey, M., & Zaragoza, M. (1985). Misleading postevent information and memory for events: Arguments and evidence against memory impairment hypotheses. *Journal of Experimenal Psychology: General, 114*, 1–19.

Mehl, P. (1912). Beitrag zur Psychologie der Kinderaussage. *Archiv für Kriminologie— Anthropologie und Kriminalistik, 49*, 193.

Melkman, R., & Deutsch, C. (1977). Memory functioning as related to developmental changes in the bases of organization. *Journal of Experimental Child Psychology, 23*, 84–97.

Melkman, R., Tversky, B., & Baratz, D. (1981). Developmental trends in the use of perceptual and conceptual attributes in grouping, clustering, and retrieval. *Journal of Experimental Child Psychology, 31*, 470–486.

Miller, P. H. (1983). *Theories of developmental psychology.* New York: W. H. Freeman.

Neil v. Biggers, 409 U.S. 188 (1972).

Nelson, K. (1983). The derivation of knowledge and categories for event representation. In E. K. Scholnick (Ed.), *New trends in conceptual representation: Challenges to Piaget's theory?* Hillsdale, NJ: Erlbaum.

Nelson, K., & Gruendel, J. M. (1981). Generalized event representations: Basic building blocks of cognitive development. In A. Brown & M. Lamb (Eds.), *Advances in developmental psychology* (Vol. 1). Hillsdale, NJ: Erlbaum.

Paris, S. G. (1978). The development of interference and transformation as memory operations. In P. A. Ornstein (Ed.), *Memory development in children.* Hillsdale, NJ: Erlbaum.

Rosenthal, R., & Rubin, D. B. (1982). A simple, general-purpose display of magnitude of experimenal effect. *Journal of Educational Psychology, 74*, 166–169.

Saks, M. J. (1974). Ignorance of science is no excuse. *Trial, 10*, 18–20.

Shiffrin, R. M., & Schneider, W. (1977). Controlled and automatic human information processing: II. Perceptual learning, automatic attending, and a general theory. *Psychological Review, 84*, 127–190.

State v. Chapple, 135 Ariz. 281, 294, 660 P.2d 1208, 1221 (1983).

Stern, L. W. (1910). Abstracts of lectures on the psychology of testimony and on the study of individuality. *American Journal of Psychology, 21*, 270–282.

Stern, L. W. (1939). The psychology of testimony. *Journal of Abnormal and Social Psychology, 34*, 3–20.

Stovall v. Denno, 388 U.S. 293 (1967).

Tulving, E., & Thompson, D. M. (1973). Encoding specificity and retrieval processes in episodic memory. *Psychological Review, 80*, 352–373.

United States v. Smith, 736 F.2d 1103, 1105-1106 (6th Cir. 1984).

Watkins, M. J., & Tulving, E. (1975). Episodic memory: When recognition fails. *Journal of Experimental Psychology: General, 104*, 25–29.

Wells, G. L. (1978). Applied eyewitness testimony research: System variables and estimator variables. *Journal of Personality and Social Psychology, 36*, 1546–1557.

Wells, G. L., & Hryciw, B. (1984). Memory for faces: Encoding and retrieval operations. *Memory and Cognition, 12*, 338–344.

Wells, G. L., & Lindsay, R. C. L. (1983). How do people judge the accuracy of eyewitness identifications? Studies of performance and a metamemory analysis. In S. Lloyd-Bostock & B. R. Clifford (Eds.), *Evaluating witness evidence*. Chichester, England: Wiley.

Wells, G. L., & Loftus, E. F. (Eds.) (1984). *Eyewitness testimony: Psychological perspectives*. Cambridge, England: Cambridge University Press.

Wells, G. L., & Murray, D. M. (1983). What can psychology say about the Neil vs. Biggers criteria for judging eyewitness identification accuracy? *Journal of Applied Psychology, 68*, 347–362.

Wigmore, J. H. (1909). Professor Munsterberg and the psychology of evidence. *Illinois Law Review, 3*, 399–445.

Woocher, F. D. (1977). Did your eyes deceive you? Expert psychological testimony on the unreliability of eyewitness testimony. *Stanford Law Review, 29*, 969–1030.

Yarmey, A. D. (1979). *The psychology of eyewitness testimony*. New York: Free Press.

Author Index

Subject Index